Indian Affairs and the Administrative State in the Nineteenth Century

The framers of the Constitution and the generations that followed built a powerful and intrusive national administrative state in the late eighteenth and nineteenth centuries. The romantic myth of an individualized, pioneering expansion across an open West obscures nationally coordinated administrative and regulatory activity in Indian affairs, land policy, trade policy, infrastructure development, and a host of other issue areas related to expansion.

Stephen J. Rockwell offers a careful look at the administration of Indian affairs and its relation to other national policies managing and shaping national expansion westward. Throughout the nineteenth century, Indian affairs were at the center of concerns about national politics, the national economy, and national social issues. Rockwell describes how a vibrant and complicated national administrative state operated from the earliest days of the republic, long before the Progressive era and the New Deal.

Stephen J. Rockwell is an Associate Professor of Political Science at St. Joseph's College in Patchogue, New York. He taught in the Political Science and Public Administration programs at the University of Michigan–Flint and worked as a Senior Research Analyst at the Brookings Institution in Washington, DC. He is the coauthor (with Peter Woll) of *American Government: Competition and Compromise* (2001) and coeditor (with Peter Woll) of an anthology entitled *American Political Ideals and Realities* (2000).

Indian Affairs and the Administrative State in the Nineteenth Century

STEPHEN J. ROCKWELL
St. Joseph's College, New York

CAMBRIDGE
UNIVERSITY PRESS

CAMBRIDGE UNIVERSITY PRESS
Cambridge, New York, Melbourne, Madrid, Cape Town, Singapore,
São Paulo, Delhi, Dubai, Tokyo, Mexico City

Cambridge University Press
32 Avenue of the Americas, New York, NY 10013-2473, USA

www.cambridge.org
Information on this title: www.cambridge.org/9780521193634

First published 2010

Printed in the United States of America

A catalog record for this publication is available from the British Library.

Library of Congress Cataloging in Publication data

Rockwell, Stephen J., 1966–
Indian affairs and the administrative state in the nineteenth century / Stephen J. Rockwell.
p. cm.
Includes bibliographical references and index.
ISBN 978-0-521-19363-4 (hbk.)
1. Indians of North America – Government relations – History – 19th century. 2. Indians of North America – legal status, law, etc. – History – 19th century. 3. Federal government – United States – History – 19th century. 4. Administrative agencies – United States – History – 19th century. 5. United States – Territorial expansion. 6. United States – Politics and government – 19th century. 7. United States – Ethnic relations – Political aspects – History – 19th century. I. Title.
E93.R63 2010
323.1197–dc22 2009042793

ISBN 978-0-521-19363-4 Hardback

To Mom and Dad

It does not seem a great task to attend to the business of directing the management of about three hundred thousand Indians; but when it is considered that those Indians are scattered over a continent, and divided into more than two hundred tribes, in [the] charge of fourteen superintendents and some seventy agents, whose frequent reports and quarterly accounts are to be examined and adjusted; that no general rules can be adopted for the guidance of those officers, for the reason that the people under their charges are so different in habits, customs, manners, and organization, varying from the civilized and educated Cherokee and Choctaw to the miserable lizard-eaters of Arizona; and that this office is called upon to protect the Indians, whether under treaty stipulations or roaming at will over his wild hunting-grounds, from abuse by unscrupulous whites, while at the same time it must concede every reasonable privilege to the spirit of enterprise and adventure which is pouring its hardy population into the western country; when these things are considered, the task assigned to this bureau will not seem so light as it is sometimes thought.

– Dennis Cooley, Commissioner of Indian Affairs, 1866,
quoted in Gary L. Roberts, "Dennis Nelson Cooley," in
Robert M. Kvasnicka and Herman J. Viola, eds.,
The Commissioners of Indian Affairs, 1824–1977
(Lincoln: University of Nebraska Press, 1979), 105

Contents

Acknowledgments

Research remains a deeply collaborative process. I am profoundly grateful for the help I've received as I've worked on this book.

I am grateful for the generous institutional support provided at various stages of this project by Brandeis University, the Gordon Center for American Public Policy, the Brookings Institution, the University of Michigan–Flint, and the Thompson Center for Learning and Teaching. Fordham University gave the project its start, at least indirectly, and I remain indebted to Fordham for the confidence and support it offered many years ago. My thanks, too, for the generous support given by St. Joseph's College, particularly through the Faculty Development Small Grants program and through the award of a Summer Research Grant. The staff at the National Archives in Washington were always helpful and generous with their time, as were the librarians and staff at Brandeis, Brookings, the University of Michigan–Flint, Fordham, and St. Joseph's College. Research like this cannot move forward without your help. Thanks.

I am grateful for the comments and advice offered over many years by my colleagues and friends. The scholars who read and commented on this manuscript for Cambridge University Press offered insightful and helpful practical suggestions for shortening and improving the book. Albert Price read several versions of the manuscript, including suffering valiantly through the early versions and responding honestly, helpfully, and with good humor. Steven Fuchs, Peter Woll, Fred Woodward, and Bill Altermatt also contributed suggestions and insights as the manuscript progressed. Shep Melnick, Sidney Milkis, and Morton Keller were in this from the beginning. I am deeply grateful for their commitments to me and for their patience as I pursued an unconventional topic. Thanks to Peter Skerry for his unwavering support for my research and for his influence on my technique (particularly in showing me how well the telephone works). I have had many excellent contacts at the Bureau of Indian Affairs, far too numerous to name here. I always found the Bureau's personnel to be helpful and open when treated with the respect they deserve for operating in such a complicated policy field. My thanks, too, for the contributions and the time offered by tribal leaders and others as I did field research over the years. These discussions deepened my understanding of the bureaucratic dynamics involved in U.S. Indian policy.

I am indebted to many scholars whose work precedes my own. The work that went into each source cited in the notes is deeply appreciated. I'd like to single out the efforts of the historians Francis Paul Prucha, Ronald Satz, Grant Foreman, and William Goetzmann, upon whose work much of my understanding of Indian affairs and the nineteenth century rests. I'd also like to highlight my debt to James Q. Wilson and Daniel Carpenter. Their work has been instrumental in helping me clarify my understanding of organizations and bureaucracies. I also owe a great debt to Vine Deloria Jr. Many years ago, Professor Deloria responded to an inquiry from me, a graduate student unknown to him and half a continent away, asking about general directions for my research. In a brief note on a postcard, he suggested that investigating discretionary authority at the Bureau of Indian Affairs would prove fruitful. He was right.

I have been lucky to run across many people whose contributions to this work may not be terribly obvious, but without whom this book could never have been completed. These folks include, in no particular order, John and Patricia Schmitt (plus Meaghan, Ryan, Stephen, and Peter), Matthew and Michelle Rorke (and Kevin), Steve and Nicole Pierce (and Rebecca and Owen), Hank Lutton, Glen Weiss and Ann Ginsberg (plus Zachary and Madeline), Lonnie and Dara Meiner, Doug Katz, Jean-Paul and Jennifer Vest, whoever fixed the television at the Minneapolis airport Hilton, Zoe Fidelman, Walter Nicklin, Martha Doughty, DJ Trela, Martha Bayles, Steve and Angie Jones, Mike and Amy Price, Rod and Rachel March, Bruce Wilson, Doug Wilson, Joanne and Brian Specht, Cora Jones, Martin Levin, Heather Scott, Fred Dews, Susan Stewart, Jon Shields, Crystal Pepperdine, Peggy Kahn, Derwin Munroe, Bill Laverty, Viki Zavales, Stephanie Greco Larson, James Kloppenberg, Raymond D'Angelo, Ted McGlone, Sister Elizabeth Hill, Sister Loretta McGrann, Sister Margaret Buckley, Robert Jones, Elaine Crane, Paul Cimbala, Cheryl and Tal Ninyo and the Ninyo and Mallenbaum families, and Danielle, Sarah, Emily, and Christine Kadtke.

The book is dedicated to my parents, Ronald and Patricia, both of whom have combined genius, love, and professionalism with unshakeable support for their children. I am grateful, too, for the support of my brothers Kenny and David, who have always been there to remind me that there are more important things to do than work. Thanks to Adina, Kim, and the kids.

My grandparents contributed in many ways to the completion of this project, too, and they are not forgotten.

Finally, I have been lucky to fall in with the excellent people at Cambridge University Press, who have shepherded this manuscript through the review and production processes with professionalism, efficiency, and good judgment. In particular, thanks to Lew Bateman, Emily Spangler, Anne Lovering Rounds, Laura Lawrie, Mark Fox, and Marc Anderson.

Introduction

Big government won the West.

In the early republic, policymakers and administrators at the national level utilized the treaty system to order and control relations with Indian nations, and they used a string of government trading houses known as the factory system to pacify affairs on the U.S. frontiers. Together with trade regulation and licensing systems, government policy and public officials drove the lucrative fur trade into the control of large and accountable major firms, while limiting the potential for costly conflicts that would threaten the new nation's survival. In the 1830s, the federal government oversaw the forced removal of a hundred thousand Indians from their homes in the Southeast, relocating them on administratively manageable reservations west of the Mississippi River. Other removals in other parts of the continent fill the nineteenth century. Throughout the heart of the nineteenth century, political leaders and public administrators isolated and contained Indians on reservations and in areas in the recently acquired West, extending federal jurisdiction and administrative structures into new areas and finally across the continent. Throughout these years, policymakers and administrators designed and effected a massive land transfer program that allotted millions of acres of tribal lands to individual Indian and non-Indian landowners, an effort which reached its peak after passage of the General Allotment Act, or Dawes Act, in 1887.

These efforts were difficult and complicated, yet the Indian Office in the nineteenth century effectively administered national policy related to westward expansion and achieved its primary mission in each major era of Indian policy. Indian Office personnel administered national policies in volatile, diverse, and rapidly shifting administrative environments, and remained responsive to powerful and shifting interests both inside and outside of government. Acquisition of territories in the Great Plains, Texas, Arizona, New Mexico, California, Washington, Oregon, and eventually Alaska and Hawaii brought novel challenges. As the nation moved west, the interests involved in frontier affairs evolved and developed: fur traders and land companies gave way to railroad and mining companies, settlement interests, farmers, and developers. To the government's interactions with the tribes of the East were added interactions with the tribes of the Southwest, the Northwest, California, and the Great Plains. To missionary societies and religious groups advocating the interests of Indians as individuals were added philanthropic humanitarians and nonsectarian Friends of the Indian. And to the main goals – pacification, removal, and containment – were added an unending and always evolving series of subordinate aims: administrators designed and implemented national social policies and programs extended goods and services to Indian populations, opened and administered reservation and off-reservation schools, initiated training and vocational programs, and undertook programs in health care, forestry, irrigation, and the development of infrastructure and natural resources.

These were not minor or tangential affairs, somehow to the side of or beneath the "important" aspects of U.S. history and development. They are not outliers. Significantly, in each major era of Indian policy, and in each region into which the United States moved, "the Indian question" existed near the center of concerns about the nation's future. Indian affairs were absolutely critical to virtually all calculations of interest, of politics, of economy, of social situation, and of national survival and future development. The founding generation, the Jacksonians, and later Americans created effective administrative procedures and structures, and accepted discretionary authority exercised by creative field agents, commensurate with the need and course of U.S. interests. In the nineteenth century, those interests centered around expansion. Our romantic false memory of an individualized, pioneering expansion across a remote and unpeopled West obscures recognition of federally led and nationally coordinated administrative and regulatory activity in the late eighteenth and nineteenth centuries.

A major argument of this book is that we need to reassess the nineteenth-century administrative state. James Q. Wilson writes, for example, in a passage typical of many scholars' approach to nineteenth-century administration,

> During the first half of the nineteenth century, the growth in the size of the federal bureaucracy can be explained, not by the assumption of new tasks by the government or by the imperialistic designs of the managers of existing tasks, but by the addition to existing bureaus of personnel performing essentially routine, repetitive tasks for which the public demand was great and unavoidable. The principal problem facing a bureaucracy thus enlarged was how best to coordinate its activities toward given and noncontroversial ends.[1]

[1] James Q. Wilson, "The Rise of the Bureaucratic State," reprinted in *Current Issues in Public Administration*, 6th ed., ed. Frederick S. Lane (Boston: Bedford/St. Martin's, 1999), 41.

Elsewhere in the same article, Wilson – again, like many public administration scholars – identifies the Interstate Commerce Commission as the first significant federal effort to regulate the economy, suggests that the tasks of the nineteenth-century military and its officers were minor and easily controlled by political leaders, and writes that "before the second decade of this [twentieth] century, there was no federal bureaucracy wielding substantial discretionary powers."[2] Many other scholars have stated similar conclusions, and these conclusions dominate the literature. Daniel Carpenter, for example, in his influential book, *The Forging of Bureaucratic Autonomy*, writes,

> Through most of the 1800s, administrative capacity in the United States – the collective talent of bureaucracies to perform with competence and without corruption or malfeasance – was the minimally sufficient ability to distribute federal largesse to electorally favored constituencies. The possibility of employing bureaucracies to address national problems, the possibility of bureaucratic planning, was almost entirely removed from the American political imagination.[3]

A careful look at expansion and Indian affairs, however, reveals a vibrant, complicated federal bureaucracy, planning and performing complex and difficult tasks in politically charged environments, full of debate over means and ends and carried out with vast grants of discretionary authority to federal field agents deployed across the continent, and doing so long before the Civil War and the New Deal. At the same time, civil administrators in a host of venues were given primary responsibility for organizing, controlling, and directing settlement and expansion. From surveyors, treaty commissioners, and explorers to trading house factors, local agents, boards of inquiry, and scientific and engineering outfits within the military, nineteenth-century civil administration is the focal point of federal activity. The regular military was never far behind, as enforcer and deterrent, but it rarely operated as

[2] Wilson, "Rise of the Bureaucratic State," 57.

[3] Daniel P. Carpenter, *The Forging of Bureaucratic Autonomy: Reputations, Networks, and Policy Innovation in Executive Agencies, 1862–1928* (Princeton: Princeton University Press, 2001), 47. The implications of this view have been outlined by many authors, including perhaps most prominently Theodore Lowi, who in *The End of Liberalism* takes to task the extensions of delegated power and administrative responsibility he identifies with modern liberal government. Lowi writes, for example, "The first century was one of government dominated by Congress and virtually self-executing laws.... It was due to this quite special and restricted use of government that Congress could both pass laws and see to their execution." Theodore J. Lowi, *The End of Liberalism: Ideology, Policy, and the Crisis of Public Authority* (New York: Norton, 1969), 128. This vastly oversimplifies the nation's first century of public administration and overestimates Congress's ability – and its desire – to direct and control that administration. Lowi's assertions about the nation's first century are made in service of a normative argument about the legitimacy of the administrative state. That argument is not supported by the historical record.

the first line of expansion. Civil administration inside and outside the military – the Indian Office as well as the General Land Office and bodies like the Post Office, the Customs Service, and the U.S. Corps of Topographical Engineers – represented the core of national administrative efforts in the nineteenth century. Public administration, not military force and not simple, unsupervised demographics, conquered the North American continent in the years from the early republic to the New Deal.

In fact, what we find in the late eighteenth century and throughout the nineteenth century is the administrative state. John Rohr's definition, from his classic book, *To Run a Constitution: The Legitimacy of the Administrative State*, is helpful:

> When I speak of the "administrative state," I mean the political order that came into its own during the New Deal and still dominates our politics. It is the form of government that Dwight Waldo described so eloquently four decades ago in his political science classic *The Administrative State*. Its hallmark is the expert agency tasked with important governing functions through loosely drawn statutes that empower unelected officials to undertake such important matters as preventing "unfair competition," granting licenses as "the public interest, convenience or necessity" will indicate, maintaining a "fair and orderly market," and so forth.
>
> The administrative state is not confined to regulating industry. Its writ runs to defense contracting and procurement, military and diplomatic policy, and the institutions of mass justice that manage problems in public assistance, public housing, public education, public health, disability benefits, food stamps, and so forth.[4]

Rohr's description of the administrative state applies almost precisely to government activity promoting and managing expansion and Indian affairs. The only difference is in the timing: the administrative state defined by Rohr and Waldo existed in concrete and influential form throughout the nineteenth century.

Recognizing the contribution of the Indian Office and other administrative efforts managing national expansion reorients our understanding of the constitutional legitimacy of the federal administrative bureaucracy. Their rhetoric of limited government notwithstanding, the founding generation and subsequent generations built complicated and influential administrative structures to direct and oversee national expansion. Indian policy was a common denominator of the national government's creative activities in the eighteenth and nineteenth centuries. It stood at the center of regulatory activity, at the intersection of church and state, at the core of policy development, the focus of debates on federalism and government involvement in the economy, the creative force behind developments in public administration, and the lynchpin of national survival and expansion. Expansion and Indian affairs are what the federal government was doing *before* – before

[4] John A. Rohr, *To Run a Constitution: The Legitimacy of the Administrative State* (Lawrence: University Press of Kansas, 1986), xi (internal reference omitted).

the New Deal, before the Progressives, before the Civil War, and before the Jacksonians.

Introduction to Chapters

National administration in expansion policy and Indian affairs is the main subject of this book. Chapter 1 reviews our national myth of North America as largely uninhabited wilderness, and the assumption that expansion was an inevitable result of demographic factors and an open West. Persistent stereotypes and assumptions have encouraged scholars to overlook expansion as the first national policy supported by a variety of government institutions and numerous individual functionaries. Alexis de Tocqueville, for example, usually implied or simply stated that North America was either uninhabited or inhabited only by a few doomed native peoples. This attitude blinded him to the many situations in which Indians outnumbered white settlers, and he failed to recognize the demands citizens were making on the American government for services, regulation, and protection, and he failed to understand the interplay between Western policy and the established communities in the East. Tocqueville overlooked Indian agents, land agents, and other personnel when he wrote of American administrative functions being split among local and town officials, and when he wrote that "the [national] state has no administrative functionaries of its own, stationed on different points of its territory."[5] More recently, scholars such as Stephen Skowronek, Theda Skocpol, Daniel Carpenter, Richard Bensel, and others have overlooked or minimized the administrative necessities of subduing a continent and its inhabitants, and the requirements of organizing, planning, and controlling the expansion of a new nation's people and industry. Scholars who have glimpsed the more vibrant state active in these years have tended to downplay that state's scope and significance, often surrendering the clear import of their own evidence and reverting to ingrained understandings of the early state as "prebureaucratic," more potential than real. Very few of these scholars have included careful examination of Indian affairs, expansion, or the bureaucracy before the Jacksonian era. Chapter 1 offers an assessment of the literature on state development and the development of public administration, introduces a working definition of big government, and summarizes the contours of big government in the eighteenth- and nineteenth-century United States.

The main sections that follow examine expansion, Indian affairs, and the administrative state in the era of the factory system, the era of Indian removal, and the era of the reservations. Within these sections, chapters focus on three main themes: (1) national authority over a coordinated set of policies to manage expansion and Indian affairs; (2) the broad discretion

[5] Alexis de Tocqueville, *Democracy in America* (New York: Vintage, 1945), vol. 1, 92–3.

given to the executive branch and, in particular, to its field agents, as the preferred means of accomplishing clear but general objectives in a variety of unique and rapidly changing circumstances; and (3) the persistent and sometimes consciously crafted illusion of failure that surrounded, and continues to surround, the administrative activity of the Indian Office in the nineteenth century.

In the first major era of federal Indian policy, national policy and administrative efforts pacified the early frontier through diplomacy and regulations governing land and trade policy. The treaty system organized relations with Indian nations, and helped institutionalize federal government control over land, trade, and diplomacy in service of a coordinated, national effort. The national trading houses, together with a series of licensing and bonding measures, aimed to supervise trade with the Indians and oversee (in some cases eliminate) private traders, thereby limiting opportunities for unscrupulous traders or unauthorized intruders to set off a general conflict. The factory system also aimed to provide Indians with goods at a substantial discount from what the free market might provide, allowing them to trade skins for blankets and other goods – which would not only promote good relations but would help the Indians deal with the diminishment of land and game.

In the second major era of federal Indian policy, the federal government removed more than one hundred thousand Indians from southern states and relocated them on reservations west of the Mississippi River. Removal's roots were planted earlier, at least as far back as the founding era; the heyday in the Jacksonian period saw pressured removals gradually replaced by the use of direct force. And while removals from the Southeast are the most well known, removals took place across the continent and continued throughout the nineteenth and twentieth centuries. Removals were extraordinary administrative undertakings, as we will see, necessitating planning and discretionary decision making by field officers from both the civilian and military wings of the War Department.

In the third major era of Indian affairs, the national government isolated and contained Indian populations on administratively manageable reservations, shrinking reservation lands as Indian defenses weakened. Reservations were intimately tied to the removal policy, and after the height of removal reservations became the centerpiece of U.S. policy toward Native Americans. The point of reservations was to isolate Indian populations in places that were administratively controllable and where administration could be used to further U.S. expansion and development goals. Reservations were important parts of U.S. nation-building, both in areas settled by whites and in U.S. attempts to restructure and reorient native governing and community systems. Beginning in the reservation era and gaining full force in the 1870s, the United States allotted two-thirds of remaining tribal lands to individuals, in an effort to destroy tribal entities as political and social communities. Allotment, too, is an essentially administrative undertaking, involving surveying, recordkeeping, adjudication of disputes, enforcement of decisions, and so on.

United States expansion to the West never relied solely or even primarily on the military as the foundation of state power and authority. The military played an important role, one often underestimated, but its responsibilities were almost always subordinate to the effort to manage the U.S. expansion through civilian administrative mechanisms. The treaty system, national trade and intercourse laws, and gradual extension of national jurisdiction over frontier areas speak to this effort, borne of the early republic's military weakness and economic instability relative to Indian and European powers and out of a fear that unnecessary conflicts with Indians would jeopardize money, lives, and national security. Moving west by exterminating Indians was at first impractical and always costly, as well as a violation of American founding ideals. From its earliest days, the United States set out to negotiate and sign treaties – however flawed that process was – and to civilize Indians for eventual assimilation – however misguided *that* objective was. Conquest was to be had in battle only if necessary; otherwise, the path of conquest would be laid by federally controlled administrative mechanisms. States delegated policymaking and administrative primacy regarding expansion to the national government. Congress delegated power and discretionary authority to the president and to the executive branch's administrative offices, such as the War Department and, later, the Department of Interior. Agents of these departments designed and implemented Indian policies and administered Indian affairs across the continent with substantial effectiveness in the century and a half before the New Deal.

The wisdom and justice of United States policies toward American Indians are questionable, at best, and in many cases the policies were abominable and their effects tragic. Removals and reservations would today be called ethnic cleansing, and a century of initiatives designed to pacify, remove, and then isolate and contain native populations is a deplorable legacy. It is no less deplorable, and may even be more so, because proponents used the rhetoric of legalism, restraint, and high ideals to justify it. It is an error to see this history as a mistake, though, a failure of a weak state to control its agents and its citizens. Choosing to view the history of Indian policy as inept or tragically corrupt absolves public officials from responsibility for the course of national expansion. To dismiss the Indian Office itself as corrupt or poorly managed is to contribute to the expansion myth and shift responsibility for the horrors of the United States' Indian relations to the vagaries of fortune, luck, and evil men. That myth absolves the representatives and citizens of the United States of blame and responsibility, and overlooks the extensive scope of administrative mechanisms and activity designed and implemented by national officials and federal agents, often working in conjunction with state and local individuals. Expansion and Indian affairs arose from the careful, planned, and effective actions of reasonable and often well-meaning people. The rapidity and thoroughness with which the federal government pacified, removed, contained, and dispossessed American Indians and tribes across North America is an awesome display of coordinated public administration at the national level.

I

The Myth of Open Wilderness and the Outlines of Big Government

The romantic myth of Western settlement omits the federal government's critical role in promoting and managing expansion and development. The image of an open wilderness, slowly peopled by rugged pioneers who built towns and communities and small businesses independent of the national government, is false. The understanding of "government" and public administration as late entries upon the stage, come to constrain and oppress the individualism and free spirit of the American pioneer, is similarly false. Nevertheless, understanding of the West remains obscure to almost all but historians of the West itself. As a result, the development of government administrative structures to plan and manage westward expansion remains largely hidden.

The North American continent was not open wilderness. The land supported and sustained hundreds of sovereign political communities with millions of people – farmers, traders, and hunters, husbands, wives, and children, living in houses, tepees, and pueblos, and living everywhere from New England to Florida, from the old states of the Southeast to the Ohio Valley, from the Mississippi Valley to Arizona, the Pacific Northwest, California, and along the Great Plains from the Dakotas to Texas. The fact of these communities, and the fact that they were, in many cases, politically and militarily sophisticated enough to threaten the very existence of the United States, is a truer starting point for understanding the development of the national government and its administrative structures.

An open wilderness is easy to conquer – individual pioneers can do it. The myth never requires, and therefore never sees, the extensive activities of the national government. A peopled continent – and a dangerous continent, and a complicated continent – immediately reveals the need for, and presence of, indispensable coordinating activity and administrative structures. Moreover, the constantly changing nature of U.S. relations with diverse American Indian nations – from those nations east of the Mississippi in the years of the early republic, to the Southeastern nations and nations west of the Mississippi through the early part of the nineteenth century, to completely different cultures, structures, and environments as the United States moved west through Mexico and the Southwest, and then back again to the Dakotas at the close of the nineteenth century – suggests the variety and rapidly shifting nature of political and administrative contexts confronting federal administrators.

Millions of People with Diverse Communities and Interests

The Hollywood version of our history – or the dime novel version, or the James Fenimore Cooper version, for that matter – simplifies Indians and Indian affairs, leaving no need for government, management, and administration. Simple and rare Indians create no great obstacles to U.S. expansion. Thus the mythic view hides the actions of government officials. The reality of the situation in North America quickly suggests that expansion couldn't have been as easy as it looks in the theater.

Persistent stereotypes have hobbled understanding of Indian affairs since the days of Columbus. These stereotypes obscure the size and significance of American Indian populations, the diverse and complicated political interests involved in white–Indian relations, and the humanity of Indian leaders and communities. They also obscure the reasons why government involvement was so essential to the orderly and effective continental expansion of the United States. The stereotypes must be rejected in order to clear a path for understanding the complexity of Indian affairs, and thus the complexity of politics and public administration related to U.S. expansion.[1]

Between 75 million and 112 million people lived in the Americas in 1492; some estimates range as high as 145 million people. Between 12.5 million

[1] See, e.g., Robert F. Berkhofer Jr., *The White Man's Indian: Images of the American Indian from Columbus to the Present* (New York: Vintage, 1978); Richard Slotkin, *Regeneration Through Violence: The Mythology of the American Frontier, 1600–1860* (New York: HarperPerennial, 1996 [1973]). For illustration of the staying power of these stereotypes in American culture, see the essays in Peter C. Rollins and John E. O'Connor, eds., *Hollywood's Indian: The Portrayal of the Native American in Film* (Lexington: The University Press of Kentucky, 1998); Carter Jones Meyer and Diana Royer, eds., *Selling the Indian: Commercializing & Appropriating American Indian Cultures* (Tucson: University of Arizona Press, 2001); Ward Churchill, *Fantasies of the Master Race: Literature, Cinema and the Colonization of American Indians* (Monroe, ME: Common Courage Press, 1992). Recent scholarship in Indian affairs law demonstrates how thoroughly (and dangerously) these stereotypes continue to permeate U.S. legal and political decisions. See, e.g., N. Bruce Duthu, *American Indians and the Law* (New York: Viking, 2008); David E. Wilkins and K. Tsianina Lomawaima, *Uneven Ground: American Indian Sovereignty and Federal Law* (Norman: University of Oklahoma Press, 2001); Kevin Bruyneel, *The Third Space of Sovereignty: The Postcolonial Politics of U.S.-Indigenous Relations* (Minneapolis: University of Minnesota Press, 2007); Robert A. Williams Jr., *Like a Loaded Weapon: The Rehnquist Court, Indian Rights, and the Legal History of Racism in America* (Minneapolis: University of Minnesota Press, 2005).

and 18 million people lived in North America, with roughly 1.2 million people in the Pacific coastal region, 3.8 million around the Great Lakes, and 2.7 million in California, the Great Basin, and the Plains. Henry Dobyns estimated that about 1.1 million people lived from the Gulf of Mexico across east Texas, close to 700,000 in Florida, and about 2.2 million from Florida up the East Coast to Massachusetts. He estimates about 5.25 million in the Mississippi River valley, including the Missouri, Ohio, Kentucky, and Tennessee areas – for a total of between 16 and 18 million people in what is now the continental United States.[2]

These were not scattered, roaming populations. They were often agricultural communities, settled in cities as large as Cahokia, near present-day St. Louis, with an estimated 40,000 inhabitants. Numerous cities of over 10,000 people dotted the landscape; Florida in 1500, for example, contained roughly 150 communities of 2,000 or more inhabitants.[3] Native cities lie under many major U.S. cities, and these communities were connected: native trade routes are the geographic basis for the U.S. interstate highway system,[4] and native trading networks extended for thousands of miles. This networked complexity belies the image of isolated Indian communities in idyllic settings, unfamiliar with trade or with strangers. This was not a sleepy, frozen frontier waiting for the arrival of John Wayne or Kevin Costner to start the action; it was an energetic, constantly evolving kaleidoscope of diversity, uncertainty, trade, and politics.

Even as Indian populations declined because of European exploration, colonists and then the United States continued to confront region after region in which Indians were substantial parts of the population, often outnumbering whites. Russell Thornton estimates that by 1800, about six hundred thousand Indians remained in what is now the lower forty-eight states.[5]

[2] David E. Stannard, *American Holocaust: The Conquest of the New World* (New York: Oxford University Press, 1992), 11, 266–8, and Appendix 1. Stannard's appendix offers an excellent short summary of population studies and how estimates have changed over time. See also the works of Henry Dobyns, especially his seminal study, "Estimating Aboriginal American Population: An Appraisal of Techniques with a New Hemispheric Estimate," *Current Anthropology* 7 (1966); and *Their Number Become Thinned: Native American Population Dynamics in Eastern North America* (Knoxville: University of Tennessee Press, 1983); Russell Thornton, *American Indian Holocaust and Survival: A Population History Since 1492* (Norman: University of Oklahoma Press, 1990); Lenore A. Stiffarm with Phil Lane Jr., "The Demography of Native North America: A Question of American Indian Survival," in *The State of Native America: Genocide, Colonization, and Resistance*, ed. M. Annette Jaimes (Boston: South End Press, 1992), 26–7. For a helpful chart comparing scholars' estimates of native populations at contact, see Paul Stuart, *Nations Within a Nation: Historical Statistics of American Indians* (New York: Greenwood Press, 1987), 51.

[3] Dobyns, cited in Stiffarm and Lane, "Demography," 29.

[4] Jack Weatherford, *Indian Givers: How the Indians of the Americas Transformed the World* (New York: Fawcett Columbine, 1988), ch. 13.

[5] Thornton, *Holocaust*, 90.

Other estimates place this number closer to 1.5 million or 1.8 million,[6] at a time when the entire U.S. population stood at roughly 5 million.[7] Through the expansion era, the United States would deal with millions of American Indians living in settled, stable communities, or seasonally migrating across established and familiar regions. And although these numbers do not approach the several hundred millions of North American inhabitants with which we are familiar today, the numbers are substantial and – perhaps even more important – native populations inhabited the same areas that whites would come to desire most energetically. Henry Brackenridge, an investor in Ohio lands with links to George Washington, Thomas Jefferson, and Albert Gallatin, wrote of Indian mounds along the Ohio and Scioto Rivers that "all of these vestiges invariably occupy the most eligible situations for towns or settlements."[8] The best lands, the most fertile valleys, the easiest places to cross rivers and canyons and ranges and deserts, places near water, places protected from weather, places on ancient roads and waterways suitable for residence, agriculture, trade – whites confronted Native Americans at the crucial and valuable places where whites wanted to settle, build farms and cities and ports, and run railroads.

The image of hundreds of North American communities supporting millions of American Indians clashes with the vast open spaces and small populations characteristic of films and novels about the West. But the numbers and the nature of native communities are not the only popular culture stereotypes that obscure the realities of the West and American Indians. Common stereotypes present Indians as a single, monolithic group, usually one amalgamating the Plains cultures of the mid- to late nineteenth century. Yet Indian nations are diverse. Farming nations in the Southeast, fishing tribes on the Great Lakes or in the Pacific Northwest, hunting tribes of the Great Plains, Comanche traders on the lower Plains, Pueblos of the Southwest – all possess unique cultures, histories, backgrounds, and religions. The stereotype hides the diversity of the tribes and bands with which the United States dealt in the eighteenth, nineteenth, and twentieth centuries. The stereotype of a monolithic group also obscures the fact that Indian nations' interests shift, just like those of all other nations. The Seminole had different interests in 1825 than they had in 1925, and different than they have in 2010. The Nez Perce Indians of the Northwest had interests and goals in 1840 that differed from their interests and goals in the 1870s, and their interests and goals

[6] Stiffarm and Lane, "Demography," 37.

[7] Richard B. Morris, ed., *Encyclopedia of American History*, 6th ed. (New York: Harper & Row, 1982), 649.

[8] Quoted in Judith Nies, *Native American History: A Chronology of a Culture's Vast Achievements and their Links to World Events* (New York: Ballantine, 1996), 196.

would shift subtly every year as circumstances on the ground changed: personalities change, relationships with the United States, England, and other tribes evolve.

Given this diversity, it is easy to understand why tribes do not always, or even often, share the same interests or behave as a cohesive group. The Lakota and the Crow, the Navajo and the Hopi, the Cherokee and the Seminole – and bands and groups within any of those tribes – have independent interests in policy issues depending on matters of leadership, era, politics, and so on. Tribes in close proximity often competed with each other, giving them different goals and interests. Distant tribes, with vastly different societies, pursued completely different goals and reaped different benefits or costs from national policies.

The misperception of Indians as a monolithic group with shared interests often seems to suggest that managing or representing those interests at the level of the national government is relatively simple. (Leave aside for the moment that the Bureau of Indian Affairs only became an ally and advocate of Indians during the New Deal, if even then.) Administrators at the War Department and the Indian Office did not and could not approach Indian affairs as a homogeneous set of interests when negotiating treaties, controlling land exchanges, or implementing trade and social policies. In dealing with multiple cultures in a broad variety of changing and evolving policy and administrative circumstances, the Indian Department has far more in common with the State Department than it does with a typical "client" agency.

Beyond the tribes, individual Indians are far more diverse in interests and individual character than the stereotypes ever suggest. The images of the "good Indian" and the "bad Indian" coexist, and both serve to hide what should be an obvious fact: Indians are people. Attitudes differ, change, and evolve; personal motives enter into political issues; and not all Indians agree. Asking "What is the Indian position" on an issue, whether the topic is twenty-first-century gaming or nineteenth-century demands for removal, yields more questions than answers. Which Indian? Which tribe? When? Who's asking? As a parallel, consider asking, What do Africans think about global warming? The question itself seems absurd. The diversity and complexity of Indians in reality far outstrip the stereotypes. When John Ross wrestled with the question of Cherokee alliance with North or South in the early days of the Civil War, he did not approach the issue as a noble savage or as a bloodthirsty warrior; he approached it as a skilled, veteran international diplomat concerned with both success, victory, and the well-being of an often fractured and contentious constituency.[9] The same is true of

[9] Ari Kelman, "Deadly Currents: John Ross's Decision of 1861," in *Major Problems in American Indian History*, 2nd ed., ed. Albert L. Hurtado and Peter Iverson (Boston: Houghton

Osceola, Crazy Horse, Geronimo, Looking Glass, and Chief Joseph, and of ordinary Indian men, women, and children throughout years of constant upheaval and critical decision making.

Individuals within tribes had diverse opinions on the issues of the day, just as Indians today, in different parts of the country and within a particular tribe, do not hold a single, monolithic view on issues like gaming. And, as anywhere else, even where there is agreement on a basic policy (like gaming), there is disagreement on the details (location, management companies, business plans, contractors). At contact, Indians disagreed over the proper course to follow in dealing with the newcomers. Later, some Indians in the 1820s and 1830s favored removal, for a variety of different reasons, even as many others opposed the idea with force. Individuals in the reservation era split over questions of whether to continue armed resistance against U.S. encroachment or accept terms of peace; whether or not children should be given over to government boarding schools, and why; whether or not contracts with mining or railroad companies or with cattlemen were in the community's best interest. One of the most effective U.S. tactics in battling and influencing Indian nations has always been to take advantage of the diversity of opinion in native communities, to divide and conquer – to encourage factional infighting and make incremental headway toward U.S. goals. If some Indians want to remove in 1830, for example, let them argue it out with their opponents, weakening a nation's cohesion. Then move those who will go, and deal with the others – numerically and politically weakened – later.

Two other stereotypes persist in white relations with American Indians. The stereotype of the deficient Indian centers on the image of Indians in terms of what they lack, at least from the observer's point of view. In various cases, Indians are seen as lacking Christianity, manufactured goods, civilization, morals, intelligence, potential, and so on. This stereotype drives many aspects of U.S. Indian policy. Damaging, too, is the "vanishing Indian" stereotype that assumes the inevitable defeat – through extinction or assimilation – of American Indians.[10]

These facts may seem simple and obvious, but they are too easily – and too often – overlooked. Stereotypes of Indians – as small in number, as a homogeneous group, as divided into caricatures of good and bad Indians – are part of the reason why expansion as a public policy issue, and the difficulty of managing expansion, are absent from so many works on American political and bureaucratic development. Considering Indians as few in number, as

Mifflin, 2001); Joseph T. Glatthaar and James Kirby Martin, *Forgotten Allies: The Oneida Indians and the American Revolution* (New York: Hill and Wang, 1996); Laurence M. Hauptman, *Between Two Fires: American Indians in the Civil War* (New York: Free Press Paperbacks, 1996).

10 See Berkhofer, *White Man's Indian.*

easy to deal with, and as inevitable losers facing the unstoppable advance of the United States dictates a particular historical tale. If Indians and Indian affairs were as the stereotypes suggest, there might *not* have been much need for government, policy, and administration. But: if Indians are diverse culturally, tribally, and individually; if they are complicated politically; if they disagree with each other, from tribe to tribe and individual to individual; and if there are hundreds of tribes and millions of people – then the task of managing U.S. expansion looks much, much more difficult. It becomes like many other areas of public policy – a charged political arena peopled by astute, savvy, and changing individuals, interests, and tribal groups, building alliances and coalitions, seeking advantages, testing strengths and weaknesses, vying for public opinion, and playing the institutions of various governments against each other.

Myth and Assumptions in the Literature

Scholarship on American state and administrative development tends to ignore or marginalize expansion and Indian affairs, and to replace study, analysis, and evidence regarding early administrative eras with presumptions about simple issues and meager, uncoordinated responses. This has had devastating effects on our understanding of the scope and complexity of the federal government's operations in the late eighteenth and nineteenth centuries.

Indians are simply invisible in many works. Some authors choose to dismiss Indian affairs as unique or unusual. Daniel Carpenter, for example, explicitly excludes Indian affairs from his analysis of the Interior Department. Carpenter's study of bureaucratic autonomy offers no analysis of the Indian Office or the Bureau of Indian Affairs during a century of policy encompassing the factory system, the end of the factory system, Indian removal, reservations, allotment, and leasing.[11] William Novak, in his thorough study of state-level regulation in the nineteenth century, largely avoids the topic of federal-level regulation and explicitly opts out of addressing Indian affairs, acknowledging the topic as a major piece of the puzzle in understanding the nineteenth century but one beyond the scope of his research.[12] Indians, Cherokees, and Thomas McKenney do not appear in the index for Matthew Crenson's book on Jackson-era bureaucracy, despite the significance of Indian removal in the Jackson years. For a book on

[11] Daniel P. Carpenter, *The Forging of Bureaucratic Autonomy: Reputations, Networks, and Policy Innovation in Executive Agencies, 1862–1928* (Princeton: Princeton University Press, 2001), 12, 37ff.

[12] William J. Novak acknowledges that Indian affairs, public lands, public defense, public finance, public works, natural resources, slavery, and a host of other areas fall outside his scope. William J. Novak, *The People's Welfare: Law & Regulation in Nineteenth-Century America* (Chapel Hill: The University of North Carolina Press, 1996), e.g., 16, 53.

Jacksonian bureaucracy to overlook McKenney – the chief administrator for Indian affairs for Jackson, and for the country generally since 1816 – is remarkable.[13] McKenney gets one passing reference in Daniel Feller's book on Jacksonian land policy, along with a few scattered references to Indian removal.[14]

Some scholars have included but oversimplified Indian affairs. Leonard White, in *The Jeffersonians*, states that he will not address the process of dispossessing Indians of their lands because he considers that to have been a political, rather than an administrative, problem.[15] This is far from the truth, as we will see, but it speaks to the deep denial of academic analysts about the planning and effort it takes to conquer a continent using primarily administrative, rather than military, means. Even Laura Jensen, who does an admirable job of returning consistently to the Indian context in her study of early social provision, has a relatively oversimplified understanding of Indian affairs dynamics. Whereas some authors tend to overlook the complexity and moral disaster associated with U.S. Indian policy, Jensen's statements about U.S. policy as one close to a policy of extermination are well-meaning, but oversimplified and misleading, as we will see.[16]

Failing to examine the relationship of Indian affairs to other issues causes confusion in some works. Carpenter, for example, follows White and characterizes the Interior Department as "a kit bag of programs and bureaus that bore no relation to one another – land management, patent administration, pension distribution, Indian affairs."[17] Yet, as Jensen shows, Indian affairs, land management, and pension distribution had been intricately connected since the Revolution, something that Washington and others acknowledged for decades as the national government crafted coordinated responses to the needs of veterans, Indians, speculators, white settlers, and numerous other interests.[18] Peter Onuf's study of early land policy largely ignores the foundation of the nation's land policies in Indian affairs and the efforts made by the national government to secure peace and title to lands, a prerequisite for the ordered expansion and settlement that he so thoroughly documents.

13 Matthew A. Crenson, *The Federal Machine: Beginnings of Bureaucracy in Jacksonian America* (Baltimore: The Johns Hopkins University Press, 1975).

14 Daniel Feller, *The Public Lands in Jacksonian Politics* (Madison: University of Wisconsin Press, 1984), 128 and 14, 94, 111, 197–8.

15 Leonard D. White, *The Jeffersonians: A Study in Administrative History, 1801–1829* (New York: Free Press, 1951), 498 n4.

16 Laura Jensen, *Patriots, Settlers, and the Origins of American Social Policy* (Cambridge: Cambridge University Press, 2003), e.g., at 12, 135.

17 Carpenter, *Forging*, 51.

18 See Jensen, *Patriots*; Peter S. Onuf, *The Origins of the Federal Republic: Jurisdictional Controversies in the United States, 1775–1787* (Philadelphia: University of Pennsylvania Press, 1983); Reginald Horsman, *The Frontier in the Formative Years, 1783–1815* (Albuquerque: University of New Mexico Press, 1975).

Onuf overlooks the careful creation of circumstances involving Indian affairs that allowed for economic development. Phrases like "Congress's overriding concern with revenue"[19] dot the discussion, overlooking Congress's equal (at least) concern for national security in potentially hostile territories. Onuf seems to begin with the myth of open wilderness, as if the land were already in the safe and secure hands of the new Union.[20]

Several recent works carefully delineate the scope of early national government activity, yet even these fail to examine expansion and Indian affairs fully and carefully. Jerry Mashaw, for example, provides a thorough explication of administrative law in the early republic from 1787 to 1801. Yet Mashaw, like other writers, trivializes Indian affairs generally and war with Indians in particular. Mashaw discusses the factory system only briefly, in a footnote, and he also relegates to a footnote the vast authority delegated to the president throughout the 1790s to enable responses to threats from abroad.[21] Also footnoted are delegations of authority to the president in 1799 to furnish tribes with animals and farming implements, regulate trade, and to preserve peace on the frontiers.[22] Why these are addressed in footnotes rather than in the main text is not explained, but the choice suggests that the author does not consider the topics significant enough to crack the main line of analysis. Several references to the Indian trade, licensing systems, and legislation are not examined further. Mashaw also excludes expansion, Indian affairs, land policy, international relations, and trade regulation from his list of "the big operations" of the government.[23] Max Edling, who examines the role of the military in the West to good effect, repeats the tendency to underestimate the difficulty and significance of expansion, Indian affairs, and administration.[24] Richard John's excellent study of the Post Office and its relationship to national expansion makes only brief reference to Indian affairs, even though treaties were frequent prerequisites to the construction of post roads and Indians were constant participants in controversies regarding the mails.[25]

[19] Peter S. Onuf, *Statehood and Union: A History of the Northwest Ordinance* (Bloomington: Indiana University Press, 1987), 30.

[20] Onuf, *Statehood and Union*, 15. Carol Sheriff similarly overlooks Indian affairs and the land acquisition process in her study of the Erie Canal: Carol Sheriff, *The Artificial River: The Erie Canal and the Paradox of Progress, 1817–1862* (New York: Hill and Wang, 1996).

[21] Jerry L. Mashaw, "Recovering American Administrative Law: Federalist Foundations, 1787–1801," *The Yale Law Journal* 115 (April 2006), 1300, notes 134 and 135.

[22] Mashaw, "Recovering," 1301 n136. With other similar issues, Mashaw hedges on an explanation for such broad delegations of power, calling the reasons "not always obvious."

[23] Mashaw, "Recovering," 1338.

[24] Max M. Edling, *A Revolution in Favor of Government: Origins of the U.S. Constitution and the Making of the American State* (Oxford: Oxford University Press, 2003), e.g., 139, 146.

[25] Richard R. John, *Spreading the News: The American Postal System from Franklin to Morse* (Cambridge, MA: Harvard University Press, 1995), 97, 134.

Without a full and nuanced approach to Indians and expansion, scholarship has tended to marginalize or trivialize state activity and bureaucratic development. Without Indians and expansion, such development can look meager and haphazard, and conclusions rest on our collective myths and presumptions about the early republic and the nineteenth century.

To begin, it is important to note that studies of American political development and the development of public administration at the national level usually overlook or quickly dismiss the years before the Civil War, particularly the years before the Jackson administration. Notable exceptions by a few authors like Laura Jensen and Matthew Crenson offer different models for approaching those years, but if one looks to leading authors like Stephen Skowronek, Theda Skocpol, Richard Bensel, Daniel Carpenter, and others, one finds brief references and broad assumptions about those early years. Despite what look like thorough efforts in the past twenty years or so, then, careful study of public administration and the administrative state in the nineteenth century is still a largely untapped area of inquiry.

In his landmark *Building a New American State*, for example, Stephen Skowronek looks at almost nothing before the Jacksonians, save for a brief glance at the period immediately following the War of 1812.[26] Richard Bensel, in his well-received *Yankee Leviathan*, brushes quickly past the early era and exemplifies the predominance of Skowronek's assertions about the absence of a sense of the state in early America. Bensel writes, in a footnote, "The interpretation put forward here *assumes* little preexisting state-centered orientation on the part of the participants in Union or Confederate public life."[27] He views state-building as haphazard, with little recognition by the participants of a statist perspective.

Terminology and language trivialize and marginalize the early state, with little or no supporting evidence or clear definition of terms. In his perfunctory discussion of the "early" state, Skowronek refers to the state as "meager,"

[26] Stephen Skowronek, *Building a New American State: The Expansion of National Administrative Capacities, 1877–1920* (Cambridge: Cambridge University Press, 1982).

[27] Richard Franklin Bensel, *Yankee Leviathan: The Origins of Central State Authority in America, 1859–1877* (Cambridge: Cambridge University Press, 1990), 98 n6 (emphasis added). Bennett and Bennett, in their study, *Living with Leviathan: Americans Coming to Terms with Big Government*, skip directly to the Jackson era, and then they skip forward from the 1830s to the 1860s with no analysis of the years in between. Their entire discussion of the United States before the Civil War runs to roughly four and a half pages. Linda L. M. Bennett and Stephen Earl Bennett, *Living With Leviathan: Americans Coming to Terms with Big Government* (Lawrence: University Press of Kansas, 1990). Even Desmond King and Rogers Smith, in their study of racial institutional orders, fail to discuss explicitly the period before the Civil War in their section on bureaucracy and in their discussion of Carpenter's omission of race. This is a remarkable oversight given the authors' main contention that race needs to be a larger part of political development research. See Desmond S. King and Rogers M. Smith, "Racial Orders in American Political Development," *American Political Science Review* 99 (February 2005), 85–6.

and he refers to its "tiny" army.[28] Daniel Carpenter writes of "feeble" public authority at the national level, quoting Tocqueville, and he writes that executive departments were "only quiet and quiescent spectators" in national debates over policy and legislation.[29] No evidence is offered. Bensel, in *Yankee Leviathan*, repeatedly marginalizes the pre–Civil War state, even as he obliquely refers to the demanding responsibilities faced by that state. The discussion is marked by assertion and presumption, not by evidence: "Up to the point of capture [of the state by northern Republicans], the American state had been *little more than* an arena in which contending forces and coalitions in the national political economy competed over decisions related to continental settlement and foreign policy."[30] Carpenter similarly mentions conquest and "managing of lands" almost in passing,[31] and Bensel writes that "The [Republican] platform did not reveal any inclination to regulate investment or direct economic activity beyond the *mild manipulations* of land distribution, development of rivers and harbors, and a tariff on imports."[32]

The trivializing phrases judge and dismiss issue areas that would seem to be fairly important, like continental conquest, settlement, and foreign policy. Why assume that activity regulating investment and directing economic activity in *land*, a centerpiece of the new nation's security, economy, and future, is "mild"? Similarly, again from Bensel: "Restricted to a *very few functions* such as the collection of customs duties and delivery of the mail, the federal government contained no statist-bureaucratic element that could prepare for the secession crisis."[33] What are the other functions? And why presume that they are so simple? Finally, harkening back to terms like "meager" and "feeble," Bensel adds: "Because northern nationalists and southern separatists so completely divided the terrain of the antebellum political system, no purely statist program could develop the *anemic apparatus* of the federal government."[34] Such an assertion is in dire need of deeper definition and analysis.

All of this leads to a particular set of assumptions about policy and public administration at the national level. Federal activity is presumed to have been as simplistic, disorganized, and marginal as the issues themselves. Skowronek writes, "The path that had been traveled in the development of early American government did not anticipate the need for a strong national administrative arm."[35] He adds, "There were no foreign enemies posing

28 Skowronek, *Building*, 8.
29 Carpenter, *Forging*, 38.
30 Bensel, *Yankee Leviathan*, 2 (emphasis added).
31 Carpenter, *Forging*, 37.
32 Bensel, *Yankee Leviathan*, 67 (emphasis added).
33 Ibid., 85 (emphasis added).
34 Ibid., 91 (emphasis added).
35 Skowronek, *Building*, 4.

a threat to security, and internal social conflict could be diffused through movement to the frontier."[36] The first part of this is inaccurate; the second is much more difficult than the passage suggests. Relying on Bensel and one other source, Skocpol writes, "Only during the Civil War did a Republican-run crusade to save a northern-dominated nation temporarily transfer the locus of sovereignty to an activist federal government."[37] We will see that this is also exaggerated, as the federal government had been "activist" and at the center of sovereignty from the earliest days of expansion policy. Bensel writes, in his opening paragraph, "Other than these pleas to a return to 'the Constitution as it was,' the modern state's inheritance from the antebellum period was nil. In that sense, then, an account of American state formation can begin with the Civil War with little lost in historical continuity or theoretical generality."[38] This is wildly overstated.

Trivializing the scope and role of the early American state plays havoc with our understanding of national administrative capacity and bureaucratic development. Asserting the general absence of important or complicated federal duties, and presuming a small, anemic governing structure, scholars pass quickly beyond any deeper inquiry into the scope and nature of early bureaucracy. The subtitle of Matthew Crenson's *Building the Invisible Orphanage* is "*A Prehistory of the American Welfare System*"; his book on Jacksonian land policy is subtitled, "*Beginnings of Bureaucracy in Jacksonian America.*" Without further explanation, he passingly refers to the "*non*bureaucratic forms of government administration" before the Jacksonians which would have to be "abandon[ed]" as bureaucratic forms were "superimposed upon the business of the national government."[39] Carpenter writes that "Americans regarded [early] bureaucracies as brute administrative units, not planning or policymaking organizations,"[40] and he writes, "The possibility of employing bureaucracies to address national problems, the possibility of bureaucratic planning, was almost entirely removed from the American political imagination."[41] Public administration scholar David Rosenbloom regularly refers to these years as "prebureaucratic," and speaks of later eras having to "retrofit" the administrative state.[42] Michael Nelson

36 Ibid., 7.

37 Theda Skocpol, *Protecting Soldiers and Mothers: The Political Origins of Social Policy in the United States* (Cambridge, MA: Harvard University Press, 1995), 68.

38 Bensel, *Yankee Leviathan*, ix.

39 Crenson, *Federal Machine*, ix; emphasis in original.

40 Carpenter, *Forging*, 40.

41 Ibid., 47.

42 David H. Rosenbloom, "Retrofitting the Administrative State to the Constitution: Congress and the Judiciary's Twentieth-Century Progress," *Public Administration Review* 60 (January/February 2000); see also Laurence E. Lynn Jr., "The Myth of the Bureaucratic Paradigm: What Traditional Public Administration Really Stood For," *Public Administration Review* 61 (March/April 2001), 147.

calls the "status of administration" "still nascent in the early nineteenth century," and refers to "the limited demands" placed on that government. Nelson follows Crenson in arguing that "administrative agencies at this time were not organized bureaucratically," and that bosses were able to order and oversee underlings effectively.[43] Ira Katznelson, even as he offers a sophisticated look at the military before the Civil War, offers a similar review of the significant activities of the early state and then retreats to characterizing the United States central bureaucracy as "small and limited," at least in comparative perspective.[44] All of this assumes a certain past, one resting on assumption and assertion rather than on evidence and analysis.[45]

Similar presumptions infuse presentations of the public administrators working for the federal government. Martin Shefter refers to federal employees as "gentlemen dilettantes."[46] Matthew Crenson rests on the old saw about the Washington administration's reliance upon "fitness of character," rather than formal rules and regulations, to organize administration.[47] Carpenter offers the idea of a "clerical" state, inhabited by administrators who were little more than clerks following orders without contributing anything notable in the way of innovation or creativity. Notably, Carpenter's analysis of "the clerical state" prior to the Jacksonians runs just slightly more than one paragraph.[48] Yet it is hard to categorize Benjamin Hawkins, longtime federal agent to Indians in the South, or Henry Schoolcraft, writer and longtime northern agent, as "clerks." It is hard to imagine Andrew Jackson, military leader and treaty commissioner, as a clerk. It is hard to categorize Secretary of War Henry Knox or longtime Indian Office head Thomas McKenney as gentlemen dilettantes. Such presentations reinforce a lasting impression of simplicity, smallness, and extremely limited scope – an impression that is supported more by our collective presumptions and prejudices than it is by analysis, research, and evidence.

The effect of so many terms like "prebureaucratic," "meager," and "feeble" so often and so easily passed off as analysis is significant, discouraging further inquiry and reinforcing presuppositions about the early American

43 Michael Nelson, "A Short, Ironic History of American National Bureaucracy," *The Journal of Politics* 44 (August 1982), 755–6. See also 768, arguing that federal functions did not change through the early and middle nineteenth century. Nelson relies on the same narrow group of authors, including Skowronek, White, and Crenson.

44 Ira Katznelson, "Flexible Capacity: The Military and Early American Statebuilding," in *Shaped by War and Trade: International Influences on American Political Development*, ed. Ira Katznelson and Martin Shefter (Princeton: Princeton University Press, 2002), 89.

45 For a review of traditional thinking and approaches to the development of public administration in the United States, with a call for a more historically careful approach, see Lynn, "Myth"; David H. Rosenbloom, "History Lessons for Reinventors," *Public Administration Review* 61 (March/April 2001).

46 Quoted in Skocpol, *Protecting*, 74.

47 Crenson, *Federal Machine*, x.

48 Carpenter, *Forging*, 40–1.

state without offering much evidence to justify the conclusions. It is hard to know what to make of a "tiny" army that can remove one hundred thousand Indians a thousand miles to the west, against their will; it is hard to know what to make of a meager government that can dispossess millions of American Indians and contain them on administratively manageable reservations, all the while organizing land transfers and channeling expansion of a nation across a continent.

Such problems are exacerbated by use of a narrow and self-reinforcing set of sources. The work with the most impact on the topic has clearly been Skowronek's *Building a New American State*, but it is important to remember that Skowronek's conclusions about early America's sense of statelessness rest on the works of three scholars who did not live in the United States: Hegel, Marx, and Tocqueville. These are curious choices, even given Tocqueville's uncanny ability to get many things right about Americans. But Tocqueville is notoriously weak on expansion and Indian affairs, and it is an odd choice to rely on these three writers for such important conclusions about such an amorphous, intangible concept as a sense of a state. The impact is significant: in the relatively limited literature on state development, especially for years prior to the Civil War, Skowronek is the foundation source for many other works. Carpenter and Bensel, for example, rely heavily on Skowronek. Skocpol relies heavily on Skowronek and Bensel. Michael Nelson quotes Skowronek on the duties of the early government but retreats, with Skowronek, to a conclusion that its tasks (maintaining a continental legal order, fighting wars, expropriating Indians, securing new territories, maintaining international diplomacy, and fostering economic development) created only a small bureaucracy with modest functions, a "tiny" army, and an engineers corps with "a few frontier patrols."[49] The sources tend to wrap into each other, simultaneously reinforcing each other and dampening further inquiry. The marginalizing and self-referencing approaches taken by various authors are significant because they discourage further analysis into state issues and the responses that tended to enhance centralization and extend state power.

Authors occasionally hint at the presence of something not fully uncovered or examined, only to back away from deeper investigation and return to their primary subjects. Crenson notes that "There may have been some respects, of course, in which the national government was always bureaucratic." He looks to the rule of law here, but asserts that "the formal rules and regulations – of a bureaucratic order," or the idea of "organizational impersonality," "were not realized in the conduct of everyday government business for more than a generation."[50] Crenson's presentation is similar

49 Nelson, "Short, Ironic History," 755–6.
50 Crenson, *Federal Machine*, x.

to those by Skowronek and Skocpol, both of whom acknowledge the presence of state structures even in the early republic but who both quickly dismiss them as relatively unimportant, especially – as Skowronek classically asserted – because they created no sense of the state. Mashaw, too, flinches at the implication of an administrative state in the eighteenth century. After his impressive list of national actions in the republic's opening decades, Mashaw drifts back to calling the government's efforts "relatively feeble"; only "around the edges of these dominant themes of development and defense, familiar modern concerns and administrative techniques began to emerge."[51] After favorably mentioning administrative developments and alluding to the Federalists' "strenuous efforts" and innovations, Mashaw reverts to evaluating "the power of the government to command both allegiance and obedience" as "suspect to say the least."[52] He concurs with Shefter's assessment that the state had both "weak parties and a weak bureaucracy," and "glimpse[s]" only the "beginnings" of the idea of a hierarchically organized civil service.[53] He writes that "The idea of agencies as expert administrators – indeed the very idea of public administration – lay far in the future."[54]

Part of the confusion stems from the role played by the military in American state development. War, crisis, and military development are classic engines of state development and centralization. Failing to look carefully at expansion and Indian affairs, scholars have simultaneously understated the military's development and overemphasized its significance.

The U.S. military is generally presumed to have been small and largely unnecessary, especially before the Civil War, and it is simultaneously presumed to have been dominant. Max Edling, for example, summarizes the early republic, writing that "The Federalist peace establishment came to exist of a small regular army, which served as a border constabulary securing western expansion by overcoming the Indian tribes that stood in the republic's way."[55] Theda Skocpol writes that after a "loosely coordinated" revolution against the British the United States "found itself facing westward toward a huge continent available for conquest from always worrisome yet militarily unequal opponents."[56]

Skocpol rests her assertion on just a few sources, including Bensel, Morton Keller, Samuel Huntington, Seymour Martin Lipset, and Skowronek – none of whom look carefully at conflict and war before the Civil War. Given the

51 Both quotations are in Mashaw, "Recovering," 1277.

52 Mashaw, "Recovering," 1318.

53 Ibid., 1318–19.

54 Ibid., 1342.

55 Edling, *Revolution*, 225; see also 140, 141.

56 Skocpol, *Protecting*, 44.

voluminous studies of Indian policy and expansion-related conflicts written by historians looking specifically at these issues, the choice of sources is curious, misleading, and instructive. Indian nations at the end of the Revolution were more than matches for a weakened and tired United States, a fact known to George Washington, Henry Knox, and many others, as well as one common to literature on Indian affairs and expansion. Arthur St. Clair, whose defeat at the hands of a pan-Indian confederacy in 1791 included the loss of a huge part of the U.S. army, would be surprised to hear his adversaries described as "worrisome yet militarily unequal."[57] The same can be said of William Henry Harrison, who had his hands full in the Old Northwest, the series of American commanders who failed to drive the Seminoles out of Florida, and the military leaders who lost battle after battle to American Indian opponents on the Plains and in the West.

Scholars have tended to make two mistakes when it comes to understanding the military and state-building in the United States. First, in assuming a relatively open West – worrisome opponents but not significant ones – scholars have failed to look carefully at development in the military. The military's roles and its development, however, are far more extensive than scholars usually assume. Author Terry L. Anderson counts as many as 1,800 battles between Indians and whites in the period from 1790 to 1897; the vast majority of these took place between 1830 and 1880.[58] Before the Civil War, expenditures on the military "dwarfed all other outlays," in Ira Katznelson's words, running at least 72 percent of total expenditures and up to 94 percent of total expenditures each year but one between 1808 and 1848, and running to about half of federal outlays from 1848 to 1861.[59] Numerous studies demonstrate extensive activity and bureaucratization in military organization.[60] Dismissing the U.S. wars as minor policing actions discourages study and inevitably overlooks the statist dimensions of more than a century of warfare with militarily challenging opponents, whether the opponents were the Iroquois Confederacy or Tecumseh's confederacy in the early republic, the Cherokee, Seminole, and Osage during removal,

[57] Cf. Stephen Aron, "Lessons in Conquest: Towards a Greater Western History," *The Pacific Historical Review* 63 (May 1994), 137; Leroy V. Eid, "American Indian Military Leadership: St. Clair's 1791 Defeat," *The Journal of Military History* 57 (January 1993), and see n4.

[58] Terry L. Anderson, *Sovereign Nations or Reservations? An Economic History of American Indians* (San Francisco: Pacific Research Institute for Public Policy, 1995), 70.

[59] Katznelson, "Flexible Capacity," 91–3. Katznelson acknowledges the key role played in these years by expansion, Indian removal, and Indian-related warfare. See 98–9.

[60] Harry M. Ward, *The Department of War, 1781–1795* (Pittsburgh: University of Pittsburgh Press, 1962); Francis Paul Prucha, *The Sword of the Republic: The United States Army on the Frontier, 1783–1846* (Bloomington: University of Indiana Press, 1977); Mark R. Wilson, *The Business of Civil War: Military Mobilization and the State, 1861–1865* (Baltimore: The Johns Hopkins University Press, 2006).

or the Nez Perce or Sioux or Kiowa of the later nineteenth century's Indian wars.

The second mistake that scholars make is to assume that the military would be the primary locus of state-building; failing to see a fully developed, fighting military, and assuming a dearth of civilian administrative requirements, scholars have concluded that American state development was minimal. Yet Katznelson insightfully argues for a softer understanding of the military, pointing out that the U.S. military is not best understood in a comparative context with Europe in terms of its gross size or expense, but in its "flexible capacity" to serve effectively in a number of different roles, and to expand and contract as necessary, in changing environments. This understanding has much in common with Edling's description of the framers' design for national military capacity.[61] More fundamentally, the early and nineteenth-century United States is not dominated by its military, and military solutions were usually not the first choice for policymakers. It is crucial to recognize that the military was never the primary locus of administrative development in a United States committed to expansion through civilian administrative mechanisms.

The best scholarship in American state and administrative development is scholarship which addresses history directly and carefully. Works and portions of works that delve deeply into history, rather than relying on presumptions, provide instructive lessons. Laura Jensen finds significant examples of programmatic social policies before the Jacksonians. Skocpol's analysis of social policy *after* the Civil War is justifiably a landmark in the field. Bensel's careful and thorough attention to the historical record *during* the Civil War years turns up significant findings about state-building in the North and the South. The portions of works by Skowronek, Crenson, and Carpenter that focus on the historical record of the late nineteenth and early twentieth centuries are likewise much stronger than their too-brief dismissals of what had gone before.

These works stumble primarily when they draw comparisons with earlier eras that have not been carefully examined. Bensel's analysis, for example, runs into problems when making comparisons with an earlier era that he has not examined in detail. About the North Bensel writes, "The Union, while only a little better organized, possessed at least an administrative shell."[62] This is an odd way to describe what we will see develop in the seven decades from the founding to the dawn of the Civil War. Of the South, Bensel writes that "In creating the administrative apparatus necessary to orchestrate the southern war effort, the Confederate state started from scratch."[63] This is

[61] Katznelson, "Flexible Capacity"; Edling, *Revolution.*

[62] Bensel, *Yankee Leviathan*, 99.

[63] Ibid., 99.

inaccurate. The South had, for generations, prevailed upon and relied upon extensive administrative capacity at the national level to manage land and trade relations with Indians, control and channel expansion and settlement, and, finally, to remove Indians forcibly from its midst. It was only after demanding and witnessing the uses of state power and authority that the South seceded, and even then its new government was built on the institutional structures and laws of the previous union, as Bensel notes. Bensel may be correct that what drove secession was the South's calculation that the national government by the late 1850s was heading in a direction counter to its own interests. Yet even if that is correct, the South did not have to start from scratch when it came to administration. It knew what big government could do, and how it did it.

Max Edling has recently reinterpreted the formation of the United States as "a revolution in favor of government." While his study sees much of the federal government's power in the early years as potential, he argues that the authority in particular to tax and to raise militaries without limit were carefully and consciously secured. Edling writes, "[T]he Federalists developed an idea of an American state that possessed powers similar to contemporary European states, yet was shaped by the predominant American mode of antistatism."[64] My argument suggests that leaders in the federal government quickly put such potential powers into practical effect.

The Outlines of Big Government

What we find in the nation's first century and a half is what is today called big government. Big government in the American context is the combination of (1) national, programmatic social, economic, trade, and regulatory policies touching the lives of millions; (2) the bureaucratic capacity, discretionary authority, and administrative autonomy to plan, to innovate, and to effectively implement policies and programs; and (3) an awareness, a sense of the state, seamlessly and inextricably woven into the fabric of everyday life and never far from the consciousness and activity of American society. Understood in these terms, "big government" characterizes the United States long before FDR and the New Deal, long before the Progressives, and long before the Civil War. Even long before Andrew Jackson.

While my working definition is a loose one, authors, pundits, and politicians have used the phrase "big government" for many years with no definition at all.[65] In those works and in others, it becomes a term that refers

[64] Edling, *Revolution*, 10.

[65] In addition to ubiquitous usage of the phrase in contemporary politics, see, e.g., Mashaw, "Recovering," 1281–2; Bennett and Bennett, *Living with Leviathan*; King and Smith, "Racial Orders," 84; R. Shep Melnick, "An American Dilemma," *Wilson Quarterly* 23 (Autumn 1999). In *Defending Government: Why Big Government Works* (Upper Saddle

to a variety, a combination, or a conjunction of factors. It is imprecise and subjective, meaning different things to different people at different times. My understanding of big government is a conceptual idea, akin to, but not identical to, Skowronek's notion of a "sense of the state," which he describes as "the sense of an organization of coercive power operating beyond our immediate control and intruding into all aspects of our lives."[66] It is similar, too, to Edling's concept of a state that can be thought of in terms of how "light" and "inconspicuous" it is.[67] "Big government" used herein includes a sense of the state, perhaps of lightness or heaviness, as essential components, but it is also more than that. Big government used herein relates closely to J. P. Nettl's classic notion of the state as a conceptual variable,[68] and it also relates to discussions of the "federal presence" in Western history, an imprecise concept that has inspired calls for more clarity and rigor.[69] "Big government" has definiteness beyond a "sense" or a "presence," brought to it by the existence of programs and regulations that affect, order, and manage aspects of millions of lives, and by the active institutional ability to design those efforts and influence the people they affect. Big government thus combines ability and execution with awareness (or sense) of the government's scope and efforts on the part of the citizenry.[70]

I make no judgment here about the merits of "big government." The term is used today mostly as a pejorative, and that sense can easily be applied to the state in the nineteenth century. The state's role in protecting and promoting

River, NJ: Prentice Hall, 2000), Max Neiman focuses on government size, particularly as a function of receipts and outlays, but nowhere does he actually define "big government" in normative terms. Thomas McCraw offers only a slight refinement: "big government (or, more precisely, a powerful and well-developed state apparatus)." Thomas K. McCraw, "Business & Government: The Origins of the Adversary Relationship," *California Management Review* 26 (Winter 1984), 44. Mashaw does try to clarify what he calls "the big operations" of government – which he seems to limit to revenue collection and the Post Office – as those governmental functions "involving a *substantial* number of federal employees and reaching a *large* proportion of communities." Mashaw, "Recovering," 1338 (emphasis added). Elsewhere, Mashaw offers a list of government efforts, which he identifies as "what we would now characterize as welfare state activity," but he follows the list with the vague clarification that "none of these operations was very large." Mashaw, "Recovering," 1338.

66 Skowronek, *Building*, 3.

67 Edling, *Revolution*, 224.

68 J. P. Nettl, "The State as a Conceptual Variable," *World Politics* 20 (July 1968).

69 Karen R. Merrill, "In Search of the 'Federal Presence' in the American West," *The Western Historical Quarterly* 30 (Winter 1999).

70 My definition of "big government" attempts to give the phrase more clarity than it usually is afforded, but beyond a certain point I am not sure that big government can, or even should, be precisely defined. Efforts to pin down government size or scope by looking at budgets, expenditures, number of employees, or public opinion, for example, offer a misleading kind of precision, one that sacrifices meaning for measurable data points, or what Max Neiman calls "single-factor explanations." Neiman, *Defending Government*, 9.

slavery, in controlling labor, and in the continental expropriation of millions of American Indians, including the horrible destruction and demoralization of individuals and communities, parallels closely contemporary criticism of big government. Yet big government often suggests to more sympathetic observers an effort to do good, to use the powers of an organized society to improve living conditions and order a complicated world, to redistribute resources more fairly and to help take care of society's members when they need help, when they grow old, when they meet with misfortune. These aspects of big government are also part of the nineteenth century experience. My point is not to argue for or against the *idea* of big government, as a good thing or a bad thing. My argument is merely that we should think about our country's roots and foundations in such terms.

Big government is not new, it is not unusual, it is not unexpected. Questions about its legitimacy fall silent when we recognize the hand of the founding generation in building it. Edling calls the national government under the Constitution "a government that had the right to mobilize the full resources of society at will and, therefore, a government that promised to be powerful whenever it had to be."[71] Appeals to return to a simpler time, a time before big government, when freedom reigned and government was small and limited – those are appeals to a mythical place that never existed in the United States.

National Policies in the Early Republic and the Nineteenth Century

Much of this book will focus on federal policy toward American Indians, regulation of land and expansion policies, and extensive national economic and trade regulation. In addition to these aspects of big government activity, it is important to recognize here that national, programmatic social policies involving pensions, education, health, and vocational training touched the lives of millions of people in the late eighteenth and nineteenth centuries. Benefits flowed to individuals and to groups; they flowed to citizens and, importantly, to noncitizens. They flowed as the result of services rendered, for exchanges of land and goods, as the result of feelings of compassion and charity, and in ways that were intimately intertwined with considerations of moralism, religion, patriotism, benevolence, and nationhood.

Nationally administered social policies in the nineteenth century are extensive. Laura Jensen has traced the ways in which land bounties and military pensions for revolutionary and other veterans served as programmatic social policy.[72] Jensen finds important education programs reinforcing

[71] Edling, *Revolution*, 192; also 8, 220, and generally. Regarding the legitimacy of the administrative state, see, e.g., John A. Rohr, *To Run a Constitution: The Legitimacy of the Administrative State* (Lawrence: The University Press of Kansas, 1986); Theodore J. Lowi, *The End of Liberalism: Ideology, Policy, and the Crisis of Public Authority* (New York: Norton, 1969).

[72] Jensen, *Patriots*.

land and pension policies in the early republic, Skocpol adds important information about these efforts during and after the Civil War, and Crenson, Katznelson, and Margaret Weir all consider education and schooling as closely related to development of a social welfare state.[73] Jerry Mashaw adds long lists of national attention to veterans' disability pensions, seamen's hospitals, and disaster relief.[74] Michelle Landis details the history and development of disaster claims, seeing in the process the origins of the American welfare state.[75]

Remarkably, but in line with my analysis above, these authors have generally ignored or marginalized the array of programmatic social policies targeted to noncitizen Indians and Indian communities throughout the nineteenth century, the inclusion of which extends the scope of nineteenth-century federal activity in the realm of social policy and entitlements.[76] From 1778 to 1871, for example, at least 120 U.S. treaties with Indians included education provisions.[77] Government efforts to provide and promote agriculture, domestic manufactures, and private property ownership through treaty, law, and administration fall under the rubric of education, as these efforts aimed at assimilating Indians to European–U.S. lifestyles. Aid from the federal government to missionaries, and support from federal agents for their efforts, added to the national government's education policies. Civilization programs, federal funding, treaty provisions, and missionary societies together evolved into an educational system with hundreds of schools, serving tens of thousands of students.[78]

73 Matthew A. Crenson, *Building the Invisible Orphanage: A Prehistory of the American Welfare System* (Cambridge, MA: Harvard University Press, 1998), 22.

74 Mashaw, "Recovering," 1277–82, 1321, 1338.

75 Michele L. Landis, "'Let Me Next Time Be "Tried by Fire"': Disaster Relief and the Origins of the American Welfare State 1789–1874," *Northwestern University Law Review* 92 (Spring 1998).

76 Jensen's approach and definitions encompass Indian affairs within the ambit of programmatic entitlements: *Patriots*, 3, 8, 12, 25. Landis fully integrates Indian affairs into her analysis by including Indian-related claims in her study of disaster relief. Landis, "Disaster Relief."

77 Jon Reyhner and Jeanne Eder, "A History of Indian Education," in *Teaching American Indian Students*, ed. Jon Reyhner (Norman: University of Oklahoma Press, 1994), 37.

78 The federal government played a primary and direct role after the Civil War; before the Civil War, it supported missionary efforts with funds and other aid. Reports of the exact numbers of schools and students vary, as does the level of federal support and control. According to an 1888 report, 38 federal Indian schools educated 1,159 students in 1825; in 1861, 162 schools served 5,950 students; in 1886, 531 schools educated more than 21,000 students. See Meyer Weinberg, *A Chance to Learn: The History of Race and Education in the United States* (Cambridge: Cambridge University Press, 1977), 183, Table 26. David Wallace Adams finds 200 schools (114 boarding schools and 86 day schools) serving more than 8,000 students in 1885; by 1890, 246 schools were servicing more than 12,000 students; and by 1900 more than 21,500 students attended 307 schools. David Wallace Adams, *Education for Extinction: American Indians and the Boarding School Experience, 1875–1928* (Lawrence: University Press of Kansas, 1995), 58, Table 2.2.

Since the early nineteenth century, the United States has obligated itself to provide health care, physicians, and medical supplies to Indians through treaties, laws, and the trust responsibility.[79] Historical works on particular tribes and eras are replete with examples of federal agents working on vaccinations, quarantines, sanitation, irrigation, and other health care–related areas. This is perhaps not surprising: looking at the state level, William Novak finds "an extensive regulatory regime in early America that regularly held private liberty, property, and contract subject to restriction in the interest of public health, safety, comfort, and well-being," including powers of quarantine, authority to address public health nuisances, regulations addressing public morality and sexual conduct, a system of public health inspections and vaccinations, and public works that targeted health-related issues: "drainage, sewers, waste and garbage removal, and water treatment and distribution."[80]

All of these policies were tied closely to expansion efforts, as we will see in following chapters. "Social policies" were not sharply separated from other areas of expansion policy, and other federal policies affected millions of people when they engaged issues of group membership and identification, morals and lifestyles, and religious observance. National efforts to regulate land, trade, the economy, internal improvements, and a host of other issue areas comprise an organized set of policies affecting all aspects of life in the early republic and the nineteenth century, especially in the West but also in the East.

The details of national social policies extant in the late eighteenth and nineteenth centuries are far beyond the scope of this book. We will touch on some examples, particularly in the context of Indian affairs, but the task of examining particular policy areas in the nineteenth century will remain largely unconquered for the time being. The focus of this study is on the

[79] E.g., the Miami Treaty of 1826 provided annual cash payments for the "poor and infirm." J. Diane Pearson, "Lewis Cass and the Politics of Disease: The Indian Vaccination Act of 1832," *Wicazo Sa Review* 18 (Autumn, 2003), 30 n11. The Treaty of Washington (1836) with the Ottawa Indians of Michigan included $2,000 for medicine and health care. Hauptman, *Between Two Fires*, 132. Health care provisions were included in treaties with the Kiowa and Comanche (1867), the Crows (1868), and the Eastern Band of Shoshoni (1868): Stephen J. Kunitz, "The History and Politics of US Health Care Policy for American Indians and Alaskan Natives," *American Journal of Public Health* 86 (October 1996), 1464; Timothy M. Westmoreland and Kathryn R. Watson, "Redeeming Hollow Promises: The Case for Mandatory Spending on Health Care for American Indians and Alaska Natives," *American Journal of Public Health* 96 (April 2006), 601.

[80] William J. Novak, "Private Wealth and Public Health: a critique of Richard Epstein's defense of the 'old' public health," *Perspectives in Biology and Medicine* 46 (Summer 2003), S183; see also Novak, *The People's Welfare*. Interestingly, the earliest public quarantine act cited by Novak is from 1662, and addressed Indians and servants. Novak, *The People's Welfare*, 215.

main threads of expansion and Indian policy, and on public administration and bureaucracy.

Bureaucratic Autonomy in the Early Republic and the Nineteenth Century

As studies have overlooked social provision to American Indians and the federal government's extensive regulatory role in areas like land and trade, they have often overlooked the bureaucracy set in place to design policies and deliver benefits and goods, and the dynamics of that process. Extensive programmatic policies and administrative efforts addressed and targeted American Indians, for example, with important parallels to programs involving U.S. citizens (as well as important differences). These programs existed long before the advent of Jacksonian "democracy." As we will see, these programs cannot be dismissed as unfulfilled rhetoric masking expansionist or exterminationist policies, nor can they be dismissed as inept or corrupted failures of good intent. They were often effective and helpful; they were often effective and detrimental and demoralizing. And they point to the existence of extensive administrative structures, with administrators in the nation's capital and across the continent helping to design, implement, evaluate, and adjust policies, programs, and administrative mechanisms.

The presumed absence of bureaucratic ability, capacity, structure, innovation, and planning has discouraged generations of scholars from looking for, much less carefully examining, complicated early policies. Yet bureaucratic autonomy in the United States exists in a significant way as early as the late eighteenth century, and persists throughout the nineteenth. Bureaucratic autonomy and administrative capacity are forged early in our national history.

James Q. Wilson describes bureaucratic autonomy as both external and internal. External autonomy, he writes, is equivalent to jurisdiction or domain: "Agencies ranking high in autonomy have a monopoly jurisdiction (that is, they have few or no bureaucratic rivals and a minimum of political constraints imposed on them by superiors). The internal aspect of autonomy is identity or mission – a widely shared or approved understanding of the central tasks of the agency."[81] We will see both exhibited persistently at the Indian Office. More recently, Daniel Carpenter has offered one of the most thorough studies of bureaucratic autonomy. His understanding begins with a straightforward approach: "Bureaucratic autonomy occurs when bureaucrats take actions consistent with their own wishes, actions to which politicians and organized interests defer even though they would prefer that other actions (or no action at all) be taken..."[82] Autonomy prevails when agencies can establish political legitimacy. This legitimacy

[81] James Q. Wilson, *Bureaucracy: What Government Agencies Do and Why They Do It* (New York: Basic Books, 1989), 182; see the discussion generally in chs. 10–11.

[82] Carpenter, *Forging*, 4.

includes a reputation for expertise, efficiency, or moral protection, and it is characterized by "a uniquely diverse complex of ties to organized interests and the media."[83] This constellation of dynamics, Carpenter argues, induces politicians "to defer to the wishes of the agency even when they prefer otherwise."[84] For Carpenter, the "primary marker of bureaucratic autonomy is entrepreneurial policy innovation," and "the key prerequisite for autonomy is bureaucratic reputation."[85]

The War Department and, within it, the Indian Office, exercised bureaucratic autonomy in the early republic and throughout the nineteenth century. The Indian Office quickly built a reputation for expertise, and became the leading institution for designing and administering expansion-related Indian policies – often in the face of concerted opposition from local and national economic and policy leaders. Secretaries of War including Henry Knox and Henry Dearborn exemplified defense and national security expertise. The Indian Office and its leaders, including John Mason (son of George Mason) and Thomas McKenney, successfully built reputations as national experts on Indian trade, the treaty process, voluntary and forced removals, and reservation administration, along with a panoply of civilian measures that pursued the nation's social policy initiatives.

As the century progressed, the civilian Indian Office (later the Bureau of Indian Affairs) developed and sustained a reputation as the leading expert agency dealing with Indian affairs, and it successfully thwarted repeated attempts to transfer its responsibilities to the military. The agency's defenses highlight the complexity of the ties it had developed, its reputation, and the complicated nature of administration in the nineteenth century. The persistence of the factory system against growing opposition in the 1810s and early 1820s, the ability of the Indian Office and military to resist calls for forcible Indian removal into the 1830s, conflicts over reservation policy (including the field service's creation of police forces and judicial systems), and the continuity of treaty-related operations even after Congress ended treaty-making in the 1870s all point to the independent and autonomous ability of the agency to conduct its affairs. The networks and complications that Carpenter suggests protect bureaucratic autonomy in the twentieth century were at play throughout the nineteenth as well.

The Indian Office exhibited the ability to innovate, plan, and exercise discretionary authority. Oftentimes, innovations in Indian affairs ran counter to the wishes of some or most political leaders; Indian police forces and the development of reservations against demands for removals of Indian communities are two good examples. At times, the factory system, the reservation system, allotment, criminal justice and law enforcement policies, economic development, even aspects of the treaty system existed either without the

[83] Ibid., 4.
[84] Ibid., 4.
[85] Ibid., 33, 17.

presence of statutory authority, or under color of vague and broad delegation of discretionary authority. Expansion in general is a planned endeavor, driven by numerous and diverse bureaucratic units involving national security planning, planning for recordkeeping of plattes and deeds, planning for the movement and location of populations, planning wagon and canal and railroad routes, planning educational and other social programs. The standard argument about early bureaucratic activity erroneously draws sharp contrasts with the modern state. Carpenter, for example, writes, "[N]othing so distinguishes twentieth-century bureaucratic government from its predecessors as its ability to plan, to innovate, and to author policy."[86] Richard McCormick writes, "A paucity of planning also characterized government in the party period.... 'Policy' was little more than the accumulation of isolated, individual choices, usually of a distributive nature."[87] To the contrary: the factory system, Indian removal, the reservation system, and allotment are all about long-range planning, combining innovative broad and immediate responses, taking place with direction by experts within the Indian Office. The ability to plan, innovate, and author policy is not a distinguishing feature of the "modern" state.[88]

The real failing of works like Wilson's and Carpenter's is not in their understanding of how bureaucratic autonomy is forged and maintained. Their understanding of these dynamics is helpful and validated by the histories of many agencies. The problem lies in the timing. Bureaucratic autonomy does not wait to be forged until the late nineteenth or early twentieth centuries. It is forged in the days of the early republic, and it is forged out of necessity and practical decision making. Congress could not oversee field activities closely, and the volatility of the frontier frequently left Congress and the courts lagging behind events and inexpert at addressing complicated circumstances. The capacity to innovate and the process of building a reputation went hand in hand, and they both started early.

The Critical Contributions of Street-Level Operators

Many scholars recognize that government was critical to expansion and Indian affairs, and to land and trade and other developmental policies, throughout the nineteenth century. Few political and administrative development scholars, though, have examined carefully exactly *how* those policies were designed and administered, and have thus overlooked the critical component of public administration identified by scholars such as Michael Lipsky and Wilson: street-level bureaucrats, or operators.[89]

[86] Ibid., 5; see also 9: "core properties of the twentieth-century policy state – planning and discretionary innovation."

[87] McCormick, quoted in Carpenter, *Forging*, 60.

[88] See Carpenter, *Forging*, 28.

[89] See, e.g., Michael Lipsky, *Street-Level Bureaucracy: Dilemmas of the Individual in Public Services* (New York: Russell Sage Foundation, 1983); Wilson, *Bureaucracy*.

Political development literature and public administration scholarship alike have seriously oversimplified the difficulty and complexity of expansion. As a result, both of these literatures have generally underestimated the creativity, innovation, and discretionary activity necessary to bring it about. Both of these literatures have all but ignored the role of operators in the nineteenth century, choosing instead to assume that they were clerks, following orders in the pursuit of simple distributory policies. This is far from accurate. It is, instead, an application of the long discredited politics-administration dichotomy, which sees administration as the mere carrying out of decisions made by leaders at higher levels. The discipline of public administration has dispensed with the myth of the politics-administration dichotomy in studies of modern bureaucracies. We must do the same when we examine bureaucratic activity in the nineteenth century, and realize that operators in the nineteenth century were no more robotic and compliant than are operators today. In fact, given the state of communications and technology, and the significance and volatility of administrative endeavors related to expansion, operators in the nineteenth century may have been *more* innovative, more independent, and more autonomous than the micro-managed, cellphone- and laptop-hobbled operators of today.

It is important that the dynamics of operators, bureaucratic autonomy, organizational culture, and planning and innovation presented by authors like Carpenter, Skocpol, and Wilson in other contexts are applicable to earlier eras. It means that we can study and understand how these early agencies functioned, and how they developed. Important roles, for example, were filled by leaders at the Bureau of Indian Affairs. This "mezzo-level," as Carpenter calls it,[90] engaged in policy design and oversight. Often expert and professionalized, the number one and number two posts at the Indian Office are a far cry from the incompetence and corruption that outside observers usually assume to have been dominant. John Mason, Thomas McKenney, and Charles Mix are just a few of many long-tenured, expert leaders. Carpenter is correct to highlight the importance of the mezzo-level in forging autonomy and in developing innovations, and he is correct to highlight the ability to learn and innovate.

But there is much more to bureaucratic autonomy and innovation than the mezzo-level leadership, regardless of whether the organization under analysis is making counterterrorism policy in 2010 or Indian policy in 1810. Operators and street-level bureaucrats are a tremendously significant part of the overall picture. Operators at the Indian Office were some of the era's chief innovators. It was often the operators and field agents – not the leadership – who were in "the best position to experiment, learn, and innovate."[91] Interestingly, the dynamics that put field operators in such an important role

[90] See Carpenter, *Forging*, 11ff., 18ff., and throughout.
[91] Carpenter's words, describing mezzo-level leaders, *Forging*, 21.

are the same as those identified by Carpenter as the factors that make mezzo-level leaders important in innovation: durability, constancy, discretion, and legitimacy. Innovation does benefit from constancy, contact, and networks; in Indian affairs, those dynamics describe field operations as much as they describe relationships at the headquarters level.

Carpenter, like many scholars, downplays the role of operators: "Even under the merit system, although they have administrative discretion, operators have little ability to shape the agencies for which they work."[92] "Shape" is a little vague, but the point here is unmistakable. Carpenter continues: "Nineteenth-century politics commissioned a state equipped to perform little more than the delivery of mail, the routine taxing of imported goods, and the rote distribution of pensions and public lands. Bureaucrats as clerks did not innovate; they took orders."[93]

To the contrary: operators in Indian affairs – dealing with land, trade, and security concerns, as well as programmatic social policies – innovated within broad grants of discretionary authority. Operators played important roles in defining the contours of policy, as when the factory system was developed and eventually eliminated following input from field agents. Executive branch agents designed the factory system and Indian removal, and field agents sparked both the reservation and allotment systems. Most of these policy "eras" were being developed and refined in the field and in executive branch agencies long before Congress got around to legislating. Innovative details – on the negotiation of treaties, on the details of removal, on the leasing of Indian lands for stock grazing or settlement, and in many other areas – came from field agents at the cutting edge of policy. Operators were often free to modify policies and programs: sometimes to the benefit of local interests, sometimes in opposition to national policy goals, and sometimes to moderate aggressive national policies like removal – against the wishes of non-Indian interests – to ameliorate some of the heavy damage done to Indian communities. And these dynamics are true not only for Indian agents but also for operators at the Post Office, the General Land Office, the Coast Guard, the military, and numerous other government agencies.

A Sense of the State

In the most influential book yet written on the development of the American state, Stephen Skowronek defined the "sense of the state" as "the sense of an organization of coercive power operating beyond our immediate control and intruding into all aspects of our lives."[94] Skowronek continued, after noting the presence of a state before the Civil War, to make a landmark assertion: "The exceptional character of the early American state is neatly summarized

[92] Carpenter, *Forging*, 20.
[93] Ibid., 60.
[94] Skowronek, *Building*, 3.

in the paradox that it failed to evoke any sense of a state."[95] Skowronek seriously underestimated the perception and presence of the state's role in everyday affairs in the nineteenth century. A more careful analysis of the late eighteenth and nineteenth centuries reveals a clear sense of the state, among both citizens and (especially) noncitizens, particularly if we recast the definition as a sense of a state presence seamlessly and inextricably woven into the fabric of everyday life.

This should not be too surprising. It has been twenty-five years since *Building a New American State* appeared, and in the intervening years we have had numerous careful and important efforts to define and discover what the state was actually doing in these years. I suggest that the body of work taken as a whole, together with the contribution I've tried to make here, recommends to us a new starting point. By a new starting point, I mean reversing the approach that assumes a world of limited government and which has generally seen government activity as exceptional, and which usually reverts to a conception of the dominance of limited government soon after highlighting the exceptions. *The new starting point should assume big government.* The exceptional moments are those free of governmental impact, free of that sense of the state.

Analysis of government, especially at the federal level, needs to leave behind the popular myth of limited government and recognize the strong, intentional, and influential role played by the national government in social provision, expansion, Indian affairs, and administrative development. We also need to get past the rumor of absent sense of the state, and recognize that millions of U.S. citizens and American Indians looked to the federal government and its agents as the appropriate locus of decision-making authority in critical aspects of their everyday lives: land, trade, the economy, national security, foreign policy, and expansion. The era saw regulations cast at the federal level that touched land, trade, alcohol, weapons, education, health care, job training, income stabilization, and pensions. Parties and courts were active elements in this world, but their contribution was complemented by a web of forces including sectional and regional politics and party groupings, by an occasionally active and influential Congress, by a consistently active and engaged presidency, and by autonomous bureaucratic units enjoying substantial discretionary authority and innovating creatively in the field.

The national government not only managed and regulated; it intruded. The nineteenth century abounds with examples of the federal government interfering with or managing affairs to the dismay of individuals and businesses. Citizens and organizations petitioned regularly for federal military and development aid and regularization of laws that they believed would be to their benefit, yet simultaneously resented government efforts to manage their affairs. Speculators and settlers looked to the federal government for

[95] Ibid., 5.

official sanction of actions planned or taken in the field. The United States assumed final say over the dispensation of lands and the legality of efforts to organize, distribute, and settle lands in the West, wherever the West happened to be. Many saw the Indian Country of the West itself as a giant obstacle created and maintained by the federal government.[96] Federal agents enforced trade and land laws, removed squatters from unceded lands, and protected commercial routes and trading parties. Civilian and military officers seized goods and stores from unlicensed traders, impeded movement of individuals and parties without proper passports and documentation, and arrested and imprisoned violators of the laws. Agents at federal outposts like Fort Kearny in Nebraska supplied wagon trains, provisioned migrant companies, tended to the sick and wounded, shod horses – and they also imposed rules and regulations on the great migrations regarding everything from campground locations to the nature and makeup of wagon trains allowed to move on to the West. Scientists, explorers, surveyors, merchants, suppliers, all confronted forms of government control as they worked westward. The maps they used, the goods they bought, the land titles they held, their safety in travel, all relied on the actions of the federal government in exploring and surveying, publishing, regulating, negotiating and ratifying treaties, registering deeds, and defending transportation routes. Westering individuals, farmers, hog producers, saloonkeepers, traders, hunters, mountain men, fur traders, shipowners, sailors – all risked facing off with agents of the federal government in one way or another. No person in North America in the nineteenth century could have avoided regular contact with forms of government, public policy, regulation, and control. This world actively engaged the talents and lives of national leaders in governing institutions at the federal, state, local, and tribal levels, and of millions of citizens and noncitizens receiving employment, pensions, education, grants, job training, infrastructure, housing, health care, goods and services, cash payments, and much more. A sense of the state came with the territory.

[96] David Lavender, *The Great West* (Boston: Houghton Mifflin, 2000 [1965]), chs. 1–2, 51, 204.

2

Managed Expansion in the Early Republic

Thomas Jefferson, the patron saint of limited government, established a land office before the Revolution to sort through and organize the complicated claims and legal implications of speculation in the western portions of Virginia. Jefferson championed royal and colonial government channels as the appropriate paths for managing land speculation, stabilizing cessions from Indians, and establishing title to Western lands – often in opposition to the crafty and creative efforts of pioneering individuals.[1] It is President Jefferson who maintained and expanded the Washington administration's efforts to regulate the fur trade in the early republic, and it is Jefferson who convinced Congress to give the president authority over other areas of the western economy, such as the alcohol trade. It is Jefferson, of course, who sparked the nation's most famous federal enterprise in scientific and military exploration, the Lewis and Clark expedition, in support of a vast extension of U.S. authority across North America; Jefferson made parallel efforts in the Southwest[2] and drove an aggressive land acquisition policy over and above the prominent example of the Louisiana Purchase. And it is Jefferson who is credited with the first serious proposals for Indian removal, a giant public policy effort to relocate hundreds of thousands of American Indians from their homes east of the Mississippi. It is also Jefferson who promoted the use of federal mechanisms to educate a national populace, and to remove whites who had settled west of the Mississippi, and to remove blacks out of the United States. The icon of limited government had a lot of practical ideas about how to use government to achieve public ends. And

[1] Anthony F. C. Wallace, *Jefferson and the Indians: The Tragic Fate of the First Americans* (Cambridge, MA: Harvard University Press, 1999); Dumas Malone, *Jefferson the Virginian* (Boston: Little, Brown, and Company, 1948), 257–9; Jeff Madrick, *The Case for Big Government* (Princeton: Princeton University Press, 2009), 31–7.

[2] William H. Goetzmann, *Army Exploration in the American West, 1803–1863* (Lincoln: University of Nebraska Press, 1959), 33.

they were not merely ideas – many became policies crafted and put into motion.

The last thing that national leaders like Jefferson wanted after the Revolution was another war. With an economy in trouble and with regional issues threatening the tenuous bonds of union, neither nationalists nor regional expansionists could afford the costs or risks of another major conflict. Europeans hovered on the United States' borders, and powerful American Indian nations and alliances threatened the fragile peace. Conflict with Indians could easily flare into a broader Indian war, which could then ignite another international conflict if the Europeans jumped into the fray. To avoid such a disastrous chain of events, the new republic's leaders had to control and manage the major elements that, if allowed to pursue their own individualized self-interests, could precipitate a conflict: traders, tribes, white settlers, land speculators, and the states themselves.

At the heart of these efforts emerged a commitment to craft expansion policy at the national level, and a dedication to managing expansion policies by controlling critical aspects like military planning, land policy, communications, and infrastructure. Indians were central players in land, trade, and expansion policies, and so Indians were critical participants in considerations of war and peace on the continent. A complicated array of economic, diplomatic, and social policies, backed up by military deterrence and the use of force, characterized U.S. policy and administration in Indian affairs specifically and in expansion policies generally. The federal government played a leading role in these years through extensive domestic policymaking, management, and public administration. The American administrative state was born early, and despite its youth set to the task of a careful and managed expansion westward.

The Significance of Indian Affairs

Indians and Indian affairs lay at the heart of social, economic, and political development in the years of the early republic. The era's culture, security issues, and land and trade policies cannot be understood without American Indian participants.

Scholars have long recognized the critical importance of Indians in early American mythology and cultural development. Indians played a crucial role in establishing "the American" as a distinct and discrete concept. Robert Berkhofer Jr. writes that Indians were essential to the development of higher forms of art and literature unique to America in the early republic.[3] Our unique system of government draws considerably from native governmental

[3] Robert F. Berkhofer Jr., *The White Man's Indian: Images of the American Indian from Columbus to the Present* (New York: Vintage, 1978), 86. See also Richard Slotkin, *Regeneration Through Violence: The Mythology of the American Frontier, 1600–1860* (New York:

forms, particularly those of the Iroquois confederacy, as evidenced in the writings of such notables as Franklin, Madison, Jefferson, and Adams – all of whom studied native governance extensively and applied what they learned to American independence and constitutionalism.[4] Indians were critical to the burgeoning study of nature and science, too: expeditions such as the landmark journey of Lewis and Clark captured public imagination with Indians and the West, and helped build a nation psychologically and scientifically, by providing information about the western territories and the people who lived there. This information would prove essential for future social, economic, and military endeavors.[5] Throughout the era, images of Indians entwined with ideas about social destiny, mankind's place in America, and territorial expansion, promoting and justifying the policy and administrative precedents that formed the foundation for continental conquest and the rise of the United States. Americans arts, culture, and science rest on information, speculation, and imagination about American Indians.

The importance of Indians in the early United States extends far beyond cultural dynamics and inquiries into the American psyche – Indians were critical to national security, a basic fact of national land policy, and an integral part of national trade policy. In the late eighteenth century, the United States was a weak power relative not only to the European forces arrayed around the continent but also relative to many Indian nations. The nation's future relied upon avoiding conflicts that it could ill afford to fight, either in terms of its fledgling economic circumstances or from the standpoint of public confidence in the new national government. Conflict with Indian nations threatened renewed conflict with Britain, France, or Spain – or all three – putting the entire American experiment at risk. After a brief period of failed aggressiveness toward Indian nations immediately following the Revolution, federal policy focused on maintaining peace and order. Peace was expedient, less costly than war, and held more promise for the nation's ultimate survival. Order promised predictability and control – it aimed at preventing surprises, even small ones, that could grow into larger problems.

HarperPerennial, 1973); Russel Blaine Nye, *The Cultural Life of the New Nation* (New York: Harper, 1960), 244.

[4] Donald Grinde, "Iroquoian Political Concept and the Genesis of American Government," in *Indian Roots of American Democracy*, ed. José Barreiro (Ithaca, NY: Akwe: Kon Press of Cornell University, 1992); Jack Weatherford, *Indian Givers: How the Indians of the Americas Transformed the World* (New York: Fawcett Columbine, 1988), ch. 8. See also Francis Paul Prucha, *American Indian Treaties: The History of a Political Anomaly* (Berkeley: University of California Press, 1997), 68; Gordon S. Wood, *The Americanization of Benjamin Franklin* (New York: Penguin, 2004), 72–8.

[5] See, e.g., Goetzmann, *Army Exploration*, ch. 2.

These concerns dominated American political thinking in the nation's early years. As early as 1783, George Washington linked Indian affairs with control and settlement of the West. In a letter to James Duane in which he argued for peace with the Indians and the establishment of trading relations, Washington wrote of the need to order Indian affairs:

> Unless some such measure as I have here taken the liberty of suggesting are speedily adopted one of two capital evils, in my opinion, will inevitably result, and is near at hand; either that the settling, or rather overspreading the Western Country will take place, by a parcel of Banditti, who will bid defiance to all Authority while they are skimming and disposing of the Cream of the Country at the expence of many suffering Officers and Soldiers who have fought and bled to obtain it, and are now waiting the decision of Congress to point them to the promised reward of their past dangers and toils, or a renewal of Hostilities with the Indians, brought about more than probably, by this very means.[6]

Washington expressed a concern that persisted throughout most of the nineteenth century: that inattention to the frontier invited dire consequences. Washington worked to secure the frontier not just to reward veterans, but in the interests of nation-building. In the same letter, Washington continued:

> [T]he Settlemt. of the Western Country and making a Peace with the Indians are so analogous that there can be no definition of the one without involving considerations of the other. for [*sic*] I repeat it, again, and I am clear in my opinion, that policy and oeconomy point very strongly to the expediency of being upon good terms with the Indians . . .[7]

Other leaders of the era also recognized the central importance of Indian affairs. In the 1780s, the governor of Virginia wrote to the governor of South Carolina, suggesting a southern confederacy for managing Indian affairs: "If this is not done, there is too much reason to apprehend that continued encroachment [by whites] will be made upon their [Indian] land and, of course, the frontiers of each state laid waste in its turn in revenge for the injuries."[8]

[6] George Washington to James Duane, September 7, 1783, in *Documents of United States Indian Policy*, 2nd ed., ed. Francis Paul Prucha (Lincoln: University of Nebraska Press, 1990), 2. For more on this letter and its context in the debate over federal control of Western lands, see Robert F. Berkhofer Jr., "Jefferson, the Ordinance of 1784, and the Origins of the American Territorial System," *The William and Mary Quarterly* 29 (April 1972), 237–8 and generally; Reginald Horsman, *Expansion and American Indian Policy, 1783–1812* (Norman: University of Oklahoma Press, 1992 [1967], 6ff.; Wiley Sword, *President Washington's Indian War: The Struggle for the Old Northwest, 1790–1795* (Norman: University of Oklahoma Press, 1985), 26ff.; Walter H. Mohr, *Federal Indian Relations, 1774–1788* (New York: AMS Press, 1971), 101. See also Laurence F. Schmeckebier, *The Office of Indian Affairs: Its History, Activities and Organization* (Baltimore: The Johns Hopkins University Press, 1927), 11ff.

[7] Washington to Duane, September 7, 1783, in Prucha, *Documents*, 2.

[8] Quoted in Mohr, *Federal Indian Relations*, 140.

Military security and control of a peaceful frontier were indispensable to national survival, economic development, and physical expansion. Washington spent much of his early career in pursuits tied closely to Indian affairs, surveying lands in western Pennsylvania and fighting in the French and Indian War. His experience in Indian affairs typified the era; the list of characters active in the early republic indicates the constant presence of Indian affairs in the life of the eighteenth and early nineteenth centuries. Benjamin Franklin, Patrick Henry, James Wilson, Thomas Jefferson, Alexander Hamilton, Oliver Wolcott, Henry Dearborn – many leaders from the battles and strategic thinking of the Revolution – state governors and legislators, frontier leaders and challengers, people engaged in Western land speculation, trade, shipping, canals, transportation, newspapers – all had direct experience and connections with the details and patterns of land politics, trade, and Indian affairs. Indians and Western activity permeated discussions of the nation's future, in complicated discussions of economic power, demographics, and party politics.[9]

Land and territory anchored the era's events. Today, we are accustomed to strong ties between government and business interests, and we expect ambitious people in positions of authority to have extensive connections with the business sector. Those connections define and drive today's politics. In the eighteenth and nineteenth centuries, such connections centered on land. Powerful economic combinations and alliances had designs on the early frontier, and these interests maintained pressure on public officials. Land interests had been united around the desire to obtain Indian land and expand westward since well before the Revolution, but securing land was not as easy as simply squatting and claiming ownership. Disputes arose over particular tracts of land, especially from Indians who had occupied the lands for generations. Philosophical arguments divided republican philosophers and land speculators, the former favoring small farmers and small plots of land, whereas speculators and larger land companies pressed the government to dispense land in huge parcels so that intermediary companies and speculators could dispense them to farmers or others as they saw fit. Different interests and ideologies split over the propriety of gaining formal

[9] Charles Royster, *The Fabulous History of the Great Dismal Swamp Company: A Story of George Washington's Times* (New York: Vintage, 1999), 8, 58–9, 129–34; Francis Jennings, *The Creation of America: Through Revolution to Empire* (Cambridge: Cambridge University Press, 2000), 64, 123–6, 231–2; Randolph C. Downes, *Council Fires on the Upper Ohio* (Pittsburgh: University of Pittsburgh Press, 1989 [1940]), 59–64; Michael Allen, "Justice for the Indians: The Federalist Quest, 1783–1796," *Essex Institute Historical Collections* 122 (1986); Francis Philbrick, *The Rise of the West, 1754–1830* (New York: Harper, 1965), ch. 5; Andrew R. L. Cayton, "'Separate Interests' and the Nation-State: The Washington Administration and the Origins of Regionalism in the Trans-Appalachian West," *The Journal of American History* 79 (June 1992); Richard R. John, *Spreading the News: The American Postal System from Franklin to Morse* (Cambridge, MA: Harvard University Press, 1995).

land cessions and negotiated agreements with Indians – versus a simpler, but riskier and costlier, conquest by force.[10]

Lands were key to expansion, and key to gain. In all regions of the nation, land companies and development interests pressured the federal government to negotiate treaties and redistribute land. These interests agreed that land acquisitions needed to be secure enough, and organized enough, to protect investments. Secure title and physical safety were integral parts of successful expansion, and interested parties looked to the federal government to provide opportunities, protect investments, and coordinate expansion.

The politics of these matters were intricate. As much as the companies wanted government support for and protection of investments, they also wanted to maximize their own gain – goals that sometimes collided. When Virginia offered to cede land to the federal government in 1781, for example, speculators and land companies urged the Continental Congress to reject the deal because the cession would have defeated the claims of some of the biggest companies and most powerful players in the areas north and west of the Ohio River. Congress accepted Virginia's cession, though, as the demands for public revenue from land sales and for grants for veterans of the Revolution prevailed – an example of the significant power and influence the national government had against speculators and company interests.[11] Much of the action centered in the Old Northwest, with the Ohio Company at the forefront pressing for federal action and sparking the Northwest

[10] See Laura Jensen, *Patriots, Settlers, and the Origins of American Social Policy* (Cambridge: Cambridge University Press, 2003), 136ff.; Peter S. Onuf, *Statehood and Union: A History of the Northwest Ordinance* (Bloomington: Indiana University Press, 1987); Peter S. Onuf, *The Origins of the Federal Republic: Jurisdictional Controversies in the United States, 1775–1787* (Philadelphia: University of Pennsylvania Press, 1983); Daniel Feller, *The Public Lands in Jacksonian Politics* (Madison: University of Wisconsin Press, 1984), chs. 1–3; Cayton, "'Separate Interests,'" 47; Earl S. Pomeroy, *The Territories and the United States, 1861–1890: Studies in Colonial Administration* (Seattle: University of Washington Press, 1947), 96–8; Berkhofer, "Jefferson"; Rudolf Freund, "Military Bounty Lands and the Origins of the Public Domain," *Agricultural History* 20 (1946), reprinted in Vernon Carstensen, ed., *The Public Lands: Studies in the History of the Public Domain* (Madison: University of Wisconsin Press, 1968), 26–31. On military bounty lands, see also Malcolm J. Rohrbough, *The Land Office Business: The Settlement and Administration of American Public Lands, 1789–1837* (New York: Oxford University Press, 1968), ch. 4; Freund, "Military Bounty Lands." On land companies, see Shaw Livermore, *Early American Land Companies: Their Influence on Corporate Development* (New York: Octagon, 1968); Carstensen, "Introduction," in Carstensen, *Public Lands*. On corporations, charters, and contract generally, see William J. Novak, *The People's Welfare: Law & Regulation in Nineteenth-Century America* (Chapel Hill: The University of North Carolina Press, 1996), 105–11.

[11] Royster, *Dismal Swamp Company*, 298. On state cessions to the new national government, and their effects on land companies, investors, and expansion and development, see also Livermore, *Land Companies*, chs. IV and V; Rohrbough, *Land Office Business*, ch. 1; Carstensen, "Introduction"; Payson Jackson Treat, "Origin of the National Land System under the Confederation," *American Historical Association Report*, 1905, vol. 1, reprinted in Carstensen, *Public Lands*; Onuf, *Statehood and Union*; Onuf, *Origins*, ch. 4.

Ordinance as a means of protecting and organizing settlement.[12] A new land act, passed in 1800, began another era in land policy in the region that, combined with peaceful relations with Indians and Ohio's entry as a state in 1803, accelerated settlement to the area. White settlement drove new efforts to finance and build infrastructure like canals and the national road.[13]

Outside the Old Northwest, other states and regions saw their own interactions of speculators, settlers, frontiersmen, Indians, and land policies through state and federal governments. Land speculation and efforts to seize territory animated affairs in New York after the Revolution and into the nineteenth century. These efforts involved many of the era's leading figures, in New York and nationally: Alexander Macomb, for example, "the most ambitious of all the speculators in northern New York," was closely tied to influential national figures like Gouverneur Morris, financier Robert Morris, and Secretary of War Henry Knox.[14] As New York worked to build its roads and canals, local and state officials worked with federal planners and federal funds to negotiate and sign treaties for Indian land cessions. Federal officials helped remove the Indians from the path of development; federal laws controlled actions, and in fact are, even today, at the center of controversies in New York over land ownership of vast upstate regions. Access to Indian lands in New York State was crucial for national development, too. New York's development of canals and other infrastructure was critical to the development and growth of New York City, but, more important, these efforts were central to national plans to settle the West. Once the Erie Canal opened in 1825, settlement in Michigan, Illinois, and Wisconsin exploded, and access to those regions' resources helped bind those areas and

[12] Reginald Horsman, *The Frontier in the Formative Years, 1783–1815* (Albuquerque: University of New Mexico Press, 1975), 36–8; also see Rohrbough, *Land Office Business*, 10–12; Freund, "Military Bounty Lands," 23ff.; Onuf, *Statehood and Union*, 42–3. On the Northwest Ordinance, land policy, and restrictions in the Old Northwest, see Onuf, *Origins*; Fred Anderson and Andrew Cayton, *The Dominion of War: Empire and Liberty in North America, 1500–2000* (New York: Viking, 2005), 190ff.; Beverly W. Bond Jr., "American Civilization Comes to the Old Northwest," *The Mississippi Valley Historical Review* 19 (June 1932), 7ff.

[13] Horsman, *Frontier*, 73–4. These issues were all closely connected. The Louisiana Purchase, for example, sparked efforts to secure areas and roads in upstate New York and in the Old Northwest. Mary P. Adams, "Jefferson's Reaction to the Treaty of San Ildefonso," *The Journal of Southern History* 21 (1955), 181, 182ff. A federal agreement with Ohio set aside 3 percent from public land sales for state highways, which also led to the opening of mail routes. Bond, "American Civilization," 12–13. On land policy and administration generally, see Rohrbough, *Land Office Business*; Andro Linklater, *Measuring America: How an Untamed Wilderness Shaped the United States and Fulfilled the Promise of Democracy* (New York: Plume, 2003); Onuf, *Statehood and Union*, 22–4, 41–2; Pomeroy, *Territories*, 1–5; Harry L. Coles Jr., "Applicability of the Public Land System to Louisiana," *Mississippi Valley Historical Review* 43 (1957), reprinted in Carstensen, *Public Lands*, 216.

[14] Horsman, *Frontier*, 27–8.

northern Ohio to the United States.[15] Canals such as Erie relied on prior land acquisition, often from Indians.

Similar dynamics characterized the Old Southwest, as treaties, law, and military activity opened areas for white settlement and exploding non-Indian populations between 1810 and 1820. Extinguishing Indian title was a critical dynamic, allowing early population expansion into some areas like Alabama that had benefited from land cessions and delaying expansion into areas like Mississippi that had not yet secured title to Indian territory.[16] The attractive southern Indian lands of the Yazoo territory, for example, involved foreign trade with France and Spain and high-profile investors from New England, and became a cause célèbre in national and international politics for decades even after John Marshall's landmark U.S. Supreme Court ruling in *Fletcher* v. *Peck* (1810).[17]

With wide variation in details but not in the significance of land itself, other southern states and regions confronted the hunger for land, the value and importance of land policies, and the fact that when land was concerned, so were American Indian nations and communities.[18] Congress created boards to handle conflicting land claims in Louisiana in the early 1800s;

[15] Laurence M. Hauptman, *Conspiracy of Interests: Iroquois Dispossession and the Rise of New York State* (Syracuse: Syracuse University Press, 1999). See also Ronald E. Shaw, *Canals for a Nation: The Canal Era in the United States, 1790–1860* (Lexington: The University Press of Kentucky, 1993) 48; Carol Sheriff, *The Artificial River: The Erie Canal and the Paradox of Progress, 1817–1862* (New York: Hill and Wang, 1996); Onuf, *Origins*, ch. 5; Livermore, *Land Companies*, 197–209.

[16] See Thomas D. Clark and John D. W. Guice, *The Old Southwest, 1795–1830: Frontiers in Conflict* (Norman: University of Oklahoma Press, 1996 [1989]), 164–5 and ch. 11. On the role of federal road and other projects in shaping and encouraging settlement in the region, see Clark and Guice, *Old Southwest*, 174ff.; Joyce Purser, "The Administration of Indian Affairs in Louisiana, 1803–1820," *Louisiana History* 5 (Fall 1964); R. S. Cotterill, "Federal Indian Management in the South, 1789–1825," *The Mississippi Valley Historical Review* 20 (December 1933); Jared W. Bradley, "William C. C. Claiborne, the Old Southwest and the Development of American Indian Policy," *Tennessee Historical Quarterly* 33 (Fall 1974); Henry deLeon Southerland, Jr., and Jerry Elijah Brown, *The Federal Road through Georgia, the Creek Nation, and Alabama, 1806–1836* (Tuscaloosa: The University of Alabama Press, 1989); James W. Silver, "Edmund Pendleton Gaines and Frontier Problems, 1801–1849," *The Journal of Southern History* 1 (August 1935), 324; Benjamin Hawkins, *A Sketch of the Creek Country, in the Years 1798 and 1799 [1848] and Letters of Benjamin Hawkins, 1796–1806 [1916]* (Spartansburg, SC: Reprint Co., 1974), 174ff., 242.

[17] See, e.g., C. Peter Magrath, *Yazoo: The Case of* Fletcher *v.* Peck (New York: Norton, 1966); Florette Henri, *The Southern Indians and Benjamin Hawkins, 1796–1816* (Norman: University of Oklahoma Press, 1986), 144–5; Clark and Guice, *Old Southwest*, 69ff.; Tim Alan Garrison, *The Legal Ideology of Removal: The Southern Judiciary and the Sovereignty of Native American Nations* (Athens: The University of Georgia Press, 2002); Livermore, *Land Companies*, 146–62.

[18] On complexity and the federal role in the South, see, e.g., Cynthia Cumfer, "Local Origins of National Indian Policy: Cherokee and Tennessean Ideas About Sovereignty and Nationhood, 1790–1811," *Journal of the Early Republic* 23 (Spring 2003); Mary Elizabeth

in five years, the boards heard sixty-five hundred claims. Inquiries were still open in 1835; by 1837, most had been settled by administrative adjudication, although some were not settled until after the Civil War.[19] Georgia officials, working to secure the state's lands and protect its claims, decided in 1802 to cede much of what would become Alabama and Mississippi to the federal government – with the expectation that federal officials would work to quiet Indian claims and remove Indians from Georgia's borders as part of the process of settling and integrating those regions. Georgia's compact with the United States, and its expectations of national administrative activity, would become central to demands for Indian removal in the 1820s and 1830s.

The politics of trade were important and intricate, too – and also involved American Indians and their communities and nations in central roles. Most importantly, American Indian labor and lands across the continent anchored the lucrative international fur trade. Furs were highly valued in Europe and also in Asia, encouraging fur trading on both coasts of North America and throughout the interior. The fur trade fueled an international economy that included trappers and hunters as well as corporate middlemen, translators, guides, suppliers of boats, packs, horses, and other tools – and eventually auctioneers, shippers, shipbuilders, loggers, and seamen. Indians traded furs for kettles, knives, weapons, powder, textiles – whatever they needed or wanted, providing markets for a broad array of manufactured goods in North America.[20]

Philosophical arguments raged as independent traders competed with large, organized trading interests like the British-influenced Panton, Leslie and Company, North West Company, and Hudson's Bay Company, and American organizations like the Missouri Fur Company, tied closely to

Young, *Redskins, Ruffleshirts, and Rednecks: Indian Allotments in Alabama and Mississippi, 1830–1860* (Norman: University of Oklahoma Press, 1961), 12–13, ch. 3; Ira Katznelson, "Flexible Capacity: The Military and Early American Statebuilding," in *Shaped by War and Trade: International Influences on American Political Development*, ed. Ira Katznelson and Martin Shefter (Princeton: Princeton University Press, 2002); Michael D. Green, *The Politics of Indian Removal: Creek Government and Society in Crisis* (Lincoln: University of Nebraska Press, 1985); Clark and Guice, *Old Southwest*.

19 Coles, "Public Land System," 217–18.

20 On the global nature of trade, see Hiram Martin Chittenden, *The American Fur Trade of the Far West*, Vol. 1 (Lincoln: University of Nebraska Press, 1986 [1935]), 6; Bond, "American Civilization," 15. Edling writes of the early years of the republic, "[F]luctuations in international trade left virtually no American unaffected. This of course meant that the regulation of commerce was one of the most important ways in which the [national] government influenced the well-being of its citizens." Max M. Edling, *A Revolution in Favor of Government: Origins of the U.S. Constitution and the Making of the American State* (Oxford: Oxford University Press, 2003), 85. Even canal building had deep international connections, in the transfer of expertise and technology. Shaw, *Canals*.

Thomas Hart Benton, and John Jacob Astor's American Fur Company. Astor's efforts in the Pacific Northwest in 1811 and 1812 were part of American efforts, on the heels of Lewis and Clark, to secure Oregon for the new republic; his efforts in Michigan and around the Great Lakes, like the efforts of others, were essential components of the economy of the new nation and its relations with England and Indian nations in the Old Northwest before, during, and after the War of 1812. Astor's importance should not be underestimated. The historian John Denis Haeger places Astor at the center of the development of American business and American industrialization as early as the 1780s. Haeger argues that Astor's contributions to specialization, market control, and business influence on national affairs predate analyses that place these developments later, in the 1840s or with the coming of the railroads.[21]

Astor and the fur trade encouraged exploration and settlement, and were in turn encouraged by those efforts, connecting closely trade, land interests, speculation, Indians, and the military. That does not mean that speculators and traders agreed on policy: traders and settlement interests often held fundamentally different visions of how the land should be used and organized, and how Indians should fit into any area's business. Traders wanted Indians to hunt and collect skins and furs, and to buy manufactured goods. Land interests often wanted just the opposite: they wanted Indian lands transferred to non-Indians, and they wanted the Indians to disappear and stop frightening potential settlers. Big money and powerful influences did not always agree on how to deal with the Indian context, but they could not escape it.

Other sectors of the new republic's economy also could not escape the Indian context. In his Report on Manufactures, Hamilton emphasized that "There are scarcely any manufactories of greater importance" than that of skins.[22] Hamilton highlighted the relationship between tanneries as a manufacturing sector and the impact of cattle raising on agriculture and national expansion. Here, trade and manufacturing shared a direct link to land acquisition, bringing the national economy into close contact with Indian affairs. Tension between Indian communities and whites often arose over the extensive and expanding lands needed for raising cattle, which impacted hunting grounds and areas Indians used for agriculture.[23]

[21] John Denis Haeger, *John Jacob Astor: Business and Finance in the Early Republic* (Detroit: Wayne State University Press, 1991), 35–41; see also David Lavender, *The Fist in the Wilderness: A Narrative History of the American Fur Trade* (Garden City, NY: Doubleday, 1964); Richard R. John, "Elaborations, Revisions, Dissents: Alfred D. Chandler, Jr.'s The Visible Hand after Twenty Years," *Business History Review* 71 (Summer 1997).

[22] Alexander Hamilton, "Report on Manufactures," in Alexander Hamilton, *Writings* (New York: Library of America, 2001), 717.

[23] Clark and Guice, *Old Southwest*, 113.

Elsewhere in the Report on Manufactures, Hamilton wrote of the "high importance" of the manufacture of gunpowder, intimately related both to the trade in skins and also to affairs in the West.[24] Hamilton wrote of firearms and other weapons, "There are already manufactories of these articles, which only require the stimulus of a certain demand to render them adequate to the supply of the United States."[25] Hamilton recommended an annual purchase and the creation of arsenals to ensure against surprises and encourage the industry, and he even suggested that weapons manufacturing might be best left to government and not to private industry. In any case, Hamilton recognized and promoted the arms trade – not surprising given his background and the situation of the early United States. Supplying the nation's military, its militias, and its citizens was then, as it is now, an important and profitable business. Early manufacturers of weapons and powder, like the DuPonts of Delaware, had considerable interests in and potentially great profits from U.S. and other activities involving American Indians. The military was a major customer: Cincinnati got its start as the major supply point for Fort Washington, for example; Alabama alone was home to fifty-seven forts from the 1820s to the Civil War.[26]

The southern regional economy also included Indians in critical roles. Cotton involved Indians, both as laborers and also as competitors against non-Indian growers and plantation owners. Cotton growing expanded on Indian lands just as it did in white-controlled areas in the South. Indian-run agriculture and domestic industries offered white women opportunities for employment, affecting both economic and social affairs in the region. Slave-owning Indians competed with slaveowning whites. Free Indian country gave hope of sanctuary to Southern slaves, and frightened southern slave-holders with the prospect of slaves' escape and potential rebellion, perhaps in alliance with Indians. And, of course, land was a piece of trade once again: as cotton exploded in the South, land and labor remained central issues in the region's life. Indian lands and Indian competition, and tense race relations generally, became unavoidable. And while trade encouraged federal trading factories and supported manufacturing interests, agriculture and slavery incited Georgians and other southerners to work diligently toward obtaining Indian lands and destroying competing communities.[27]

[24] Hamilton, "Report on Manufactures," 729.

[25] Ibid., 713.

[26] See Stephen Aron, "Lessons in Conquest: Towards a Greater Western History," *The Pacific Historical Review* 63 (May 1994), 139; Bond, "American Civilization"; Katznelson, "Flexible Capacity," 90–1; Anderson and Cayton, *Dominion of War*, 133; Clark and Guice, *Old Southwest*, 202. See Edling, *Revolution*, 76 and chapter 5 generally, on the interrelationship of military and fiscal powers, commercial regulation and development, and treaty enforcement. See also Andrew C. Isenberg, "The Market Revolution in the Borderlands: George Champlin Sibley in Missouri and New Mexico, 1808–1826," *Journal of the Early Republic* 21 (Fall 2001).

[27] Henri, *Hawkins*, 145–51.

In these sectors of the economy and in others, American Indians and Indian nations were centrally important to the new nation's economic and political present and future. In a volatile world, trading interests in agriculture and in manufactured goods wanted frontiers secured for trade, they wanted competitors excluded, and they sought protections and advantages for their investments. As with the issue of land, the drive for safety, efficiency, and profit put a premium on stability, predictability, and order in expansion and Indian affairs.

Federal expenditures in the republic's early decades reflect the importance of Indian affairs. The historian Walter H. Mohr reports that the United States' expenditures on Indian affairs in 1776, primarily expenses for treaties and goods, reflect at least about 10% of the new nation's income in the era.[28] The Secretary of War in 1839 reported that the "consideration in money or in lands" for purchase of more than 419 million acres of Indian land, from 1795 to 1838, exceeded $81.6 million.[29] Historian Stephen Aron tallies war with Ohio Indians as costing the United States $5 million between 1790 and 1796, accounting for 80 percent of the federal budget during the Washington administration.[30] Close to 60 percent of the federal government's expenditures in 1799 and 1800 went to the War and Navy Departments,[31] with expenditures for the War Department representing approximately 25 percent of total federal expenditures. By 1836, War Department expenditures (including the Indian Office) had risen to more than 39 percent of total federal outlays.[32] Ira Katznelson examines data regarding military expenditures, in total and in relation to U.S. expenditures generally, finding that pre–Civil War military expenditures spiked, as would be expected, during the years of the Creek conflict, Tecumseh's confederacy, and the War of 1812. In this era, military expenditures approached 70 percent of the federal budget.[33] Indian Department expenditures are relevant as well, varying widely but running to as much as 9 percent of War Department expenditures in 1796 and 1818, 19 percent in 1825 and 1826, 13 percent in 1830, 25 percent in 1832, and 27 percent in 1833.[34]

[28] Mohr, *Federal Indian Relations*, 194–5. Mohr makes his calculation based on data for 1786, which he calls a time of "profound peace."

[29] Quoted in Paul Stuart, *Nations Within a Nation: Historical Statistics of American Indians* (New York: Greenwood Press, 1987), 78.

[30] Aron, "Lessons," 139.

[31] United States Bureau of the Census, *Historical Statistics of the United States: Colonial Times to 1970*, 2 parts (Washington, DC: U.S. Bureau of the Census, 1975), 1115; Richard B. Morris, ed., *Encyclopedia of American History*, 6th ed. (New York: Harper & Row, 1982), 736.

[32] *Historical Statistics*, 1115; Morris, *Encyclopedia*, 737.

[33] Katznelson, "Flexible Capacity," 92–3; see also *Historical Statistics*, 1114–15. The number of enlisted men in the U.S. Army, Navy and Marine Corps also spiked during the Indian conflicts and War of 1812, peaking at about forty-five thousand people. Katznelson, "Flexible Capacity," 98; see also Edling, *Revolution*, 138.

[34] *Historical Statistics*, 1115.

Such numbers are tricky because they tell only part of the complicated story of conquering a continent largely through peaceful administrative measures. For example, the War Department reported that the Indian Department's total expenditures from the Declaration of Independence to 1820 were just under $6 million.[35] However, the War Department also tallied total expenditures incurred by the United States under the 1802 compact with Georgia, which ceded the state's western lands to the United States in exchange for a federal commitment to extinguish Indian title to the lands. The 1824 report was written well before Jacksonian Indian removal, and during a period of relative peace that saw Georgia clamoring for federal enforcement action. In contrast to the $6 million figure for Indian Department activities from the 1780s to 1820, this report found that more than $7.7 million of *total* expenditures had been incurred from 1802 to 1824 on the Georgia context *alone*.[36] This larger figure – representing almost 2 percent of total U.S. expenditures in the period – includes expenditures for land purchases, claims, treaty negotiations, purchase of reservation land, and annuities. The Georgia case suggests that expansion is not a series of simple, robotically administered, and narrowly confined organizational activities; because they are not simple, expenditure or employment figures arranged according to discrete organizational units hardly tell a full and nuanced story. To the contrary, at any given time and place expansion operations were complicated, coordinated, and multifaceted interactions involving a variety of experts, agencies, motives, authorities, and institutions.

Beyond establishing the concept of the American, the life of the early republic focused on security, land, trade, political development, and frontier politics – and all of these issues revolved around Indians. In the agricultural lands of the south, in the fur trading west, in the finance houses of New York, Philadelphia, and Boston, among canal developers and road builders in upstate New York and the Old Northwest, among shippers, traders, settlers, farmers, and land speculators, and in the concerns for national security and development, Indian affairs were at the heart of all that mattered.

Nationalizing Expansion

In the years of the early republic, the federal government consolidated and expanded its authority to control and regulate the nation's land and trade policies, and its relations with vitally important Indian nations. Delegating

35 The figure includes roughly $1.5 million for treaties, and $3.3 million for expenditures in the Indian Department. "Expenditures for the Indian Department since the Declaration of Independence," December 7, 1820, in *American State Papers – Indian Affairs* [ASPIA] (Washington, DC: Gales and Seaton, 1834), vol. II: 209–12.

36 The actual figure is $7,735,243.52½. "Statement of the amount of expense incurred by the United States, under the compact with the State of Georgia of April 24, 1802," March 27, 1824, in *ASPIA*, II: 463.

dominant authority for expansion and territorial growth to the federal government was not the only option available to policymakers confronting an unstable and threatening frontier in the late eighteenth century. Considering the factors that had contributed to the colonies' rebellion against British efforts to exercise centralized control, centralizing authority over the frontier might seem surprising. As would be the case in later years, interests fought over the issue. State officials and many citizens recognized that granting authority in expansion-related matters to the federal government surrendered decision making and implementation authority to the control of a new, national government apparatus. This surrender – although based on clear evidence that multiple jurisdictions were unable to manage Indian affairs effectively – did not happen easily.

The federal government eventually assumed responsibility for directing and administering the two most significant aspects of expansion: land policy and trade policy. The treaty system, regulations governing land purchases, and formal boundary lines addressed issues of land policy. Management of trade policy included licensing systems, regulation of entry to markets and behavior within markets, and a network of government-run trading posts called the factory system. The factory system extended federal influence over Indians' internal affairs through civilization initiatives and social policies, and served as an institutional cornerstone for organizing disparate administrative efforts.

The Nationalization of Expansion Policy

The American Congress took over Indian affairs from the colonies in the Revolutionary era. Just prior to the founding of the American republic, centralized control of Indian affairs dominated British policies. These approaches had evolved from the colonies' failures in earlier eras when central control had eased: competition between colonies and the volatility of relations with Indians in these years had fostered uncertainty, increased expense, and invited disaster. European powers' centralizing policies and administrative experiences influenced choices in the new republic. Most observers recognized the failure of the colonies' fragmented efforts to deal with Indian affairs, the dangers posed by states operating independently on security issues, and the necessity of a coordinated approach. The new nation needed to manage and control rivalries between the new states if it were to survive.[37] Yet states often wanted to pursue their own policies, and wanted to support state officials and economic interests that could be at odds with

[37] Colonial practices included government approval of land sales, bans on the private purchases of land from Indians, public monopolies on the Indian trade, and regulated licensing of private traders, including bonding and forfeiture requirements. Commissioners and other officials administered the various mechanisms. Stephen Saunders Webb, *1676: The End of American Independence* (Syracuse: Syracuse University Press, 1995); Francis Jennings, *The Invasion of America: Indians, Colonialism, and the Cant of Conquest* (New York: Norton,

the interests of other states or of national leaders. The federal government's assumption of authority was not easy, and years of negotiation with the states were necessary to secure federal preeminence.

In 1775, the Continental Congress established northern, southern, and middle departments to manage Indian affairs. The first commissioners selected for the middle department – Benjamin Franklin, Patrick Henry, and James Wilson – reflect the seriousness with which the members approached Indian affairs. Efforts to establish federal dominance over Indian affairs continued through the Articles of Confederation and on into the Constitutional Convention, but a consensus had long existed among nationalists that Indian affairs were predominantly a federal matter.[38] As early as 1786, echoing earlier statements, the Continental Congress declared the national government's authority over Indian affairs in an Ordinance for the Regulation of Indian Affairs. The preamble states that "the United States in Congress assembled... have the sole and exclusive right and power of regulating the trade, and managing all affairs with the Indians not members of any of the states; provided that the legislative right of any state within its own limits be not infringed or violated."[39] The 1786 Ordinance established northern and southern administrative districts, each headed by a superintendent.

The 1786 ordinance nods to the power of states to control affairs within their own limits, and Congress drew clearer lines almost immediately. Only a month after passage of the Northwest Ordinance in 1787, which set guidelines for organizing the territory west of the Appalachians, a special committee blamed state actions for troubles in the Indian administration's southern department. States were treating directly with Indian tribes and assigning lands independently, the committee found, much as the colonies had done. The committee's report reiterated the necessity of peace on the frontier and noted that encroachments by states on Indian lands "appear to demand the serious attention of Congress, as well because they may be unjustifiable as on account of their tendency to produce all the evils of a general Indian war on the frontiers." The committee argued strenuously that despite the

1976), 130; Francis Paul Prucha, *The Great Father: The United States Government and the American Indians* (Lincoln: University of Nebraska Press, 1986), 5–44; *Laws of the Colonial and State Governments, Relating to Indians and Indian Affairs, from 1763 to 1831 Inclusive* (Stanfordville, NY: Coleman, 1979 [1832]); on trading houses, see Allen W. Trelease, *Indian Affairs in Colonial New York: The Seventeenth Century* (Lincoln: University of Nebraska Press, 1997 [1960]), ch. 2, esp. 46, 132; Jerry L. Mashaw, "Recovering American Administrative Law: Federalist Foundations, 1787–1801," *The Yale Law Journal* 115 (April 2006), 1318.

38 Prucha, *Great Father*, 35, 50; Prucha, *American Indian Treaties*, 68.

39 "Ordinance for the Regulation of Indian Affairs," August 7, 1786, reprinted in Prucha, *Documents*, 8.

wording of the 1786 Ordinance reserving powers to the states, the powers of treating and managing Indian affairs

appear to the committee to be indivisible, and that the parties to the confederation must have intended to give them entire to the Union, or to have given them entire to the State.... The laws of the State can have no effect upon a tribe of Indians or their lands within the limits of the state so long as that tribe is independent, and not a member of the state ...[40]

Private interests provided strong support for national management of Indian affairs and of land and trade policy. Settlement and development efforts by private parties often hinged on an active role by the federal government in protecting and promoting stability and security, both of lives and of investments. The Ohio Company, for example, committed to purchasing land in the Old Northwest after the Revolution on condition that Congress provide for a governmental organization that would attract settlers. Historian Wiley Sword summarizes the situation in the Old Northwest in the nation's early years this way:

It is difficult to perceive that there was ever a greater impetus for legislative action during the formative years of our nation than in the spring and summer of 1787.... In this crisis [Secretary of War Henry] Knox well understood the significance of the burgeoning difficulties with the western Indians. Exposed to increasingly severe raids along the frontier, the Kentucky settlements were vehemently demanding protection, and as a result pressure continued to emanate from the settlers' parent state, Virginia. Because the hostile Indians dwelled within the federal government's new western territory, the governor of Virginia even went so far as to petition Congress early in June, 1787, for pacification of the region.[41]

These and other interests looked to the national government to manage and pacify expansion, generating strong support from interests that understood the pitfalls of uncoordinated, even competitive, land and security policies designed and administered independently by the states.

[40] "Committee Report on the Southern Department," August 3, 1787, reprinted in Prucha, *Documents*, 10. The report allowed for special circumstances which might allow a state authority over Indian territory, but the thrust of the report was that jurisdiction in most cases resided solely with the federal government. See also Cayton, "'Separate Interests,'" 63, for an example of the stern federal response to state meddling in Indian affairs and a strongly worded assertion of the federal government's sole authority. On making Indians a federal responsibility through the 1790 Trade and Intercourse Act, and controlling land transfers, see also Dian Million, "Policing the Rez: Keeping No Peace in Indian Country," *Social Justice* 27 (Fall 2000), 105–6; Joseph T. Glatthaar and James Kirby Martin, *Forgotten Allies: The Oneida Indians and the American Revolution* (New York: Hill and Wang, 1996), 289ff.

[41] Ray Allen Billington, *The Westward Movement in the United States* (New York: Van Nostrand, 1959), 30; Sword, *President Washington's Indian War*, 45–7. See also Cayton, "'Separate Interests,'" 51ff.

Land and the Treaty System

Federal treaties became the dominant mechanism for transferring land from Indians, and reliance upon the treaty system cemented the federal government's preeminence in Indian affairs and expansion policy. The dynamics of the treaty system evolved over time, as did the system's administrative requirements, but treaties remained at the heart of nation-to-nation relations even after Congress formally ended treaty making in 1871. Federal treaties were, and are, the cornerstone of U.S. relations with Indian nations. The Constitution makes it clear that treaties are the supreme law of the land, and the founding generation understood treaties as significant international commitments: treaties had legal and moral status above and beyond the laws and regulations that peppered Indian affairs and expansion policies.[42]

As the new republic struggled to stabilize its Indian policy, false steps illustrate the fact that nothing in Indian administration and policy was inevitable. Following the Revolution, the United States initially sought to treat with Indian nations as conquered nations, under the theory that the defeat of the British consequently meant a defeat of Britain's Indian allies. Indians, of course, did not see it quite this way. Nevertheless, U.S. treaty commissioners immediately after the Revolution sought to dictate terms and set boundary lines without offering compensation for land cessions. This method dominated affairs in the northwest and the middle Atlantic, evidenced in the Treaties of Fort Stanwix (1784), Fort McIntosh (1785), and Fort Finney (1786), among others.

The new government's efforts to deal with Indian affairs, though, were constrained by the weak position of the United States relative to the Indian nations and by efforts by leaders in states like New York, North Carolina, and Georgia to conduct their own Indian relations. The early decision to treat Indians as conquered peoples was a conscious choice that looked toward eventual conquest of lands desired by settlers and states, but the United States lacked the raw power to drive policy the way it wanted. By the late 1780s, the Indians who had signed treaties had become dissatisfied and further conflict loomed. Confronted with the risks of continuing its aggressive stance, the federal government narrowed its demands and began to treat Indians as independent sovereigns, reverting to European practices of negotiation (instead of simple declaration of boundaries), to payment for cessions, and to purchasing right of soil from Indians. Secretary of War Henry Knox pushed for this change, which became standard practice by the

[42] On treaties generally, see Prucha, *American Indian Treaties*; Prucha, *Great Father*, ch. 1; Horsman, *Frontier*. Garrison, *Legal Ideology* offers a detailed description of variations and interpretations of the treaty system as it developed to the Jackson era, highlighting the different interpretations laid out by state authorities, especially judges, at a time when southern states were trying to circumvent established treaty concepts in order to facilitate Indian removal.

close of the 1780s with compensation paid for earlier cessions and by the payments included in the treaties signed at Fort Harmar in January 1789.[43]

The federal government asserted the authority to control Indian land cessions in the 1790 Trade and Intercourse Act. Section Four of the Act stated, in clear terms:

> That no sale of lands made by any Indians, or any nation or tribe of Indians within the United States, shall be valid to any person or persons, or to any state, whether having the right to pre-emption to such lands or not, unless the same shall be made and duly executed at some public treaty, held under the authority of the United States.[44]

Time and again, contentious relations between state and federal officials resolved themselves in favor of federal authority. In New York, state officials tried to direct Indian affairs after the Revolution and into the nineteenth century. The federal government worked closely with state interests in the Empire state, particularly those led by Governor George Clinton, in a series of federally sanctioned agreements and treaties that were at times heavily influenced by New York, at times in disregard of federal authority.[45] The federal government also had trouble in the South, particularly with North Carolina soon after the Revolution and with Georgia heading into the nineteenth century. The organization and sophistication of the southern tribes, together with the slave context and continuing tensions with Spain and France, complicated matters considerably. Nevertheless, the federal government managed to work effectively toward federal dominance, sometimes by physically excluding state officials from treaty negotiations.[46] The federal government also worked to defuse tensions lit by state officials and settlers. The United States, for example, defused southern efforts to start an Indian war in 1795. Secretary of War Timothy Pickering wrote to Governor William Blount, "It is plain that the United States are determined, if possible, to avoid a direct or indirect war with the Creeks. Congress alone are competent to decide upon an offensive war, and congress have not thought fit to authorize it."[47]

The treaty system incurred substantial costs. Individual treaties cost tens of thousands of eighteenth- and early-nineteenth-century dollars for administrative expenses, payments, and goods and presents. The Continental Congress appropriated $10,000 for presents to be distributed at a council in Pittsburgh in 1776, and another $10,000 for a council in 1778; a 1798

[43] Berkhofer, *White Man's Indian*, 143.

[44] *U.S. Statutes at Large*, 1:137–8, reprinted in Prucha, *Documents*, 15.

[45] See, e.g., Prucha, *American Indian Treaties*, 43–8 and 48 n17; 113–15, 144–5.

[46] See, e.g., Prucha, *American Indian Treaties*, 59–66; the exclusion of Georgia's representatives from the treaty at Coleraine in 1796 is discussed at 96–100.

[47] Quoted in Prucha, *Great Father*, 69; see also 69ff.; Prucha, *American Indian Treaties*, ch. 2; Cayton, "'Separate Interests.'"

treaty signed with the Cherokee at Tellico in Tennessee saw $5,000 worth of goods distributed at the site. $20,000 was distributed at the landmark Treaty of Greenville in 1795, $10,000 at a treaty in New York, $6,000 at Colerain in Georgia in 1796. The sums increased with time, especially as the United States began paying off tribes' debts to trading companies with monies committed during treaty negotiations. In 1805, for example, a treaty with the Chickasaws committed $20,000 "for the use of the nation at large, and for the payment of the debts due to the merchants and traders." The United States promised $200,000, to be held by the government at six percent interest, in exchanging Creek lands surrounded by Georgia for lands in the West. At a treaty with the Potawatomis in 1826, the federal government distributed presents worth more than $30,000.[48] By 1829, the total congressional appropriation just for treaty annuities amounted to $214,590.[49] Leading Indian law scholar Felix Cohen estimated that by 1947, $800 million had been paid out just for Indian land cessions, not including administrative and military costs.[50] Billions of dollars in treaty-guaranteed benefits and programs continue today.

Federal treaties gave local individuals cause for concern, because they brought thousands of Indians together in an era when rumors of Indians gathering could throw an entire region into a panic. The Creek treaty of 1790 gathered two thousand Creeks, and twelve hundred Cherokees met with William Blount, governor of the Territory Southwest of the Ohio, at Knoxville in 1791. Over a thousand gathered at one treaty in New York, 1,600 at another; 1,390 Miamis attended a treaty with William Henry Harrison in 1809, 3,000 attended a treaty at Greenville with Harrison and Lewis Cass in 1814, and 1,000 more attended at Prairie du Chien in 1825.[51]

48 Prucha, *American Indian Treaties*, 30, 31, 89, 93, 96, 100, 110; quoted in *American Indian Treaties*, 110; 124, 138.

49 Prucha, *Great Father*, 171.

50 Cited in Terry L. Anderson, *Sovereign Nations or Reservations? An Economic History of American Indians* (San Francisco: Pacific Research Institute for Public Policy, 1995), 74.

51 Prucha, *American Indian Treaties*, 80, 86, 95, 122, 130, 141. Efforts like these were a constant feature of national administration. The United States made treaties with the Cherokees, for example, in 1785, 1791, 1798, 1804, 1805 (two), 1806, 1816 (two), 1817 (two), 1819, and 1835. William G. McLoughlin, *Cherokee Renascence in the New Republic* (Princeton: Princeton University Press, 1986), 28–9. Treaties were made with the Miami and Chippewa in 1818, 1819, 1820, 1821, 1825, 1827, 1837, 1854, 1855, and 1863. Duane Champagne, *Chronology of Native North American History: From Pre-Columbian Times to the Present* (New York: Thomson Gale, 1994), 133. Lawmaking was a constant, too: the United States passed major laws on land, trade, or administrative issues involving Indian affairs in 1785, 1786, 1787, 1790, 1793, 1799, 1800, 1802, 1817, 1822, 1830, 1832, 1834, 1837, 1847, 1849, 1862, 1864, 1867, 1869, 1870, 1871, 1882, 1884, 1885, 1887, 1888, 1889, 1891, 1892, 1893, 1897, 1898, and 1899. Patricia Nelson Limerick reports that Congress passed 375 land laws between 1789 and 1834. *The Legacy of Conquest: The Unbroken Past of the American West* (New York: Norton, 1987), 61.

The Scope of Federal Government Activity

The early federal government worked to regulate other aspects of expansion and Indian relations. New federal regulations and social policies aimed at controlling traders, restricting alcohol and weapons trading, and influencing the development of native peoples. National trade regulations supervised economic sectors, and the factory system of government trading houses managed diplomacy and trade. The federal government quickly extended its activities into a wide variety of expansion-related policies and programs.

Early Regulations and Social Policy

Congress established several mechanisms to support the goals of the treaty system and minimize conflicts arising from trade between Indians and whites. Congress enacted a licensing system to regulate the Indian trade as early as 1776, with modifications appearing regularly. Throughout the years of the early republic, regulations mandated the posting of bonds, outlined restrictions on what goods could be traded and where transactions could take place, and even addressed the personal characteristics of traders themselves.[52] Congress established penalties to punish violators. The 1790 Trade and Intercourse Act also set punishments for crimes committed by whites against Indians in Indian country. It is important to note that such laws and regulations were aimed at whites more than at Indians.

Controlling trade in firearms and liquor was critical to trading regulations, because they were commodities likely to encourage conflict between Indians and whites. Prohibitions and controls on trade in these items date to the earliest days of the colonies. Early U.S. efforts to control the trade struggled, in part because of the blurred lines of authority between local, state, and federal authorities. Continuing problems arising from the whiskey trade brought increasing complaints and demands for help from the federal government.[53] Jefferson eventually took the lead in convincing Congress to expand the president's power to control the alcohol trade, after he was only partially successful in convincing state and territorial leaders to do so. Alcohol prohibition in Indian affairs would have a long and checkered history – in large part because alcohol played a central role in furthering diplomacy and land cessions, and helped drive frontier economies through supply to Indians, the military, and others on the frontier. Yet the historian William Unruh demonstrates that it was the absence of federal authority

[52] Katherine Coman, "Government Factories: An Attempt to Control Competition in the Fur Trade," *Papers and Proceedings of the American Economic Association*, Vol. 1 (April, 1911).

[53] Prucha, *Great Father*, 98–102; William E. Unruh, *White Man's Wicked Water: The Alcohol Trade and Prohibition in Indian Country, 1802–1892* (Lawrence: University Press of Kansas, 1996).

that often provoked states and territories to regulate alcohol more strictly, after demands for greater federal control had gone unmet.[54] The federal government also took the lead in trying to extend and enforce criminal justice protocols in and around Indian country, and in trying to maintain peace by overseeing and adjudicating claims from depredations and other problems allegedly caused by Indians or whites.[55]

These regulatory and compensatory efforts related closely to the government's efforts to "civilize," educate, and protect Indians, and social policy initiatives characterized the early republic's efforts to pacify and manage its frontier. Education provisions in Indian affairs go back to the republic's early years. A 1789 treaty with Oneida, Tuscarora, and Stockbridge was the first to contain education provisions.[56] Treaties obligated the United States to provide instruments of husbandry at least as early as 1791, to help teach Indians to become yeoman farmers.[57] Senecas petitioned George Washington in 1791 for teachers; a 1794 treaty with the Stockbridge and an 1803 treaty with the Kaskaskias provided funds for education.[58] An 1804 treaty with the Delawares provided ten years' and $3,000 worth of instruction and materials in agriculture and domestic arts.[59] A treaty with Seminoles ratified in 1823 included $1,000 per year for a reservation gunsmith and a

[54] Unruh, *White Men's Wicked Water*.

[55] Prucha, *Great Father*, 103ff., 107; John K. Mahon, *History of the Second Seminole War, 1835–1842* (Gainesville: University of Florida Press, 1992), 59, 164; Larry C. Skogen, *Indian Depredation Claims, 1796–1920* (Norman: University of Oklahoma Press, 1996); Clark and Guice, *Old Southwest*, 209ff. Citizens submitted claims for more than a quarter million 1987 dollars in 1813–1814 (Clark and Guice, *Old Southwest*, 126), and Skogen reports that, while payouts were difficult to secure, people entered thousands of claims with federal agents. Landis notes that disaster relief, including Indian affairs, expanded "vastly" during the Jefferson, Madison, and Monroe administrations. Michele L. Landis, "'Let Me Next Time Be "Tried by Fire"': Disaster Relief and the Origins of the American Welfare State 1789–1874," *Northwestern University Law Review* 92 (Spring 1998), 977–8; see also 977 n53, 982 n81, 983 n87, 1005–8, 1024–7. See also Mashaw, "Recovering," 1295 (demands for post roads, service), 1297 (in its first twelve years, the U.S. House of Representatives received nearly three thousand petitions "for relief of some sort"); Mark R. Wilson, *The Business of Civil War: Military Mobilization and the State, 1861–1865* (Baltimore: The Johns Hopkins University Press, 2006), 8, describing demands for reimbursements for volunteer regiments in the War of 1812 and the Mexican War.

[56] Jon Reyhner and Jeanne Eder, "A History of Indian Education," in *Teaching American Indian Students*, ed. Jon Reyhner (Norman: University of Oklahoma Press, 1994), 37.

[57] Joan Greene Orr, "Civilize the Indian: Government Policies, Quakers, and Cherokee Education," *The Southern Friend* 10 (1988), 28, citing the Treaty of Holston with the Cherokees, 1791. See also Clark and Guice, *Old Southwest*, 27ff.

[58] Ronald Rayman, "Joseph Lancaster's Monitorial System of Instruction and American Indian Education, 1815–1838," *History of Education Quarterly* 21 (Winter 1981), 396; see also Meyer Weinberg, *A Chance to Learn: The History of Race and Education in the United States* (Cambridge: Cambridge University Press, 1977).

[59] Robert M. Owens, "Jeffersonian Benevolence on the Ground: The Indian Land Cession Treaties of William Henry Harrison," *Journal of the Early Republic* 22 (Fall 2002), 420.

reservation blacksmith, and $1,000 per year for twenty years to maintain a school.[60]

Legislation also promoted education among Indian populations. The Continental Congress donated $500 to Dartmouth for the education of American Indians in 1775. Commissioners of the Northern Department for Indian affairs were directed to comply with Dartmouth's requests for financial support from the federal government.[61] Education and social policy provisions were part of federal Trade and Intercourse Acts as early as 1793, and beginning in 1802 Congress provided $15,000 per year "to provide Civilization among the Indians."[62] Following negotiations between missionaries and members of the executive branch, the Civilization Fund of 1819 built on these and other efforts by allocating $10,000 annually for education and other efforts. The Civilization Fund included provisions for agriculture and "reading, writing, and arithmetic" as assimilation methods. Negotiations produced contracts spelling out the duties of the missionaries and the responsibilities of the government, and committed the Secretary of War to instruct federal agents to provide buildings and tools to the Indians working with the missionaries.[63] The Civilization Fund lasted until 1873, at which point the U.S. government had become even more directly involved with educating Indians.[64]

To help meet its commitments, the United States from the dawning of the republic actively supported the work of missionaries and missionary societies among Indians. Gideon Blackburn received government aid from Jefferson and Dearborn for a Presbyterian school among the Cherokees in 1803; Cyrus Kingsbury received government aid from Crawford's War Department in 1816 for the first mission of the American Board of Foreign Missions at Brainerd, Tennessee. As in other aspects of expansion policy, monetary amounts rarely tell the entire story. While grants such as these were relatively small early on, sometimes on the order of only a few hundred dollars, they established close links between religious groups and federal agents and set precedents for government aid. Indian agents and

60 Mahon, *Second Seminole War*, 47. On the significance of blacksmiths see, e.g., Glatthaar and Martin, *Forgotten Allies*, 70; Washington Irving, *The Adventures of Captain Bonneville* (Washington, DC: National Geographic, 2003 [1837]), 11.

61 Mohr, *Federal Indian Relations*, 196. See also Patricia A. Carter, "'Completely Discouraged': Women Teachers' Resistance in the Bureau of Indian Affairs Schools, 1900–1910," *Frontiers* 15 (1995); Weinberg, *A Chance to Learn*.

62 Reyhner and Eder, "Indian Education," 37; Weinberg, *A Chance to Learn*, 181.

63 Orr, "Civilize," 28; William G. McLoughlin, *Cherokees and Missionaries, 1789–1839* (Norman: University of Oklahoma Press, 1995), 3, 105ff.; see also Bernard W. Sheehan, *Seeds of Extinction: Jeffersonian Philanthropy and the American Indian* (New York: Norton, 1973), ch. 5. See also Young, *Redskins*, 8ff., 23ff.; Daniel Feller, *The Jacksonian Promise: America, 1815–1840* (Baltimore: The Johns Hopkins University Press, 1995), 142–5.

64 Reyhner and Eder, "Indian Education," 38, 45.

trading house factors were ordered to assist missionaries in the administration of farming, education, and other programs, support which was often more important to the missionaries' efforts than cash would have been. The responsibility of factors and Indian agents to provide help and support for the missionaries provided legitimacy and institutionalized protection for their efforts. And the give-and-take between federal support and "private" activity could be quite close. Reverend Cyrus Kingsbury of the American Board of Commissioners for Foreign Missions solicited and obtained funds from the federal government for buildings, teachers, equipment, and supplies. In return, Kingsbury worked hard to comply with federal reporting requirements.[65]

As head of the Indian Department after 1816, Thomas McKenney promoted education, civilization, and government ties with religious organizations, including an extension of Kingsbury's educational model and various initiatives to supply stable funds for such purposes. The bill creating the Civilization Fund gave the president broad authorization to appoint and regulate teachers of agriculture and reading, writing, and arithmetic:

> That for the purpose of providing against the further decline and final extinction of the Indian tribes, adjoining the frontier settlements of the United States, and for introducing among them the habits and arts of civilization, the President of the United States shall be, and he is hereby authorized, in every case where he shall judge improvement in the habits and condition of such Indians practicable, and that the means of instruction can be introduced with their own consent, to employ capable persons of good moral character, to instruct them in the mode of agriculture suited to their situation; and for teaching their children in reading, writing, and arithmetic, and performing such other duties as may be enjoined, according to such instructions and rules as the President may give and prescribe for the regulation of their conduct, in the discharge of their duties.[66]

By 1822, as the factory system era wound down, the United States operated eleven principal schools and three subordinate schools, with 508 instructors. By 1824, thirty-two schools pursued U.S. goals, with close to a thousand students; by 1830, when the movement started to slow, there were fifty-two schools and over fifteen hundred students.[67] By 1834, the United States was committed to $35,500 earmarked for schools under treaty provisions; by 1845 the annual sum in twenty-four treaties exceeded $68,000.[68] As just one example in a particular context, between 1817 and 1852 the

[65] Rayman, "Joseph Lancaster," 397–9.

[66] Quoted in Schmeckebier, *Office of Indian Affairs*, 39; the appropriation was not repealed until 1873 (Schmeckebier, *Office of Indian Affairs*, 39 n63).

[67] Leonard D. White, *The Jeffersonians: A Study in Administrative History, 1801–1829* (New York: Free Press, 1951), 505–6; Prucha, *Great Father*, 152, 154.

[68] Prucha, *Great Father*, 153; Prucha, *American Indian Treaties*, 12.

United States appropriated more than half a million dollars to meet treaty provisions for Choctaw education alone.[69]

The Factory System

A network of trading houses, called factories, became the administrative centerpiece coordinating many of the national government's efforts. The factory system created a series of not-for-profit, government-run trading houses that intentionally undersold private traders in dealings with the Indians. The government would purchase items for the factories, ship the goods, and then sell them under the aegis of the factor, an appointed position in the War Department. By underselling private traders and pushing them out of the trade, policymakers hoped that Indians would be less likely to be wronged (or feel that they had been wronged) by unscrupulous independent profit-seekers; as such, the likelihood of conflict could be reduced. The factories served as a tool of diplomacy, of peace and order on the frontier. Healthy trade relationships would bind the Indians to the United States, and Indian debts to the trading houses could be paid in land cessions. Factors provided a stable government presence on the frontier, they could help missionaries and others inculcate white and Christian values among the Indians, and the factories could coordinate the government's domestic and "civilization" initiatives. Factors became a lynchpin of the civilization efforts, dispensing agricultural goods, encouraging domestic activity, and providing a stable presence for Indians, missionaries, settlers, and traders in volatile areas. Through the factories, and together with the licensing and bonding system established by the Trade and Intercourse Acts and the cooperation of missionaries with government designs, federal authorities believed that they could control the frontier well enough to reduce costs in money and lives and control threats to the nation's security.

Henry Knox and George Washington designed the factory system and convinced Congress to authorize and fund it. Although the system did not spring from the lobbying of private parties, large trading interests became important constituencies that worked during the factories' early years to perpetuate the system. By design, government regulations benefited large trading interests. Policymakers persistently rejected proposals for a government monopoly over the Indian trade, as the factories and the trade regulations intentionally drove the nongovernment trade into the hands of large, well-funded, and presumably more responsible corporations. John Astor, for example, worked closely with the Indian Office and with other engines of the government in planning and operating his ventures in Astoria and in the fur trade.[70] The losers in this scheme were independent traders,

69 Prucha, *American Indian Treaties*, 12.

70 See, e.g., Lavender, *Fist in the Wilderness*; Haeger, *John Jacob Astor*; Jack Weatherford, *Native Roots: How the Indians Enriched America* (New York: Crown, 1991), 76–7.

who often could not afford the bonding requirements, who lacked access to government officials who controlled dispensation of trade licenses, and who policymakers believed represented the greatest threats to peace and order on the frontier. Independent traders were also more likely than representatives of major trading companies to be allied with foreign interests on U.S. borders.

Small and independent traders had mixed feelings about the factory system. To their benefit, the system promised to help pacify frontier areas and establish a stable federal presence. One of the avowed goals of the factory system was to drive Indians into debt, thereby making Indians favorably disposed to extinguishing their debts through land cessions; white settlers and land interests, especially, appreciated this aspect of the policy. On the other hand, regulations cut into independent traders' ability to conduct trade relations on their own terms. Further, the federal government acted not only as a competitor, but also as an obvious ally of large trading companies.

As the years of the factory system passed, two dynamics evolved. First, local and independent traders increasingly came to see the government's activities as a threat. Second, over time even the system's large trading allies came to see the factories as an unwanted competitor. After federal activity had facilitated their success, many of the larger interests, Astor in particular, came to oppose the system. These interests would eventually coordinate a successful attack on the factories. This attack distorted the factories' primarily diplomatic and pacification objectives, and obscured the system's history of effectiveness. The big companies' lobbyists would weave the story of the factories into a tale of administrative incompetence and government mismanagement.

A total of thirty factories operated at one time or another at key sites in the U.S. westward advance, including Detroit, Fort Mackinac, Fort Wayne, Green Bay, Sandusky, and Chicago; eight factories operated in the southeastern states, and eight more on the Mississippi River from Minnesota to Arkansas, Natchitoches, and Fort Osage. The factory system carried through four administrations, defended by presidents against increasingly resistant private interests.

Federal Activity in Other Areas

Federal efforts to manage expansion were not limited to Indian affairs, and Indian affairs were hardly the only important area of public policy to come under control of the national government in the late eighteenth century.

The Land Ordinance of 1785 set out guidelines for settlement, sales, and control of land, and established the Office of Geographer of the United States. Surveying lands and sectioning territory was a labor-intensive effort undertaken by federal authorities, often (especially later) contracted out to representatives of concerns like the Ohio Company. Overseeing federal agents at offices like the far-flung General Land Office, and contracted parties doing the federal government's work, invited efforts to standardize and coordinate efforts in the field, and of course these efforts too involved the interplay of government, private, and political issues.[71]

Federal involvement in internal improvements in the early nineteenth century is obscured by high profile presidential vetoes like Madison's veto of the Bonus Bill in 1817, Monroe's veto of the Cumberland Road Bill in 1822, Jackson's veto of the Maysville Road Bill in 1830, and Polk's veto of the Rivers and Harbors Bill in 1846.[72] George Washington, though, favored the public construction of roads and canals, both to serve as sparks to commerce, spurs to his own investments, and as guarantors of national security and settlement.[73] Ronald Shaw argues convincingly that Jefferson and the Democrats generally evolved into strong supporters of the national government's participation in internal improvements, despite common assumptions to the contrary. The Natchez Trace between Natchez and Nashville, surveyed and built by the army under Jefferson and thus "a pioneer Federal internal improvement project," affected communications, military preparedness and deployment, and trade and settlement.[74] In the same year as the Cumberland Road Act – 1806 – Congress paid to survey and improve the federal road from the Ocmulgee River to the Imbigbee, including the building of bridges and construction of causeways.[75] Congress appropriated $20,000 in 1824 for a road from St. Augustine to Pensacola, to bolster communications and security in Florida as tensions increased in the 1820s.[76] The Santa Fe Trail, initially surveyed at the end of the factory system era, was "arguably the most successful of the early nineteenth-century federal

[71] Linklater, *Measuring America*; Mohr, *Federal Indian Relations*, 104; R. Douglas Hurt, *The Ohio Frontier: Crucible of the Old Northwest, 1720–1830* (Bloomington: University of Indiana Press, 1996); Rohrbough, *Land Office Business*.

[72] Shaw, *Canals*, 199ff., and ch. 1. See also Southerland and Brown, *Federal Road*, ch. 1; Feller, *Public Lands*, xii–xiii, 48–66. The use of the veto adds to the argument that the presidency in this era was a major player in domestic policy.

[73] Anderson and Cayton, *Dominion of War*, 183–4.

[74] Clark and Guice, *Old Southwest*, 87. Illustrating the power and influence of Indian nations at the time, the Cherokees' refusal to allow the United States to cross its lands in 1801 forced the new post road to Nashville, rather than Knoxville. Clark and Guice, *Old Southwest*, 86–7. See 177 and ch. 5 generally for a discussion of the significance of the Natchez Trace and other federal roads in the South. See also Southerland and Brown, *Federal Road*; Ronald N. Satz, *Tennessee's Indian Peoples: From White Contact to Removal, 1540–1840* (Knoxville: University of Tennessee Press, 1979), 52.

[75] On the significance of the Cumberland Road, see Arthur H. Cole, "Cyclical and Sectional Variations in the Sale of Public Lands, 1816–1860," reprinted in Carstensen, *Public Lands*, 236. Travelers understood that the federal road from the Ocmulgee was a government project, and credited the president. Clark and Guice, *Old Southwest*, 175. On the federal road through Georgia and Alabama, see Southerland and Brown, *Federal Road*.

[76] Mahon, *Second Seminole War*, 67; see 133 for other Floridian demands for roads.

road-building programs, which sought to expand commerce and integrate distant regions into the national market economy."[77]

In the canal era, state and private interests peppered the federal government with requests for aid. The federal government played key roles in obtaining land from Indians, a crucial stage in development too often overlooked or touched on only fleetingly by scholars of the canal era. The government then made land available to states and developers by means that included land grants, foreshadowing railroad-era policy.[78] Monroe signed the General Survey Act of 1824, which paved the way for federal sponsorship and expertise, and Jackson signed internal improvement bills encompassing over one million dollars annually. In the canal context alone, and in addition to its critical role in land issues, the federal government contributed funds, bought stock subscriptions, lent and paid for expert help in planning and construction, and helped coordinate efforts. Federal troops protected companies and put down violence. Nationalist and expansionist values and rhetoric – like calling federally subsidized canals "national waterways" – motivated canal developers and popular opinion, even when states or private interests were doing the building.[79] Canal development aided expansion more deeply than can be assessed simply by looking at economic returns, as development encouraged population movement and bound sections of the country together just as the railroads would do in later years.[80]

Roads, canals, and other improvements brought administration. The Corps of Topographical Engineers has roots in the years after the War of 1812, and by the mid-1820s the Corps was working on a national road between New Orleans and Washington, supervising construction of the Cumberland Road, constructing the Chesapeake and Ohio Canal, working on the Coast Survey and the Lighthouse Board, making improvements on the Ohio and Mississippi Rivers, surveying Nantucket and Marblehead, sponsoring the survey of the Santa Fe Trail, and surveying routes for private railroads.[81] The Board of Engineers was another specialized administrative unit, aiding particularly in canal development and expansion; the Bernard Board coordinated strategic coastal defenses with inland communications,

77 Isenberg, "Market Revolution," 464.

78 Grants of four and a half million acres supported canal activity, with Ohio, Indiana, Illinois, and Wisconsin benefiting in the 1820s and 1830s, and Michigan and Wisconsin benefiting in the 1850s and 1860s. Shaw, *Canals*, 225; see also Hauptman, *Conspiracy*; Sheriff, *Artificial River*.

79 Shaw, *Canals*, 18, 199ff.

80 Shaw notes, for example, that although the Chesapeake and Ohio Canal cost $14 million and repaid less than 2 percent of the cost to build it, "It was typical of the Canal Era, a canal that could not fulfill its original goals but nevertheless left an undeniable mark on the growth of towns and cities along its banks." Shaw, *Canals*, 106; see also 142.

81 Goetzmann, *Army Exploration*, 3–61; J. E. Kaufmann & H. W. Kaufmann, *Fortress America: The Forts that Defended America, 1600 to the Present* (Cambridge, MA: Da Capo Press, 2004), 191.

transportation, and militias; other efforts combined land acquisition, materials procurement, and construction to build, maintain, and administer forts, supply depots, arsenals, and navy yards.[82] All of these efforts sparked complaints about federal activity, and also demands for greater federal involvement and expertise.[83]

Adding to the national government's presence on its lands and borders, the government relied on a system of naval stations to provide an effective presence around the globe after the War of 1812. Just as the nation's Indian policies were designed to ward off the need to use expensive and unpredictable force, "The essential objective [of the naval stations] was to show the flag in foreign ports, and ensure an intermittent presence sufficient to discourage any thoughts of aggression by the new states or the native population."[84] Long courtesy visits encouraged social contacts and enabled negotiated approaches to conflicts. After 1808, federal efforts inhibited the slave trade, especially in patrolling the African and United States coasts. Slavers established routines for evading the U.S. efforts and for slipping into U.S. ports, but ships and slaves were still seized by federal ships.[85]

Other federal agents filled the landscape. Federal customs service officials were among the most visible early federal agents in the East. Customs officials engaged in a broad variety of tasks involving immigration, collecting funds for the relief of sick and disabled seamen, directing hospitals and

[82] Robert G. Athearn, *Forts of the Upper Missouri* (Englewood Cliffs, NJ: Prentice Hall, 1967); Emanuel Raymond Lewis, *Seacoast Fortifications of the United States: An Introductory History* (Annapolis: Naval Institute Press, 1979), 37ff.; Kaufmann and Kaufmann, *Fortress America*, 205–9.

[83] Congress received numerous state requests for canal aid during Jefferson's presidency. Shaw, *Canals*, 24. In the 1820s, Calhoun – who in 1819 called for army engineers to guide a national system of internal improvements – sent the Board of Engineers in answer to requests for help from the Morris Canal in New Jersey and the Chesapeake and Delaware Canal Company in 1823. Shaw, *Canals*, 200. Federal involvement affected canal building in the South, as well. Georgia's Governors David Mitchell and George Troup pressed for internal improvements after the War of 1812 and into the 1820s, with a combined nationalism and hopes for sparking economic development across Georgia, even if little work was ultimately accomplished in the state. The South, though, does not seem to have pressed for aid from the national government as strongly as other regions did, nor did it build as much as other states. Shaw, *Canals*, 122–5. Even when the federal government did not ultimately back canal projects, the expectation and hope existed. New York developers believed, for example, that the federal government would back its canal project financially and pointed to Gallatin's report promoting road and canal projects to bolster their argument. Congress even passed a bill with funding for New York's canal, but President Madison vetoed it. Sheriff, *Artificial River*, 20–1; Shaw, *Canals*, 26–9, 199.

[84] Jean Heffer, *The United States and the Pacific: History of a Frontier* (Notre Dame: University of Notre Dame Press, 2002), 75; see also 79.

[85] George Francis Dow, *Slave Ships and Slaving* (Mineola: Dover, 2002 [1927]), 272–9, 321, 338; see also Iver Bernstein, "Securing Freedom: The Challenges of Black Life in Civil War New York," in Ira Berlin and Leslie M. Harris, eds., *Slavery in New York* (New York: New Press, 2005), 306.

other services, enforcing state and federal health laws and quarantines, and collecting bonds from crew members bound for foreign ports.[86] Federal appointees ran territorial governments and represented federal goals, regulating and nurturing important sectors of regional and national economies like dairy farming and hog production, and even laying down "morals" legislation.[87] Congress declared postal service to be under monopoly federal control as early as 1786. Unlike the federal–local tensions that typified territorial politics, Wesley Everett Rich writes that there was little opposition to congressional supremacy in administering the mails.[88] This control gave the federal government responsibility for general guidelines and administration covering affairs across the country and expansion into newly acquired areas, and established the federal government's authority to control important and lucrative matters such as the building of post roads, the subsidizing of the stagecoach industry, and the letting of valuable contracts to mail carriers and others associated with the business of the Post Office. Congressional authority over post roads "had major implications for the pattern of everyday life, since it virtually guaranteed that the postal network would expand rapidly into the transappalachian West well in advance of commercial demand," historian Richard John writes. "Not until the 1830s, *after* the national market had been established, would private entrepreneurs begin to compete against the government in an organized way." Later, Congress defended and tightened its monopoly against competition and "private expresses" with the Post Office Acts of 1845 and 1851.[89]

Efforts by the national government to control the identification of people by race or other categories, and to enforce through such distinctions the goals of public policy, are further examples of state activity that should not be overlooked. Efforts to regulate membership and identity extend as far back as distinctions made by enumerators regarding race in the 1790 Census.[90]

[86] Melvin Dubnick, "Customs Service," in *A Historical Guide to the U.S. Government*, ed. George T. Kurian (New York: Oxford University Press, 1998), 144–5.

[87] E.g., Hurt, *Ohio Frontier*, ch. 8. Territorial laws, for example, denounced "idle, vain, and obscene conversation, profane cursing and swearing," and forbade "servile labor" on the Sabbath. Bond, "American Civilization," 27–8.

[88] Wesley Everett Rich, *The History of the United States Post Office to the Year 1829* (Cambridge, MA: Harvard University Press, 1924), 63, 111.

[89] John, *Spreading the News*, 45, 54, 49, 160ff.

[90] Rogers M. Smith, *Civic Ideals: Conflicting Visions of Citizenship in U.S. History* (New Haven: Yale University Press, 1997); Jack D. Forbes, *Africans and Native Americans: The Language of Race and the Evolution of Red-Black Peoples*, 2nd ed. (Urbana: University of Illinois Press, 1993); Circe Sturm, "Blood Politics, Racial Classification, and Cherokee National Identity: The Trials and Tribulations of the Cherokee Freedmen," *American Indian Quarterly* 22 (Winter 1998); Clark and Guice, *Old Southwest*, ch. 12; Bonita Lawrence, "Gender, Race, and the Regulation of Native Identity in Canada and the United States: An Overview," *Hypatia* 18 (Spring 2003), 16; Melissa Nobles, "History Counts: A Comparative Analysis of Racial/Color Categorization in U.S. and Brazilian Censuses," *American Journal of Public Health* 90 (November 2000), 1738.

Immigration policies provide another long line of federal interventions and efforts to exercise control in identity and membership issues.[91] The national government imposed political and racial categorizations through censuses, treaties, immigration acts, and other laws, excluding or including individuals and groups in policies and administrative jurisdictions. Making such distinctions, whether they were based on political or racial categories, or a combination thereof, involved the national government and its agents in major decisions with significant effects on Indian and non-Indian individuals and communities. By these methods the United States was, of course, doing more than merely extending its own jurisdiction over Indian and other communities. It was simultaneously narrowing the scope and relevance of native and ethnic autonomy, traditions, cultures, and decision-making methods.[92]

Expansion policies were nationalized, coordinated, and planned, and they affected virtually everybody at some level. In the earliest years of the republic, the national government was a major player in issues of land, trade, the economy, war, diplomacy, expansion, infrastructure, settlement, criminal justice, education, health, and identity. As national policies and presence led and managed movement west, public administrators, bureaucracy, and a sense of the state were inevitable.

[91] In the Naturalization Act of 1798, for example, Congress raised from five to fourteen the number of years an immigrant must have lived in the United States before becoming a citizen. Anthony M. Platt and Jenifer L. Cooreman, "A Multicultural Chronology of Welfare Policy and Social Work in the United States," *Social Justice* 28 (Spring 2001), 95.

[92] The Indian Office's operations, and indeed those of the national government generally in Indian affairs, can be seen in terms of what Desmond King and Rogers Smith have labeled "racial institutional orders." Desmond S. King and Rogers M. Smith, "Racial Orders in American Political Development," *American Political Science Review* 99 (February 2005), 75. On roles, identity issues, and related issues generally, see Eva Marie Garroutte, "The Racial Formation of American Indians: Negotiating Legitimate Identities within Tribal and Federal Law," *American Indian Quarterly* 25 (Spring 2001); Lawrence, "Gender"; Forbes, *Africans*; Sturm, "Blood Politics"; Ruth Wallis Herndon and Ella Wilcox Sekatau, "The Right to a Name: The Narragansett People and Rhode Island Officials in the Revolutionary Era," in *Major Problems in American Indian History*, 2nd ed., ed. Albert L. Hurtado and Peter Iverson (Boston: Houghton Mifflin, 2001); Laurence M. Hauptman, *Between Two Fires: American Indians in the Civil War* (New York: Free Press Paperbacks, 1996), 68.

3

Tippecanoe and Treaties, Too

Executive Leadership, Organization, and Effectiveness in the Years of the Factory System

William Henry Harrison is perhaps best remembered for dying a month after his coatless inaugural address in 1841. At the time, though, Harrison was recognized as one of the nation's most famous military and political figures. Perhaps the most memorable campaign slogan in American history, "Tippecanoe and Tyler, Too" recalled for voters Harrison's most notable contribution: his 1811 victory at Tippecanoe over a pan-Indian confederacy, following Tecumseh and aligned with the British, that threatened to close off the lands to the West and stifle U.S. expansion into the Ohio region.

Landmark battles and groundbreaking victories involving American Indians led Harrison to the presidency, and catapulted the careers of many other officials in politics and government in the opening decades of the nineteenth century. In the race against Harrison, for example, Martin Van Buren's running mate was Richard M. Johnson – widely credited with actually killing Tecumseh, and known to be the driving force behind the popular and effective Choctaw Academy school, founded in 1825. Andrew Jackson, in some ways Harrison's opposite number in the South, rode a military background built in large part on Indian affairs into the presidency. Yet a focus on the military events of the early nineteenth century obscures what men like Harrison did far more often and with far quieter effectiveness: they managed the orderly acquisition of lands and territories in the West. The process was difficult: slow, incremental years of building relationships, trading, negotiating, pressuring, cajoling, and cheating. Affairs were dominated by complicated and laborious preparations for treaty negotiations, including supplying thousands of participants with goods and provisions; by constantly surveying and marking boundaries; and by efforts to dampen conflict and ward off explosive violence. Much of Harrison's career is that of a diplomat and administrator, the longtime governor of the Indiana Territory. Hundreds of other public officials worked diligently to avoid the costs and risks of war. In assessing "Mad" Anthony Wayne's contribution to the conquest of the Old Northwest, for example, the historian Robert Owens ranks Wayne's skill and service negotiating the Treaty of Greenville in 1795 above Wayne's historic military victory in 1794.[1]

This is not to suggest that westward expansion in the early nineteenth century was uniformly peaceful, legal, and orderly. It wasn't. But behind the battles like Fallen Timbers and Tippecanoe lay a constant march of treaties based on careful negotiation and diplomacy; decades of land cessions nudged along by sporadic violence, piecemeal encroachment, and manufactured debt crises in Indian communities; and efforts to reeducate, "civilize," and cleanse native communities of their traditions, religions, and relationships. As in much of human history, major battles reveal occasional failures of the mundane, civilian administration that tries to keep the world just this side of upheaval. Looking eagerly west, the United States entrusted its dreams of expansion to public administration: the treaty system, land and trade regulations, civilization initiatives, and the factory system. Civilian administrators would carry the nation westward, supported but rarely outrun by a rising military and its aggressive frontier advocates. The goal of their endeavors would be the pacification and dispossession of American Indians, and their efforts would be successful.

Managed Expansion and the Presidency

The executive branch stood at the forefront of establishing federal authority and administrative control over expansion. Washington and later presidents led the administration of treaty policy, the factory system, and trade and intercourse regulations. These initiatives, often originating with the president and his top advisors, gradually quieted relations on U.S. borders and also relations between the federal and state levels. The contention and volatility among these forces during the 1790s, politically and militarily, gave way to an organized and ordered relationship pursuing peaceful and managed expansion after the turn of the century.

Presidents in the early republic were keenly aware of the seriousness, volatility, and comprehensive relevance of Indian affairs in national policy. Presidential leadership, innovation in the executive branch, and persistent pressure on Congress drove policy initiatives in Indian affairs. Congress responded by enacting presidential requests, by delegating broad responsibility for administration to the president and the executive branch, and by sanctioning practical developments in policy and administration. Congress granted the president virtually unlimited discretion to appoint personnel, to

[1] Robert M. Owens, "Jeffersonian Benevolence on the Ground: The Indian Land Cession Treaties of William Henry Harrison," *Journal of the Early Republic* 22 (Fall 2002), 408; see also Andrew R. L. Cayton, "'Separate Interests' and the Nation-State: The Washington Administration and the Origins of Regionalism in the Trans-Appalachian West," *The Journal of American History* 79 (June 1992), 54.

issue trading licenses and regulations governing their issue and forfeiture, to make exceptions licensing foreign traders and allowing them to continue in the fur trade, to issue regulations concerning administration of the Indian Office, to establish criminal justice procedures and guidelines through treaty and other mechanisms, to remove squatters from unceded Indian lands, to establish the method and means of acquiring and distributing goods for presents and annuities, to decide how to distribute annuities, to make important decisions about the character and disposition of various public lands, to employ teachers and send them among the Indians in pursuit of "civilizing" the Indians, and to design and implement guidelines for record-keeping and other administrative functions. Congress sanctioned, explicitly and tacitly, extension of such discretionary authority down through the executive branch.[2] Congress seems to have played a minimal role in oversight, evidenced by its difficulties investigating the factory system, the broad discretion granted to the executive branch in treaty making, its frequent ignorance of administrative developments in the executive branch, and the requests of its members for information and leadership.[3]

Presidents and Treaties

The president and the executive branch quickly became the center of leadership and authority in the nation's expansion policy. Nowhere is this more evident than in the treaty system. By the dictates of the Constitution, treaties involve both the executive and legislative branches of the federal government. Congress' early delegation of much of the authority for administration, and the executive's assumption of power for negotiating agreements and submitting them for a vote by Congress, represented a central component of the early executive's vast authority and Congress' willingness to allow the executive a crucial role in the affairs of the early nation's life.[4] By the end of the era, Congress was not only routinely granting the president authority to conduct important negotiations and to make key decisions about appointments, expenditures, boundaries, administration, and political relations, but it was also generally assenting to the decisions made by

2 Corwin defines "discretionary" authority generally: "duties, or powers . . . are 'discretionary,' in that the officer to whom they are entrusted is left a greater or less latitude of judgment respecting the occasion for their exercise, or the manner of it, or both." Edward S. Corwin, "The President as Administrative Chief," *The Journal of Politics* 1 (February 1939), 41. See also the discussions of discretionary authority throughout Daniel P. Carpenter, *The Forging of Bureaucratic Autonomy: Reputations, Networks, and Policy Innovation in Executive Agencies, 1862–1928* (Princeton: Princeton University Press, 2001).

3 See Jerry L. Mashaw, "Recovering American Administrative Law: Federalist Foundations, 1787–1801," *The Yale Law Journal* 115 (April 2006), 1268 and generally.

4 Leonard D. White, *The Federalists: A Study in Administrative History* (New York: Macmillan, 1948), 59; Thomas D. Clark and John D. W. Guice, *The Old Southwest, 1795–1830: Frontiers in Conflict* (Norman: University of Oklahoma Press, 1996 [1989]), 25; John J. Pitney, Jr., "The Coming Ascent of Congress," *Policy Review* 100 (April/May 2000).

executive branch officials. Washington, at first willing to request advice from the Senate instead of simply submitting treaties for consent, quickly became dissatisfied with the atmosphere in the Senate and with the Senate's desire to examine documentation from the makings of the treaties at their leisure. From this point forward Washington kept the Senate informed about negotiations but never again visited.[5]

It is no surprise, when reassessing the importance of Indian affairs and the frontier, that the familiar textbook tale of Washington going to the Senate – and leaving, vowing never to return for the "advice" part of advice and consent – involved an Indian treaty. Washington established the precedent for effective executive branch control of treaty relations with Indian nations, with congressional oversight usually a step removed and usually operating after the fact or at the behest of executive branch officials. The executive branch initiated, administered, negotiated, signed, and implemented treaties, with Congress approving or rejecting only after the bulk of the work and the negotiating had been accomplished. In the early era, Congress ratified most of the agreements; those rejected were usually re-negotiated with minor adjustments.[6]

Presidents and Regulation

Executive power in regulating licensing and alcohol was likewise forceful and leading. The executive branch designed, advocated, and administered policies in these areas, and enjoyed broad powers delegated by Congress. The president could permit licenses if he thought the public interest demanded it, for example; the president was authorized to use military force to seize goods and arrest violators; goods and peltries found with traders in violation of the laws were subject to seizure by executive branch field agents. Passports were required for foreigners who wished to pass through Indian territory. These measures were designed largely to limit the influence of British traders among the Indians and to hurt British trading interests, but they succeeded in establishing important precedents for the executive's implementation of the laws.

President Washington lobbied Congress for stringent measures in his annual messages. Washington pleaded for more help from Congress, for example, and he received a new intercourse law in 1796 that established boundary lines in the Northwest. President Jefferson continued the policies of the Washington and Adams administrations, and he requested and

[5] Francis Paul Prucha, *American Indian Treaties: The History of a Political Anomaly* (Berkeley: University of California Press, 1997), 70–9; see also 8–9, 94, 100, 135, and ch. 4.

[6] Failure to ratify a treaty did not necessarily mean that it did not go into practical effect: Congress, for example, did not ratify an 1820 treaty with the Omahas, yet the executive branch delivered promised goods to the Indians anyway and both sides respected the land cession boundaries involved. Judith A. Boughter, *Betraying the Omaha Nation, 1790–1916* (Norman: University of Oklahoma Press, 1998), 30–1.

received innovations in restrictions on the alcohol trade.[7] The 1802 Trade and Intercourse Act, which remained largely unchanged until 1834, delegated more powers and maintained the requirements of bonds and the practice of forfeiting goods for violations of trading regulations. In 1816, all but American citizens were forbidden by law from obtaining licenses to trade with Indians within U.S. boundaries. An 1822 law gave the executive even more authority, authorizing searches of traders' goods by Indian agents, military personnel, and superintendents to look for alcohol; if found, the goods were subject to seizure and bonds and licenses subject to forfeiture. While these regulations were not completely effective, they demonstrate willingness on the part of Congress to enact initiatives pressed by the president, and to provide for enforcement by granting broad powers to the president and his personnel.[8]

The executive was also instrumental in the federal government's involvement in criminal justice matters in Indian country. A 1793 Act expanded presidential authority regarding crimes committed by whites against Indians. At President Washington's urging, the 1796 Act included even more provisions for punishing crimes in Indian country. Over the years of the factory system, the executive aided in the control of horse stealing, fielding petitions from individuals and encouraging Congress to include, in early intercourse laws, rules for licensing horse purchases in Indian country and for providing funds for those who had stock stolen.[9] Echoing the opinion of leading scholars of the era's Indian affairs, Francis Paul Prucha writes, "Congress . . . in large part followed the recommendations and reports of the presidents, the secretaries of war, and other executive officials, in the directives and regulations issued by the War Department and in the decisions of the courts."[10]

[7] William E. Unruh, *White Man's Wicked Water: The Alcohol Trade and Prohibition in Indian Country, 1802–1892* (Lawrence: University Press of Kansas, 1996), 17; Peter C. Mancall, "Men, Women, and Alcohol in Indian Villages in the Great Lakes Region in the Early Republic," *Journal of the Early Republic* 15 (Autumn 1995), 427.

[8] On licensing in the factory system era, see also Andrew C. Isenberg, "The Market Revolution in the Borderlands: George Champlin Sibley in Missouri and New Mexico, 1808–1826," *Journal of the Early Republic* 21 (Fall 2001), 452. On delegation of authority to regulate Indian trade, ceded to the president, see Mashaw, "Recovering," 1299–1300. Importantly, these efforts at the federal level predate many of Novak's examples of state regulation in the same areas. See William J. Novak, *The People's Welfare: Law & Regulation in Nineteenth-Century America* (Chapel Hill: The University of North Carolina Press, 1996), 90–105.

[9] Francis Paul Prucha, *The Great Father: The United States Government and the American Indians* (Lincoln: University of Nebraska Press, 1984), 91, 106–7. The federal administrative system established to handle depredation claims by Indians and by whites is thoroughly examined in Larry C. Skogen, *Indian Depredation Claims, 1796–1920* (Norman: University of Oklahoma Press, 1996).

[10] Francis Paul Prucha, *American Indian Policy in the Formative Years: The Indian Trade and Intercourse Acts, 1790–1834* (Lincoln: University of Nebraska Press, 1962), 3; see also Reginald Horsman, *The Frontier in the Formative Years, 1783–1815* (Albuquerque: University of New Mexico Press, 1975); Curtis E. Jackson and Marcia J. Galli, *A History*

The factory system itself was a presidential policy initiative. President Washington laid out the idea for regulating trade through the factory system in his Fifth Annual Address, in 1793:

> Next to a rigorous execution of justice on the violators of peace, the establishment of commerce with the Indian nations, on behalf of the United States, is most likely to conciliate their attachment. But it ought to be conducted without fraud, without extortion, with constant and plentiful supplies, with a ready market for the commodities of the Indians, and a stated price for what they give in payment and receive in exchange. Individuals will not pursue such traffic unless they be allured by the hope of profit; but it will be enough for the United States to be reimbursed only.[11]

Congress failed to act in 1793, and Washington reiterated the idea in his address of 1794: "But I cannot refrain from again pressing upon your deliberations the plan which I recommended at the last session for the improvement of harmony with all the Indians within our limits by the fixing and conducting of trading houses upon the principles then expressed."[12]

Congress appeared doubtful at first. Officials in the House discussed the propriety of the factory system at length, in a debate touching on the relationship of the national government to the states, the relationship of economic issues to international policy and defense, and, of course, the expected cost of a federal trading house network. Opposition focused on the proper scope and nature of government activity. Zepaniah Swift of Connecticut, for example, argued that trade was "always managed better by individuals. Great loss and dilapidation are the consequences [of government involvement]; nor is it possible to guard against frauds and abuses."[13] Debate also addressed the national government's practical ability to manage and control trade, especially given the specters of waste, fraud, and abuse.[14] Agents of the Indian affairs field service helped convince the reluctant Congress to support the program. Letters from Indian agents in the field urged the creation of trading houses to limit the influence of foreign nations. After

of the Bureau of Indian Affairs and Its Activities Among Indians (San Francisco: R&E Research Associates, 1977), ch. 2; Mashaw, "Recovering," 1297–8; U.S. House of Representatives, Committee on House Administration, "The Power of the Purse," *Journal of Public Budgeting, Accounting & Financial Management* 9 (Fall 1997), 371ff.

11 Quoted in Aloysius Frederick Plaisance, "The United States Government Factory System, 1796–1822," unpublished Ph. D. Dissertation, St. Louis University (1954), 6. See also Edgar B. Wesley, "The Government Factory System Among the Indians, 1795–1822," *Journal of Economic and Business History* 4 (1932), 490–2; M. M. Quaife, "An Experiment of the Fathers in State Socialism," *Wisconsin Magazine of History* 3 (January 1920), 281; R. S. Cotterill, "Federal Indian Management in the South, 1789–1825," *The Mississippi Valley Historical Review* 20 (December 1933), 338.

12 Quoted in Plaisance, "Factory System," 7.

13 Quoted in Plaisance, "Factory System," 14.

14 See, e.g., Plaisance, "Factory System," 14–15; Katherine Coman, "Government Factories: An Attempt to Control Competition in the Fur Trade," *The American Economic Review* 2 (March, 1912); Ora Brooks Peake, *A History of the United States Indian Factory System, 1795–1822* (Denver: Sage, 1954), ch. 11; Quaife, "Experiment."

they were read before the House, members authorized $50,000 for the purchase of goods to supply the Indians within the limits of the United States. Congress made it clear who had responsibility for the program: "the sale of such goods [shall] be made under the direction of the President of the United States."[15] Congress appropriated $50,000 in 1795 for the building of government trading houses, and it formally authorized the plan in 1796.

Congress did not act to oversee the system in any kind of careful or thorough manner. For the rest of the 1790s, Congress seemed little interested in administrative details and practical management; no action was taken to renew the system's one-year initial authorization when the original Act expired. A congressional committee reviewed the factory system in 1800, but failed to draw a conclusion about the system's progress because of a lack of information.[16] Acknowledging broad presidential authority, Secretary of War James McHenry noted in 1800 that the act creating the factory system had expired, but McHenry stated that "It will of course rest with the President to continue the Factories, or Trading houses for trading with the Indians, or otherwise, as to him shall seem proper... "[17] The factories continued without formal authorization until the system was reauthorized at Jefferson's insistence.[18] Appropriations were used by the executive not for their particular purposes but for advances in policy. For example, leftover funds from the initial 1796 appropriation were used to establish four new factories in 1802.[19] In 1816, Lewis Cass recommended few changes to the system and noted that the existing laws "are fully sufficient. The executive authority is fully competent to make every alteration, which in my judgement is necessary to be made, with the exception of the annual appropriations."[20]

The president and executive branch field agents, having lobbied for the factory system and convinced Congress to create it, immediately enjoyed broad discretion over how to administer the system and evaluate its

[15] Quoted in Plaisance, "Factory System," 9. See his discussion at 8ff. for details on the field service's involvement in the congressional debates.

[16] Plaisance, "Factory System," 20ff. Claiborne, in the House, ultimately submitted a report on the Indian trade based on responses to his questions from Secretary of War James McHenry. Jared W. Bradley, "William C. C. Claiborne, the Old Southwest and the Development of American Indian Policy," *Tennessee Historical Quarterly* 33 (Fall 1974), 272. For oversight problems generally, see also Committee on House Administration, "Power of the Purse," 371ff. For more on Congress and its role in finance powers, see Max M. Edling, *A Revolution on Favor of Government: Origins of the U.S. Constitution and the Making of the American State* (Oxford: Oxford University Press, 2003), especially Part Three.

[17] McHenry to Wright, May 22, 1800, *Creek Factory, Correspondence 1795–1814*, Subgroup 42, Record Group 75, National Archives (hereafter *Creek Factory, Correspondence*).

[18] Bradley, "Claiborne," 276.

[19] Quaife, "Experiment," 281.

[20] Cass to Crawford, November 29, 1816, *Department of War, Letters Received, 1800–1823*, Subgroup 1, Record Group 75, National Archives (hereafter *War Department, Letters Received*).

activities. Public administration at the national level – administration of federal regulations and social policies, centered in Indian affairs at the heart of the new nation's economy, security, and survival – would rely on a network of federal officials exercising a delicate balance of administrative control and broad discretionary authority.

Administrative Structure and Organization

In coordinating the varied pieces of U.S. expansion policy – including the treaty system, trade regulation, civilization initiatives, and the factory system – the War Department occupied a central place. Until the creation of the Interior Department in 1849, officials of the War Department possessed primary authority for designing and administering the use of civil policies and the application of military force. Administration of Indian affairs within the Department was never haphazard – uncertain at times, confused at times, but never haphazard.

A three-level structure characterized the Indian service from its earliest days, a holdover from European practice. As territorial governor and ex officio superintendent of Indian affairs, Harrison occupied the middle tier, serving as a federal agent carrying out national policy even as he worked to extend politics, party, and security on behalf of regional populations. Harrison answered to the capital, but he also acted independently. The field agents got caught in the crossfire, never quite sure if their loyalty attached to Washington and the national government or to the complicated regional politics of their immediate supervisor, and often times patron, the territorial governor. Like many agencies, the early Indian Office suffered continual efforts to adapt and improve the details of administration as circumstances, personnel, and ideas evolved. Efforts to encourage greater efficiency and effectiveness by refining rules and clarifying lines of authority characterized Indian affairs administration throughout the era. But so did ad hoc decisionmaking, based on discretionary authority granted to governors and field agents who were tasked with using their best judgment to pursue general policies in unique and rapidly changing circumstances.

Delegating Within the Executive

The president and the War Department embarked on the factory system with broad discretionary authority over the organization of the factory system and the procedures for its administration.[21] The Act that established the trading houses in 1796 gave the president authority to establish factories at such

[21] War Department heads were responsible directly to the president, which was not true at Treasury. Corwin, "President as Administrative Chief," 34; Committee on House Administration, "Power of the Purse," 370; Mashaw, "Recovering." Mashaw lays heavy emphasis on the Treasury Department, because it is constructed and placed carefully in balance with

points which in his judgment would be "most convenient for the purpose of carrying on a liberal trade with the several Indian nations, within the limits of the United States." The Act also empowered the president to appoint an agent for each house who would serve "according to the rules and order which the President shall prescribe." The Act restricted the factors from engaging in the trade in their own interest, and it appropriated funds for the factories and for personnel to be spent largely at the president's discretion in furtherance of the system's ends.[22] President Washington quickly set about delegating authority for the details of administration.

Washington delegated authority for the trading house system to the War Department, and Secretary of War Timothy Pickering decided for strategic reasons to build the first factories in the Southern region. Pickering made decisions concerning the division of congressional funds among the factories, as well as the purposes for which those funds would be used. Because the factories had diplomatic and international goals as well as economic, military, and social goals, such decisions pursued multiple and diverse ends. Pickering coordinated factory placement with the federal military presence, the influence of other nations and the relative power of different tribes, and also the need to effect a presence in areas crucial to national expansion. Pickering chose the general locations for the new factories, but he left the exact placement and other specific decisions to local field agents. Congress left many of the details of administration to the War Department: Pickering's successor, James McHenry, was one of a long line of secretaries who "found it necessary to formulate his own regulations to supplement those made by Congress."[23]

The system was never static; reorganizations and efforts to clarify and improve administration and lines of authority were common. Factor Thomas Linnard, for example, sent intelligence reports to the Trade Superintendent

oversight institutions. The independence and autonomy of the War Department, and of the Indian Office, are addressed only briefly in Mashaw's article, at 1284–5 and 1299–1301.

[22] *U.S. Statutes at Large*, 1:452–3, reprinted in Francis Paul Prucha, ed., *Documents of United States Indian Policy*, 2nd ed. (Lincoln: University of Nebraska Press, 1990), 16–17.

[23] Plaisance, "Factory System," 34. The General Land Office also sported a three-level structure, and numerous organizations relied on administrative discretion to create and implement policy. See Malcolm J. Rohrbough, *The Land Office Business: The Settlement and Administration of American Public Lands, 1789–1837* (New York: Oxford University Press, 1968), ch. 4, 74, 51ff.; Andro Linklater, *Measuring America: How an Untamed Wilderness Shaped the United States and Fulfilled the Promise of Democracy* (New York: Plume, 2003); Peter S. Onuf, *Statehood and Union: A History of the Northwest Ordinance* (Bloomington: Indiana University Press, 1987), 22–4, 41–2; Emanuel Raymond Lewis, *Seacoast Fortifications of the United States: An Introductory History* (Annapolis: Naval Institute Press, 1979), 21; Rita W. Cooley, "The Office of the United States Marshal," *The Western Political Quarterly* 12 (March 1959), 124ff.; Frederick S. Calhoun, *The Lawmen: United States Marshals and Their Deputies, 1789–1989* (New York: Penguin, 1991); and the essays in Vernon Carstensen, ed., *The Public Lands: Studies in the History of the Public Domain* (Madison: University of Wisconsin Press, 1968).

as well as to the Secretary of War. He continued to send reports to both offices even after Trade Superintendent John Mason, in an effort to clarify the lines of authority, had directed that intelligence reports be sent to the War Department and not to him.[24] A succession of Secretaries of War tried to distinguish clear lines between the civilian service and the military, even though both arms operated out of the War Department. McHenry, for example, requested that the Treasury Department keep separate accounts for the civilian factory system.[25] In 1801, Secretary of War Henry Dearborn outlined his own division of responsibilities within the War Department.[26] Dearborn would set policy, and he issued detailed directions for procedures such as the construction of factory buildings. His subordinate, William Irvine, handled the daily operations of the system.[27] Following Irvine's death, Dearborn initiated a reorganization in 1805. William Davy became Irvine's replacement as the Indian trade superintendent; his experience in the private sector was expected to help him in the post. Davy tried to separate military supply and the system for supplying the Indian trade, believing that this would help the factory system operate more efficiently. Despite these efforts, the close relationship between military and civilian operations in the field perpetuated confusion between the two wings of Indian affairs well after the Indian Office was moved to the new Interior Department forty-four years later.

The executive branch and Congress sometimes worked together to clarify, refine, and improve organizational arrangements in Indian affairs. Congress followed Davy's efforts with a new factory system act in 1806. The 1806 reorganization gave official birth to an expert section on Indian affairs in the War Department, called the Office of Indian Trade and led by a Superintendent.[28] More important, the creation of the Office of Indian Trade formally separated nonmilitary Indian affairs from military concerns,

[24] E.g., Linnard to Mason, February 16, 1811, Linnard to Marian, April 10, 1811, Linnard to Mason, February 1, 1813, Linnard to Mason, March 20, 1813: *Natchitoches-Sulphur Fork Factory, 1809–1821, Letters Sent*, Subgroup 61, Record Group 75, National Archives. See also Secretary of War to Johnston, September 24, 1803, *Department of War, Letters Sent, Secretary of War-Indian Affairs 1800–1824*, Subgroup 2, Record Group 75, National Archives (hereafter *War Department, Letters Sent*); Irvine to Wright, October 20, 1801, Clay to Halsted, April 15, 1802, Davy to Halsted, January 6, 1806, Mason to Halsted, November 28, 1810, *Creek Factory, Correspondence*.

[25] McHenry to Samuel Meredith, March 8, 1797, cited in Plaisance, "Factory System," 36.

[26] Dearborn to Irvine, May 11, 1801 cited in Plaisance, "Factory System," 46–7.

[27] Plaisance, "Factory System," 34ff.

[28] Prucha, *Great Father*, 121. Reorganizations in this era were common, and were undertaken both statutorily and internally at Treasury, at the War Department, in the Navy, inside the Army (after St. Clair's defeat is an early example; an 1818 reorganization was the basis for the Quartermaster's Department that served as backbone of the North's Civil War effort), and at the Office of the Superintendent of Indian Trade, later the Indian Office, later the Bureau of Indian Affairs informally, later codified under that heading. Cf. Peake, *History*, ch. 2; Wesley, "Government Factory System," 493ff.; Paul Stuart, *Nations Within a Nation: Historical Statistics of American Indians* (New York: Greenwood Press, 1987), 127; Mark R.

even though both continued to operate out of the War Department. The Superintendent of Indian Trade became the historical forerunner of the position of Commissioner of Indian Affairs. Officials within the executive branch spearheaded another internal reorganization in the 1820s, as the factory system wound down. In 1824, Secretary of War John Calhoun established the Bureau of Indian Affairs within the War Department and assigned Thomas McKenney to lead the office. McKenney later claimed to have written the organic statute for the Bureau that was eventually formally enacted by Congress.[29] Calhoun's belief at this time was that the end of the trading house system in 1822 would lead to more work in Indian affairs, not less, and to a commensurate need for more personnel and more regulation. Congress confirmed the position of Commissioner eight years later, but not without some surprise. Leonard White relates a tale that illustrates the discretion afforded the War Department, and the lack of oversight by Congress, in the early years. John Cocke, chairman of the Committee on Indian Affairs in the House, discovered Calhoun's "bureau" in 1826. Cocke wrote, "[Y]ou mention a Bureau where the affairs of the Government with the several Indian tribes appear to be transacted – they have searched in vain for the law establishing that office.... The Committee have directed me to inquire when, and by what law, the said Bureau is authorized."[30] Having delegated administration of Indian affairs to the executive branch, Congress would always have difficulty when it came to oversight.

Executive activity at the Office of Indian Trade looks very similar to the jobs done today by modern agency heads. John Mason held the Superintendent's post from 1807 to 1816, and Thomas McKenney held it from 1816 until the end of the factory system in 1822. Leadership by these two men provided stability and expertise at the top of the Indian service bureaucracy for much of the factory system era. Mason spent time reporting to the Secretary of War, making suggestions, answering questions, lobbying for staff and resources, and explaining delays and mistakes.[31] He served

Wilson, *The Business of Civil War: Military Mobilization and the State, 1861–1865* (Baltimore: The Johns Hopkins University Press, 2006), 37.

29 Thomas L. McKenney, *Memoirs, Official and Personal* (Lincoln: University of Nebraska Press, 1973 [1846]), 58. Given the significant role played by McKenney and other War Department and Indian Office leaders in writing legislation, the presumption of congressional direct dominance in nineteenth-century lawmaking is overstated. See, e.g., Michael Nelson, "A Short, Ironic History of American National Bureaucracy," *The Journal of Politics* 44 (August 1982), 754.

30 Quoted in Leonard D. White, *The Jeffersonians: A Study in Administrative History, 1801–1829* (New York: Free Press, 1951), 507.

31 On communications with superiors, see, e.g., Mason to Dearborn, January 18, 1808, March 30, 1808, January 10, 1809; Mason to Gallatin, September 30, 1808, November 24, 1810; Mason to Eustis, December 19, 1811, November 3, 1812; Mason to Armstrong, February 15, 1813: *Office of Indian Trade, Letters Sent, 1807–1830*, Subgroup 4, Record Group 75, National Archives (hereafter *Office of Indian Trade, Letters Sent*).

as a liaison with Congress, offering expertise, information, and a base of communications between the executive branch and key committees and members in Congress – even as he lobbied for resources, autonomy and turf, and tried to stay away from partisan fighting by protecting a reputation as a nonpartisan expert administrator and not a policymaker.[32] He worked with organized groups and private interests with a stake in Indian affairs like the Quakers, suppliers of blankets and other goods, and manufacturers of gunpowder, rifles, and ammunition.[33] Mason worked to promote domestic manufactures.[34] He tried to work out procedures for supply and purchasing, he negotiated on prices for goods, procured goods and oversaw procurement by others, he oversaw arrangements for shipping and transport, and he worked with his field agents to refine and improve the process where possible. Mason supervised the maintenance of the Office's records, which came in handy when field records were lost by accident and in the midst of confusion during the War of 1812, when some of the factories were destroyed. Mason also made demands on officials in the capital to protect and secure the Office's records during the threat of British invasion.[35] All the while Mason strove to be cognizant of the particular and personal struggles that affected the activities of his field agents. Mason worked in personnel selection, too, handling applications for jobs and submitting recommendations to the president for approval. He delegated hiring authority of lower

[32] On relations with Congress and committees, see, e.g., Mason to Dearborn, January 16, 1809; Mason to Newton, January 16, 1809; Mason to Anderson, April 12, 1810; Mason to Smith, February 21, 1811; Mason to Rhea, June 5, 1812; Mason to King, February 27, 1815: *Office of Indian Trade, Letters Sent.* See also Mason to Clay, February 9, 1816; Mason to King, February 23, 1816: *Vol. C, Roll 3, M16, Office of Indian Trade, Letters Sent, 1807–1830*, Subgroup 4, Record Group 75, National Archives (hereafter *Office of Indian Trade, Letters Sent, Roll 3, M16*); McKenney to Adams, June 11, 1816: *Vol. C, Roll 4, M16, Office of Indian Trade, Letters Sent, 1807–1830*, Subgroup 4, Record Group 75, National Archives (hereafter *Office of Indian Trade, Letters Sent, Roll 4, M16*). On advice, recommendations, negotiations, and requirements for goods, see, e.g., Mason to Dupont Nemours & Co., December 28, 1807, March 23, 1808; Mason to Jefferson, January 26, 1808; Mason to Varnum, April 9, 1812; Mason to Davy, April 16, 1815: *Office of Indian Trade, Letters Sent.*

[33] On Astor, see, e.g., Mason to Eustis, February 3, 1810; Mason to Diaz, December 10, 1810 and June 13, 1811; Mason to Astor, June 12, 1815: *Office of Indian Trade, Letters Sent.* See also McKenney to Astor, April 29, 1816, *Office of Indian Trade, Letters Sent, Roll 4, M16.*

[34] See, e.g., Mason to Southard, January 15, 1808, *Office of Indian Trade, Letters Sent.*

[35] On recordkeeping, shipping, standardization, exchange of information and developments, and other communications with the field service, see, e.g., Mason to Johnson, January 19, 1808; Mason Circular to Linnard, Hogg, Gaines, and Treat, March 18, 1808; Mason to Johnston and Sibley, May 20, 1808; Mason to Irwin and Varnum, September 9, 1808; Mason Circular to Factors, July 20, 1810; Mason Circular to Factors, August 31, 1810; Mason Circular to Factors, April 16, 1811; Mason to Rawlings, March 15, 1814; Mason to Varnum, July 25, 1815: *Office of Indian Trade, Letters Sent.* See also Prucha, *Great Father*, 121, 164–5.

positions to officers in the field.[36] Organizing and clarifying internal administrative mechanisms received constant attention. Mason worked diligently to standardize and organize recordkeeping, salaries, instructions, duties, and lines of authority, and he tried to keep the field service informed about relevant political and legal developments at the capital and internationally.

The three-level administrative system in Indian affairs is a holdover from British practice, and despite years of adjustments the Indian Office's formal structure has always included a middle level with significant influence.[37] Diverse tasks and responsibilities have characterized Indian affairs for two centuries: diplomatic relations and politics between nations and communities; scientific and geographic tasks like negotiating and supervising the drawing of boundaries; mediation among private and public interests among both whites and Indians; and maintenance of goodwill. The varied responsibilities given to Indian department superintendents under the British imperial system included "protecting the Indians as well as they could from traders and speculators, negotiating the boundary lines that were called for after 1763, distributing presents given to the Indians in the attempt to gain and maintain their goodwill, and enlisting Indians in wartime to fight on the British side. The superintendents, too, exercised what control they could over the fur trade, although management of the trade remained to a great extent in colonial hands."[38]

Regional superintendents' duties were carried over to the new American superintendents created under the 1786 Ordinance. Careful instructions governed the actions of the superintendents, with Henry Knox understanding that activities would be controlled by a combination of formal guidelines and restrictions with a healthy amount of personal discretion and personal ability.[39] The system encouraged active involvement by regional supervisors.

[36] Chester L. Guthrie and Leo L. Gerald, "Upper Missouri Agency: An Account of Indian Administration on the Frontier," *The Pacific Historical Review* 10 (March 1941), 49; Cotterill, "Federal Indian Management," 336; Peake, *History*, ch. 3, 237; a few examples are in Benjamin Hawkins, *A Sketch of the Creek Country, in the Years 1798 and 1799 [1848] and Letters of Benjamin Hawkins, 1796–1806 [1916]* (Spartansburg, SC: Reprint Co., 1974), including Hawkins to Burges, February 1, 1797, 68; Hawkins to Barnard, March 7, 1797, 96; Hawkins to McHenry, February 23, 1798, 293. On personnel issues, see, e.g., Mason to Irwin, May 6, 1809; Mason to Gallatin, January 29, 1810; Mason to Madison, August 10, 1812, and August 27, 1812; Mason to Varnum, June 21, 1815; Mason to Madison, November 13, 1815: *Office of Indian Trade, Letters Sent.* See also Mason to Clay, February 9, 1816, *Office of Indian Trade, Letters Sent, Roll 3, M16*; McKenney to Walmer, April 15, 1816, McKenney to Macon, April 17, 1816, McKenney to King, April 18, 1816: *Office of Indian Trade, Letters Sent, Roll 4, M16.*

[37] Jackson and Galli, *History*, chapter 7; Viola, *Thomas L. McKenney*, ch. 6.

[38] Prucha, *Great Father*, 21.

[39] Walter H. Mohr, *Federal Indian Relations, 1774–1788* (New York: AMS Press, 1971), 106–7; see, e.g., Prucha, *American Indian Treaties*, 117ff. Instructions were also given to at least

Most often, territorial governors like Harrison served as ex officio Superintendents of Indian Affairs, linking federal authority with regional and local interests. After statehood, Indian superintendents served as the regional directors of Indian affairs administration. Regional supervisors controlled the intersection of federal and local powers and demands. Superintendents were forbidden from engaging in the Indian trade for personal gain, but they possessed the authority to grant trading licenses and enforce trade regulations. They were responsible for general diplomatic duties, and appointed agents for special diplomatic missions.

Throughout the era, territorial governors dealt with Indian affairs and often complained of the time and effort those affairs took – few of the territories ever escaped Indian affairs for very long. Lewis Cass, governor of Michigan and with a long career in federal affairs, complained in 1815:

> ... at Detroit my situation is at all times very unpleasant and sometimes very unsafe. Surrounded by drunken lawless Indians, doubtful friends and secret enemies, without any physical force at my disposal, and breaking in upon me at all hours of the day; their conduct and demands may easily be conceived. It is a literal fact, that I have been compelled, more than twenty times to hide myself, to avoid their importunities.[40]

Cass, of course, understood Indians' central role in the politics and economics of territorial Michigan. He negotiated the important Treaty of Saginaw (1819) and the Treaty of Chicago (1833), and oversaw the Treaty of Washington (1836) after his successes in Michigan had led him to the post of Secretary of War.[41] As governor, Cass encouraged trade and the local economy by allowing the American Fur Company to import up to eight thousand gallons of liquor to Mackinac Island to smooth the fur trade and help John Astor compete with British traders.[42] Cass reported that thirteen people worked in his Indian Department in Michigan, responsible for roughly nine thousand Indians in the immediate vicinity of the Detroit agency, and excepting "the immense number of individuals" who annually visited the city. Cass also pointed out the importance of the island of Michilimackinac, which one day hosted more than eighteen hundred Indians, by Cass's estimate.[43] Such vast and important duties helped make Indian superintendents powerful

some Indian agents: Clark and Guice, *Old Southwest*, 43; and to officials at specific treaties: Clark and Guice, *Old Southwest*, 147ff. The War Department also spelled out the duties of personnel at the Corps of Engineers in instructions that are very similar to those sent to Indian Office personnel, especially in their delineation of discretionary authority within clearly described, overarching guidelines. William H. Goetzmann, *Army Exploration in the American West, 1803–1863* (Lincoln: University of Nebraska Press, 1959), 7ff.

40 Quoted in White, *Jeffersonians*, 508.

41 Charles E. Cleland, *Rites of Conquest: The History and Culture of Michigan's Native Americans* (Ann Arbor: University of Michigan Press, 1992), 212ff.

42 Ibid., 178–9.

43 Cass to Crawford, September 27, 1816, November 29, 1816, *War Department, Letters Received.*

figures on the frontier. The historian James P. Ronda calls William Clark, territorial governor of Missouri from 1813 to 1820, "the single most important American officer in the West," responsible (by Clark's own account in 1815) for making policy for sixty-four thousand native people in twenty-two tribes and bands – with another one hundred thousand Indians on the outskirts of his domain. Clark supervised six agents, three subagents, and six interpreters.[44]

Below the superintendents were Indian agents and factors charged with the hands-on duties of Indian administration in the field. Early on, "agents" had responsibilities for wide areas and extensive diplomatic duties. "Factors" remained tied to particular fixed posts and were responsible primarily for administration of the trading houses, and less so for diplomacy and formal negotiations. As the factory system took root, factors became increasingly involved with a host of tasks related and unrelated to the trade. Later, at the same time as the trading houses were declining, local agencies in the East and on reservations became more fixed and the term "agent" came to refer to local officials responsible for circumscribed areas or for affairs with particular tribes or reservations.

Indian agents' duties were broad and generalized. Commissioner T. Hartley Crawford described the local agent's duties this way: "He is the Representative of the Government to attend to the complaints of the Indians[,] supply their wants, redress their grievances[,] soften their ruggedness, change their habits and ameliorate their condition."[45] The historian Ronald Satz elaborates: "Agents had responsibilities to both the Indians and whites. They were to punish unruly Indians, settle disputes between tribes or between whites and Indians, oversee the expenditure of funds for improving the education, and general conditions of the Indians, disburse annuities and gifts, license Indian traders, and settle their claims."[46] Benjamin Hawkins, twenty years agent to the southern Indians, left a thorough record of his various duties and the role they played in the pacification of the South. Hawkins wrote of

[44] James P. Ronda, "Red-Head's Domain: William Clark's Indian Brokerage," in *Between Indian and White Worlds: The Cultural Broker*, ed. Margaret Connell Szasz (Norman: University of Oklahoma Press, 1994), 82–3.

[45] Quoted in Ronald N. Satz, *American Indian Policy in the Jacksonian Era* (Lincoln: University of Nebraska Press, 1975), 182.

[46] Satz, *American Indian Policy*, 182. Hawkins even drew up rules for making written claims for lost property or property allegedly stolen by Indians: see Hawkins, *Sketch*, 341. The established bureaucratic authority, agents, and procedures involved in claims involving Indian affairs adds a stable and consistent element to the analysis presented by Landis, which focuses primarily on the case-by-case approach Congress used to address claims. See Skogen, *Indian Depredation Claims*; Michele L. Landis, "'Let Me Next Time Be "Tried by Fire"': Disaster Relief and the Origins of the American Welfare State 1789–1874," *Northwestern University Law Review* 92 (Spring 1998), esp. 981ff.

the press of responsibilities in terms remarkably similar to those expressed by Lewis Cass above: "I am surrounded with difficulties.... I have some white women and children who have been robed and striped of their clothing now depending on me for aid, and I meet some Spanish interposition.... I am surrounded with one hundred Indians daily; all of them with complaints, and my health is fast declining..."[47]

Lists of the agents' tasks hint at the divided loyalty that complicated their activities. Their diverse tasks set agents (and factors) between tribes, individual Indians, and whites, without a clear sense of priorities or loyalty. Agents could not be neutral, as they were charged with "improving" the condition of Indians and not simply overseeing actions taken by others. Yet they were also responsible to whites, controlling Indian populations and securing payment for infractions. Agents licensed traders, and thus they had to make decisions about individuals' character and suitability, and they were responsible for bonds and other negotiations and agreements. The agents, subagents, and factors were the center of federal power in the field, but from the earliest days their jobs were complicated by having to balance their activities delicately between conflicting obligations and divided loyalties.[48]

[47] Quoted in Florette Henri, *The Southern Indians and Benjamin Hawkins, 1796–1816* (Norman: University of Oklahoma Press, 1986), 125.

[48] See, e.g., Henri, *Southern Indians*, 126ff.; Michael D. Green, *The Politics of Indian Removal: Creek Government and Society in Crisis* (Lincoln: University of Nebraska Press, 1985), 51. An 1822 statement of expenditures lists some of the Indian Department's tasks, referred to as "contingent expenses, as buildings and repairs, tools, and general expenses of smithshops, expresses, transportation, laborers, removal of Indian emigrants, repairing agricultural implements, and expenses incident to executing the intercourse per act of March, 1802." "Statement of the Expenditures of the Indian Department," January 15, 1822, in *American State Papers – Indian Affairs* (Washington, DC: Gales and Seaton, 1834) (hereafter *ASPIA*), vol II: 268. An 1826 report enhanced the list further, listing as contingent expenses "pay of blacksmiths and strikers, and interpreters; hire of expresses; expense of coal, iron, and steel for the blacksmith shops; of rations issued to Indians under the act of 13th May, 1800; of rations at the distribution of annuities; of transportation of annuities; of medical attendance, &c. on sick and distressed Indians; of visits of deputations of Indians to the seat of Government, under the act of 13th May, 1800, before referred to; of prosecuting murderers and others violating the laws regulating intercourse with Indian tribes; of building and repairing agency houses; of tools and implements of husbandry and manufacture for Indians; payments of claims of citizens and Indians adjusted at the Department of War, when the amount cannot be recovered agreeably to the intercourse law, or there is no annuity to pay it from, and for which, in such cases, the Government is liable, &c. &c. &c." "Statement showing the amount of disbursements in the Indian Department for the years 1824 and 1825," April 20, 1826, in *ASPIA*, II: 669. On field service tasks, see also George D. Harmon, "Benjamin Hawkins and the Federal Factory System," *The North Carolina Historical Review* 9 (January–October, 1932), 144; Joyce Purser, "The Administration of Indian Affairs in Louisiana, 1803–1820," *Louisiana History* 5 (Fall 1964), 401–2; Guthrie and Gerald, "Upper Missouri Agency," 47 (quoting Benjamin O'Fallon); George S.

Fifteen agents and ten subagents were on the payroll by 1818; seventeen agents, twenty-five subagents, thirty-four interpreters, and twenty-one blacksmiths were on the roll in 1822.[49] Figures like these generally omit ad hoc local appointments and other assistants, as agents and factors frequently hired people for tasks that came up in the course of business. Leonard White recognized the "great" volume of activity in the field and its daily press even upon figures at the headquarters level, and he reported the total payroll as over $67,000.[50] Positions in the Indian service were desirable, with good pay and "good opportunities for influence and advancement."[51]

The people in the Indian service were not amateurs. Personnel at all levels reflected the fact that Indian affairs was a specialized policy field demanding skilled personnel, and the realization that Indian affairs was a high-profile and politically significant field involving national security and economic and political development.

Early trade superintendents at the capital, like later commissioners, combined expertise and political connections. John Mason, son of George Mason, was president of the Bank of Columbia in Washington when he took the job of trade superintendent. Mason's political and business acumen served him well as the factory system expanded, and he oversaw efforts to formalize recordkeeping and standardize activity in the field.[52] Thomas McKenney was a former Georgetown merchant with banking and management experience; he served in Maryland and Washington during the War of 1812. The thirty-one-year-old McKenney replaced Mason, apparently winning his appointment on the strength of a friend's recommendations and the fact that one of his store's customers was President Madison.[53] By the time he left the public service in the 1830s, McKenney had kept his post

Gaines, "Notes on the Early Days of South Alabama," reprinted in *The Alabama Historical Quarterly* 26 (Fall/Winter, 1964); Peake, *History*; Wesley, "Government Factory System," 496ff.; Wayne Morris, "Traders and Factories on the Arkansas Frontier, 1805–1822," *The Arkansas Historical Quarterly* 28 (Spring 1969), 31ff.

49 Prucha, *American Indian Policy*, 54–5; White, *Jeffersonians*, 508–9. The list of Indian Department employees reported in 1822 includes blacksmiths and interpreters as well as agents, subagents, and superintendents; a note at the end acknowledges that "Besides the interpreters and blacksmiths mentioned in the preceding statement, who may be considered as regularly employed, there are others, particularly interpreters, temporarily employed in the Indian Department, in cases of emergency, or at Indian treaties, where no regular interpreter is at hand." "Names and pay of all the persons employed in the Indian Department," April 12, 1822, in *ASPIA*, II: 364–71. The note is at the bottom of 366.

50 White, *Jeffersonians*, 508–9.

51 Wesley, "Government Factory System," 503; see also Quaife, "Experiment," 282.

52 See Prucha, *Great Father*, 121; Peake, *History*, 42–4, 120ff.; McKenney to Irwin, May 28, 1817, in Lyman Copeland Draper, ed., *Collections of the State Historical Society of Wisconsin*, Vol. VII (Madison: Wisconsin Historical Society, 1908 [1876]), 271ff.

53 Viola, *Thomas L. McKenney*, 4–5.

at the top of the Indian service through the political roller coaster of the 1820s, working for Madison, Monroe, John Quincy Adams, and Andrew Jackson, and becoming the nation's leading civilian expert on Indian affairs. The men appointed or elected as Secretaries of War and territorial governors also reflected the complicated policy and political issues in play in Indian affairs – men like Henry Knox, Henry Dearborn, Lewis Cass, and William Clark, who served as an Indian agent (1807–13), territorial governor of Missouri (1813–20), and superintendent of Indian affairs after Missouri gained statehood (1822–38). Harrison was Wayne's aide-de-camp at the landmark Treaty of Greenville in 1795, later registrar of the land office at Cincinnati, then Secretary of the Northwest Territory. He represented the Territory in Congress, and his abilities allowed him to pass safely from the Adams administration into the Jefferson administration.[54]

Selecting the personnel on the front lines of Indian affairs reflected a variety of goals, and also commonly included components of expertise and likely effectiveness along with political considerations. Here, and importantly, effectiveness and potential skill tended to outweigh political patronage when the dynamics of professionalism and patronage came into conflict. Territorial governors were often politically connected and trusted: Washington put many allies from the Revolution into positions of authority in the Old Northwest. Harrison survived into the Jefferson administration and proved a very effective force for Jefferson's policies, reflecting Jefferson's commitment to an effective administrator despite the change in party leadership. Further down the hierarchy, early Indian agents tended to be experienced in public affairs and knowledgeable about local conditions. Benjamin Hawkins of North Carolina had extensive congressional experience and served in the south from 1796 to 1816; Silas Dinsmoor of New Hampshire, a veteran of the navy, worked with the Cherokee and then the Choctaws from 1796 to 1813; Return J. Meigs, a military leader in the Revolution and later a legislator for the Northwest Territory, served as Cherokee agent from 1801 to 1823.[55]

Factors, responsible for a host of politically sensitive administrative duties, came from a variety of geographic areas and were chosen through a variety of selection methods. While the agency often selected employees

[54] Robert M. Owens, "Jeffersonian Benevolence on the Ground: The Indian Land Cession Treaties of William Henry Harrison," *Journal of the Early Republic* 22 (Fall 2002), 408 n7, 410.

[55] Green, *Politics of Indian Removal*, 50. See also Guthrie and Gerald, "Upper Missouri Agency," 48 n4; Draper, *Collections*, 269–70; Harmon, "Benjamin Hawkins," 138–9; Purser, "Administration," 402–9; James W. Silver, "Edmund Pendleton Gaines and Frontier Problems, 1801–1849," *The Journal of Southern History* 1 (August 1935). Cotterill finds that the Indian service before 1812 "had been conducted on a relatively high plane. The agents had been men of ability and integrity . . . " Cotterill, "Federal Indian Management," 346.

with an eye toward patronage and party politics, expertise and experience were also important criteria in selecting personnel for sensitive posts. Factors came primarily from the Northeast and Virginia, with a decided bias toward those areas out of which the Indian Office operated: at first Philadelphia, and, following the office's move to Georgetown, the District of Columbia. Virtually all of the early factors were Easterners with little knowledge of or experience with frontier life, the treatment of animal skins, or relations with Indians. With time, though, more attention was paid to matching applicants with the demands of the job. Increasingly, men who had prior business experience were appointed to be factors. This shift paralleled a gradual redefinition of the factory system as the era progressed – as the system effectively pacified the eastern regions, its diplomatic and social mission became increasingly forgotten in lieu of a focus on the economics of the Indian trade.[56]

From its earliest days, then, the structure of the Indian service reflected a number of important and persistent characteristics: a stable three-level hierarchy, ongoing efforts to clarify lines of authority and refine the duties and responsibilities of particular jobs, and an effort to satisfy the difficult requirements of a volatile and unique policy area with a direct impact on the early nation's economic and political development.

Administration of the Treaty and Factory Systems

Efforts to clarify lines of authority and regularize Indian Office operations in the capital have often been far less important to the operations of the service than have been the situational imperatives faced by operators in the field. The Indian affairs bureaucracy within the War Department evolved steadily in the nineteenth century's opening decades, with different regions and localities facing different problems and having different histories of U.S.–Indian relationships. These dynamics have driven real decision-making authority to the local level of the Indian service for more than two centuries. In the factory system era, the Indian Office leadership effectively communicated a clear mission and general guidelines for behavior in the field, and combined these with broad grants of discretionary authority. This allowed agents and factors to act in whatever manner they thought would best further the Office's goals. The result was an effective administrative endeavor, one which accomplished its goals, but one characterized by local, case-by-case decision making by field agents.[57]

56 Plaisance, "Factory System," 414ff.

57 See Michael Lipsky, *Street-Level Bureaucracy: Dilemmas of the Individual in Public Services* (New York: Russell Sage Foundation, 1983) and James Q. Wilson, *Bureaucracy: What Government Agencies Do and Why They Do It* (New York: Basic Books, 1989), for discussions of situational imperatives and the important role of operators in public administration.

Mission

The interaction of local circumstances, individual priorities, and discretionary authority invited inconsistency at the local level, as we will see in the next chapter. These centrifugal forces might have sent the entire system spinning out of control if not for the government's effectiveness at defining a clear mission and purpose for the factories and the treaty system.

The treaty system has characterized U.S.–Indian relations for more than two hundred years. The relative positions of the United States and Indian nations have evolved and shifted over time, meaning that early treaties and later ones are the products of vastly different political circumstances. The fundamental reliance on treaties, though, reflects core principles in U.S. understanding of American Indian nations.

The treaties and the treaty process accomplished a number of objectives important to the United States. Treaty negotiations provided a means of recognizing or building a sense of friendship; they provided a vehicle by which the United States could provide presents to Indians, honoring a long-standing tradition in Indian–colonial relations; they provided an opportunity for the United States to make a show of force. The treaty documents themselves established formal relations, set land boundaries, provided for roads and infrastructure development, and bound Indians to the United States exclusively in security and trade relationships. Treaties were important for Indians, too: they addressed issues of concern, such as white encroachments on Indian lands and exchange of accused criminals or stolen goods, they recognized Indian nations as political communities involved in high-level negotiations, and they provided a reference point for addressing later issues.[58] Before 1812, treaties filled many functions, chief among them recognition of power and political relationships, cession of lands, arrangement of boundaries, establishment of trade and criminal justice regulations, and commitment to civilization and social policy resources. Between 1812 and the removal era of the 1830s, the treaties continued to fulfill many of these roles, but they were often treaties of peace, reestablishing relations after the war, and providing a vehicle by which tribal land was increasingly exchanged for lands in the West. With the treaty system, the United States acknowledged its basic objectives: expansion, order, legalism based on written agreements, and (ideally) controlled expenditures. The nation's leaders hoped to manage expansion through the treaties and avoid the monetary and moral costs of naked conquest. U.S. reliance on treaties highlights the focus its leaders put on civilian negotiation, diplomacy, and public administration.[59]

58 See Prucha, *American Indian Treaties*, 1–19, 24–7, 122–3; Wesley, "Government Factory System," 490–2; Harmon, "Benjamin Hawkins," 145.

59 Owens, "Jeffersonian Benevolence," 410; Cynthia Cumfer, "Local Origins of National Indian Policy: Cherokee and Tennessean Ideas About Sovereignty and Nationhood, 1790–1811," *Journal of the Early Republic* 23 (Spring 2003), 31–2.

The factory system was an intimate relation of the treaty system. The factories aimed to pacify relations on the frontier by limiting potential conflict between settlers and Indians, and to provide an engine that would gently force Indians to cede ever more lands to the United States. The factories would also establish a stable civilian federal presence near Indian country that could oversee trade, enforce regulations, report on rapidly changing situations, and promote social policy initiatives like small farming. Jefferson offered a candid description of the philosophy behind the factory system in an 1803 letter to Harrison, then governor of Indiana Territory:

> When they [Indians] withdraw themselves to the culture of a small piece of land, they will perceive how useless to them are their extensive forests, and will be willing to pare them off from time to time in exchange for necessaries for their farms and families. To promote this disposition to exchange lands, which they have to spare and we want, for necessaries, which we have to spare and they want, we shall push our trading houses, and be glad to see the good and influential individuals among them run in debt, because we observe that when these debts get beyond what the individuals can pay, they become willing to lop them off by a cession of lands.
>
> At our trading houses, too, we mean to sell so low as merely to repay us cost and charges, so as neither to lessen nor enlarge our capital. This is what private traders cannot do, for they must gain; they will consequently retire from the competition, and we shall thus get clear of this pest without giving offence or umbrage to the Indians. In this way our settlements will gradually circumscribe and approach the Indians, and they will in time either incorporate with us as citizens of the United States, or remove beyond the Mississippi.[60]

By reducing the chances for independent traders to take advantage of Indians in trade relations, the factory system tried to lessen the chance that a trade dispute would erupt into a larger regional conflict. A pacified frontier and carefully managed relations held the promise of a peaceful and ordered process for obtaining lands from Indians, as Jefferson pointed out. The same process created opportunities to promote U.S. social goals such as farming, thrift, education, and other activities by which those Indians who did not move west could merge with the expanding white society. As late as 1816, Secretary of War William Crawford reiterated the factory system's focus on peace, not profit: "That inducement [for continuing the factory system], if it exists at all, must be found in the influence which it gives the Government over the Indian tribes within our limits, by administering to their wants, increasing their comforts, and promoting their happiness. The most obvious effect of that influence is the preservation of peace with them, and among themselves." Crawford acknowledged that private traders could certainly

[60] Thomas Jefferson to William Henry Harrison, February 27, 1803, reprinted in Prucha, *Documents*, 22–3. On Jefferson, removal ideas, and the debate among historians, see Owens, "Jeffersonian Benevolence," 406. On the factory system's peaceful goals, see Isenberg, "Market Revolution," 446–7, 450ff.; Owens, "Jeffersonian Benevolence," 405.

gain the Indians' land much more quickly than the government could, but warned that such a course would result in "continued warfare, attended by the extermination or expulsion of the aboriginal inhabitants of the country to more distant and less hospitable regions."[61]

Treaties and Administration

Treaty making required a host of administrative actions situated in the executive branch, under the president's authority. When George Washington decided never to return to the Senate for "advice and consent" regarding treaties, he cemented into place executive branch dominance in the complicated process of preparing for and negotiating treaties in the field.

Treaties often involved extensive activity in the capital itself: Indians often wanted to travel to the U.S. capital to make their claims and negotiate with federal officials. As time wore on, government officials tried to discourage such visits because of their expense and because they were time-consuming administrative hassles. Housing, feeding, and entertaining visiting Indians – and accounting for these expenses, all the while evaluating expenditures for waste and abuses – was a complicated, difficult, and uncertain business. A constant stream of lobbyists, delegations, contractors, suppliers, hoteliers, restaurateurs, and travel agents worked the important area of Indian affairs, sometimes responding to legitimate needs and at other times taking advantage of Indians, the federal government, or both.[62]

In the field, treaties were high profile events. Major Lawrence Taliaferro, who directed Indian affairs in the upper Mississippi region for twenty years, described an 1824 event at Prairie du Chien that had been in the works for more than a year. He described the arrival of 385 Sioux and Chippewa Indians:

> There was a halt before entering the town, at the "Painted Rock," where, after attending to their toilet and appointment of soldiers to dress the columns of boats, the grand entry was made with drums beating, many flags flying, with incessant

[61] Quoted in Prucha, *Great Father*, 127. On the factory system generally, see Peake, *History*; Wesley, "Government Factory System"; Harmon, "Benjamin Hawkins," 139–147; Willoughby M. Babcock Jr., "Major Lawrence Taliaferro, Indian Agent," *The Mississippi Valley Historical Review* 11 (December 1924), 361. George S. Gaines's memoirs provide a good first person account of the factory system's operations in Alabama. Gaines, "Notes." On efforts to regulate trade before the factory system, see Royal B. Way, "The United States Factory System for Trading with the Indians, 1796–1822," *Mississippi Valley Historical Review* 6 (1919), 220–4; Quaife, "Experiment," 278–9.

[62] Viola, *Thomas L. McKenney*, 130ff.; Herman J. Viola, *Diplomats in Buckskins: A History of Indian Delegations in Washington City* (Bluffton, SC: Rivilo Books, 1995). The Secretary of War, for example, asked agent Hawkins to discourage Indians from trying to visit the capital. The Indians, he wrote, "must be taught that the Agents are the immediate Representatives of the Government... " Secretary of War to Hawkins, November 26, 1800, *War Department, Letters Sent.*

discharges of small arms. All Prairie du Chien was drawn out, with other delegations already arrived, to witness the display and landing of this ferocious looking body of true savages.[63]

Practical administration supported the pomp and circumstance. Responsibilities associated with negotiating and signing treaties included managing diplomatic relations and politics between Indian nations and communities; pursuing scientific and geographic details like negotiating and supervising the surveying of lands and the drawing of boundaries; mediating among private and public interests among both whites and Indians; and maintaining the goodwill and trust of important players. The negotiating process depended heavily upon presents given to Indians, which had to be purchased, shipped, and distributed in the field. Presents included goods, but also symbolic items like flags and peace medals. Peace medals, like other goods, had to be crafted and minted by artisans working for the federal government, either directly or under contract; as with coins today, disputes broke out around the design and quality of the medals. Indians had their own tastes, too, and these tastes varied by person and by tribe – making even this small piece of treaty making fairly complicated.[64]

Because treaties were often made with large numbers of people and were planned for months in advance to compensate for the slow pace of communication and travel, provision of goods was an important and complex administrative task. Thousands of Indians attended some of the treaties, and they required thousands of pounds of meat, flour, and other foodstuffs – and, in many cases, considerable amounts of alcohol to help U.S. representatives grease the wheels of exchange. McKenney estimated in 1826 that a monthlong conference attended by 5,000 Indians on his tour of the Great Lakes required at least 225,000 pounds of beef, and a like amount of flour; supplies for a treaty near Green Bay in 1827 included 116 barrels of whiskey.[65]

Factors supplied many of the goods, and agents and factors tried to navigate payment via allocated funds and/or treaty provisions and annuities; factors often worked with regular contractors near the trading houses to obtain the provisions. Issues arose regarding cost savings: Jonathan Halsted, for example, the factor near Fort Wilkinson, touted his efforts to supply nearly one thousand Indians at the Creek treaty of 1802. Halsted provided goods at roughly one-fifth of the $10,000 cost of the same goods obtained through contractors.[66] Provisions often included items like wineglasses, tea

[63] Quoted in Roy W. Meyer, *History of the Santee Sioux: United States Indian Policy on Trial*, revised edition (Lincoln: University of Nebraska Press, 1993), 39.

[64] See Viola, *Diplomats in Buckskins*, chs. 5 and 6; Prucha, *Great Father*, 173–6; Isenberg, "Market Revolution," 457.

[65] Viola, *Thomas L. McKenney*, 136.

[66] Henri, *Southern Indians*, 173–4.

and coffeepots, paper, sealing wax, brandy, and cigars. Interestingly, supplying the government agents could cost much more than supplying the Indians: whereas the government spent about ten cents per day per Indian at the 1802 treaty, it spent about ten *dollars* per day for each treaty commissioner.[67]

Choosing treaty commissioners was a complicated task. Another indication of the importance of Indian affairs in these years, many of the era's leading figures served repeatedly as treaty commissioners, with agents, governors, and military leaders often doing double duty as treaty commissioners. As much as the federal government sought to control the treaty process in practice – and did control it legally – the reality of politics in the new republic demanded that some attention be paid to state and local interests as well as to private concerns. Treaty commissioners often doubled, working for a level of government as well as for a private company. The same was true of the survey teams that worked to mark off boundaries and lines. Commissioners usually operated under fairly detailed guidelines that recommended boundaries and suggested prices to be paid for certain parcels of land. Often, the commissioners received guidance about priorities and how hard they were to push for certain cessions. At the same time, the commissioners enjoyed broad discretion to make judgments as they saw fit.

Indian agents, the local experts on Indian affairs, were often closely connected with treaty negotiations. Agents' duties for treaties and in other areas developed as the intercourse acts and other measures aimed at regularizing and clarifying Indian affairs and trade regulation. Agents' duties became more specific with time, reporting requirements became more extensive, and they were tasked with assessing the condition of Indian populations, learning the natural history of the areas in which they worked, and evaluating Indian progress toward "civilization."[68]

Perhaps the most volatile element of treaty making from the federal government's standpoint was American responsibility for removing whites who encroached upon Indian lands before cession by Indians, or who willingly violated boundary lines established by treaty. The president possessed authority to remove white settlers who had unlawfully encroached on Indian lands which had not been ceded to the United States. Examples in which the U.S. Army removed white settlers, burned their homes and crops, and threatened other disciplinary action dot the years of the early republic. Federal troops removed intruders from Cherokee lands, for example, in 1797–98, 1803, 1804, 1805, 1808, 1809, and 1810. The 1797 effort saw twelve hundred troops remove white squatters from Cherokee lands, burning cabins and wrecking fences.[69] A letter from the War Department advised Indian

[67] Ibid., 174.
[68] Prucha, *American Indian Policy*, 54.
[69] Cumfer, "Local Origins," 31, 23, 40.

agent Benjamin Hawkins, in 1805, that "It is the express direction of the President, that any white settlers, who may intrude on the Indian lands, be removed by military force, without delay. You will please to carry this direction into effect, in all cases which may happen in your Agency."[70] In a later example, E. P. Gaines placed his federal troops in the middle of Georgia's conflict with the Creeks in 1825 to stop Governor Troup from surveying Creek lands before that was allowed by treaty stipulations.[71]

As much as authorities might have preferred to avoid this task, the necessities of the situation often demanded that the military act. Squatters and others threatened the main goals of U.S. policy, the peaceful and orderly transfer of Indian lands to the United States. Federal personnel forced white settlers off of cleared land and burned homes on the frontier.

Administration at the Factories

The factory system is the institutional forerunner of the modern Bureau of Indian Affairs. The factories and the factors resided at established locations and sought to control and regulate geographic areas and certain populations, dynamics which make them the antecedents of modern Indian agencies and superintendents.

Factors operated in virtually all of the era's issues: they established a peaceful and orderly federal presence on the frontier, they were involved in regulating Indian trade and enforcing licensing and other measures, they negotiated day-to-day issues of land, trade, and criminal justice among Indian and non-Indian populations, and they oversaw efforts to influence Indian behavior and social development. Factors were involved in diplomatic and intelligence activity, and they were a central component of treaty making – with roles ranging from supply and provisioning to negotiations and management of the long administrative path to a treaty. Factors were the local manifestation of regularized federal authority. Physical stability, a broad mandate, and wide discretionary authority over day-to-day events made the factory system a critically important example of the federal government's efforts to extend basic administrative and bureaucratic control over national expansion.

70 War Department to Hawkins, June 28, 1805, *War Department, Letters Sent.*

71 Silver, "Edmund Pendleton Gaines," 331–2. For other examples, see Treat to Waterman, December 13, 1806, *Arkansas Factory, Letters Sent and Received, 1805–1810*, Subgroup 27, Record Group 75, National Archives (hereafter, *Arkansas Factory, Letters Sent and Received*); War Department to Hawkins, November 6, 1809, War Department to Neely, November 17, 1809, Secretary of War to Meigs, January 14, 1804, Dearborn to Wilkinson, April 30, 1802: *War Department, Letters Sent*; Meigs to Calhoun, September 6, 1819, and accompanying Memorial against the War Department's action: *War Department, Letters Received.* See also Prucha, *Great Father*, 108–14; Prucha, *American Indian Treaties*, 64–65; Babcock, "Major Lawrence Taliaferro," 372; Purser, "Administration," 406–7, 413.

As early as 1795, a standardized list of instructions and guidelines for behavior communicated to factors the mission and purpose of the factory system. The instructions clearly stated the diplomatic and long-term peace-keeping mission of the factory system, underscoring the essential principle that the factories were not in operation for purposes of profit and gain. Factors were not to be mere businessmen. Rather, factors were federal agents bringing peace and order to frontier areas.

The instructions began with a general statement of the factory system's mission and its relationship to the broader goals of U.S. policy. The first two of eighteen points outlined in Factor Edward Price's instructions, for example, clarified the principle and object of the trade to be carried out under the factory system.

1. The principle of the trade is to furnish Indians with goods at such moderate price that the sales may simply reimburse to the U.S. the principle cost and all charges, which cost of charges you will find in the Invoices which will be delivered to you by the Purveyor.
2. The object of this trade is [that] by supplying the Indians on such easy terms to manifest the liberality and Friendship of the United States and thus by the ties of interest and gratitude secure their attachment and lay the Foundation of a lasting peace.[72]

The first point immediately established the factory as a not-for-profit enterprise, while outlining fundamental operating principles for the factor. The inclusion of invoices as a reference point for pricing in the field was an effort to standardize and control the activities of the factor and the factory. In the second point lay the overarching mission of the system: securing peace and friendship, anticipated to be the outcome of the Indians' gratitude at being supplied on good terms by a benevolent nation.

The final point in Price's instructions offered guidelines for ethical behavior, reinforcing the factor's mission: "I close these instructions suggesting to you the necessity of kind and friendly treatment of the Indians who may visit your station, and of perfect candor in all your dealings with them. Patience in particular will be requisite, caution when any of them get drunk. To avoid the latter you will use your endeavors with the influential men among them to draw them off from the station as soon as their attack is over and until then you may contrive as above suggested to make them small issue of rum." This point suggests the sincerity with which field agents were to carry

[72] "Instructions to the Factor, 1795 & 6," *Creek Factory, Correspondence*. Slightly different but essentially identical instructions are reprinted in Coman, "Government Factories"; Wesley, "Government Factory System," 491–2, 499–500; Nella J. Chambers, "The Creek Indian Factory at Fort Mitchell," *Alabama Historical Quarterly* 21 (1959), 15–18. See also Hawkins, *Sketch*, 190–2.

out the mission of the factory system; their orders to be fair and friendly to the Indians were very clear. Finally, factors operated under considerable restrictions designed to keep them from taking advantage of situations for personal gain. They were prohibited, for example, from any personal involvement in the Indian trade. This restriction aimed to further the factory system's goal of benefiting Indians and reducing the chances for Indian–white conflicts.

The system's paternalism is evident in these instructions, but so is the system's peaceful purpose. Regardless of the larger motives of the government's policy, regardless of whether Knox, Washington, Jefferson, and others sought by the factory system to drive Indians into debt or otherwise gain land cessions, and regardless of how policy was meant to complement the treaty process and facilitate white settlement, the factors were ordered to behave and act in a fair and benevolent fashion. Given prevailing attitudes toward the Indian presence, and given the persistent fear and unfamiliarity with Indian cultures, these instructions are quite extraordinary and they should not be interpreted as simple demands on the professional behavior and demeanor expected of government officials. The heads of the Indian department were aware that they had a volatile situation on their hands, and they were at pains to make this clear to their field agents. Field agents were granted discretion in many matters, but the factors and field agents were not given official leeway to cheat or mistreat Indians. The instructions opened and closed with statements to this effect, and they are more clear on this point than on any other. Nor should the passages be read as gratuitous or fatuous; the debate over the factory system centered on the practical gains to be had on behalf of the United States, but it also included a sincere effort at benevolence toward Indians. The ability to rationalize Indian policy as beneficial to both the United States and to Indians has often been self-serving and sometimes absurd, but it is a perpetual hallmark of federal policy toward American Indians and should not be too quickly rejected as consciously hypocritical.

Somewhat less clear than the factory system's mission were the procedures and formal rules governing factors' tasks in operating the factories. The factory system demanded the completion of tasks associated with the establishment of the trading posts, including maintaining stocks and running the factories, and tasks associated with the factor's role as the local representative of the federal government. Review of the factor's duties reveals the extent of those duties, and also illustrates just how quickly the Indian field service came under formal rules and constraints. The list of standardized procedures is far too long to be covered in full here. What is significant for the purposes of this study is how early the Indian Office's leadership tried to establish rules and procedures governing operating behavior, and the effort at standardization the office made in an effort to professionalize and make coherent the diverse operations of the Indian field service.

Each factor first needed to establish the trading post itself. The factor surveyed the general area in which the government had chosen to locate a factory, and decided upon a suitable position for the factory buildings. The factor – working with whatever help he could gain from Indian agents, local traders, and others – considered local trading routes and habits, geographical features such as rivers and hills, and the availability of supplies. Having chosen a location, the factor was responsible for erecting the government buildings; this required gathering building supplies and coordinating labor, usually personnel from the local military command. Factors were given control over these proceedings as a necessary concession to the vagaries of local conditions.[73]

Factors managed day to day operations at the factories. Among the most basic of tasks was becoming familiar with the local traders and suppliers, many of whom were involved with the factory as intermediaries. Point 5 of Price's instructions introduced James Seagrove as "the Superintendent of Indian Affairs in Georgia." Seagrove was to alert the local Indians about the factory and its guidelines and, if possible, provide Price with an interpreter. At the same time as they were becoming familiar with the operations of the factory, factors were ordered to familiarize others with the store's daily operations, laying the foundation for a continued and professionalized Indian service. The rigors of frontier life were not underestimated in this vein, either: Point 8 of the instructions, after establishing two assistants, ordered Price to familiarize the assistants with the factory's business "that in case of any interruptions in your attention they may be able to continue."

Factors were responsible for trading factory goods for animal skins brought in by Indians, which required making judgments about the value of skins, furs, or other goods traded for factory stores. This required intimate knowledge of the fur trade as it operated in the field, in the capital and along the East Coast, and internationally, since trades at the factory had to account for the future disposition of furs and skins. Having accepted goods in trade at the factory, usually skins obtained by Indian hunters, the factors were responsible for keeping and storing the furs until they could be shipped back to the capital. Point 7 of the instructions informed Price that the Purveyor would supply him with information regarding the saving and packing of peltries, a difficult and specialized skill unfamiliar to most new factors. Many of the peltries spoiled due to inexpert packing and storage, and suppliers and the head office repeatedly reminded factors of the necessary

73 Price to Hopkins, February 5, 1798, *Creek Factory, Letters Sent, 1795–1816*, Subgroup 43, Record Group 75, National Archives (hereafter *Creek Factory, Letters Sent*); see also Peake, *History*, ch. 3.

techniques. This activity took time and patience, and quickly became one of the most important and time consuming aspects of the factor's job. Local experts offered frequent tips to factors on topics like the proper timing of shipments and the method of assessing the quality of skins.[74]

Factors sent requests back to the capital ordering goods that they believed were appropriate or necessary for their local trade.[75] This encouraged the factors to become specialists on the specific tastes, needs, and development of the local Indians. Good judgment and experience were needed to determine what might be saleable and desired. Orders had to be submitted months in advance due to the slow pace of communications and transportation of the goods themselves. Having ordered goods, factors were responsible for receiving, inspecting, and accepting or rejecting goods shipped to them. Often this required travel to regional supply areas, such as Savannah or New Orleans. Factors dealt with suppliers, conducted sales and credit transactions, and managed the rejection of goods and claims for losses.

Factors were responsible for much more than running the trading post. Point 10 of Price's instructions made him responsible not only for the goods of his store, but also for $1,500 in goods to be delivered to the Creeks as part of their annuity under treaty with the United States. These treaty-related goods were to be kept separate from the operations of the factory. Requirements like this overlapped the tasks of the Indian agents, involving both factors and agents in negotiating and implementing treaties. This makes sense, given the primary role of the factories in maintaining peace and order on the frontier and given their stability as stationary outposts and therefore good communications and distribution centers. Overlap between factors' and agents' duties, though, blurred the lines of operating procedures: the records of the Creek factory, for example, showed considerable debts drawn against the Creeks' annuity payments by Indian Agent Benjamin Hawkins, which required the factor not only to verify and record such transactions but also to come to conclusions about what might be a valid charge and what might not be.[76]

Agents and factors also shared duties associated with granting trading licenses, an endeavor that required federal officials to evaluate the character of an applicant and become responsible for the bonding requirements. Price

74 Saul to Treat, June 2, 1806, *Arkansas Factory, Letters Sent and Received*. On transportation of merchandise, see Peake, *History*, ch. 6; Wesley, "Government Factory System," 496–9; Morris, "Traders and Factories," 31–2; Aloysius Plaisance, "The Chickasaw Bluffs Factory and Its Removal to the Arkansas River, 1818–1822," *Tennessee Historical Quarterly* XI (March–December 1952), 47–8.

75 For details of goods, prices, etc., see Peake, *History*, ch. 5; Wesley, "Government Factory System," 496–9; Chambers, "Creek Indian Factory," 21–2; Morris, "Traders and Factories," 45; Aloysius Plaisance, "The Arkansas Factory, 1805–1810," *Arkansas Historical Quarterly* 11 (1952), 191–2; Plaisance, "Chickasaw Bluffs Factory," 43ff.

76 Chambers, "Creek Indian Factory," 25.

also had authority to grant passes and to issue permits for purchasing horses from Indians.[77]

Point 12 of the instructions placed Price in charge of hospital stores for the troops stationed near the factory. Price would hold these stores, relinquishing them only for signed requests from the surgeon which would indicate the name of the sick person for whom they were taken. This and the other points that deal with relations between the military garrison and the factory placed Price and other factors in the middle of the garrison's affairs. Relations with local military and others using the store's services made the factor a de facto creditor, and left him responsible for collecting debts and for taking action against defaulters. Factors were also responsible for protecting their factory's goods against theft by local white settlers, Indians, or, often, the local military personnel. Relationships between the factor and the local military garrison, supposedly the factory's protection, were often very important – and often very tense.

The central office at the capital attempted to standardize recordkeeping, reporting, and accounting throughout the factory system era. Factors were expected to keep records of all transactions, stocks, and clients. The variety of standard records included daily ledgers, account books, quarterly reports, notebooks, and copies of incoming and outgoing correspondence. Daybooks were kept coterminous with transactions, journals served as a revised chronology of transactions, and ledgers listed transactions by account and included an index. Factors were also expected to make periodic reports to the central office, noting their sales, outstanding credits and debts, and so on. Factors were sent periodic updates, revisions, and new instructions for recordkeeping, and regularly received comments, advice, and criticism on the quality of their records.[78] The formal instructions also required factors to "keep a regular and frequent correspondence" with the

[77] Price to Thomas, May 27, 1797, Price to James Burges, February 27, 1797, *Creek Factory, Letters Sent*. On passports, see Gaines, "Notes," 170. Choctaw agent Silas Dinsmoor demanded proof of ownership and travel passports for slaves passing his agency on the Natchez Trace, strictly applying the law in a manner sure to anger and frustrate settlers and traders. Dinsmoor even detained slaves belonging to Andrew Jackson. See Clark and Guice, *Old Southwest*, 135. Tasks for Hawkins and Price also included granting permits for things such as removing hogs to market, collecting mortgages, and collecting money for slaves. Harmon, "Benjamin Hawkins," 148 n38, 150. Hawkins kept notes of towns, inhabitants, and traders, including their property holdings, character, and so on. See Hawkins, *Sketch*, 168ff.

[78] An 1824 War Department report, for example, noted the revised and enlarged rules and regulations governing the Indian Department, and focused attention on the "Forms... prepared and forwarded to the superintendents of the Indian schools, which have produced a system in their reports, out of which a general exhibit of all that relates to this branch of the Indian Department can be furnished with facility and accuracy, at the close of each year." *ASPIA*, II: 523. The Indian Office is hardly unique: see Paul Wallace Gates, "The Homestead Law in an Incongruous Land System," *The American Historical Review* 41 (July 1936), 665 n47, noting the "hundreds of volumes of abstracts in the General Land Office,

Purveyor, and with the Department of War when appropriate. This led factors to report frequently on intelligence matters, general occurrences, and even on leadership and attitudes among the Indians.

The Effectiveness of Public Administration in Indian Affairs

Treaties provided a stable and, over time, a progressively more standardized method of recognizing sovereignty, acknowledging land cessions, drawing boundaries, describing future benefits and social policy goals, outlining criminal justice procedures, and controlling the encroachments and behavior of whites. Controlled by the federal government, the treaties and trade and intercourse laws effectively managed expansion westward. As mechanisms not only for dealing with Indians but also for standardizing the transfer of formal title from Indians to private landholders, treaties were the federal government's chosen instrument for acting as the essential middleman.

The absence or ineffectiveness of federal efforts related to treaties is often overplayed and oversimplified. The United States was able to meet obligations when it wanted to; and it certainly maintained a presence that was neither "light" nor "inconspicuous"[79] – particularly when it forcibly removed white trespassers from Indian lands.[80] A different, yet illuminating, example of the treaty system in action comes from the journals of Josiah Gregg, a

Department of the Interior, Washington, the listing of which would be almost impossible and equally futile." See also Arthur H. Cole, "Cyclical and Sectional Variations in the Sale of Public Lands, 1816–1860," reprinted in Vernon Carstensen, ed., *The Public Lands: Studies in the History of the Public Domain* (Madison: University of Wisconsin Press, 1968), 230–1, describing existing data that goes back to 1801 and is very useful for the period 1816–1860; Robert W. Harrison, "Public Land Records of the Federal Government," *Mississippi Valley Historical Review* 41 (1954), reprinted in Carstensen, *Public Lands.*

79 Edling, *Revolution*, 224.

80 E.g., see Cumfer, "Local Origins," whose evidence suggests the effectiveness of federal efforts to remove intruders and the significant impact of the federal role on Tennessee in the 1780s and 1790s, and generally; Ira Katznelson, "Flexible Capacity: The Military and Early American Statebuilding," in *Shaped by War and Trade: International Influences on American Political Development*, ed. Ira Katznelson and Martin Shefter (Princeton: Princeton University Press, 2002); Green, *Politics of Indian Removal*; Clark and Guice, *Old Southwest.* The federal government exercised its power and authority *when necessary* to pursue managed expansion; when pursuit of that mission benefited from letting white intruders flex their muscles, federal officials were content to lay off and encourage tension, carefully managed conflict, and further land cession. Scholars who see white encroachment into Indian territories as evidence of the federal government's weakness, or its "commitment incapacity," overlook the careful, complex calculations behind decisions about when to intervene. E.g., see Nelson, "Short, Ironic History"; Owens, "Jeffersonian Benevolence," 409 and 412 n16; and Robert O. Keohane, "International Commitments and American Political Institutions in the Nineteenth Century," in Katznelson and Shefter, eds., *Shaped by War and Trade*, 67, which overplay federal inactivity and weakness.

nineteenth-century trader. Gregg speaks directly to the effect of government activity in securing trading routes, and also – no less importantly – of the awareness that individuals had of these efforts. Passing Council Grove (in present-day Kansas) in 1831, Gregg dispels what he calls a "romantic sort of interest" that might be associated with the place in the minds of the reader as a meeting place for exotic native populations and "lurking savages." In particular, he replaces that myth with "the facts":

> The facts connected with the designation of this spot are simply these. Messrs. Reeves, Sibley, and Mathers, having been commissioned by the United States in the year 1825 to mark a road from the confines of Missouri to Santa Fe, met on this spot with some bands of Osages, with whom they concluded a treaty whereby the Indians agreed to allow all citizens of the United States and Mexico to pass unmolested, and even to lend their aid to those engaged in the Santa Fe trade; for which they were to receive a gratification of eight hundred dollars in merchandise.

The place and the route remained safe, and "from the borders of Missouri to those of New Mexico not even an Indian settlement greeted our eyes." That safety and the absence of Indians was a government-constructed outcome, and Gregg knew it. The freedom of the prairie described so movingly by Gregg toward the end of his journal – "the wild, unsettled, and independent life of the prairie trader" – was made possible by the prior action and continuing oversight of the federal government.[81]

The factories were effective, too. The system maintained its funding base for many years and contributed to a relatively peaceful and widespread settlement east of the Mississippi. No major Indian wars broke out near the factories. Early reports on the factory system were positive, and Jefferson echoed Knox's argument that peaceful trading relations were a more expedient and cost-effective method of securing and advancing peace and order in the American West. In the system's early years, Jefferson asked Congress to expand the system: "Instead, therefore, of an augmentation of military force proportioned to our extension of frontier, I propose a moderate enlargement of the capital employed in that commerce as a more effectual, economical, and humane instrument for preserving peace and good neighborhood with them."[82] Trade regulations complementing the factories encouraged concentration of authority and control of the fur trade. As planned, this benefited

81 Josiah Gregg, *The Commerce of the Prairies*, ed. by Milo Milton Quaife (Lincoln: University of Nebraska Press, 1967), 32, 30, 326. The road bill Gregg discusses was introduced by Thomas Hart Benton in the Senate in 1825, and signed by President Monroe. Gregg, *Commerce*, 12 n10. See also Isenberg, "Market Revolution," 462.

82 Quoted in Plaisance, "Factory System," 30. Administration and planning were also critical parts of Jefferson's response to the possibility of conflict following the Louisiana Purchase. Isenberg, "Market Revolution," esp. 445, 456ff.; Mary P. Adams, "Jefferson's Reaction to the Treaty of San Ildefonso," *The Journal of Southern History* 21 (1955), 174–5, 184ff.

American companies, helped to exclude foreign competition, and nurtured the nation's economy while securing its frontier regions. Later, individuals like William Crawford and Thomas McKenney argued for great expansions in the system. Prucha points out that the vehement and sustained opposition to the factories pressed by organized competitors such as John Astor indicate the significant role they played in the Indian trade.[83] Until it was dismantled in the 1820s, the factory system did exactly what it was supposed to do.[84]

This adaptive structure and its creative operators had some success with their social policy initiatives, as well. Recognizing the paternalism and ethnocentrism that characterized social policy related to American Indians in the early republic, the Indian service nevertheless claimed some success in its efforts to encourage farming and domestic manufactures, and to bring its definition of "civilization" and Christianity to eastern Indians. Efforts to promote farming, literacy, and home manufactures often met their purposes.[85]

More important to the development of public administration and social policy in the United States, perhaps, is the fact that the Indian Office's

[83] Prucha, *Great Father*, 134.

[84] Isenberg, "Market Revolution," 454–8; 461. While most scholars of the factories agree that they were generally successful in their diplomatic mission, Royal B. Way argues that the factories hurt U.S.–Indian relations and encouraged Indian alliances with European powers. Way, "United States Factory System." Chittenden also deems the factories largely a failure, and ascribes the failure to the government's inability to compete with private traders. He lays particular emphasis on the government's decision to use a mixed system of licensing, with different rules for credit and other issues constraining the factories but not private companies. Chittenden thus evaluates the system primarily as an economic enterprise, and overlooks many of the diplomatic and expansion-oriented purposes of the system. Paradoxically, too, Chittenden sees the factories as economically successful enough to have attracted the ire of the private companies, which ultimately drove the factories to extinction. See Chittenden, *American Fur Trade*, 1:14–17. For varying evaluations of the system, often driven by how significant the author considers the system's economics to be as a criterion for evaluation, see Peake, *History*, chs. 12–13; Cotterill, "Federal Indian Management," 339, 341, 345–6, 351; Wesley, "Government Factory System," 509–10; Coman, "Government Factories," 386–8; Harmon, "Benjamin Hawkins," 151–2; Way, "United States Factory System," 233–5; Purser, "Administration," 417–19; White, *Jeffersonians*, 503. Morris, "Traders and Factories," 48 evaluates the Arkansas factories. For discussions of contemporary criticism and support of the factory system, see Peake, *History*, chs. 11–13; George Sibley, August 18, 1811, reprinted in George Sibley, "Extracts from the Diary of Major Sibley," reprinted in *Chronicles of Oklahoma* 5 (June, 1927), 199–200; Coman, "Government Factories," 374ff.; Quaife, "Experiment," 288.

[85] Bernard W. Sheehan, *Seeds of Extinction: Jeffersonian Philanthropy and the American Indian* (New York: Norton, 1973), ch. 9; Ronald Rayman, "Joseph Lancaster's Monitorial System of Instruction and American Indian Education, 1815–1838," *History of Education Quarterly* 21 (Winter 1981), 400–5; Daniel Walker Howe, "Church, State, and Education in the Young American Republic," *Journal of the Early Republic* 22 (Spring 2002).

activities in the new republic reveal ideological and institutional foundations for social policy designed and funded at the federal level and administered by federal agents. While the government struggled to find the right mix of public activity, private input, and religious work, leaders and operators of the day clearly accepted the idea that the federal government had an appropriate role to play in regulating trade, criminal justice, alcohol, and weapons to shape the development of the frontier. The federal government had a role to play in education and in subsidizing farming and certain manufactures, always with close interrelations between profit and the economy, on one hand, and social development in a republic, on the other. Despite its paternalistic underpinnings, early attention to the welfare of individual Indians set a pattern that would continue in Indian affairs into the twenty-first century. The factory system stood at the center of many initiatives that promoted civilization, education, and vocational training among Indian populations.

One of the best measures of the effectiveness of the federal effort to pacify Indian affairs in the early republic, and to extend dominion, legitimacy, and a sense of the national state to whites in the West is visible in the debates undertaken regarding federal policy and power, and in the reflexive consideration given to federal policy and judgment. Extensive debate took place among whites concerning the proper scope and extent of national power vis-à-vis the states, and the amount of deference owed to national policy. Such debates, together with actions against federal efforts, demonstrate the pervasiveness and conspicuousness of federal policies, as well as the legitimacy already enjoyed by the federal government. As backwoods settlers worried about federal rules, treaty boundaries and exclusions, and the threat of being removed by federal troops and having "their" property and crops destroyed – as they debated the legality and propriety of what they were doing – as they uneasily ignored or violated federal guidelines – the federal government existed as an intrusive, present, influential, and, in many cases, determinative force. At one point, concerned about the federal government's reactions, white intruders on Indian lands even went so far as to fire weapons through their own clothing, to establish claims of self-defense against an anticipated federal legal action, which was working diligently to uphold treaty obligations.[86]

The administrative mechanisms put in place by the federal government to support the treaty and factory systems relied on localized decision making within general guidelines and a clearly articulated mission. This combination

[86] See Cumfer, "Local Origins"; Cayton, "'Separate Interests'"; Clark and Guice, *Old Southwest*; Tim Alan Garrison, *The Legal Ideology of Removal: The Southern Judiciary and the Sovereignty of Native American Nations* (Athens: The University of Georgia Press, 2002). The weapons story is in Cumfer, "Local Origins," 21.

effectively pacified Indian relations with the young United States. As treaties and the factories developed and as field agents increasingly made their own decisions in unique, volatile circumstances, a culture of local, discretionary decision making took deep root. This discretionary culture would sometimes look to contemporary observers and to later historians like failure and incoherence, but it was the key to effective public administration of national policy in the factory system era.

4

The Key to Success and the Illusion of Failure

There are three reasons why it is easy to overlook the effectiveness of public administration in Indian affairs. The first reason is that evaluations of Indian policy and administration in American history have a tendency to focus on the problematic nature of the values and purposes driving government policy. The era's social policies ranged from paternalistic to culturally destructive, and they deserve criticism. Yet administrators often made progress, as they defined it; the era's administrators effectively pursued the goals they set for themselves. And we must remember that "civilization" and other social goals were never the primary purpose of U.S. Indian policy. When evaluations focus exclusively on social policy issues, the effectiveness of agents administering treaties, factories, and economic regulations are obscured. The same is true of focusing on warmaking and military conflict for evidence of state-building and state effectiveness – warmaking, conflict, and extermination were never first goals of the American state. Then, as now, they were rhetorically attractive at times and served in practice as a backup, a deterrent, a last measure. The state's primary goal in the era of the factory system was ordering and managing peaceful and economical continental expansion. Federal agents administering the treaty and factory systems in the early republic accomplished that goal with considerable success.

There is a second reason why it is easy to overlook the effectiveness of Indian affairs administration. Indian affairs administration was effective precisely because it recognized the fluid and volatile dynamics surrounding local circumstances and local relationships with particular Indian tribes, leaders, and events. Discretion and judgment in such an administrative environment were central to effective pursuit of organizational goals. Administration of Indian affairs thus rested upon the necessity of creativity, discretion, and uniqueness in pursuit of the clearly defined mission. Indian affairs administration was never uniform in its details, and it is not uniform now – so any inquiry into administrative development that looks too narrowly for uniformity and consistency, or that sees inconsistency as evidence of chaos or failure, is frustrated. The broad discretion allowed to field agents to pursue clear and accepted goals, and the unique circumstances and personalities driving the details of administration, led to administration that was inconsistent, not uniform. This inconsistency is precisely why Indian affairs administration *was* so effective, because field agents embraced and carried out their roles of resolving disputes and solving problems with one eye on volatile local circumstances, and another on the broader mission of the treaty and factory systems.

Finally, there is a third reason why it's easy to overlook the Indian service's effectiveness: powerful interests worked purposely to discredit the service. Certain interests benefited from discrediting the Indian Office's efforts, especially as time wore on. Policy goals and the interests involved in Indian affairs shifted constantly, and by the end of the factory system new directions in Indian policy were needed in the old states of the East and in the fresh areas of the West. Those interests seized upon the inconsistencies of Indian affairs administration in order to discredit the service – as a way of redirecting the course of Indian policy to serve evolving purposes. It is no accident that we have a distorted understanding of government administration in the republic's first thirty years. Many people wanted it that way.

Administrative Discretion

Indian affairs administration has always had something of a split personality, as it simultaneously strives for an orderly pursuit of shared goals in a system of continental administration, on the one hand, and encourages local discretionary authority attuned to specific circumstances, on the other. Throughout the Indian service's history, amid the effort to meet important goals, rules and formal constraints have multiplied – including standardized operating procedures covering the numerous tasks for which field personnel were responsible, and regular reporting requirements for accounting and oversight. Paradoxically, rather than binding operators' behavior, the multiplication of rules and guidelines has more often worked to free field agents to operate on their own discretion.

The Indian service's reliance on discretionary actions on the part of field agents gave those agents great freedom. As treaty commissioners and factors came to realize that waiting for instructions or guidance from the capital was an ineffective and even potentially dangerous way of resolving problems or foreseeing future requirements in the field, they capitalized on the freedom they were granted to make their own decisions. Field operators could act in accordance with their instructions, and defend their actions against complaint by appealing to higher authority. The same operators could also ignore or liberally misinterpret their orders, if those orders conflicted with the operators' own judgment – they could then fall back on their discretionary authority and the precedents for such action in order to defend and justify acting on their own best judgment. And, as people still do today, anyone could blame the rules for suboptimal outcomes – rules that could be condemned as too vague, or too constricting, depending on the circumstance.

Administrative Discretion

Treaty commissioners enjoyed extensive discretionary authority to arrange for treaty negotiations, arrange for provisions and presents, make agreements, select boundaries, and establish payment amounts and methods.[1] For this reason, and given the importance of Indian affairs, the men who served as treaty commissioners were usually experienced leaders from civilian or military backgrounds: treaties ratified before 1830 are dominated by the signatures of future Treasury Secretary Oliver Wolcott, longtime Indian agent Benjamin Hawkins, George Rogers Clark, Arthur St. Clair, Henry Knox, William Blount, Timothy Pickering, Anthony Wayne, James Wilkinson, William Henry Harrison, Return J. Meigs, Henry Dearborn, William Hull, Peter Chouteau, Lewis Cass, Andrew Jackson, William Clark, Ninian Edwards, Auguste Chouteau, David Meriwether, John Calhoun, and George Sibley. Harrison signed thirteen treaties; Lewis Cass signed twenty; William Clark signed thirty-one.[2]

Indian agents and factors in the early Indian Service were also given broad grants of discretionary authority with which to carry out their missions.[3]

1 "The sum to be given must from the nature of the business principally depend on your judgment and discretion." Secretary of War to Hawkins, Wilkinson, and Anderson, May 5, 1803, *Department of War, Letters Sent, Secretary of War-Indian Affairs 1800–1824*, Subgroup 2, Record Group 75, National Archives (hereafter *War Department, Letters Sent*). See also Francis Paul Prucha, *American Indian Treaties: The History of a Political Anomaly* (Berkeley: University of California Press, 1997), 27, 28, 30, 43, 105, 117. Jefferson granted Harrison "full power to conclude and sign any Treaty or Treaties, which may be found necessary with any Indian Tribes North West of the Ohio, and within the Territory of the United States, on the subject of their boundaries or Lands," and Calhoun gave Cass and other commissioners similar broad discretion in 1818. See Prucha, *American Indian Treaties*, 119, 136, 99–100. Holding such discretionary authority over the terms of treaties gave these regional officers influence over hundreds of thousands of dollars worth of public funds to be distributed to Indians in future years.

2 Author's count, based on data presented in Prucha, *American Indian Treaties*, Appendix B. Commissioners were also chosen with respect to geography; see Prucha, *American Indian Treaties*, 43 n4.

3 For examples of acknowledgment of discretionary authority and action in sales, salaries, and other activities, see Treat to Davy, June 23, 1805, Shee to Treat, circular of November 24, 1806, Treat to Shee, December 31, 1806: *Arkansas Factory, Letters Sent and Received, 1805–1810*, Subgroup 27, Record Group 75, National Archives; Halsted to Clay, May 10, 1802, Halsted to Secretary of War, October 9, 1802, Halsted to Shee, January 23, 1807, Halsted to Eustis, April 26, 1811: *Creek Factory, Letters Sent, 1795–1816*, Subgroup 43, Record Group 75, National Archives (hereafter *Creek Factory, Letters Sent*); Price to Hawkins, August 17, 1797, Hawkins to Price, October 20, 1797, Secretary of War to Halsted, November 12,

This authority reflected the distant and varied nature of the agents' and factors' duties, and also the important and volatile nature of Indian affairs. The presence and importance of powerful, diverse tribes dictated the nature and course of early Indian policy. Tribes' real power in the field forced accommodation to differences in local policy and administration. Treaties often followed a standard template, but usually included unique provisions related to specific events, land features, and personal relationships relevant at a particular place and time. Local expertise and experience had to be capitalized upon among Indian agents and factors, who were expected to rely on their judgment in furthering the goals of Indian policy.

The factors' instructions reflected this fact, offering general guidelines for operating in unexpected circumstances – and leaving room for factors to stray from the guidelines when they believed it necessary in order to pursue the service's objectives. Point 3 of the factors' instructions, for example, acknowledged that such basic tasks as pricing goods for sale at the factory could not be controlled from headquarters. Its plea for consistency must have sounded futile even in 1795:

> 3. To provide against the numerous accidents and losses to which the trade will be liable, percentage should be added to the price of goods beyond the first cost and charges. This is to be considered as a general rule. You may find it necessary, however, to depart from it by charging lower, and some higher in order the better to satisfy the Indians in the course of trade; but, it will be important to first arrange on the proper prices and afterwards to adhere to them steadily. The Indians will then know what to depend on, and not have their jealousy excited by the apprehension of unfair dealings which a fluctuation of prices would be apt to beget.[4]

This point overlooked significant difficulties. First, factors were frequently unaccustomed to the frontier generally and to the Indian trade in particular.

1802: *Creek Factory, Correspondence 1795–1814*, Subgroup 42, Record Group 75, National Archives (hereafter *Creek Factory, Correspondence*); Secretary of War to Hawkins, November 26, 1800, Secretary of War to Meigs, February 19, 1803, November 23, 1803, *War Department, Letters Sent*; Mason to Johnson, November 11, 1808, Mason to Gaines, August 28, 1810, Mason to Clark, August 7, 1815: *Office of Indian Trade, Letters Sent, 1807–1830*, Subgroup 4, Record Group 75, National Archives (hereafter *Office of Indian Trade, Letters Sent*); McKenney to Saul, May 13, 1816: *Vol. C, Roll 4, M16, Office of Indian Trade, Letters Sent, 1807–1830*, Subgroup 4, Record Group 75, National Archives (hereafter *Office of Indian Trade, Letters Sent, Roll 4, M16*); Irwin to McKenney, August 10, 1818, in Lyman Copeland Draper, ed., *Collections of the State Historical Society of Wisconsin*, Vol. VII (Madison: Wisconsin Historical Society, 1908 [1876], 276–7; McKenney to Rawlings, April 18, 1817, quoted in Aloysius Plaisance, "The Chickasaw Bluffs Factory and Its Removal to the Arkansas River, 1818–1822," *Tennessee Historical Quarterly* XI (March–December 1952), 49–50.

[4] "Instructions to the Factor, 1795 & 6," *Creek Factory Correspondence.*

Identifying appropriate prices took time, as factors learned what the going rates were in various areas, what contractors charged for shipping, how many goods were liable to be lost in shipping, and so on. Further, the trade was not nearly as predictable as these instructions imply: weather, the international market for skins and peltries, theft, and regional differences all combined to make predictions unreliable and supply of the stores – from Indians and from the capital – unpredictable. To know and to be able to predict accurately based on these contingencies in order to set prices and hold them close to buyers' expectations was extremely unlikely. Factors quickly found that the costs of doing business were high, due in large part to goods lost on their way to the stores and to variations in markets. The effort to tie prices to the Purveyors' invoices and to set predictable prices proved difficult.

Point 4 of the instructions added more variables to the mix. Point 4 noted that if the factory-area market value for peltries was high enough that resale of the peltries after shipping to Philadelphia would incur losses, the prices of other goods at the factory were to be inflated. The factor thus had almost complete discretion to alter and adjust prices however he saw fit: allowing him to set goods' prices based on two different markets for peltries (Point 4) and to anticipate damage and losses (Point 3) meant, in effect, that a wide range of prices could be justified under the factor's guidelines.

Leadership at the Indian Office condoned and encouraged the exercise of discretion. John B. Treat's tenure as factor in Arkansas provides an example of the discretion and authority granted to field agents. Controversy arose around Treat's factory after the Morgan-Bright company received a license to trade in the area. Locals feared that Morgan-Bright had been granted a monopoly. Secretary of War Dearborn wrote Treat in late spring of 1806 to the effect that the president, when he granted Morgan and Bright a license to trade up the Arkansas River, had not intended to create a monopoly. All other traders were welcome to apply to Treat for licenses, and Morgan-Bright "ought not to keep a Store at Arkansas to trade with the Indians."[5]

The exact nature of the license from the president to Morgan-Bright, or the functionings of their stores, are less at issue here than the apparent confusion in the field and the use of the factor as the closest federal agent to address the situation. The Secretary authorized Treat to grant trading licenses as he saw fit, to take "suitable bonds" (the amounts were unspecified), to prohibit liquor sales, and to act in a policing capacity. One section of Treat's instructions from Dearborn, in particular, illustrates the vast discretionary authority given to the factor:

> [I]f any Person, or Persons heretofore licensed, or to whom you may grant licenses, should be guilty of makeing [sic] or attempting to make impressions on the minds of

[5] Dearborn to Treat, April 29, 1806, *Arkansas Factory, Letters Sent and Received.*

the Indians unfavorable to the Government of the U.S. or to its views in relation to Indian affairs, especially in relation to our Factories, you will on receiving suitable evidence of such conduct or of any other improper conduct consider the license to any such Person, or Persons as forfeited, and will annul them accordingly. – And in cases where sufficient Legal evidence can be obtained to prove a forfeiture of bonds, given on the receipt of a license, prosecutions should be commenced for the penalty of the Bonds.[6]

The case is important because of the broad grant of authority given to the factor. Treat was given power to grant licenses and to investigate, charge, and sentence violators of the licensing regulations. The characteristics of "suitable evidence" were left undefined, as were the boundaries of the comments or other "improper conduct" that would qualify as unfavorable. The forbidden action – giving Indians "unfavorable" impressions of the United States – is extremely vague. Such power over traders' bonds and livelihoods indicates the scope of federal authority on the frontier. Treat was placed in the middle of all this, and he was forced to deal with the complaints. "It has been my endeavour to appease and convince them that our Govt shews no partiality, But are desirous to prevent unprincipled Individuals from going into the Indian Country – that no exclusive privileges are given."[7] Trade Superintendent Davy wrote to Treat, sanctioning Treat's use of his judgment to resolve various matters: "no blame can attach to any subordinate agent who has only to do his duty in executing as far as circumstances will admit the trust confided to him."[8] Treat reported almost three months later

[6] Dearborn to Treat, April 29, 1806, *Arkansas Factory, Letters Sent and Received*. See also Chester L. Guthrie and Leo L. Gerald, "Upper Missouri Agency: An Account of Indian Administration on the Frontier," *The Pacific Historical Review* 10 (March 1941), 47; Irwin to McKenney, September 29, 1817, in Draper, *Collections*, 273–4; Frank L. Owsley Jr., "Benjamin Hawkins, the First Modern Indian Agent," *Alabama Historical Quarterly* (Summer, 1968), 10. Licensing was sometimes at odds with the factories themselves: Irwin to McKenney, September 29, 1817, in Draper, *Collections*, 274–5; McKenney to Irwin, July 5, 1821, in Draper, *Collections*, 280–2. See also Wayne Morris, "Traders and Factories on the Arkansas Frontier, 1805–1822," *The Arkansas Historical Quarterly* 28 (Spring 1969), 29, on how agents' and factors' tasks differed, and Edgar B. Wesley, "The Government Factory System Among the Indians, 1795–1822," *Journal of Economic and Business History* 4 (1932), 487 n1, on how agents and factors generally developed different relationships with the traders as a result. I think both Morris and Wesley underestimate the level of overlap between factors and agents in administering various aspects of policy.

[7] Treat to Dearborn, March 27, 1806, *Arkansas Factory, Letters Sent and Received*.

[8] Davy to Treat, May 16, 1806, *Arkansas Factory, Letters Sent and Received*. Upon assuming his responsibilities, Davy tried to direct details of field operations from the capital. See Davy to Halsted, e.g., November 8, 1805, October 5, 1805, June 17, 1806, *Creek Factory, Correspondence*. Davy even went so far as to dictate the precise measurements and layout of factory buildings: Davy to Peterkin, July 30, 1802, *War Department, Letters Sent*. Halsted repeatedly tried to convince Davy that administering the factories from the capital was ineffective and counterproductive. In contrast, Mason generally supported his field officers' judgment, even when he believed it to be silly: in a letter to Sibley, Mason wrote, "I have

to say that much of the tension had been quelled, due in part to the territorial governor sending Treat several blank licenses with which Treat could carry out his new mandate and demonstrate the absence of a monopoly control by Morgan-Bright.[9]

Treat also exercised considerable discretionary authority when he established a second factory store without authorization from headquarters. Treat wrote to his superior that he wanted to establish a second trading house to counter some of the dynamics of the Morgan-Bright company; he wanted to take over a good location from a trader who was retiring, and establish a second store. Treat tried repeatedly to obtain authorization for the second store; receiving no response to his inquiries, he took advantage of the absence of explicit limits on his authority in the case and established the store based on his own discretionary authority. Superintendent John Shee finally gave an official acknowledgement of Treat's initiative well after the fact, writing in July 1807 that while the second store was "commendable," "I must observe to you that matters of this kind require to be duly authoriz'd."[10] Importantly, Shee did not reprimand Treat; in fact, he praised him. Shee's response was bound to encourage such active decision making on the part of the field agents, and is an early example of the home office remaining silent on sensitive questions until the outcome of field action became apparent.

Other factors routinely acted on their own discretion. In moving his factory from its original location at Colerain, Edward Price made numerous practical administrative decisions on his own authority. Like Treat, Price learned that his recommendations from the field were often followed, and he developed a habit for acting on his own judgment. He wrote in 1798 that he expected approval for an appointment he had made to an official post, but he had not yet heard back. He needed to wait for the official decision, he wrote, but he had expectations that he would be approved, "as they have hitherto been governed by my reports on these points."[11] In the spring of 1798, Price purchased a wagon and a team of horses for the factory after tiring of relying on the resources of contractors. Price acknowledged that he had not received explicit permission for the purchase when he wrote to the Secretary that he would purchase another team and wagon if the first purchase was approved.[12]

sent you the wigs whimsical as the thing is as the object is to work influence thro' these said wigs.... I trust however you will see that those who are to wear them make use of them." Mason to Sibley, May 15, 1809, *Office of Indian Trade, Letters Sent*. McKenney reversed course, and at the start of his tenure made decisions about the benefit of certain particular goods requested by the factors. See McKenney to Simpson, May 9, 1816, May 14, 1816, May 17, 1816, *Office of Indian Trade, Letters Sent, Roll 4, M16*.

[9] Treat to Dearborn, July 13, 1806, *Arkansas Factory, Letters Sent and Received*.

[10] Shee to Treat, July 14, 1807, *Arkansas Factory, Letters Sent and Received*.

[11] Price to Wallace, October 15, 1798, *Creek Factory, Letters Sent*.

[12] Price to Secretary of War, March 7, 1798, *Creek Factory, Letters Sent*.

While discretion could support action, it could also support inaction. When orders conflicted with the factor's assessment of a situation, the factor could choose to interpret the orders in a manner consistent with his own judgment. Before finally moving his store upriver, for example, Price had delayed the action. Asked why he had not yet moved the factory, Price responded that he had received no formal instructions to do so.[13] There is a telling backstory here: Price didn't want to move the store. In a letter to his superiors, he questioned the move's wisdom in the context of the factory system's mission of dealing with the Indians: "I find the lower part of the [Creek] Nation much averse to our taking away the store and we have experienced a considerable influx of skins this spring. I am decidedly of opinion to answer the views of govern't in accommodating the Creek nation a store ought to be continued at or near this place."[14] Price had used his discretion, relying on the absence of clear, formal orders, to delay the store's move.

Price hinted at the delicate line in play in matters of discretionary authority when he discussed the Indian trade with a Captain Meals. Price wrote to Meals, in August 1797,

> I am restricted from doing any business on my private acc'ts. [accounts] as there is an officer for the particular purpose of making all purchases for the US. I have made it a rule not to purchase or sell out of the line laid down but in cases of necessity. . . . I am convinced I could have saved money to the public had I conceived myself at liberty to act discretionally.

Price reveals two important things here. First, he tells the Captain that his actions in this case are constrained by his limited authority, and that – were they not so – the factory might be doing much better. Price thus uses the formal guidelines to absolve himself of responsibility for the store's effectiveness, and also to help him avoid entering into a deal with Meals. He suggests, in short, that his discretionary authority is constrained. At the same time, though, Price suggests that he is free to act "out of the line laid down" when necessary – so it is, after all, ultimately up to his own discretion when to act and how to act. Price was able to influence the running of the store and delay its move – which accorded with his view of the store and his own mission – by relying on the absence of clear directions from his superiors. Yet he took decisive action by hiring more assistants without orders when he believed that acting was in the best interests of the store and the factor.

The Indian Office's imprecise guidelines and the necessity of granting authority to field agents led to agents acting, or not acting, based on their individual opinions of the best way to pursue the service's goals. Over time,

[13] Price to Capt. E. Waterman, April 3, 1797, Price to Secretary of War, June 27, 1797, *Creek Factory, Letters Sent.*

[14] Price to Barnard, May 18, 1797, *Creek Factory, Letters Sent.*

field personnel became increasingly able to justify their actions, or inactions, by appeal to specific guidelines mandating behavior – or by appeal to a growing history of having had discretionary decisions sanctioned after the fact. This process helped free the factors to operate largely on their own best judgment.

The factory system set important precedents for a federal administrative capacity marked by institutional adaptability and driven by personal creativity and initiative. By centering administration of the factories at the local level and granting federal officers broad discretionary authority, the factory system's administrators were free to adapt the system as time moved on and circumstances evolved. Indian Office leadership made continual adjustments and refinements to the institution's mechanisms, and they quickly developed a tradition of deferring, often silently, to the recommendations and actions of the field service. This encouraged the field service to take action, insulated the leadership from complaints, and cast the leadership in a role that reacted to complaints and serious issues in the field – other issues could be left to the field service to handle. This quickly developed into a dynamic administrative mechanism with great flexibility, great ability to meet changing circumstances in pursuit of clearly defined ends. It also developed a system that insulated leadership from responsibility for localized decision making.

Discretion and the Personalization of Administration

The Indian Office's culture of discretionary authority and localized decision making rested administrative effectiveness on the talents and decisions of individuals in the field. Free to rely on or dismiss the agency's many rules and constraints, field agents' personal abilities and individual priorities determined the outcomes of problem solving and dispute resolution. Given the broad array of tasks and responsibilities facing factors, this kind of decision making could be crucial. Factors frequently faced choices about prioritization, for example: stock furs, hire a translator, resolve a dispute, or fill out the ledger and daybook? Handle matters independently, through superiors, or go to the local garrison commander? Press a charge against locals, or let it go? Individual responses to these kinds of questions not only dictated the nature of business around any given factory, but could also dictate what did or did not get done.

Far distant from superiors and high level officials, affairs in the field were heavily influenced by personal relationships in play at any given place and time. Good personal relationships could minimize conflict and maximize cooperation; poor relationships could frustrate administration and threaten the Indian service's mission. For example, factories were often located near military posts, to take advantage of communication and coordination benefits that arose from proximity. Point 9 of the factors' instructions outlined the relationship between factories and local military garrisons. Point 9 told the factor that the commanding officer at a nearby military post "will at all times furnish you with necessary guards. One great object of their service is to protect this Indian trade."[15] The military, according to factors' instructions, supported and protected the factories. Written rules, though, never necessarily determine the course of events in the field. Lines of authority and rules of cooperation between the civilian and military authorities in the field were not set deeply enough that military officers reflexively supported the civilian mission of the factories or submitted to the supervision of factors. Civil-military relations in the field depended instead upon particular relationships among field officers. Contentious relations between Factor Edward Price and the local military garrison near the Colerain factory in Georgia, for example, constrained Price's effort to administer the store and pursue the mission of the factory system.[16]

Factors' personal relations with other interests also played a key role in what happened around the factory, and in *how* it happened. Price's relations with other local interests appeared strained. He implicated local traders for many of the difficulties he faced supplying and managing the store, but the friction with the military garrison made it even more difficult for Price to manage disputes with local traders. At one point, Price was forced to beg for security from the military commander with whom he had had abrasive relations almost since he'd arrived. Incidents between the factor, locals, and the military garrison disrupted factory activities, hindered Price's ability to

[15] "Instructions to the Factor, 1795 & 6," *Creek Factory Correspondence*.

[16] See, e.g., Price to Tench Francis, December 1, 1795, December 4, 1795, December 26, 1795, Price to Maj. Constant Freeman, January 5, 1797, Price to Gaither, August 14, 1797, January 8, 1798, January 29, 1798, Price to Lt. Webb, February 4, 1798, *Creek Factory, Letters Sent*. Price appealed directly to his and others' instructions in these battles: he wrote, for example, "When the department of war directed me to make any tolerable conveniences I thought requisite for the factory they instructed me to appeal to no other person's judgment than my own for the propriety thereof[,] and will you show me instructions stating that your decision is to be the umpire in such cases." Price to Gaither, January 22, 1798, *Creek Factory, Letters Sent*. See also Johnston to Secretary of War, May 21, 1806 and July 3, 1806, *War Department, Letters Received, 1806–1824*, Subgroup 3, Record Group 75, National Archives. See also Prucha, *Great Father*, 163; Linnard to Mason, January 4, 1811 and March 25, 1812, Fowler to McKenney, April 14, 1817, *Natchitoches-Sulphur Fork Factory, 1809–1821, Letters Sent*, Subgroup 61, Record Group 75, National Archives; Mason to Eustis, December 19, 1811, Mason to Secretary of War, September 14, 1812, *Office of Indian Trade, Letters Sent*; McKenney to Irwin, August 7, 1816, *Office of Indian Trade, Letters Sent, Roll 4, M16*. On civil-military relations in the field, see Willoughby M. Babcock Jr., "Major Lawrence Taliaferro, Indian Agent," *The Mississippi Valley Historical Review* 11 (December 1924), 364, 366; Ora Brooks Peake, *A History of the United States Indian Factory System, 1795–1822* (Denver: Sage, 1954), 239, 249; Wesley, "Government Factory System," 502–503; Nella J. Chambers, "The Creek Indian Factory at Fort Mitchell," *Alabama Historical Quarterly* 21 (1959), 32–3; Hawkins to Gaither, April 22, 1798, in Benjamin Hawkins, *A Sketch of the Creek Country, in the Years 1798 and 1799 [1848] and Letters of Benjamin Hawkins, 1796–1806 [1916]* (Spartansburg, SC: Reprint Co., 1974), 305–6.

maintain the stores and keep records of the store's transactions, and placed at risk the furs and other goods kept at the store.

Inconsistent Administration

Personalized administration in Indian affairs, coupled with a clear sense of overarching purpose, was integral to the field service's ability to handle unique and changing circumstance while simultaneously keeping an eye on broader purposes. Yet the important role played by individuals in the Indian service had significant ramifications on administration. Field administration cannot be made uniform and predictable when it relies on local circumstance and personalities to find the best course by which to pursue broad goals effectively.

Administration in any one place could be inconsistent from agent to agent and from factor to factor, as changes in personnel brought new and different priorities, introduced new methods of problem solving and dispute resolution, and upset established local relationships. Each new agent exercised his freedom to pursue personal objectives, and each new agent built or destroyed relationships with local leaders and others. Local agents' varied tenure and experience contributed to, or detracted from, the stabilizing forces of institutional memory.

The impact of personal influences on administration meant that local dynamics changed when personnel changed. In the context of the Indian Office in the eighteenth and nineteenth centuries, turnover in personnel could ruin institutional memory. New factors and new local agents were sometimes completely unaware of the recent course of events in a particular place. This was a key problem with the Office's reliance on a clear mission, since dedication and allegiance to the service's objectives alone bestowed neither an awareness of particular field situations nor the ability to handle them and get along with people at the local level. Any change of personnel could cause a disruption, as relationships shifted, as local participants struggled to understand changes, and as new personnel were forced to adapt to what had gone before.

The historian Aloysius Plaisance argues that turnover in the position of factor contributed to administrative problems and to a general discontinuity in administration, and he estimates that factors needed two to three years to learn the local market.[17] Factor John Treat provides an example. Treat wrote, early in his tenure, that he believed the prices being charged at Arkansas to be among the highest of the factories; two months later, he wrote that he was mistaken. This kind of learning process was typical of the era's field administration, and it suggests not only a learning curve for

[17] Aloysius Frederick Plaisance, "The United States Government Factory System, 1796–1822," unpublished Ph.D. dissertation, St. Louis University (1954).

new employees but also the extent to which they were dependent on (and susceptible to) the information provided to them by others in the field.[18]

Turnover in an evolving administrative environment could promise important *benefits* for the larger mission, however. Dynamics in Indian affairs encouraged short-term and ad hoc decision making in the field, and turnover could provide a rationale (or even a motor) for shifts in policy direction, like a harsher or softer tone in diplomatic relations. Turnover provided a rationale for "mistakes," like willfully misinterpreting boundary lines or informal agreements in favor of the United States, "errors" or "misunderstandings" that furthered the government's expansionist goals.[19] Turnover, of course, could bring new approaches to old problems; sometimes institutional memory is an obstacle.

The critical element in the Indian service's effectiveness, the discretion to make quick decisions in the short term, was intimately connected to both turnover and short tenure in the field, and to the expectation that the factory system – then removal, then reservations, then assimilation – would solve "the Indian problem." Factors rarely seem to have considered local decisions in light of possible long-term ramifications, aside from a commitment to the purposes behind the factory and treaty systems. Part of this relates to the way the mission was constructed and understood. Indian policy in general has always tended to promote the impression that policy will solve "the Indian problem," and do so rather quickly. Field officers were to keep the peace and manage expansion, but their focus was the geographical and temporal *now*. The volatility of Indian affairs made field service as much a process of putting out fires and defusing tensions as an endeavor with long-term goals. Part of this results from the reactive nature of Indian affairs administration, which rewards efforts to respond to events and resolve issues quickly, before they can grow into more serious issues. It is difficult to fault field agents for their short-term views, yet these views created a mélange of local, ad hoc decisions in response to immediate problems, sometimes with little attention to future implications. Personnel changes and personalized administration helped factors achieve the broader mission of the factory system but resulted in myriad paths being blazed in pursuit of general goals.

Inconsistent Administration Within Policy Eras

The other important ramification of the key role of the individual operator in Indian affairs was that administrative techniques and decisions differed by place, a result of individual efforts and priorities as well as of the diversity in

[18] Treat to Davy, August 25, 1805, Treat to Saul, October 11, 1805, *Arkansas Factory, Letters Sent and Received*.

[19] See, e.g., Cynthia Cumfer, "Local Origins of National Indian Policy: Cherokee and Tennessean Ideas About Sovereignty and Nationhood, 1790–1811," *Journal of the Early Republic* 23 (Spring 2003), 30–1.

conditions, issues, and people that characterized areas of the field service's responsibilities. Personalized administration, the accumulation of decisions and histories, and the vast differences in circumstances and populations even east of the Mississippi created unique dynamics and outcomes from place to place. Beneath the Indian service's commitment to overarching and well-stated objectives, consistency in detail did not exist. Agents and factors might agree on the objectives, and be remarkably successful in achieving those objectives – but how they did so varied considerably across the continent.[20]

Two issues from the earliest years of Indian policy, alcohol and credit, illustrate how discretion and personalized administration of Indian service rules created inconsistencies across the factory system. Point 16 of the factors' instructions offered ambiguous guidelines regarding the supply of rum to Indians. Despite the volatility rum brought to the frontier, Price's instructions gave him wide discretion in supplying rum and suggested only a few limits which can hardly be called orders:

> It would have been extremely desirable to carry on this trade without the use of rum, but from an apprehension that the habits of the Indians in this respect could not be controlled, that article may be provided. Still, however, you are to use your endeavors by friendly advice to the Indians to persuade them to let it alone, taking care not to excite their disgust. But, if you see that rum must be sold to them, let it be in such small quantities as may guard them against drunkenness during their continuances at the post, for which you will give them this reason: "That while trading you desire them to remain sober that they may know what they do and be satisfied that the trade is perfectly fair and honest." When they are ready to depart such quantities as they may desire to carry with them and your stock will allow for sale to them may be delivered.

Factors could invoke these instructions to issue – or to refuse to issue – alcohol; the instructions also allowed alcohol to be issued to some and not to others, at the factor's discretion. Alcohol restrictions and enforcement of other related rules varied from place to place as a result of local dynamics, local personalities, and the level of tension or unrest at any given time. It would have been impossible to standardize the issuing of alcohol or to predict, in any area surrounding any factory, how the policy would be carried out at any given time.[21]

[20] See, e.g., Treat to Davy, August 25, 1805, Treat to Saul, October 11, 1805, Shee to Treat, October 6, 1806, Treat to Shee, January 8, 1807, *Arkansas Factory, Letters Sent and Received*. Irvine was told to leave some things to the discretion of field agents, especially decisions as locally particular as pricing: "something, however, must be left to the discretion of the Agents, they must govern themselves by circumstances, and by the prices current in the country where they may be stationed." Secretary of War to Irvine, July 31, 1802, *War Department, Letters Sent*.

[21] See Babcock, "Major Lawrence Taliaferro," 364–5; Peter C. Mancall, "Men, Women, and Alcohol in Indian Villages in the Great Lakes Region in the Early Republic," *Journal of the Early Republic* 15 (Autumn 1995); Irwin to McKenney, March 10, 1817, in Draper,

Issuing credit to Indians or to white traders proved an even thornier problem for factors. A consensus surrounded the idea that issuing alcohol complicated matters and invited conflict and confusion, even if it could grease the wheels of land cessions and other negotiations. No consensus surrounded the question of whether to allow purchases on credit. The tradition of the hunting economy around the factories called for advances to be made to Indians in the form of weapons, ammunition, and supplies to be used in the hunt. Afterwards, these advances would be paid back out of skins or other fruits of the hunt. The use of credit in Indian relations had long been practiced by European powers, and many Indians had become accustomed to it.

The practice had some risks, though. Some Indians considered goods issued as credit to be presents, rather than loans. In other cases, tribes returning from a hunt met rival traders, who purchased the Indians' goods without regard for the Indians' prior commitments to merchants or to a factor who had extended credit to pay for the hunt in the first place.[22] Merchants who had advanced the credit then felt abused, and the credit system encouraged conflicts between Indians and whites, and between whites and whites, by providing frequent chances for parties to feel abused. Importantly, some American officials and field personnel also believed that credit was antithetical to the values of prudence and thrift that they were working to instill in the Indian population. They also worried that credit perpetuated hunting, in direct opposition to government efforts to establish farming among the Indians as a way of ameliorating the effects of dwindling hunting areas while simultaneously nurturing the republican benefits of settled agricultural communities.[23]

Instructions and factors' experiences with the credit issue highlight the problem of trying to standardize the factors' administrative decisions in

Collections, 270–1; Peake, *History*, 222–4; Owsley, "Benjamin Hawkins," 10; Morris, "Traders and Factories," 47–8; Royal B. Way, "The United States Factory System for Trading with the Indians, 1796–1822," *Mississippi Valley Historical Review* 6 (1919), 228–9.

22 Katherine Coman, "Government Factories: An Attempt to Control Competition in the Fur Trade," *Papers and Proceedings of the American Economic Association* 1 (April 1911), 372.

23 For discussion of the credit issue, see Joseph Patrick Key, "Indians and Ecological Conflict in Territorial Arkansas," *The Arkansas Historical Quarterly* 59 (Summer 2000), 129ff.; Peake, *History*, ch. 7, 218–30; George D. Harmon, "Benjamin Hawkins and the Federal Factory System," *The North Carolina Historical Review* 9 (January–October 1932), 149–50; McKenney to Irwin, May 28, 1817, in Draper, *Collections*, 272; George S. Gaines, "Notes on the Early Days of South Alabama," reprinted in *The Alabama Historical Quarterly* 26 (Fall/Winter 1964), 198; Coman, "Government Factories," 372; Plaisance, "Chickasaw Bluffs Factory," 52ff. Plaisance's article also shows the changes in priorities that arose as different factors, with different attitudes about credit, came and went. See 53.

pursuit of the factory system's mission. Point 6 of the factors' instructions addressed the credit issue, with an astute awareness of its significance.

> 6. One of the greatest difficulties to be apprehended is the demand for goods on credit, either by the Indians themselves, or the Indian traders residing among them. But such credits are wholly inadvisable, and selling to the traders with or without credit would be subversive of the main principle, for such traders would probably sell at their usual high prices, while the true object of the U.S. is to supply the Indians at moderate prices; and with these benevolent views of the U.S. you will on all occasions endeavor to make the Indians acquainted. If difficulties should occur in carrying on the trade [because of ?] refusal of credit to the Indian traders, you will make report thereof to the Department of War stating facts, with your opinion thereon and your ideas of the best mode of furnishing supplies to the Indians to effect the salutary objects indicated in these instructions.

The instructions clearly establish the government factories in opposition to the activities of private traders, and suggest that the usual behavior of those traders is suspect. The passage begins to lay the groundwork for not trading with private traders at all, a restriction that would later hamstring the factories economically and generate much opposition. More important, Point 6 makes it clear that the object of supplying the Indians – behind which is the goal of maintaining the peace – is superior to efficient trading operations.

In a strict business sense, offering credit was a standard and accepted practice. On the other hand, encouraging good neighbors by establishing prudence, thrift, and farming culture among the Indians pushed factors to *restrict* credit. Refusing credit, though, could threaten the factory system's objective of maintaining peaceful relations with tribes accustomed to European use of presents and credit: issuing credit caused far less friction in those areas than restricting it. Recognizing the vagaries of specific situations, the War Department indicates in Point 6 that the no-credit policy may be changed if deemed necessary and if a change would further the system's broader ends. This is a strong statement from the home office regarding the factors' practices, but application of the principle would be repeatedly bent and shaped by factors – with approval from headquarters – as time wore on.

Changes and instability in these rules characterized the Trade Office's efforts to come to terms with its mandate, but it is important to note that the management level saw the credit issue as important enough that factors were *not* initially given discretion to issue credit even if they encountered resistance and felt that such a practice would be beneficial: factors had to secure permission first. It was impossible, of course, for officers at the capital to oversee private transactions in the field. In practice, and despite the instructions, factors sought advice from experienced hands in the Indian service and tended to act on their own discretion in determining if, when, and to what extent credit would be offered. Several times the central office attempted to set standards on the issuance of credit, but these attempts were often overruled in the field. The central office eventually accepted a standard of local discretion, arguing that credit be used only in special cases and with reputable individuals, but leaving all effective decisionmaking authority in the hands of local factors and agents.

By eventually allowing factors to rely on their own discretion in issuing credit, the War Department pursued the larger goals of the factory system. At the same time, the leadership continued to encourage its field administrators to make judgments based on local circumstances. Some factors issued credit, some did not, and some changed their minds depending on circumstances.[24]

Alcohol and credit, and other aspects of the factory system like pricing, stock, dispute resolution, and so on, depended heavily on circumstances, personalities, relationships, and the judgments and decisions made by local factors. While the factors worked diligently to pursue the broad objectives of national policy, their particular decisions displayed little consistency from person to person or from place to place. Factors complained that the rules were too strict and constraining, and they complained that the rules were too vague and provided too little guidance. Factors relied on their orders, and at other times relied on their judgment. Discretionary actions were overwhelmingly sanctioned by their superiors, creating an organizational culture that valued – and relied upon – individual judgment and decision making.

A Complex and Vulnerable Endeavor

Inconsistency is not necessarily bad for administration. It is not necessarily an indication of failure or incoherence. The very nature of Indian affairs administration demands inconsistency: it is an administrative environment that relies heavily on local discretion and expertise, informed by particular circumstances and unique histories among hundreds of diverse communities. The inconsistency of localized decision making is the single most important dynamic in the Indian service's effectiveness in pursuing general goals.

Yet that inconsistency has also helped to create a reputation around Indian affairs that focuses on corruption and failure, and that facilely regards inconsistency as evidence of systemic maladministration. Although many charges of corruption and maladministration in Indian affairs over the years have certainly been true,[25] it is also true that the complicated political relationships involved in Indian affairs create opportunities and incentives

[24] See, e.g., Key, "Indians and Ecological Conflict," 130; Cumfer, "Local Origins," 34–5. Treat to Dearborn, April 1, 1807, *Arkansas Factory, Letters Sent and Received*; Price to Secretary of War, November 25, 1798, Price to Barnard, October 29, 1798, Price to Hawkins, October 15, 1798, *Creek Factory, Letters Sent*.

[25] Owens writes that bribery had become a "virtual art form" in Harrison's treaty negotiations. His discussion offers an extensive catalog of factory-era negotiating tactics. Robert M.

for interested parties to discredit Indian policy and administration by targeting the Indian service. Particularly in cases where interested parties make their case to an uninformed or misinformed Congress and general public – people who often have little direct experience in Indian affairs – it is relatively easy to demonize or discredit Indian policy and its administrators in order to effect policy change or achieve specific goals. Field agents and the Indian Office in general have long been vulnerable, caught among competing – and always changing – interests. These interests have habitually seized upon administrative inconsistencies to discredit Indian policy and administration, even when those inconsistencies have been necessary parts of effective local administration. Capitalizing upon stereotypes that suggest that Indians are all the same, that Indian affairs administration should be simple, and that Indian policy should be able to "solve" the "Indian problem" quickly and easily, certain interests have consciously or out of ignorance condemned the Indian service by criticizing the nuance that lies at the heart of that service's historical effectiveness.

Interests

A complex variety of interests operated in Indian affairs in the factory system era. Federal control grew out of the power and importance of Indian nations and the risks of war, as well as the need for federal coordination of expansion and Indian policy. Concerns for national interest coexisted with concerns for human rights and the ideals of U.S. society, which included doing what was considered best for Indians and protecting them from whites. Leaders and others of the era recognized that whites caused most of the problems with Indians – from trespassing on Indian lands to harassing and crowding Indian populations. Indian policy typically promised quick resolution of "the Indian problem" to the benefit of these interests, encouraging them to see themselves as the clients and beneficiaries of Indian policy, even though many of their interests conflicted.[26]

The federal government had two motivations for controlling Indian affairs: to manage and promote expansion, and to protect Indians from being defrauded or destroyed by whites. The first made the federal government the ally of development interests seeking to take over Indian territory and integrate territory and people into the U.S. system. The second set the government up as the protector of Indians, with a presumption that

Owens, "Jeffersonian Benevolence on the Ground: The Indian Land Cession Treaties of William Henry Harrison," *Journal of the Early Republic* 22 (Fall 2002), 408, 410, 423ff., 431ff.

[26] Bradley writes that in the House of Representatives Claiborne, among others, intentionally kept the goals of the Trade and Intercourse Acts vague so that reauthorizations would appeal to different interests: the East could see federal aid and control as humanitarian, and the West could interpret the efforts as means to securing Indian lands. Jared W. Bradley, "William C. C. Claiborne, the Old Southwest and the Development of American Indian Policy," *Tennessee Historical Quarterly* 33 (Fall 1974), 275.

development interests would seek to defraud and exploit Indians. Federal agents, from the beginning, were tasked with managing affairs for the benefit of development interests while simultaneously policing those affairs to the benefit of Indians and to the *detriment* of development interests.[27] Neither Congress, nor the president, nor the Indian service itself have ever reconciled the divided loyalties.

The Indian Office received pressure from numerous directions in the factory system era. Non-Indian interests like Astor's American Fur Company, white settlers and land speculators, land companies like the Ohio Company, and suppliers of the factories and of the military – and later mining, railroad, water, and other interests – saw themselves as clients of an Indian Office and War Department dedicated to managing expansion for the benefit of U.S. social and economic development. Local and national interests like these worked to reap benefits from the factory system, from the location of forts and supply posts, and from allocation of monetary and other resources to particular areas. The military presence in Ohio and other regions, for example, provided important markets for produce, animals, and services. As the factory and treaty systems were originally, and explicitly, intended to pacify the frontier and make it safe and secure for economic development, all of these interests had good reason to see the Indian Office as working directly for their benefit. For the 1819 Treaty of Saginaw, for example, Lewis Cass hired a trader to build a council house, and also arranged loans with bankers in Detroit to pay Saginaw Chippewa the annuities that the United States had failed to render earlier. Both were necessary prerequisites for a successful negotiation. As to the loan, many of the directors of the Bank of Detroit were happy to help because they also acted as suppliers of Indian trade goods to the government.[28]

Indian interests also viewed themselves as clients of the Indian Office's activities. The Office encouraged tribes to see themselves as clients of the Indian Office by negotiating treaties on a nation-to-nation basis, recognizing political sovereignty, providing for law enforcement and punishment of whites, removing trespassers, and so on. Federal agents encouraged tribes to view treaties and protections as though they were meant to serve tribal interests, working diligently to create an atmosphere of mutual gain to manage the slow, administrative takeover of vast tracts of land. In some cases, the encouragement was justified: federal treaties and agreements were created to serve and protect Indian interests, and the Indian office and other federal personnel were the appropriate location for discussion of and attention to tribal interests. Despite much evidence to the contrary, and granting that

[27] See Laurence F. Schmeckebier, *The Office of Indian Affairs: Its History, Activities and Organization* (Baltimore: The Johns Hopkins Press, 1927), 9ff.

[28] Charles E. Cleland, *Rites of Conquest: The History and Culture of Michigan's Native Americans* (Ann Arbor: University of Michigan Press, 1992), 212.

there was much dissension among Indian populations about the worth and trustworthiness of U.S. efforts, Indian nations often viewed Indian service personnel and other federal agents as their closest, most effective, and most reliable connection to the white society on *their* borders. The fact that many of the treaties were short-term mechanisms in service of U.S. goals does not negate the fact that the Indian service encouraged tribes to see themselves as clients of the Indian Office.

Sparked by rhetoric from leaders including Washington, Jefferson, and Harrison, and from people at the Indian Office, Indian individuals also came to see themselves as clients of an Indian service dedicated to fair and just treatment and administration, with the goal of educating and civilizing individuals as a step toward Indians' eventual assimilation into white society. Eastern support of the system was based on the feeling that the Indians needed the protective arm of the government, a paternalistic view that characterized Indian affairs from its earliest days. Most Eastern newspapers supported the factories, for example, while most frontier papers called for an end to the system.[29] Indian individuals often benefited personally from treaties and other dealings with the Indian Office and the factories, whether through trade relationships or through individualized benefits like payments, land, and other goods stipulated in treaties or in side agreements.

Like interest groups today, organized interests that saw themselves as clients of the Indian affairs bureaucracy used all available means to press their demands on federal agents. Many of the development interests – both the organized interests as well as small farmers and independent settlers – worked through the executive to influence policy and administration, and of course they worked through territorial and state governments as well. Many of the more militant factions on the frontier in the nineteenth century were small farmers, independent traders, and squatters – largely unorganized interests demanding a quick end to the Indian problem by force. Testimonials sent through the executive gave voice to frontier interests. Humanitarian interests, believing themselves advocates for the interests of Indian individuals, worked through the executive branch primarily but were also open to court strategies. Tribes worked through the field service, but also lobbied presidents and congressional leaders, and used the courts to press their claims. All of these interests viewed themselves as the rightful beneficiaries of U.S. Indian policy, and worked hard to get the results that they believed they deserved.

The problem, of course, was that the demands and expectations of these groups could not all be satisfied. Despite efforts to manage such a complex constellation of interests, the combination of high expectations, divided loyalties and competing clients, and the reliance on localized and personalized administrative decision-making placed factors and field agents in perilous

[29] Plaisance, "Factory System," 577; Coman, "Government Factories," 382.

positions. Temptation to abuse authority sprouted everywhere, and many fell victim to opportunities created by discretionary authority and sporadic oversight. This is the fact of Indian affairs administration that generally receives the most attention, and many of the worst accusations against Indian service personnel have good foundations.

At the same time, however, it is important to recognize the way in which field agents were at the mercy of the interests competing for influence in Indian affairs. It has always been easy for interests involved in Indian affairs to make credible *charges* of maladministration and abuse to serve particular political ends or objectives, regardless of facts and evidence. Indian service personnel were often caught in the middle of all these interests. Charges of favoritism and criticism of factors' decisions were common. Local interests often collaborated against the factories: one factor wrote, "A member of the carters here went so far as to enter into a contract or oath not to hawl [*sic*] for the public but at their own price." "Our trade interferes with the contractors pedling [*sic*] schemes," another wrote, "and creates prejudices against us and an aversion to the success of the public institution here[.]"[30] Humanitarian interests' success in gaining federal support for civilization and other initiatives put the Indian Office in direct confrontation with the military in the field. Military officers were charged with supporting the factory system and its civilian personnel – a mission the military neither wanted nor supported. In turn, the Indian Office became a target for representatives and other officials desirous of a more muscular stance on the frontier or more direct action against Indians; at the same time, the Indian Office ran into pressure in trying to enforce licensing and other requirements.[31]

Charges against the Indian field service accumulated over time, as situations and relationships and the goals of interested parties shifted and evolved. Eventually, the charges affected the entire Indian service. Whether or not they were supported by extensive evidence, multiple and frequent charges

[30] Price to Habersham, 5 or 6/1798, *Creek Factory, Letters Sent*. See also Price to Secretary at War, April 9, 1796, and Hawkins to Price, March 9, 1797, *Creek Factory, Correspondence*: "There has been a vile attempt to prevail on the Indians to thwart the endeavours of the government"; Price to Hawkins, October 15, 1798, Price to Secretary at War, May 26, 1798, *Creek Factory, Letters Sent*.

[31] On such charges, some representative examples are included in Owens, "Jeffersonian Benevolence," 416 n23, 421, 421 n37, 424; Joseph T. Glatthaar and James Kirby Martin, *Forgotten Allies: The Oneida Indians and the American Revolution* (New York: Hill and Wang, 1996), 83; John K. Mahon, *History of the Second Seminole War, 1835–1842* (Gainesville: University of Florida Press, 1992), 70, 82ff.; Babcock, "Major Lawrence Taliaferro," 366; Joyce Purser, "The Administration of Indian Affairs in Louisiana, 1803–1820," *Louisiana History* 5 (Fall 1964), 412–14; Irwin to McKenney, n.d. [1819], in Draper, *Collections*, 277–8; Plaisance, "Arkansas Factory," 188; Plaisance, "Chickasaw Bluffs Factory," 49–50; Guthrie and Gerald, "Upper Missouri Agency," 51. Other officials operated in a similar political milieu: see, e.g., Ronald E. Shaw, *Canals for a Nation: The Canal Era in the United States, 1790–1860* (Lexington: The University Press of Kentucky, 1993), 82.

suggested to contemporaries that the Indian Office suffered from widespread and systemic corruption, abuse, and incompetence. Often, charges were brought to the national and agency-wide level by well-intentioned reformers dissatisfied with the agency's performance, particularly as that performance addressed (or failed to address) the concerns of humanitarians and the interests of individual Indians. These groups were skilled at publicizing abuses to a national audience, and the abuses were easily understood, newsworthy, and attracted attention from credible organizations. The critical point is that evaluating the charges has not always been easy; *making* the charges – in an administrative environment that was distant, obscure, and reliant upon personal decision making and discretion – has always been easy. And effective.

The End of the Factory System

The factory system's effectiveness, the effects of national expansion, and the politics of Indian affairs combined to bring the system to an end in the 1820s. By then, the system had achieved its mission in helping to pacify and order affairs on the early frontier.

The factory system was not designed to last forever, and a number of developments between 1795 and 1822 contributed to the end of the system. Southern factories stagnated after their initial successes, due to the vagaries of the trade, weather, communications, and limited funding of the system. Foreign wars and the embargo disrupted the international trading scene. Competition from large trading houses threatened the northern factories, whereas the southern factories were forbidden to trade deerskins internationally. This restriction was frequently cited in reports of the time as having a significant effect on the Southern factories' ability to move their goods, since much of the material traded by Indians were deerskins. The issuing of credit created large debts owed to individual factories.[32] Finally, early and southern factories stagnated when the action moved beyond them to the West; increased settlement also provided alternatives for both Indian and white traders. The Detroit factory, for example, was established in a high trade area with great competition; three years after its inception, Secretary Dearborn was already planning its removal.

The factories were not designed to be money makers. After several administrative reorganizations, though, and particularly after the War of 1812 had solidified U.S. control over Western regions and limited political and economic competition from European powers, observers increasingly evaluated the system as an economic endeavor. The 1806 administrative reorganization established the civilian side as its own entity, formally separated from the military even though it remained in the War Department. The split hurt the Indian Office by divorcing it from the interests supporting the military and its activities – interests which would enjoy a long run of success

[32] Plaisance, "Factory System," ch. IV.

through American history generating funds for programs supporting expansion and national defense. Isolating the factories politically and shifting the basis for their evaluation – even as the interests of some of the factory's biggest allies changed – made the system vulnerable to charges that they were being mismanaged.

Amid changes in the need for the factories and among the interests surrounding the factories' activities, the Office's leadership style also shifted. In the early years of the factory system and the early decades of the treaty system, leaders at the Office of Indian Affairs built careful alliances with influential forces in an effort to manage this environment. A variety of organized interests benefited from the activities of treaty commissioners, Indian agents, and factory system administrators, and these interests offered their support in a variety of ways in the nation's capital and in the field. The factory system, for example, enjoyed the support of presidents, the War Department, trading companies, and even many settlers on the frontier. John Mason's administration of the Office of Indian Trade in the opening years of the nineteenth century was professional and nonpartisan, yet Mason understood the need for political support among those involved in the trade. Mason's administration allowed factors and suppliers a good deal of discretion and autonomy; he opened new factories, gained authority to appoint factors and oversee aspects of the trade, and maintained good relations with suppliers, the Connecticut Land Company, and other major players. John Astor did business with the factories as early as 1808, and had consistent contact with the Superintendent's office regarding sales of skins.[33] Mason used suppliers in the West, expanding the base of people and companies who had a vested interest in maintaining the factories. At the same time, Mason deferred political decisions to the War Department, made no major recommendations on policy, and seemed generally content to receive his reauthorizations and slowly growing allocations of funds. The focus on the field service's good relations with Indians, and the ideas about the factory system's benefits for Indians, helped dampen opposition among those groups and even generated support. As long as these interests were relatively content, the factory system faced no formidable opposition and enjoyed considerable and widespread support.[34]

Mason's successor, Thomas L. McKenney, was a partisan activist who provoked Congress and his immediate executive branch superiors to intercede in the Indian Office's operations. McKenney took over the Office in 1816 and was in charge until the end of the system in 1822. Eight months

33 See McKenney to Astor, April 29, 1816, cited in Plaisance, "Factory System," 527.

34 Peake notes that Mason made various requests of the Secretary of War and Congress, which were usually granted, but her list does not include any major policy initiatives. See Peake, *History*, 187–8. On Mason's skills, see also Peake, *History*, 54, ch. 6; Coman, "Government Factories," 382–4.

into his tenure, McKenney was already advocating extensive enlargement of the factory system, including creation of a major government trading company and creation of a new trading center at St. Louis – which would compete with Astor's American Fur Company, threaten trading interests in and around St. Louis, and raise the ire of influential players like Thomas Hart Benton.[35] McKenney's endeavors led to a crackdown by Congress, most notably a refusal to allow the opening of new factories and a new requirement that the Senate approve appointments in the system.[36] Private sector entities began to criticize the system, highlighted by direct attacks from Astor's operation. Governor Ninian Edwards of Illinois reversed his earlier support and came out against the system. McKenney's practice of purchasing only in the DC area alienated Western suppliers, and ultimately they, too, attacked a system that seemed to have betrayed them.[37] Edwards had already complained of McKenney's purchasing almost exclusively at Georgetown, in contrast to Mason's careful nurturing of suppliers in Kentucky and westward. McKenney also strongly advocated restraints on private traders, a change from Mason's peaceful coexistence with other trading interests.[38]

In short, McKenney alienated the Office's allies, provoked opposition within and without the government, and failed to see that the circumstances that gave birth and purpose to the factory system were changing. The independent traders were eliminated, as Astor and a few other companies – with the help of government licensing and bonding regulations – systematically developed the mechanisms of the fur trade. The nascent trading companies nurtured by the early factory system had evolved into powerful, global firms that no longer tolerated competition from government trading houses. The diplomatic role of the factories mattered less as Indians were pacified by treaty, conflict, and settlement in New York, the Old Northwest, and the Southern states. Those states no longer needed the factories to quiet complicated and potentially explosive Indian affairs, as Indians were increasingly surrounded by whites, increasingly dependent upon government policies, and increasingly pressured to remove westward. Land companies,

35 Plaisance, "Factory System," 548ff.; McKenney to Thomas, January 3, 1817, quoted in Plaisance, "Factory System," 548–9.

36 This effort illustrates the limits of congressional oversight. Barak Owens was appointed as an assistant factor in 1818, after Congress had moved to require Senate approval of such appointments but while the Senate was in recess. The Senate subsequently rejected his appointment, but McKenney appointed Owens as "chief clerk" of the factory, a position that did not require Senate approval. McKenney thus circumvented the Senate's clear intent and action. See Plaisance, "Chickasaw Bluffs Factory," 52–3.

37 McKenney to Bronaugh, April 22, 1816, McKenney to Hall, April 23, 1816, *Office of Indian Trade, Letters Sent, Roll 4, M16.*

38 Mason had considered licenses to the large Morgan-Bright company and dealt well with the Panton-Leslie company, for example. Plaisance, "Factory System," 561.

speculators, agricultural interests – all now resented the factories and the federal presence. Territories turned into states, hunting grounds into pastures, paths into roads, and eastern Indian populations into annoyances rather than threats. As humanitarian interests effectively publicized the most heinous charges against the field service, other interests seized the opportunity to condemn the agency and Indian policies that failed to meet high expectations. The supporters of the factory system had become its opponents. Interests that had supported the factories abandoned the agency to its critics, either out of dissatisfaction or out of satisfaction and success. And interests new to Indian affairs or newly motivated capitalized on public and governmental dissatisfaction with the Indian Office's performance to argue for new policies in the East and the West.

Lobbying and pressure directed by John Jacob Astor played a critical role in ending the factories. Astor's American Fur Company and other major trading companies had benefited from federal regulations and licensing requirements, and by 1816 and through the end of the factory system in 1822 they increased pressure on the government to end the system and leave the trade to private interests. These interests worked hard to discredit the Indian service's early activities, in a pattern that has recurred throughout the history of U.S. Indian policy.

Astor undertook an extended lobbying campaign against the system. Ramsey Crooks, the manager of Astor's American Fur Company, expressed hostility toward the factories as early as 1813. Crooks's opposition suggested that he believed the Indians gained little benefit from the government trading houses, and those who did benefit were the first to cause conflict with "American settlements."[39] By 1815, the opposition effort was beginning to show progress. Ninian Edwards published a detailed critique of the system, writing that government agents lacked a personal interest in the trade and were therefore inefficient and ineffective. The placement of the factories was also ineffective, he argued, demonstrated by the fact that factors took only a small percentage of the furs in any given area. Finally, Edwards wrote, the prohibition against issuing credit handicapped the system, preventing it from outfitting its core clients, hunting parties. Edwards recommended that the government construct a single factory at St. Louis to deal with traders (not Indians).

Crooks spearheaded the lobbying effort against the factories in Washington from 1818 until 1822, reporting to Astor on the activities of relevant congressional committees and of the Office of Indian Trade. Crooks solicited comments from the Company's field agents regarding the activities

[39] Crooks to Astor, December 1, 1813, in Plaisance, "Factory System," 565.

of the factors,[40] and he used the information to nurture support in Congress. Crooks lobbied for four years, preparing groundwork and enlisting the aid of a few friendly representatives. Thomas Hart Benton, newly elected senator from Missouri and tied to the American Fur Company and to his own trading interests in and around St. Louis, became a driving force against the factories. Crooks and Russell Farnham, an American Fur Company field agent with extensive dealings in and around the factory system in the West, took up lodgings in Benton's Washington hotel.[41]

Benton cast congressional debate of the factory system's worth in terms of general policy requirements, the economic efficiency of the factories, and the threat the system posed to Western interests. In the newspaper he edited, Benton wrote that the factory system had failed to civilize or convert the Indians, that it had failed to fill "the national storehouse... with rich and precious furs," and that it could not be expanded short of a large infusion of millions of dollars.[42] His paper also criticized the centering of the system's operations in Georgetown, to the exclusion of the Western posts: "The commerce of St. Louis is therefore transferred to Washington City, and the system which drains every dollar out of the west, cannot even spare the skins which served the ancient inhabitants of this country in place of money." Benton's arguments were clever in that they emphasized the losses to the West from the factory's Eastern roots, yet at the same time Benton was able to argue to those in the trade that an expansion of the system westward posed a threat to Western trading companies and interests like his own.

Indian agents were brought in to testify against the factories. These arguments emphasized the uselessness of the factories, and the minimal inconvenience that would result from their abolition. Benjamin O'Fallon struck at the Prairie du Chien factory, arguing that contrary to its purpose, the factor's habit of trading with all comers cast the United States "in the light of a common trader," undercutting the image of strength and superiority that the nation was trying to present to the Indians.[43] Importantly, Crooks himself testified about the poor quality of the goods at the factories and the factories' stores of goods inappropriate to the Indian trade. Crooks noted that the trade had declined; this, coupled with the northwest Indians' support of the British in the War of 1812, indicated that the factories had failed to win the Indians over to the United States. Crooks testified: "The factories have now degenerated into mere places of trade, to which all colors, descriptions,

40 Plaisance, "Factory System," 567.

41 Plaisance, "Factory System," 571–2. See also Peake, *History*, chs. 12–13; Wesley, "Government Factory System," 503ff.; Coman, "Government Factories," 374ff.; Way, "United States Factory System," 230ff.; Quaife, "Experiment," 286ff.; Chambers, "Creek Indian Factory," 40ff. describes the effect of the system's closure on the Creek factory.

42 Quoted in Plaisance, "Factory System," 581–2.

43 Plaisance, "Factory System," 574.

and denominations of people resort for barter; and bear much more striking resemblance to common country stores, than to the public establishments of a benevolent Government."[44] Many of these charges were exaggerated misrepresentations of the factories' goals and effects – Andrew Isenberg calls the Crooks-Astor effort a "disinformation campaign"[45] – but the lobbying had an effect.

The local peculiarities of the Indian trade – subtle attention to which had helped make the factories successful – offered fertile soil for undercutting the factories' efforts. Opponents of the system capitalized on seeming mismanagement and congressional members' unfamiliarity with the details of localized administration to batter the system's public reputation. Benton charged the system's leaders and the factors with maladministration, poor judgment, and inconsistency. In Congress, Benton drew attention to jew's-harps sent to a factory to demonstrate how factory goods were inappropriate to the Indian trade and the goals of civilizing Indians. By mocking the jew's-harps order, Benton implied that administration was neither effective nor appropriate to the system's purposes.[46]

The jew's-harps story captures an important aspect of Indian affairs administration. Benton's argument about the jew's-harps resonated with critics and outside observers of the government's system, but the charge was misplaced. The jew's-harps in question had been specially ordered by the local factor as an item that Indians near his factory enjoyed. What looked from a distance like a frivolous or even inept order from an incompetent local administrator was, in fact, an order driven by personal knowledge of local affairs and one carefully designed to further the objectives of the factory system. Benton played on the fact that the item in question seemed incongruous with the system's purposes, and on the ignorance of congressional members and the public as to the local peculiarities that characterized the administration of Indian affairs.[47] Benton used the factors' own expertise as a weapon against them, playing to the perceptions of a public that knew more of Indian stereotypes than it did of public administration in Indian affairs.

McKenney tried to defend the Indian Office's role in the factory system by identifying the agency with special expertise. He responded strongly to

44 Quoted in Plaisance, "Factory System," 576.

45 Andrew C. Isenberg, "The Market Revolution in the Borderlands: George Champlin Sibley in Missouri and New Mexico, 1808–1826," *Journal of the Early Republic* 21 (Fall 2001), 460.

46 See Prucha, *Great Father*, 130ff. Prucha argues that Benton understood that jew's-harps were a common item in the Indian trade, yet exploited the stories for political gain. The jew's-harps story is also a focus of Way, "United States Factory System," 230ff.; Quaife, "Experiment," 288.

47 Plaisance, "Factory System," 585ff.

criticism of his field agents, arguing that the factory system had innovated by sending agents to the Indians, minimizing the drawbacks of stationary stores far from the sites of a moving trade. McKenney also recognized that the opposition to the system was coming not from neutral sources, but from the factories' competitors in the trade; he reminded Congress that these private interests had an advantage economically because they did not suffer under the same restrictions regarding the trade of alcohol. McKenney's efforts to defend specific actions, though, failed to convince representatives in Congress of the professionalism of a distant field service.

McKenney defended his administrative decisions, arguing that they cut costs and increased efficiency. Although this may have been true, it advanced the growing perception of the factories as tools of narrow economic policy rather than parts of a broader diplomatic policy. And while McKenney understood the noneconomic goals of the factory system, his use of economic defenses for his actions encouraged debate to center on those aspects – aspects that ultimately could not support a system run for no gain, which struck directly at the interests of trading companies and powerful figures like Astor, and which had lost its political allies. In a very modern sense, McKenney failed to cultivate a constituency for the factories, and he alienated the interests that were growing opposed. A defense based on expertise or good management didn't stand a chance.

Much of the criticism of the field service was plausible because, by the 1820s, the factory system was an unusual and distant administrative enterprise, the details of which were unfamiliar to many representatives and to the public. The system was thus susceptible to anecdotes about mismanagement. Factors were easy marks because the nature of their jobs placed them in the middle of multiple interests, any one of whom could be counted upon to tell a tale of how the factory system had caused harm. Left without strong allies, the system was vulnerable to attack by Western interests with intimate knowledge of Indian affairs and a deep interest in policymaking and administration. At the same time, interests that had supported the factory system in an earlier era of crisis – those in the Eastern states – no longer wanted Indians to develop into peaceful, neighborly farmers. They wanted the Indians to leave. The factory system had completed its primary mission successfully, and as a result had become obsolete as the United States moved west. Together with the changing circumstances surrounding the factory system, the system was brought to an end and the factories dismantled in the early 1820s.[48]

[48] See, e.g., Herman J. Viola, *Thomas L. McKenney: Architect of America's Early Indian Policy: 1816–1830* (Chicago: Sage, 1974); Thomas L. McKenney, *Memoirs, Official and Personal* (Lincoln: University of Nebraska Press, 1973 [1846]).

Conclusion: The Illusion of Incompetent Administration

Complicated circumstances, shifting interests, and politics – not failures in administration – spelled the demise of the factory system in the early 1820s. Opposition to the factory system, and particularly the exploitation of misleading anecdotes like that of the jew's-harps, began a recurring trend in criticism of Indian policy and administration. The factory system, like later policies, succumbed to a combination of changing circumstances, shifting interests, and shifting objectives within sets of interests. Criticisms of existing relationships were driven by charges against the field service and also by recriminations about past policies. In the factory system case, what had been an important part of ordering settlement in eastern areas was no longer relevant by the 1820s. Charges of maladministration could be used to paint the Indian Office as inept, even as the changing demands of policy animated new and shifting interests. Southeastern states would no longer be content with trade and civilization efforts – they would start to push harder for Indian removal. Settlers in the South and other areas would come to condemn federal expenditures for Indians' development, especially in social policy initiatives, and would push for removal. Humanitarian interests would split, with some recommending the continuation of factory system aspects like education and agricultural training, and others arguing that these efforts had been failures or at least would be more effective if Indians were moved further away from troublesome white populations. Stable tribes would look to self-sufficiency and recognize that the factories, and more treaties and land cessions, were not in their best interests.

At the same time, new interests – including settlers and developers in the West, tribes in the West, an increasingly militant South, and a new generation of humanitarian reformers – would seek major changes in the Indian Office's policies. Andrew Jackson would also want to see some changes. Even though the factory system had been eliminated, Jackson recognized the political potential of the Indian Office and especially of its leader, both of which had survived Astor's attacks. The Indian Office continued to function and administer the treaty system and a variety of ongoing programs through the 1820s. Simultaneously, Thomas McKenney nurtured his reputation as the nation's leading expert on Indian affairs and its administration. Jackson knew that gaining McKenney's support for Indian removal policies – especially as Jackson and McKenney were known to be political opponents – could create a formidable alliance of self-interest, expertise, professionalism, and humanitarian credibility. Convincing McKenney to support Jackson's goal of removing the Eastern Indians would be a critical part of the next era in Indian affairs, as the Indian Office and its people adapted to a new mission.

McKenney lost the factory system, but only after years of opposition from private forces like John Astor's lobbyist Ramsey Crooks, and congressional opposition from men like Senator Thomas Hart Benton. Yet even as the factory system died, the Indian Office continued on its perch at the top of Indian policy and administration. McKenney and the Indian Office continued to be the experts in charge of Indian affairs between the factory system and Removal, and they would both prove essential to passage of the Indian Removal Act.

5

Big Government Jacksonians

Andrew Jackson helped expand the scope of national administrative authority by expanding the federal government's authority over American Indians and by extending U.S. authority and jurisdiction in land and trade issues westward. It is Jackson who utilized the power of the federal government as coordinator and executor of a policy to remove American Indians from their homes east of the Mississippi, a policy founded in part on his experiences as military officer, Indian treaty commissioner, and governor of Florida territory. It is Jackson who used the authority and influence of the presidency to design and secure passage of the removal bill, and then to execute the policy. It is Jackson who sought and won vast new authority for the executive branch over the West and the dispensation of lands and privilege there. It is Jackson and his progeny who extended the scope of the federal government, on the heels of the factory system and in tandem with western expeditions, expansion policy, and Indian affairs.

The Removal era may be the most infamous time in the development of U.S.–Indian relations. Andrew Jackson's leadership of the drive to remove Indians from their homes, by force if necessary, remains a bellwether example of inhumanity in two centuries of U.S. relations with American Indians. The removal of the Five Civilized Tribes from the Southeast was not the only example of this particular federal policy, nor was removal confined to the Jacksonian era. Removals of American Indians took place before Jackson's presidency, carried through the nineteenth century, and marred the twentieth. Removals took place across the continent. Some were "voluntary," in the sense that they were not accompanied or directed by armed troops; others, like the Cherokee Trail of Tears and the Navajo Long Walk, were forced population relocations.

Removal in the Jackson era stands as a prime example of an era too long misunderstood. Removal did not just happen: populations were identified, and often intentionally fragmented; treaties were signed, censuses taken, emigrants identified and enrolled, debts paid or otherwise reconciled, disputes adjudicated. Along the path of removal, migrating populations needed routes to take, food to eat, water to drink, transportation to use, ferries to cross rivers, and, in many cases, order to be maintained – often by force. In the West, removed Indians needed land, provisions, and support. Relations with western Indians – who saw Indians removed from the East as threats to their own traditional lands and lifeways – needed to be managed and sometimes formalized through complicated, sensitive negotiations. Conflicts arose and demanded responses. New treaties, new surveys, new procedures needed to be designed and installed. Removal was always at heart an administrative endeavor, often backed up by force and the administrative structures of the military.

Indian affairs engaged the most powerful political and economic forces of the 1830s: southern agriculture, powerful Indian tribes, slavery, and the battle between states' rights and national supremacy. Removal engendered deep and heartfelt debate over American ideals and the legacy of earlier U.S.–Indian relations, including the respect owed to treaties and to Indian communities. Removal as a policy area cannot be removed from the broader context, just as the larger context cannot be understood without including Indian affairs. The process of administering removal illustrates the complicated requirements of federal policies and the intrusive effect of national administrative structures in the 1830s. At the heart of it all lay the federal government's administrative abilities, which – as in the factory era – encompassed Indian affairs, expansion, and a broad variety of contexts directly affecting the lives of millions of people.

The Significance of Indian Affairs in the Jacksonian Era

American Indians and settlement on the United States' western boundaries lay at the heart of national culture and politics in the Removal era of the 1830s. By 1830, sixty thousand Cherokees, Choctaws, Creeks, and Chickasaws lived in a twenty-five-million-acre area encompassing western North Carolina, southern Tennessee, eastern Alabama, and the northern two-thirds of Mississippi.[1] Indian removal played out in the contexts of slavery, the Seminole Wars, the Texas rebellion, and a national dialogue over the nature and expansion of the republic. Indian affairs were central to critical issues of the Jacksonian era across the nation, and the questions surrounding removal and relocation involved every region of the United States.

Indians provided a source of imagery and cultural identity, and a foundation for interpreting social and political values.[2] Indians were critical to

[1] Mary E. Young, "Indian Removal and Land Allotment: The Civilized Tribes and Jacksonian Justice," *The American Historical Review* 64 (October 1958), 31.

[2] Richard Slotkin, *Regeneration Through Violence: The Mythology of the American Frontier, 1600–1860* (New York: HarperPerennial, 1996 [1973]).

nation-building legends like those involving Daniel Boone and Davy Crockett, and to works of art like the novels of James Fenimore Cooper. Richard Drinnon writes that "Cooper's hero needed the Indians as much as they needed him": they provided the core vehicle for trying to reconcile a national expansion built on injustice with the values of justice and equality that even then lay deep in the American ethos.[3] Literature and art driven by moral questions, by stereotypes, and by the action-adventure myths of frontier life lived in the mainstream of American cultural development before the Civil War. In an atmosphere that recognized the significance of "the Indian question" to national values and national expansion, American Indians and Indian affairs stood as important players in the central issues facing Jacksonian America and its future.

More than just a cultural touchstone, Indian affairs were a major component of the slavery debate dominating the politics of the antebellum South. Indian possession of fertile lands blocked southern expansion of farming, mining, and settlement.[4] The presence of Indians and Indian nations created security issues for southern slaveholders. The Seminoles and other tribes often refused to return fugitive slaves, and Indian country – legally and in practice outside the bounds of the United States – created jurisdictional issues that complicated the lives of slaveowners trying to recover escaped slaves. Plantation owners and other southern interests petitioned the executive branch and Congress for the recovery of fugitive slaves who resided in Indian country, but these efforts could not make the general problem disappear. As long as there was Indian country, the idea of escape would occupy the minds of slaveowners and enslaved blacks. And as long as there was Indian country within state-drawn borders, whites would fear Indian-black cooperation and alliance.[5]

Affairs involving the Seminole Indians in Florida provide just one example of this complexity. In Florida, Indians and blacks had been important players in international policy from the factory era, which included attempts to seize Florida by force in 1810–14 and Jackson's invasion in 1818.[6]

[3] Richard Drinnon, *Facing West: The Metaphysics of Indian Hating & Empire Building* (New York: Schocken, 1990), 162–3.

[4] Michael D. Green, *The Politics of Indian Removal: Creek Government and Society in Crisis* (Lincoln: University of Nebraska Press, 1985), ch. 3; John K. Mahon, *History of the Second Seminole War, 1835–1842* (Gainesville: University of Florida Press, 1992), ch. 4 and generally; Tim Alan Garrison, "Beyond *Worcester*: The Alabama Supreme Court and the Sovereignty of the Creek Nation," *Journal of the Early Republic* 19 (Fall 1999), 435–6, 449.

[5] Ronald N. Satz, *American Indian Policy in the Jacksonian Era* (Lincoln: University of Nebraska Press, 1975), 4. See also George Klos, "Blacks and the Seminole Removal Debate, 1821–1835," *Florida Historical Quarterly* 68 (July 1989).

[6] Klos, "Blacks"; Mahon, *Second Seminole War*.

Slaveholding by the Seminole Indians, and the presence of free blacks in Florida, complicated the issue of Seminole removal, as Seminoles adamantly refused removal to the West without assurances that they could keep their property, including their slaves.[7] The demand for land added to the international issues and the slavery context as engines driving concerns about Florida. In 1835 and 1836, the United States brought 23,530 citizens into national military service, with about 13,000 seeing time against 4,500–5,000 Indians in Florida. In 1837, the force in Florida was close to 5,000 regulars, 4,000 volunteers, and 78 northern Indians and 100 sailors.[8] More than 2,800 Seminoles were removed by the end of the second Seminole War in 1842. Population increases and the beginnings of organized land giveaways under the 1842 Armed Occupation Act – "the direct forebear of the Homestead Act of twenty years later," in the words of historian John Mahon – marked the later years of the war.[9]

Indian affairs in one area of the South could affect the entire region. During the Seminole wars and the efforts to remove them to the West, complications and worries spilled into other contexts. The United States employed Creeks against the Seminoles, with the Creeks hoping that they might benefit from the presence of the slaves, even as the Seminoles feared being deprived of their slaves if they relocated too close to the Creeks.[10] Disruptions and troubling rumors from the West hindered federal efforts to assure eastern Indians that they would be protected in safe Western homes after being removed. As Winfield Scott began pushing Cherokee removal in 1838, there were rumors that the Indians would resist and wage a guerrilla war against whites. This complicated efforts to remove the Cherokees covered by treaty provisions, and it complicated efforts by some seven hundred Quallatown Indians to remain. Although they had long been assured that they could stay, settlers in the area worried that these Indians would become the basis for resistance efforts, or turn violent toward the white settlers. Settlers outlined their fears in hyperbolic terms to the governor.[11]

[7] Klos, "Blacks"; Francis Paul Prucha, *The Great Father: The United States Government and the American Indians* (Lincoln: University of Nebraska Press, 1984), 230; Mahon, *Second Seminole War*, ch. 4 and generally; Grant Foreman, *Indian Removal: The Emigration of the Five Civilized Tribes of Indians* (Norman: University of Oklahoma Press, 1953), 366n7. On connections between abolitionists and Indian affairs, see Kerber, "The Abolitionist Perception"; George B. Ellenberg, "An Uncivil War of Words: Indian Removal in the Press, 1830," *Atlanta History* 33 (Spring 1989), 58.

[8] The force became all regulars in 1841. Mahon, *Second Seminole War*, 188, 31, 225, 292.

[9] Mahon, *Second Seminole War*, 271, 314; see also Laura Jensen, *Patriots, Settlers, and the Origins of American Social Policy* (Cambridge: Cambridge University Press, 2003), 181–6.

[10] Foreman, *Removal*, 317.

[11] John R. Finger, *The Eastern Band of Cherokees, 1819–1900* (Knoxville: University of Tennessee Press, 1984), 20.

Southerners recognized and exploited the national context of Indian affairs. During the removal debate in the U.S. Senate, John Forsyth of Georgia and Robert Adams of Mississippi invoked as precedent for their aims earlier Indian policy in New York and New England; Jackson made the same comparison in his First Annual Message, asserting that "There is no constitutional, conventional, or legal provision which allows them [Georgia and Alabama] less power over the Indians within their borders than is possessed by Maine or New York."[12] This argument was also used in the pro-removal press.[13]

Southern references to New York suggest another fact about the significance of Indian affairs: removal era Indian affairs were not confined to the South and southern interests. Construction of New York's canals, waterways, and railroads – foundations for the rise of the Empire State – relied on the process of dispossessing and removing New York's upstate Indians.[14] The Ogden Land Company, for example, worked with leaders in Buffalo to dispossess Seneca Indians and promote the expansion of the city onto the Seneca's lands.[15] Considerable interest surrounded the 1838 sale of the Seneca's reservation lands for more than $200,000, sparking, among other things, a 256-page opposition pamphlet issued by the Quakers.[16] Efforts to dispossess Indians and develop canals and settlement were a central part of state politics, and intimately related to Martin Van Buren's efforts to grow and expand the Democratic party, both in the state and nationally.[17]

Many of the interests and individuals involved in New York's Indian affairs pressed Congress for federal action to dispossess Indians in order to support western development in Ohio and Michigan.[18] Michigan had a stake in the development of New York canals and infrastructure, and so Michigan leaders like Lewis Cass were deeply involved in Indian affairs and the dispossession of eastern Indians. Coordination between the federal government and the states, and between development and farming interests,

[12] Robert V. Remini, *Andrew Jackson and his Indian Wars* (New York: Viking, 2001), 234–5; Jackson, "First Annual Message," reprinted in Francis Paul Prucha, ed., *Documents of United States Indian Policy*, 2nd ed. (Lincoln: University of Nebraska Press, 1990), 47; Laurence M. Hauptman, *Between Two Fires: American Indians in the Civil War* (New York: Free Press Paperbacks, 1996), 5.

[13] See Ellenberg, "An Uncivil War of Words," 53–4.

[14] Laurence M. Hauptman, *Conspiracy of Interests: Iroquois Dispossession and the Rise of New York State* (Syracuse: Syracuse University Press, 1999). See also Prucha, *Great Father*, 264–6.

[15] Francis Paul Prucha, *American Indian Treaties: The History of a Political Anomaly* (Berkeley: University of California Press, 1997), 202.

[16] Ibid., 203.

[17] Hauptman, *Conspiracy of Interests*, 189.

[18] R. Douglas Hurt, *The Ohio Frontier: Crucible of the Old Northwest, 1720–1830* (Bloomington: Indiana University Press, 1996), ch. 13; Hauptman, *Conspiracy of Interests*.

secured title from Indians, removed Indians, and carved canals and other infrastructure that nurtured the rapid and successful development of the Ohio Valley and Michigan. Michigan's non-Indian population in 1820, five years before the Erie Canal opened, was 8,765; five years after the canal opened, the population had jumped to almost 32,000. In the next four years, the population almost tripled, and by 1836 the non-Indian population in Michigan was close to 175,000.[19] Similar examples exist across the frontier before the Civil War.

Indians were important elsewhere in the Midwest. Indiana residents pushed for removal of the Miami from the central part of the state from the 1820s to the Indians' eventual removal in the 1840s, in large part because white residents wanted Miami lands for canal routes, infrastructure development, and the development of the state generally. Indiana's legislature sent repeated memorials to Congress; in 1829, the state legislature wrote, "The continuance of these few savages within our limits, who claim so large a space of the best soil, not only circumscribes, in its practical effects, the usefulness of the privileges we enjoy as a free and independent State, but tends materially to impede a system of internal improvements essential to the prosperity of our citizens, and in a degree jeopardizes the peace and tranquillity of our frontier, which it is our right and duty to secure.... the large extent of country they yet claim is not only unprofitable to them, but, by its contiguity to the [Wabash] canal, is calculated to retard the settlement, the revenue, and the prosperity of the State."[20]

Westerners interested in development and growth often favored removal of small groups of northern Indians, but removal of the large, well-organized Indian nations of the South worried Western interests because of the security threat created by concentrating removed Indians in their region. Representative Samuel Vinton of Ohio, discussing the Georgia context in 1828, noted:

> At this crisis, Mr. Monroe sent a message to Congress, breathing the language of the purest benevolence, but which, I hesitate not to say, proposes the boldest experiment upon human life, and human happiness, that is to be found in the history of the world. It proposes to take a whole people, nay, more, the remnant of forty nations, from their abodes, and place them down in the recesses of a distant and forbidding wilderness....
>
> When the plan there marked out is understood by the people of the western country, it will fill them with alarm.... Such a disposition of the Indians greatly endangers the security of the whole western frontier, and renders the condition of Missouri, in particular, imminently perilous. Place around Missouri on the north and east, in conjunction with the two hundred thousand that would be there besides,

[19] Charles E. Cleland, *Rites of Conquest: The History and Culture of Michigan's Native Americans* (Ann Arbor: University of Michigan Press, 1992), 209.

[20] Prucha, *Great Father*, 258–9. The Memorial is quoted at 245.

the sixty or seventy thousand Indians of the Southwest, and what have you done! You have executed, by a single movement, the great plan of Tecumseh, that carried terror and dismay to every cabin beyond the Alleghanies . . . [21]

In 1826, the commander of the military's Western Department likened the situation in Arkansas and Texas, and in the southwest generally, to the situation that prevailed in the Northwest at the time of St. Clair's defeat.[22] Invocations of Tecumseh and a comparison with the nation's greatest defeat at the hands of an organized intertribal alliance go a long way toward suggesting the era's tension and the seriousness of Indian affairs.

Negotiations in Indian territory in the late 1830s and 1840s also involved U.S. relations with Texas and Mexico, keeping Indian affairs, as always, in the forefront of all sorts of policy areas.[23] Federal personnel at U.S. forts in the West became instrumental in managing relations among the western and removed southern Indians and in promoting farming and education. Endeavors like the 1832 Stokes Commission worked to develop and manage good relations, adjudicate disputes, and negotiate for land and for treaties of peace among the Indians. The Dodge Expedition of 1834 also sought to achieve progress toward these ends and, in the way of similar missions, worked out agreements, distributed medals and presents, and promoted communications among the tribes and between tribes and the United States.

Removal and relocation of American Indians, then, was not simply a local or regional issue; it was an issue of significance to all areas of the United States and along its borders. Even as the federal government implemented piecemeal removals in the northeast and wholesale tribal removals in the southeast, its agents pursued complicated negotiations, arrangements, and planning in the west to avoid the prospects raised by Vinton and by others. The grand design envisioned by top U.S. policymakers depended on organizing the west under federal control, utilizing civilian and military forces to control the area and nurture Indian populations to "civilization." Much of this depended upon securing peaceful relations between western Indians and eastern Indians being removed to Indian territory. The vision had many facets at different times, including ideas for Indian representation in Congress and for organized Indian government supported by an Indian multinational peace force backed by the U.S. Army. Some plans suggested that the president would eventually appoint a territorial governor and secretary, leading to an Indian confederacy with close ties to the United States.

[21] Quoted in Dale Van Every, *Disinherited: The Lost Birthright of the American Indian* (New York: Avon, 1966), 119.

[22] Brad Agnew, *Fort Gibson: Terminal on the Trail of Tears* (Norman: University of Oklahoma Press, 1980), 47–8.

[23] David LaVere, *Contrary Neighbors: Southern Plains and Removed Indians in Indian Territory* (Norman: University of Oklahoma Press, 2000), 74–7, 81ff.

With all of these regional and national interests involved directly with American Indians and tribes, it is no surprise that national politics were shot through with discussion and maneuvering around Indian affairs. Removal itself was a central issue in national politics. At the National Republican convention in December 1831, the presiding officer was James Barbour – John Quincy Adams's Secretary of War, who described the removal policy as "perhaps the most important [issue] of all" being discussed at the convention. Barbour painted Jackson as a nullifier, using Jackson's blanket dismissals of Indian treaties as evidence that Jackson had, in effect, nullified the 1802 Trade and Intercourse law which protected the Indians from intruders. Jackson's opponents attempted to use the removal issue to split Jackson's coalition. Henry Clay believed that he could use Indian issues to weaken the Democrats' strength in New York and Pennsylvania, and possibly Ohio, in the runup to the 1832 election. The National Republicans eventually censured President Jackson for not enforcing the Supreme Court's decision in *Worcester* v. *Georgia*, and Van Buren estimated that the Court's decision favoring the Cherokee Nation – which Jackson largely ignored – cost Jackson eight to ten thousand votes in New York.[24] The historian Ronald Satz calls removal "a secondary but nevertheless prominent" issue contributing to the new party system in the 1830s, as political and religious elements aligned in opposition to the policy.[25] Grant Foreman calls the removal debate "one of the bitterest debates in the history of Congress."[26] John A. Andrew writes, "More than any other topic, Indian policy delineated the emergence of a new era, of a new set of parameters to govern individual behavior and shape political policy."[27] In Georgia, according to the historian Michael D. Green, Creek resistance combined with the Governor's position on removal to spark "a national civil crisis that one federal official called more 'pregnant with threatened evil' than any 'since the formation of our Government.'"[28]

National leaders in both the Democrat and Whig factions were deeply involved in Indian affairs at both state and national levels: Jackson, Van Buren, Henry Clay, John Quincy Adams, Lewis Cass, James Gadsden, William Crawford, John Calhoun, John Marshall, even a young William Tecumseh Sherman – all were intimately and steadily engaged with Indian affairs, removal, and the Seminole War. Leading figures led the Cherokees'

[24] Satz, *American Indian Policy*, 53, 48, 52.

[25] Ibid., 28, 39.

[26] Foreman, *Removal*, 21.

[27] John A. Andrew III, *From Revivals to Removal: Jeremiah Evarts, the Cherokee Nation, and the Search for the Soul of America* (Athens: University of Georgia Press, 1992), 176.

[28] Green, *Politics of Indian Removal*, 126. For a recent, detailed discussion of the significance and political contexts of the Cherokees' situation, see Tim Alan Garrison, *The Legal Ideology of Removal: The Southern Judiciary and the Sovereignty of Native American Nations* (Athens: The University of Georgia Press, 2002).

cases before the U.S. Supreme Court: former attorney general William Wirt, the anti-Mason candidate for President in 1832, argued *Worcester* v. *Georgia* for the Cherokees before the Court; the Cherokees' other attorney, John Sergeant, received the 1832 vice presidential nomination from the National Republicans.[29] Such factors continued past the Jackson administration, too. Democrats burnished William Henry Harrison's 1840 candidacy with his Indian affairs experience and reputation, and contrasted Harrison's Indian-fighting heroism with a critique of Martin Van Buren's limited experience and less than heroic reputation. In turn, the Van Buren team emphasized the Indian-fighting background of Vice President Richard M. Johnson, widely recognized as the man who killed Tecumseh in 1813.[30] Winfield Scott's supporters trumpeted his service in Indian conflicts in the South, Florida, and the Midwest. "Van Buren's Bloodhounds" – a reference to the use of dogs in cruel campaigns against the Seminoles in Florida – became an issue in the campaign, adding fuel to an ongoing investigation of Van Buren's War Department and feeding criticism that the Seminole War had been badly run and had lasted too long.[31]

At the same time, the next generation's leaders – men like Jefferson Davis, Abraham Lincoln, Zachary Taylor, and a host of future Civil War heroes and future national leaders – were on the front lines of Indian affairs in the 1830s and 1840s. Consider the Dragoon expeditions of 1834 out of Fort Gibson in Arkansas. The regiment's officers included Jefferson Davis; Stephen Watts Kearny, who would lead the Army of the West in the Mexican War; and David Hunter, who would chair the commission that tried the conspirators in the assassination of Abraham Lincoln.[32] Washington Irving and other celebrities passed through Fort Gibson in the 1830s, illustrating the inescapable artistic and popular connections to the West and to Indian affairs.

The cost of Indian affairs in the removal era helps to illustrate its significance. Congress initially appropriated $500,000 to carry out the provisions of the original removal bill.[33] Choctaw removal ultimately cost about $5 million; the United States later paid the Choctaw $3 million, and

[29] Garrison, *Legal Ideology*, ch. 7; James R. Christianson, "Removal: A Foundation for the Formation of Federal Indian Policy," *Journal of Cherokee Studies* 10 (Fall 1985), 221–2.

[30] Robert Gray Gunderson, *The Log-Cabin Campaign* (New York: Greenwood Press Reprint, 1977 [1957]), 79–80, ch. 18; Grant Foreman, *The Last Trek of the Indians* (New York: Russell & Russell, 1972 [1946]), 123 n15. On Harrison, Indians, and the 1840 campaign, see Gunderson, *Log-Cabin Campaign*, 25, 49, 51, 73–9, 94–7, 136–7, 153ff., 272.

[31] Mahon, *Second Seminole War*, 265ff.; John Campbell, "The Seminoles, the 'Bloodhound War,' and Abolitionism, 1796–1865," *The Journal of Southern History* 72 (May 2006); Lynn Hudson Parsons, "'A Perpetual Harrow upon My Feelings': John Quincy Adams and the American Indian," *The New England Quarterly* 46 (September 1973), 374–5.

[32] Agnew, *Fort Gibson*, 116.

[33] Prucha, *Great Father*, 206.

generated about $8 million from the sale of the Choctaw lands.[34] By the 1850s, the United States had made $11.25 million from selling lands it obtained in the Treaty of Fort Jackson (1814) with the Creeks.[35] The Seminole Wars ultimately cost between $20 million and $40 million, and took the lives of more than fifteen hundred U.S. soldiers.[36] During the period of the Second Seminole War and the Removal era, expenditures on the military ranged between 50 percent and 60 percent of the overall federal budget.[37]

Indian Removal and National Supremacy

The idea of removing Indians from their homes raised fundamental questions about the nature of the federal system. Importantly, both sides in the removal debates identified the federal government as the appropriate authority to handle Indian affairs, and both sides demanded greater federal action. Anti-removal elements argued that the federal government had the responsibility to exercise its power to uphold treaties and defend Indian rights. Many states' righters rested their *pro*-removal arguments on the powers of the federal government to administer Indian affairs and remove Indians, according to earlier agreements – powers that those interests believed the federal government was not exercising. In the end, the proponents of removal succeeded only when the federal government, pushed by a forceful lobbying effort by Jackson, made removal the focus of federal Indian policy. And Jackson, despite his reputation as a limited government states-righter, had no doubt that removed Indians in the West would come under federal authority.[38] Congress gave the president broad authority to implement removal in the existing states, and vast authority over land and administration in the complicated and increasingly crowded West, where removed tribes came into volatile contact with tribes already occupying much of the land.

[34] Ibid., 219.

[35] Claudio Saunt, "Taking Account of Property: Stratification among the Creek Indians in the Early Nineteenth Century," *The William and Mary Quarterly* 57 (October 2000), 760.

[36] $20M is the most frequently cited number: see Mahon, *Second Seminole War*, 321–7; Prucha, *Great Father*, 233; Thomas D. Clark and John D. W. Guice, *The Old Southwest, 1795–1830: Frontiers in Conflict* (Norman: University of Oklahoma Press, 1996 [1989]), 251. Mahon estimates $30M–$40M, and explains that it is difficult to clarify the number because appropriations included lump sums for Indian wars; funds for the Seminole conflict are thus difficult to distinguish from funds spent on the Creek conflict of 1836. Mahon, *Second Seminole War*, 326.

[37] Ira Katznelson, "Flexible Capacity: The Military and Early American Statebuilding," in *Shaped by War and Trade: International Influences on American Political Development*, ed. Ira Katznelson and Martin Shefter (Princeton: Princeton University Press, 2002), 92–3; United States Bureau of the Census, *Historical Statistics of the United States: Colonial Times to 1970*, 2 parts (Washington, DC: U.S. Bureau of the Census, 1975), 1115.

[38] Prucha, *Great Father*, 199.

Opponents of Removal

The civilization and education policies of the factory era had worked to break down barriers between Indians and whites, and federal agents and others had touted success in "civilizing" the southern tribes. In the 1820s, Indian policy drifted between the pacification goals of the factory era and the eventual removal efforts of the Jackson era. Proponents of continuing assimilation and civilization efforts – who foresaw the Indians remaining as parts of a new American amalgamation – battled with developers and interests at the state level who understood that Indians who remained on lands in the East – well, they remained on lands in the East. Indians did not make this any easier on the pro-removal forces. The Cherokee drafted and signed a written constitution in July 1827, proclaiming the Cherokees' sovereignty as an independent nation with complete jurisdiction over its territory. The document worried the federal government and spurred Georgia to action, with the latter arguing that the idea of a sovereign government within its borders was untenable. Georgia took action to extend the authority of its government and its laws over the Cherokee territory.

Opponents of removal relied on two principal arguments, both of which centered on the federal government's role and responsibilities. Senator Theodore Frelinghuysen's famous argument against removal emphasized the sanctity of federal treaty agreements, arguing that the national government had an obligation to uphold those agreements and protect Indian civilizations against encroachments by states or by white intruders. The American Board of Commissioners for Foreign Missions, led by Jeremiah Evarts, was among the groups that lobbied in defense of Cherokees' rights. Evarts's series on the Cherokee issue and its moral importance circulated throughout the country in 1829 and 1830. Evarts used speeches and newspapers to convey his message, and organized a campaign of efforts and memorials sent to Congress against the Removal bill.

Evarts's argument, initially resting on morality and legal rights, gradually came to focus on the second antiremoval argument: the inexpediency of removal.[39] Evarts noted that removal would play havoc with Indian attitudes and with their move toward U.S.-style agriculture in the confined spaces of the East. Others, like Peleg Sprague of Massachusetts, focused on the Jackson administration's failure to take preparatory action in the West, such as signing treaties to prepare for the displacement of eastern Indians to the area. Opponents of the removal bill also focused on the substandard nature of lands in the West, for which Indians would be giving up good eastern lands that they had farmed and lived on for generations.

Some of the most prominent efforts to oppose removal took place in the federal court system. The Supreme Court promoted nationalism and state-building throughout the Marshall era, and Indian affairs followed the

[39] Andrew, *From Revivals to Removal.*

trend. In *Fletcher* v. *Peck* (1810), for example, Chief Justice John Marshall upheld states' claims to lands west of the Allegheny and Appalachian mountains, beyond the British boundary line of 1763, even though these lands had never been properly ceded by Indians. In "the Marshall trilogy," the Court clarified the relationship of Indians to the federal government and to the states. In *Johnson* v. *McIntosh* (1823), Marshall reinforced national dominion and sovereignty over its claimed territory under the "Doctrine of Discovery." In *Cherokee Nation* v. *Georgia* (1831), Marshall deemed Indian nations "domestic, dependent nations," subject to federal control. In *Worcester* v. *Georgia* (1832), the Court protected federal power against encroachment *by the states* by ruling for the missionaries and Indians over the claims of Georgia, which had attempted to extend state jurisdiction over Indian lands. The cases are landmarks in Indian sovereignty issues, but they are also crucial indicators of the scope of federal administrative capacity. In effect, even as Indian nations and opponents of removal won cases at the Court, the victories succeeded only in clarifying the appropriate locus of authority for carrying out removal policy: the federal government. The *Worcester* decision's significance, for example, lies less in the paper protections it afforded the Cherokee, and more in its clarification of the fact that the federal government, not the states, still controlled Indian policy and administration.

The Court's deference to the presidency in these cases is important to our understanding of executive and administrative power in what is erroneously considered a "state of courts and parties." In *Worcester* especially, Chief Justice Marshall avoided a head-on collision with the presidency.[40] As he had done in *Marbury* v. *Madison*, Marshall walked a fine line in the Indian cases that protected the Court's independence and authority while avoiding conflict with the more dynamic force of the executive. At the time of the ruling, the Jackson administration had already set the wheels of removal in motion, conducting treaty negotiations and other tasks; the Removal Bill had already been passed. Through a typically clever decision that took advantage of legal quirks to rule partly in favor of Worcester and the Indians, Marshall found a way to render his ruling legally unenforceable. The Court ruled that Georgia's extension of state law over Indian country was unconstitutional, and ordered the state court that had convicted the missionaries Worcester and Butler to reverse its decision and release the two. But because U.S. marshals could not be sent to enforce the decision until the Georgia court

[40] See, e.g., Vine Deloria Jr. and Clifford M. Lytle, *American Indians, American Justice* (Austin: University of Texas Press, 1992), 31–2 and ch. 2; Satz, *American Indian Policy*, 49; Prucha, *Great Father*, 212. For a review of the historiographic debate over *Worcester* and Jackson's resulting legal obligations (or lack thereof), see Tim Alan Garrison, "Beyond *Worcester*: The Alabama Supreme Court and the Sovereignty of the Creek Nation," *Journal of the Early Republic* 19 (Fall 1999), 428 and 428 n6; Garrison, *Legal Ideology*.

refused, in writing, to comply – and because Georgia had entirely boycotted the federal case – Jackson lacked legal authority to enforce the Court's decision. In effect, the Marshall Court reinforced federal control over Indian policy and helped expand federal administrative authority over the actual process of removal, even as Marshall refused to challenge the administration or Georgia. In fact, the administrative power of the executive and the speed with which administrators pushed removal and other initiatives often placed the nineteenth-century Court in positions in which its decisions and authority had been rendered moot by events unfolding in the field.[41] In short, Marshall, as usual, stood firmly for national supremacy but refused to put the Court into a head-to-head fight with the executive branch. Indian affairs remained a federal prerogative, and the executive branch retained its position of leadership.

Proponents of Removal

Often ignored or forgotten is the extent to which the *proponents* of removal looked to the federal government as the arena in which to make *their* claims. In two important respects, the critical ingredient in the removal debate was the scope and use of national power.

Initially, pro-removal forces at the state and local levels demanded national action, but were frustrated and blocked. Georgia waited years for the federal government to fulfill what Georgia officials believed was the federal government's responsibility to extinguish Indian title and remove Indians. These responsibilities, Georgia residents believed, had been incurred by the federal government in an 1802 agreement ceding Georgia's western lands to the new national government. Georgia's argument at the time of removal was that the federal government had failed to take action on its promise to clear Indian title in Georgia's territory. Georgia's press for removal was a demand for *more* federal activity, not less.

As the relative strengths of white and Indian communities evolved, eastern states became more aggressive in dealing with nearby Indians. The role of the federal government and military in policing the frontiers and reducing the chances for conflict through mechanisms like the factory system were less important by the 1820s, and the federal government's promises to secure title to Indian lands became a hot political issue. Populations in the southeast, including those in Georgia, Alabama, Florida, and Mississippi, all pressed their long-standing claims for the removal of Indians. The

[41] For example, in *U.S.* v. *Rogers*, the defendant had drowned following escape from jail before the case reached the Supreme Court. The case should have been rendered moot, but the Court was unaware of events in the field. See David E. Wilkins, *American Indian Sovereignty and the U.S. Supreme Court: The Masking of Justice* (Austin: University of Texas Press, 1997), 38ff. See also Marshall's opinion in *Johnson* v. *McIntosh* (8 *Wheaton*, 603–5), reprinted in Prucha, *Documents*, 37.

press of white settlement, and the increasing populations of settled areas in these states, made the presence of Indians a nuisance and a hindrance to development. Interests wanted land for settlement, for gold and other minerals, and for extension of the cotton culture.[42] The discovery of gold within the Cherokee nation in 1829 fed this appetite. Slaveholding interests in the South petitioned Congress for removal of potential allies to runaway slaves.[43]

Presidential and federal opposition prevailed over the states' appetites well into the 1820s. James Monroe, refusing to succumb to the states' demands, stalled removal efforts and defended federal prerogative in determining the course to be taken with regard to the Cherokees. In a special message to Congress in 1824, Monroe defended the federal government's authority in the matter with Georgia and argued that the federal government had no obligation to remove Indians by force. Even as relations with the southern states deteriorated, Monroe tried to control the debate by urging upon Congress a policy of encouraged, not forced, removal – one that would respect the treaties even as it furthered what Monroe felt was the best option, a voluntary removal of Indians to the west. Monroe led the discussion, framed much of the debate, and put forward clear suggestions for Congress. Congress followed the president's lead, with the Senate Committee on Indian Affairs adopting Monroe's system for removal. The House did not follow suit immediately, but Congress made repeated inquiries into and provisions for removal. These included various commissions, investigations, and studies designed to ascertain the prospects of removal and convince Indians to go along.[44] Congress repeatedly asked for information from the War Department on such details as the potential cost of removal, the Indians' condition, and their willingness to remove.

John Quincy Adams's administration also refused to move against the Indians. Led by intellectual precedent dating back to Jefferson and by the advice of Secretary of War Peter Porter, and with the support of missionaries Jedidiah Morse and Isaac McCoy, Adams recommended that Indians be encouraged to exchange their Eastern lands for land in the West, but he steadfastly refused to use direct force. In fact, as noted earlier, Adams positioned the military against *Georgians* who had threatened to survey Creek lands prior to treaty authorization. Adams's position respected Indian rights in the land and their option to sign or refuse to sign treaties – and it failed to satisfy Southerners.[45]

42 Daniel H. Usner Jr., "American Indians on the Cotton Frontier: Changing Economic Relations with Citizens and Slaves in the Mississippi Territory," *The Journal of American History* 72 (September 1985); Hauptman, *Between Two Fires*, 87ff.

43 Satz, *American Indian Policy*, 3–4.

44 Prucha, *Great Father*, 187ff.

45 Green, *Politics of Indian Removal*, ch. 5; Mary W. M. Hargreaves, *The Presidency of John Quincy Adams* (Lawrence: University Press of Kansas, 1985), 199–208.

The second dynamic critical to the national government's key role in removal was the election of Andrew Jackson. It is tempting to think of removal as almost a nonactivity for Jackson and the presidency, taking a cue from the familiar impression of Jackson standing idly by as Georgia and other states moved to dispossess the Indians in their midst. Jackson's famous comment defending his refusal to abide by the Supreme Court's decision in *Worcester* – "John Marshall has made his decision, now let him enforce it" – is probably apocryphal, yet it symbolizes the way in which administrative leadership in removal is often divorced from the federal government. This conception of the era obscures the politics of removal and seriously underestimates the role of the executive in designing, promoting, and implementing policy. Jackson's role was far more ambitious and proactive than the famous anecdote suggests. Rather than yield to the states and refuse to activate federal authority when ordered to do so by the Court, a more accurate understanding reveals that Jackson expanded federal powers to effect removal. Jackson even ordered federal troops to protect Creeks from Alabama squatters, resulting in the burning by federal soldiers of the town of Irwinton in 1832.[46]

States responded quickly to Jackson's election, though, pushing measures that had been bubbling through state legislatures for years. Jackson's election signaled that a major shift in federal attitude toward removal lay just ahead, and that promise of federal cooperation – and the evaporation of presidential opposition – emboldened the states. In 1828, Georgia annexed Indian lands; in 1830, it extended state laws over these areas. Jackson responded quickly, promoting removal before Congress and before the public. As was the case throughout the nineteenth century, important public policy issues surrounding expansion and Indian affairs were front and center in presidential messages offering detailed articulations of policy and purpose. Jackson's First Annual Message, in December 1829, spoke forcefully about the importance of Indian affairs, removal, and the risks Indians faced from white expansion.[47]

Jackson did not officially repudiate the treaties, as one might expect given his reputation as a states-righter and a proponent of limited government, and given that Jackson personally considered treaties and the obligations

[46] Green, *Politics of Indian Removal*, ch. 8; Sidney L. Harring, *Crow Dog's Case: American Indian Sovereignty, Tribal Law, and United States Law in the Nineteenth Century* (Cambridge: Cambridge University Press, 1994), 39. On the significance of Jackson's election, see Fred Anderson and Andrew Cayton, *The Dominion of War: Empire and Liberty in North America, 1500–2000* (New York: Viking, 2005), ch. 5, esp. 218ff.

[47] Including Indian affairs and expansion as core policy areas of the eighteenth and nineteenth centuries suggests the need to revise analyses of presidential rhetoric and public leadership in these years, such as that found in Jeffrey K. Tulis, *The Rhetorical Presidency* (Princeton: Princeton University Press, 1987).

they imposed to be "an absurdity."[48] Despite these more obvious dynamics, Jackson's actions *reinforced* the treaty system. The Indian Removal Act signed by Jackson acknowledged the sanctity of existing treaties, with Section 7 of the Act providing "That nothing in this act contained shall be construed as authorizing or directing the violation of any existing treaty between the United States and any of the Indian tribes."[49] During Jackson's presidency, sixty-seven treaties were signed and ratified, adding approximately 132 million acres of Indian land to the United States at a cost of $68 million.[50]

Jackson's expectations for removal included sweeping extensions of national authority. Removal treaties commonly included loopholes securing congressional or federal authority over Indian affairs, undercutting treaty language about postremoval Indian sovereignty. The federal government thus ensured that the treaty policy would perpetuate the bedrock principle of federal authority over Indian affairs. Once Indians had been moved west of the Mississippi River, the federal government would "circumscribe their bounds, put into their hands the utensils of husbandry, yield them protection, and enforce obedience to those just laws provided for their benefit." Jackson stated that once removal had been accomplished, "[T]here would be no question of jurisdiction to prevent the Government from exercising such a general control over their affairs as may be essential to their interest and safety."[51] And Jackson was not alone in understanding the widening scope of federal power. Historian Ronald Satz notes, "One of the interesting aspects of the voting pattern that emerged in both houses of Congress [on the Removal Bill] is that Jacksonians adhering to a political philosophy of states' rights, limited government, and retrenchment voted to provide huge expenditures for Indian removal, while National Republicans adhering to a political philosophy which encouraged federal expenditures bemoaned the 'enormous expense' removal would bring."[52] And because Indians would not be sent to areas already peopled by white settlers, the extension of federal authority and activity in these areas would, as usual, *precede* white settlement.

48 Quoted in Satz, *American Indian Policy*, 10.

49 *U.S. Statutes at Large*, 4:411–12, reprinted in Prucha, *Documents*, 53. Jackson's Secretary of War, John Eaton, argued that federal treaties cemented *state* sovereignty over Indian lands, because treaties were signed between members of the federal union (states) and Indian nations. Prucha, *Great Father*, 193. Southern jurists also crafted pro-removal legal arguments that appeared to uphold and pay respect to federal treaties. See Garrison, *Legal Ideology*.

50 Prucha, *American Indian Treaties*, 155; Remini, *Indian Wars*, 238; see also Paul Stuart, *Nations Within a Nation: Historical Statistics of American Indians* (New York: Greenwood Press, 1987), 78.

51 Jackson, quoted in Satz, *American Indian Policy*, 11; quoted in Prucha, *Great Father*, 199.

52 Satz, *American Indian Policy*, 30.

Another issue could be resolved by federal leadership in Indian removal. Federal protection of Indian interests in the South threatened further confrontation between the federal government and the states. The national effort might be put at risk if conflict erupted between the regular army and southern state militias. Part of the argument for removal laid out by Adams, Jackson, and others addressed this snag in the federal scheme. Removing Indians to the West, where they would exist independent of state boundaries, removed a key element in the national debate over states' rights. If the federal government removed the Indians and granted them title in the West, federal officials would escape a thorny legal and political issue involving state officials' interpretation of rights and privileges under the Constitution. Federal power could be used to avoid a conflict over federalism.[53]

The nullification controversy added a final facet to the interplay of removal and debates over federal authority. John Quincy Adams pointed out that southern efforts to bypass laws and treaties with Indians raised the spectre of nullification.[54] Jackson and Marshall tried to avoid open conflict, militarily or legally, with Georgia and other southern states, and Jackson also wanted to contain South Carolina's subsequent nullification threat regarding the tariff. Jackson did not want to provoke Georgia to move further toward South Carolina's position on nullification by aggressively enforcing Marshall's decision in *Worcester* v. *Georgia*. Jackson's critics ultimately foresaw a similar threat if they criticized Jackson too sharply for abandoning the Court's decision favoring the Cherokees. Jackson stood against nullification and upheld federal supremacy, as defenders of the Cherokee tempered their attacks on Jackson in order to preserve the union from a growing threat. The American Board and Frelinghuysen both came to advocate removal if a satisfactory treaty could be agreed upon.

Removal by the states would tear the fabric of federalism and the traditions of federal policy in Indian affairs. It would empower the states at the expense of the federal government and of nationalists and proponents of a strong presidency. It would leave legal and administrative oversight of Indian affairs confused and broken, even as removed Indians and western Indians, settlers, and other interests were on the verge of conflict in the West. By contrast, removal by the federal government protected and reinforced federal preeminence, avoided great risks, and built on decades of practice, law, and experience in managing Indian affairs.

National Administration in the Jacksonian Era

The debate over removal was not a debate between federalists and states'-righters – it was a debate about how to utilize federal power and about

[53] Prucha, *Great Father*, 197–8.
[54] Parsons, "'A Perpetual Harrow,'" 362–5.

how to understand and apply earlier federal commitments. All involved understood that that debate needed to be resolved at the national level itself. The removal bill gave sweeping powers to the Jackson administration to remove Indians and dispense western lands – and it placed the national administrative structure at the head of those efforts. Indian affairs continued to be directed and driven by the federal government in the 1830s and 1840s, under national guidelines and with federal personnel in key decision-making positions.

The focus on the national level in Indian affairs mirrored the national role in other areas of expansion-related policy and administration during the Jacksonian era. Removal resided among other issues, some related to Indian affairs and some not, that tested and questioned the proper scope of national administrative control of aspects of expansion.

National Administration and Indian Affairs in the Removal Era

Congress continued to delegate broad powers to the executive in the area of trade regulation. These regulations, sometimes ineffective because of the vast lands they covered, nevertheless set important precedents for federal control and executive administration. Superintendents and agents, under the direction of the president and of territorial governors acting as ex-officio superintendents of Indian affairs, were empowered to grant trading licenses and take bonds, and to search the stores and packages of traders and mete out penalties for violations of law. An Act of May 6, 1822, for example, gave the president discretionary authority to exceed statutory limits in regard to bonds taken from Indian service personnel: "[I]t shall and may be lawful for the President of the United States, from time to time, to require additional security, and in larger amounts, from all persons charged or trusted, under the laws of the United States, with the disbursement or application of money, goods, or effects, of any kind, for the benefit of the Indians."[55]

During the Jacksonian era, Congress maintained and added provisions dealing with licensing, boundaries, trade, and other issues related to Indian affairs. These were usually extensions of established trends and reflected the continuing federal role in attempts to control and order expansion policy. The landmark Trade and Intercourse Act of 1834 established specific requirements governing trading licenses, bonding procedures, seizure of goods from persons violating the regulations, criteria for denying licenses, procedures for appeal of such denials, regulations governing sales to and purchases from Indians, including but not limited to the alcohol trade, guidelines for issuing passports to Indian country, authorization for removal of white trespassers, procedures for dealing with white criminals, restrictions on purchasing land without U.S. involvement, restrictions on carrying and making communications to and from Indian country "with an intent to produce a

[55] *U.S. Statutes at Large*, 3:682–3, reprinted in Prucha, *Documents*, 35.

contravention or infraction of any treaty or other law of the United States, or to disturb the peace and tranquility of the United States," provisions for the United States to be responsible for certain categories of claims and depredations, specifications for locating the burden of proof upon whites in disputes about right of property between an Indian and a white, and even the length of time a person might be detained by the military for violating the Act (five days). The act defined Indian country and sharpened an evolving concept of boundary lines.[56]

The 1834 Indian Office Reorganization Act granted the president and agents of the executive branch vast discretionary authority to define, specify, and apply these provisions: the president received authority to issue licenses to foreign traders "under such regulations as he may prescribe," and lower officials were granted authority to make determinations regarding issuing or denying licenses, seizing goods, and revoking licenses. The president held authority to use the military to apprehend violators of the Act's provisions, and the Act stated that the superintendent of Indian affairs, agents, and subagents "shall have authority to remove from the Indian country all persons found therein contrary to law; and the President is authorized to direct the military force to be employed in such removal." The 1834 law authorized the War Department to take military measures to prevent or end wars between tribes, a matter of great import as western tribes tried to deal with removed tribes newly appearing on what they considered to be their lands. The Act authorized the president to establish subagencies and appoint subagents, provide goods and smiths, to withhold goods from certain tribes in order to be able to bring pressure upon them, and to prescribe the regulations for implementing the act itself.[57]

The national government's involvement in social policy also continued to be an important aspect of Indian affairs in the 1820s and 1830s. The federal government spent funds directly for education and other social purposes as early as the Washington administration, as we have seen. McKenney had earlier worked closely with Henry Southard, chairman of the House Committee on Indian Affairs, for a national school system for Indians. McKenney's lobbying produced a bill from the committee extending the factory system by eight factories and providing for schools for the Indians. Congress as a whole did not pass that bill in the factory era, but in 1819 it did appropriate $10,000 for a Civilization Fund to be used at the president's discretion. The president decided to use much of the money through the missionary societies, supplementing treaty annuities designated for the

56 *U.S. Statutes at Large*, 4:729–35, reprinted in Prucha, *Documents*, 64–8; Prucha, *Great Father*, 300–2.

57 *U.S. Statutes at Large*, 4:735–8, reprinted in Prucha, *Documents*, 68–71; Prucha, *Great Father*, 310, 295ff.; see also Remini, *Indian Wars*, 116ff., 233ff; Satz, *American Indian Policy*, 178–87.

tribes and earmarked for social provisions like agricultural implements and training and education.

McKenney's leadership and pressure from the executive branch were able to maintain the Civilization Fund even after the factory system was abandoned. Portions of Indian annuities were targeted for education as early as 1820, and at least $21,000 aimed in that direction by 1830. By 1834, $35,000 was committed by treaties for schools, and by 1838 the federal government was operating ninety-three schools with thirty-seven hundred students.[58] In 1839 Bureau of Indian Affairs Commissioner T. Hartley Crawford formalized the development of manual labor schools,[59] and calls for ending treaty spending on items like education in this era were met with fear of general uprising on the frontier. The presence of ninety thousand Indians just west of Arkansas and Missouri, for example, convinced a House committee looking into abrogating treaty provisions to conclude that such action would spark "an Indian war, in which all the tribes would unite."[60] Jackson promised that educational and other civilization funds would continue along with removal, as Indian service personnel coordinated and administered social policy in the new lands in the West. Jackson fulfilled his pledge,[61] and by the 1840s treaty annuities for education, mechanics, farmers, and farm implements amounted to roughly $40,000 per year. McKenney pressured field agents to support the civilization program, exhorting them to advance the program and informing them that opposition to civilization was opposition to the government. Recipients of funds received careful instructions and guidelines. McKenney used the missionary schools to inculcate attitudes favorable to removal, and he, Calhoun, and others made it clear to the societies that funds would be withdrawn if the societies did not promote U.S. policies.[62] Control of the funds gave Jackson and the removal proponents in the administration leverage over the benevolent societies. Immediately following passage of the Removal Bill, for example, Secretary of War Eaton ended the roughly three thousand dollar annual allotment that had been going to the American Board, the Bill's strongest opponent.[63]

The Indian Office's expert personnel were looked to for leadership in federal spending on social policy. Satz traces in detail how the education and civilization programs were designed, expanded, and administered, and he

[58] Meyer Weinberg, *A Chance to Learn: The History of Race and Education in the United States* (Cambridge: Cambridge University Press, 1977), 181–2; Jon Reyhner and Jeanne Eder, "A History of Indian Education," in *Teaching American Indian Students*, ed. Jon Reyhner (Norman: University of Oklahoma Press, 1994), 39.

[59] Reyhner and Eder, "History," 39.

[60] Quoted in Satz, *American Indian Policy*, 269.

[61] Satz, *American Indian Policy*, 247, 268–9.

[62] See, e.g., J. Leitch Wright, *Creeks and Seminoles: The Destruction and Regeneration of the Muscogulge People* (Lincoln: University of Nebraska Press, 1990), 230.

[63] Satz, *American Indian Policy*, 252.

writes, "Educational programs receiving support from the government were coordinated by the head of the Indian Bureau before 1832 and by the commissioner of Indian affairs after that date. These officials synthesized suggestions from field personnel, congressional leaders, secretaries of war, and other administration leaders, and their annual reports on Indian education provide insight into the federal government's motivation and effectiveness in civilizing the Indians."[64] Faced with administering the fund, Commissioner Crawford designed the details of the policy's field implementation. By the 1840s, he had had much success in instituting education programs throughout Indian country, and the programs were continued in much the same form even after the Whigs returned to power. Satz attributes some of the continuation of the programs to a strong defense of civilization funding by John Tyler's Secretary of War, John Spencer. The programs continued after the Democrats retook control in 1845.

Important earlier precedents were thus continued in these years: government cooperation with and funding for religious missionary groups; the targeting of educational services and technical assistance to specific populations; and the role of the executive in ordering and administering such programs. Federal programs sought by these initiatives to benefit and improve the lives of American Indians, to "raise" Indians to the level of whites, and to create an educated class of Indians that would be receptive to the federal government's initiatives – such as removal.

Indian affairs even brought the federal government into the health care field in a variety of ways, chief among them smallpox vaccinations. With passage of the Indian Vaccination Act of 1832, the Indian Office and War Department had effectively pushed Congress into formally providing some health care protections to Indians. At the same time, the decisions made by the Department of War and the Indian Office about whom to vaccinate and when – decisions that supported the removal policy, aided allied Indians and economic partners, and excluded Indians seen as enemies – suggest the significant autonomy and decision making that delegated power allowed to the bureaucracy. Forty to fifty thousand Indians were vaccinated under the Act's provisions, even as those vaccinations were primarily an effort to meet other policy objectives. In this case, vaccinations were less an example of generous social policymaking, and more an example of a means to facilitate removals and broader policy.[65] The Post Office worked to distribute smallpox vaccine, and surgeons at military posts in Indian country administered the vaccine. In 1831, for example, a post surgeon vaccinated seven thousand

64 Ibid., 248–9; see also 257ff.

65 See J. Diane Pearson, "Lewis Cass and the Politics of Disease: The Indian Vaccination Act of 1832," *Wicazo Sa Review* 18 (Autumn 2003), 10–11. The vaccination program was developed and sustained against the opposition of Southern states and representatives.

Creeks against smallpox; vaccinations and general health care were frequently provided at the start of and during removals.[66]

Federal Administration by the 1830s

Indian removal complemented important debates and decisions about the appropriate scope and nature of national administrative authority.

Military activity remained a familiar part of administration, far beyond the strength and power the military showed in overseeing Indian removals. The military continued to remove white trespassers who encroached on Indian lands or who outpaced land cessions. This was a dangerous duty for the soldiers, but activity of this sort is surprisingly frequent in local and regional histories. This created not only very real instances of military action against U.S. citizens, like the burning of Irwinton, but the very real *threat* of such action that hung over the lives and improvements made by squatters who did not own clear title to lands. In areas like Texas, where people faced jurisdictional disputes among Indian nations, the United States, and Mexico, settlement and other improvement became particularly risky, just like settlement in the factory era always came at the risk of having land titles and other developments quashed by national authorities.[67]

Individuals routinely confronted other government actions. In 1829, Fort Gibson commander Colonel Matthew Arbuckle began to enforce liquor laws against whiskey vendors, a process which included searches and seizures of whiskey at private stores run by a vendor who lacked a license. The matter was eventually turned over to the U.S. Attorney, yet another of the federal agents on the frontier working to establish and solidify the federal government's presence.[68] As previously noted, William Unruh finds that state liquor laws were often enacted because states were frustrated at the federal government's unwillingness to enforce federal law. Rather than being upset at the federal government's extension of its regulatory authority, state policymakers were upset that that authority was not used enough.

Civil administration, however, rather than violent conflict, more accurately typified the contribution of the military in the Jacksonian era. The government continued to build infrastructure in key areas: Zachary Taylor, for example, oversaw construction of 53 new posts, 848 miles of wagon road, and 3,643 feet of causeways and bridges in Florida in eight months

66 Green, *Politics of Indian Removal*, 169; Foreman, *Last Trek*, 123 n19.

67 On federal efforts to remove white intruders in a variety of areas during this era, see, e.g., Green, *Politics of Indian Removal*, 165, 174; Wright, *Creeks and Seminoles*, 247; Mary E. Young, "The Creek Frauds: A Study in Conscience and Corruption," *The Mississippi Valley Historical Review* 42 (December 1955), 416, 418; William D. Green, *A Peculiar Imbalance: The Fall and Rise of Racial Equality in Early Minnesota* (St. Paul: Minnesota Historical Society Press, 2007), 26.

68 Agnew, *Fort Gibson*, 36ff.

between 1838 and 1839.[69] Leaders at state and national levels, and of both parties, continued to support internal improvements and government spending throughout the Jackson era. Canal building in Indiana, for example, was spurred by federal land grants from 1827 through the 1840s. These were similar in method to the grants later given to the railroads. These canals, like Indian affairs-related activity generally, drove population growth and development westward and northward through Indiana, and the Wabash and Erie Canal has been called "the single most important development in the political and economic life of Indiana during the mid-nineteenth century."[70]

Managed land policies remained a central part of national expansion, involving large and diverse populations and animating numerous government offices in the field and in the capital, the General Land Office among them. Congress increased the staff at the General Land Office from seventeen to eighty-eight in 1835, as the nation crept west and as the office's responsibilities and importance increased.[71] Elsewhere, missionaries and other communities continued to enjoy the benefits of nearby forts, both to quiet the potential dangers posed by Indians and also because forts could provide reliable ties to the East. A bi-monthly mail courier arriving at a fort provided regular communication and mail service, for example, and the government – in its efforts to provide for communication – could sometimes be counted upon to improve roads. Roads, in turn, encouraged involvement by others working directly or indirectly for the government: surveyors, quartermasters, civilian contractors, and the like. The post at Fort Gibson, for example, became an instrumental factor in improving roads, justifying requests for federal funds to improve river navigation, and satisfying the demands of local constituencies like missionaries, traders, suppliers, and contractors.[72]

69 Mahon, *Second Seminole War*, 261.

70 Ralph D. Gray, quoted in Ronald E. Shaw, *Canals for a Nation: The Canal Era in the United States, 1790–1860* (Lexington: The University Press of Kentucky, 1993), 142. See also Carol Sheriff, *The Artificial River: The Erie Canal and the Paradox of Progress, 1817–1862* (New York: Hill and Wang, 1996), 15ff. Shaw ascribes any reluctance at the national level to provide aid for canals to sectional and state rivalries, rather than to any qualms about the constitutionality of federal aid for canal building. Shaw, *Canals*, 18, 75–6, 134–43, 153, 199. Congress also took stock subscriptions to several canals: Shaw, *Canals*, 99, 108, 117. For a discussion of the establishment and regulation of public ways at the state level, see William J. Novak, *The People's Welfare: Law & Regulation in Nineteenth-Century America* (Chapel Hill: The University of North Carolina Press, 1996), ch. 4.

71 See, e.g., Patricia Nelson Limerick, *The Legacy of Conquest: The Unbroken Past of the American West* (New York: Norton, 1987), 60; Malcolm J. Rohrbough, *The Land Office Business: The Settlement and Administration of American Public Lands, 1789–1837* (New York: Oxford University Press, 1968); Daniel Feller, *The Public Lands in Jacksonian Politics* (Madison: University of Wisconsin Press, 1984); Matthew A. Crenson, *The Federal Machine: Beginnings of Bureaucracy in Jacksonian America* (Baltimore: The Johns Hopkins University Press, 1975).

72 Agnew, *Fort Gibson*, 31ff.

William Goetzmann's study of the Corps of Topographical Engineers highlights that organization's contributions in its heyday from 1838 to the Civil War. The Army Reorganization Bill of 1838 raised the status of the Topographical Corps and expanded its size, recognizing the Corps' existence as what Goetzmann calls "a central institution of Manifest Destiny" and "a department of public works for the West." He credits the Corps with the first scientific mapping of the West, and describes how they advanced settlement "by locating and constructing wagon roads, improving rivers and harbors, even performing experiments for the location of subsurface water in the arid regions." Goetzmann also highlights the Corps' international cast of scientists, naturalists, geologists, map makers, engineers, and military personnel for the major contribution of assembling maps, statistics, and reports about the West.[73]

Government-directed exploration and development made significant contributions on the high seas in the Jacksonian era, too. The Van Buren administration initiated "the most substantial exploration ever undertaken in the Pacific," as the historian Jean Heffer describes it, "in spite of Democratic dogma, which advocated limiting activity to within federal borders."[74] On the heels of John Quincy Adams's efforts to align federal interests in supporting economic development and trade expansion in the Pacific, and with a twelve-year gestation period, the expedition was modeled on Napoleon's expedition to Egypt and involved political infighting as well as efforts to promote scientific professionalism. Six ships and 350 men, a larger effort than even Britain had ever attempted, explored the Pacific from the Antarctic to Puget Sound, returning in 1842.[75] Along with a five-ship expedition to the northern Pacific in 1852 and other endeavors, Heffer writes, "Thanks to the American Navy, the Pacific had been made a more welcoming place for mariners."[76]

On land and sea, then, public agents contributed to the life and progress of the nation. These contributions were distinctively different from the activity of private forces on the frontier, like the more familiar mountain men.

[73] William H. Goetzmann, *Army Exploration in the American West, 1803–1863* (Lincoln: University of Nebraska Press, 1959).

[74] Jean Heffer, *The United States and the Pacific: History of a Frontier* (Notre Dame: University of Notre Dame Press, 2002), 84.

[75] Heffer, *United States and the Pacific*, 84–8. This expedition crossed paths with the Nez Perce, when a landing party went inland as part of the Pacific exploration. Alvin M. Josephy Jr., *The Nez Perce Indians and the Opening of the Northwest* (Boston: Houghton Mifflin, 1997 [1965], 215.

[76] Heffer, *United States and the Pacific*, 88; see also Goetzmann, *Army Exploration*, 61. See Aristide R. Zolberg, "International Engagement and American Democracy: A Comparative Perspective," in *Shaped by War and Trade: International Influences on American Political Development*, ed. Ira Katznelson and Martin Shefter (Princeton: Princeton University Press, 2002), 39 on the varied peacetime functions of the Navy, and Katznelson, "Flexible Capacity," 92 on spending and effectiveness of the Navy.

Mountain men often worked as guides, hiring out individually or merely providing ad hoc guidance to migrants or others at way stations or even settled private trading posts. Their activity was essentially individualized and immediate, and their contribution intermittent and unorganized. By contrast, government agents provided systematic, reliable information to the broad public, at public expense and for public benefit. Their efforts sought consciously to manage expansion, further the extension of U.S. interests, and fulfill a broader and more permanent societal purpose.[77]

Federal actions inspired widespread debate. The Sabbatarian controversy, for example, began in the years following the War of 1812 and revived as Congress in 1829 considered authorizing Sunday delivery of the mails. The historian Richard John vividly demonstrates how "the critical issue was not whether a particular class of Americans had actually been harmed by the Sabbath mails, but whether the central government had acquired the capacity to shape the pattern of everyday life."[78] Debate over the appropriate purpose and scope of the federal government involved postmasters, community members active in religion, communities in general, newspaper publishers, Eastern merchants who depended on the mails to maintain contact with Western markets, canal workers, and transportation contractors and private competitors. The sweep widened as the movement to halt delivery on the Sabbath expanded to include prohibitions against private contractors transporting mail on the Sabbath (as opposed to delivery by government agents).

These issues were part of a much larger debate regarding the scope and role of the federal government and its relationship to the life of the nation's citizens, morality, economics, and expansion.[79] Sunday mail delivery and Indian removal both confronted citizens with the coercive power of the national government, and both promised the continued expansion of federal activities in areas where federal preeminence in policy and decision making were well established. Jeremiah Evarts, Theodore Frelinghuysen, Return J. Meigs Jr., Richard M. Johnson, and many others played key roles in the debates over both the Sabbatarian controversy and Indian removal. Coming on the heels, in most communities, of other expansion-related debates

[77] Water rescues provide a different model, with the federal government supplying equipment and funds to volunteers on the East Coast and the Great Lakes after establishing the U.S. Life-Saving Service in 1848. Irving H. King, *The Coast Guard Expands, 1865–1915: New Roles, New Frontiers* (Annapolis: Naval Institute Press, 1996), ch. 10.

[78] Richard R. John, *Spreading the News: The American Postal System from Franklin to Morse* (Cambridge, MA: Harvard University Press, 1995), 191.

[79] Andrew, *From Revivals to Removal*, 200ff. Involved in this debate were Southern efforts to prevail upon federal administrators, in the Post Office but also in other organizations, to defend slavery and censor public discussions. See, e.g., Henry Mayer, *All on Fire: William Lloyd Garrison and the Abolition of Slavery* (New York: St. Martin's Griffin, 1998), 196–9, 216–20.

over land, trade, and economic and infrastructure development, community members without a sense of the federal government as a familiar force in their lives would have been cloistered indeed.

Conclusion

Washington Irving began his popular 1837 account of *The Adventures of Captain Bonneville* with demands for government action. His opening paragraph condemns the government for the loss of Astoria to the British in 1814, blaming "the unfortunate supineness of the American government in neglecting the application of Mr. Astor for the protection of the American flag." Irving's concluding paragraph calls upon the government again: "The facts disclosed in the present work clearly manifest the policy of establishing military posts and a mounted force to protect our traders in their journeys across the great western wilds, and of pushing the outposts into the very heart of the singular wilderness we have laid open, so as to maintain some degree of sway over the country, and to put an end to the kind of 'blackmail,' levied on all occasions by the savage 'chivalry of the mountains.'"[80]

Like the factory system and the trade and treaty systems established in the early republic, Indian removal testifies to the important and preeminent role played by the national government in managing and organizing westward expansion. The context of removal paralleled other issues being debated, designed, and administered at the national level on behalf of a variety of diverse interests and goals. Congress and the states gave Jackson and the executive branch extraordinary authority in both the East and the West. The authority granted to the presidency in the Removal Act and the 1834 laws, together with Jackson's own actions as president, generated numerous warnings about the expansion of presidential power throughout the era and its debates over Indian affairs, removal, and other issues.[81]

Yet this is as much a story of the influence and organization of the executive branch bureaucracy, as it is a story of power delegated by Congress. On the path toward the Removal Bill, the president, the Secretary of War, and officials in the Indian Office were driving forces in the politics of removal, in the design of the authority for and direction of implementing removals, and in managing the conflict between the states and the federal government. Congress delegated control and administration of civilization programs to the executive, and took its cues on funding and the continuation of the policy

[80] Washington Irving, *The Adventures of Captain Bonneville* (Washington, DC: National Geographic, 2003 [1837]), 1, 290. Irving presents, as a serious infraction, the departure of bee hunters "without any regard to the ordinance of the American government, which strictly forbids all trespass upon the lands belonging to the Indian tribes." Irving, *Adventures of Captain Bonneville*, 13.

[81] See Prucha, *American Indian Treaties*, 164; Remini, *Indian Wars*, 235.

from that branch's experts. The executive branch sought, and won, broad decision-making and administrative authority over the scope, design, and implementation of Indian removal. The Jackson administration would set about implementing removal with broad discretion, little planning, and little congressional oversight. And notwithstanding the tragic injustice of Indian removal, implementation of removals across the continent and across time would prove horribly effective.

6

Tragically Effective

The Administration of Indian Removal

The victory of Jackson and the pro-removal forces was not based merely on better arguments or the results of the great national debate taking place. Jackson's victory rewarded the skillful use of presidential power and of executive branch administrative offices and mechanisms in service of presidential policy. By the time the Removal Bill passed in 1830, the foundations for implementing removal had already been laid. Removals would continue throughout the 1830s, throughout the nineteenth century, and on into the twentieth.

Indian removal didn't just happen. Federal authorities led in planning, coordinating, anticipating, and reacting, and they led when it came to final accountability. The nation's administrators used an established administrative structure to prepare for and execute removal. Administrators adapted the treaty process for evolving purposes, and they did the same by shaping the use of personnel, locations, infrastructure, regulations, and other administrative tools. A clear organizational mission focused administrative activity, and a combination of administrative control and broad discretionary authority characterized the activities of the military and civilian officers carrying out removals.

Executive Branch Politics in Passage of the Removal Act

Jackson argued that removal was the only way to save the Indians from the fate he said had befallen the eastern tribes in the colonial era and in the years of the early republic. Proponents of removal argued that Indians lay in the path of violent and corrupting white settlers, and that white vices like the use of alcohol hindered reformers' efforts to educate and civilize the Indians. In a western Indian country, they argued, Indians would have a better opportunity to develop and eventually join white society. The humanitarian argument *promoting* removal put antiremoval groups on the defensive, and it gave large segments of the general public as well as government officials a humanitarian rationale to support removal. The Indian Office allied with and actively encouraged humanitarian arguments in support of removal, undercutting the arguments of other humanitarian and religious groups and providing a humanitarian rationale that paved the way for alliance between the national government and powerful interests in the Southern states.[1] This was part of the genius and eventual success of the removal policy as sold by Jackson and Thomas McKenney – they made a credible, persuasive argument that removal was the best thing for the Indians.

Jackson's administration lobbied hard to get Congress to pass federal legislation authorizing removal and outlining the president's formal authority to lead the removal effort, in the East and the West. The historian Robert Remini argues that Jackson "without doubt" intended to make removal his first piece of major legislation.[2] Following his election, President Jackson took immediate action within the executive branch to strengthen the coordination and power of the executive. Jackson appointed John Eaton, a Tennessee advocate of removal, as Secretary of War, and John Berrien, a Georgia advocate of removal, as Attorney General. Jackson promoted removal in his first annual message in 1829, and presidential positions were stated clearly and explicitly in public pronouncements, messages to Congress, and letters and instructions traveling between the branches of government and between the capital and field officers. Officials in the executive branch provided Congress with recommendations and influenced debate on and passage of legislation.[3] Thomas McKenney lobbied Congress directly, beginning with his annual report in 1827.[4] Politics favored removal, too: both the House and Senate Committees on Indian Affairs were headed by Tennessee Democrats favorable to removal.

The administration also worked hard outside of the capital. Jackson enlisted McKenney, longtime head of the Indian Office and the government's premiere expert on Indian affairs, to generate public support for removal in the Northeast. McKenney wrote to the Secretary of War about the importance of gaining support from humanitarian organizations. Wanting removal to be seen as the best solution for the Indians, McKenney wrote,

> Now this is precisely the end at which every friend to the Indian should aim. It is worse than useless to take other ground. It is unkind, nay, unmerciful to the Indians, to do it. That they cannot exist in their present relations to us, I think has been shown;

[1] On divisions among the religious societies, see William G. McLoughlin, *Cherokees and Missionaries, 1789–1839* (Norman: University of Oklahoma Press, 1995), chs. 11 and 12.

[2] Robert V. Remini, *Andrew Jackson and his Indian Wars* (New York: Viking, 2001), 231, 239.

[3] John R. Finger, "The Abortive Second Cherokee Removal, 1841–1844," *The Journal of Southern History* 47 (May 1981), 223.

[4] Ronald N. Satz, *American Indian Policy in the Jacksonian Era* (Lincoln: University of Nebraska Press, 1975), 15ff.; Herman J. Viola, *Thomas L. McKenney, Architect of America's Early Indian Policy: 1816–1830* (Chicago: Sage, 1974), 210.

to flatter them with the belief to the contrary, would be fatal. The past proves it, and the present teams with admonition. Nothing could be more kind to these people, than the frank and firm answer which has been given to them. It requires, however, to make it effectual, that the bodies of citizens who have associated to meliorate and reform the condition of these people, as also all who really wish well to them, should heartily co-operate in convincing them of the destroying effects of their existing relations, and of their necessary, and final, and fatal issue, and of the vast benefits which would flow to them from a change.[5]

McKenney coordinated the battle against organized opposition. Among the most influential opponents of removal stood the American Board of Commissioners for Foreign Missions, a group of Congregationalists and Presbyterians and the leading recipient of federal funds for civilizing the Indians.[6] The Board used the press, particularly among the Indians through the *Cherokee Phoenix*, to expose early removal preparations and condemn government policy even prior to Jackson's election.[7] Jeremiah Evarts of the American Board wrote essays, circulated messages, and lobbied persistently in the nation's capital.[8] With opposition to removal centered in the American Board, Jackson set McKenney to the task of winning the group's support. McKenney failed, then used federal funds to organize and supervise a rival group, the New York Indian Board, designed to promote removal with the "understood invitation of the Executive." The New York Board gained support among Baptists, who had significant Southern and Western political influence. Isaac McCoy worked with the Board, as did Lewis Cass. The New York Board was federally subsidized, directly supervised by McKenney, and at times it used money from the Indian Office's education fund to pay for publication of McKenney's pro-removal addresses. Cass helped publicize the Board, and in turn the Board drafted memorials to Congress in favor of removal.[9]

McKenney's role in removal was crucial, and good evidence of just how important the early bureaucracy's reputation could be. Into the 1820s, McKenney had trumpeted the advances being made by eastern Indians in becoming educated, civilized, and Christianized. His reports gradually become less positive in the mid-1820s. After an 1827 tour through Indian country, McKenney began to argue that Indian progress was not proceeding

[5] Thomas L. McKenney, *Memoirs, Official and Personal* (Lincoln: University of Nebraska Press, 1973 [1846]), 334.

[6] Satz, *American Indian Policy*, 13.

[7] Viola, *Thomas L. McKenney*, 219–20.

[8] John A. Andrew III, *From Revivals to Removal: Jeremiah Evarts, the Cherokee Nation, and the Search for the Soul of America* (Athens: University of Georgia Press, 1992); Francis Paul Prucha, *The Great Father: The United States Government and the American Indians* (Lincoln: University of Nebraska Press, 1984), 202ff.

[9] Francis Paul Prucha, "Thomas L. McKenney and the New York Indian Board," *The Mississippi Valley Historical Review* 48 (March 1962).

well enough. This became the basis for arguing that civilization efforts would be more successful if the Indians were removed to the West. This change in the attitude of the nation's leading expert in Indian affairs influenced the debate over removal and encouraged some humanitarian interests back East to consider the potential benefits of a removal effort. McKenney's expertise – his experience together with his recent travels and conclusions – were looked to much as we look to experts today to provide guidance on complicated issues like global warming and health care policy. McKenney was the nation's leading bureaucratic expert in Indian affairs, and his word had weight. Federal policy and the actions of federal officials were indispensable elements in the push for Indian removal.

Jackson and McKenney used other administrative weapons in the War Department and the Indian Office to further their cause. Jackson sent secret agents into the Indian nations to promote removal and fragment opposition. McKenney ordered field agents to resist requests by Indians to visit the capital, other agents and missionaries were ordered or strongly encouraged to support removal, and federal funds flowed to the administration's supporters and dried up for its opponents. Working early in the Jackson administration to promote voluntary removal among the Creeks, McKenney discouraged Creek emissaries from pressing their case against removal in Washington. McKenney suggested to Secretary of War Eaton that the War Department recognize the group as legitimate only if they agreed to cede their lands in Alabama and remove to the West. If they refused, McKenney recommended withholding recognition, challenging the group's credibility, and creating a public impression that they were troublemakers who did not represent the majority of Creeks or their interests. This plan was put into effect. Other efforts also manipulated the power of the tribes: the War Department threatened to close local agencies near resisting tribes and leave the tribes to deal with state representatives. More effectively, Jackson ordered that annuities no longer be distributed by agents to tribal leaders, but instead agents were to distribute them per capita – this undercut the authority of antiremoval leaders, while allowing federal agents to manipulate power, wealth, and status within the tribes.[10]

The opponents of Indian removal lost the debate for many reasons. As seen in the previous chapter, among these reasons was the nature of the debate: opponents' interpretation of the federal government's obligations was met by a powerful and convincing counterargument that federal authority should be used toward different ends. Behind the public debate over the appropriate use of the federal government's authority and might in the 1820s and 1830s, though, was the use to which government agencies and operators were being put. Before and after passage of the Removal Act,

[10] Michael D. Green, *The Politics of Indian Removal: Creek Government and Society in Crisis* (Lincoln: University of Nebraska Press, 1982), 159–60; 166ff.

the War Department and the Indian Office were vibrantly alive preparing for removal, neutralizing opponents, creating supporters, and managing the outcome of legislative debate and activity in the field.

Organizational Structure and Development

Congress did not specify administrative details when it passed the Removal Bill. Much as Congress had delegated to the War Department control over the particular mechanisms of the factory system, Congress delegated to the executive branch the responsibility for establishing and overseeing the administration of removal. The Removal Bill gave the Jackson administration clear authority to direct removal and dispense lands in the West. There were those like Pennsylvania Representative Joseph Hemphill who counseled delay in order to gain a better sense of what the Jackson administration might do with the authority granted by the Removal Act, but they were voted down in the House debates. Instead, Congress handed over broad authority and resources for an undefined removal program that included the authority to exchange unorganized lands in the West and grant title to emigrating Eastern Indians.[11]

The claim that removal would not work and that the federal government was dangerously unprepared for such an important undertaking was, like so many arguments past and present, ignored. It did not matter that the administrative structure for removal was not yet in place. It did not matter that careful plans for implementation and oversight were not in place. What did matter was the extension of federal authority, the broad increase in presidential power, and the belief that trial-and-error administration, on the foundation of forty years of federal Indian policy and related policies, would manage to blaze a path for removal.

Structures for administering removal did not need to be built from scratch. The executive branch already possessed a functioning administrative structure, built up during the factory system era and dealing with treaties, diplomatic negotiation, trade and alcohol regulation, provision and supply, and education and civilization initiatives. Removal could be approached through these existing structures by established personnel, many of whom had been advocating removal and pressuring tribes to move voluntarily from both North and South throughout the 1810s and 1820s. The progression to the Removal Bill was less a change in policy than it was another stage in the development of Indian affairs. Even under Jackson, removal and its manner evolved over time, with the administration gradually pushing harder and harder for treaties and actual removal against the opposition and delaying tactics of the tribes. The biggest change after Jackson's election lay in a vigorous commitment to effecting removal, and the willingness to use force.

[11] Satz, *American Indian Policy*, 31.

The administrative adaptations, reforms, and reorganizations that characterized the factory system era continued. The War Department, the Indian Office, and Congress worked through the 1820s to try to ensure that the administrative structures surrounding Indian affairs were maintained. Secretary of War John Calhoun established the Office of Indian Affairs, which he called the Bureau of Indian Affairs, in 1824 – two years after the official end of the factory system and the demise of the Office of the Superintendent of Indian Trade, which had become the center of nonmilitary Indian policy. Calhoun appointed McKenney and two clerks, and he spelled out the duties of the office, which included supervising treaties, annuities, and expenses, administering the civilization fund, and supervising the field personnel. A letter from Calhoun to McKenney illuminates the effort to outline the commissioner's duties within the War Department, standardize lines of authority, establish responsibility, and clarify the hierarchy of the field service. The detail here illustrates how inadequately words like "prebureaucratic" characterize the Indian Office in the 1820s.

> Sir – To you are assigned the duties of the Bureau of Indian Affairs in this [War] department, for the faithful performance of which you will be responsible. Mr. Hamilton and Mr. Miller are assigned to you, the former as chief, the latter as assistant clerk. You will take charge of the appropriations for annuities and of the current expenses, and all warrants on the same will be issued on your requisitions of the Secretary of War, taking special care that no requisition be issued, but in cases where the money previously remitted has been satisfactorily accounted for, and on estimates in detail, approved by you, for the sum required. You will receive and examine the accounts and vouchers for the expenditure thereof, and will pass them over to the proper auditor's office for settlement, *after* examination and approval by you; submitting such items for the sanction of this department as may require its approval. The administration of the fund for civilization of the Indians is also committed to your charge, under the regulations established by the department. You are also charged with the examination of the claims arising out of the laws regulating the intercourse with the Indian tribes, and will, after examining and briefing the same, report them to this department, endorsing a recommendation for their allowance or disallowance. The ordinary correspondence with the superintendents, the agents, and sub-agents, will pass through your bureau.[12]

McKenney had broad responsibilities for annuities and other affairs, and the letter outlines reporting structures and lines of authority. Annuity funds, presents, personnel, buildings, transportation, and so on all needed to be coordinated and tallied by the Indian office, a daunting task. McKenney's potential powers were broad: authority over the civilization fund and the power to recommend or condemn claims, for example.

McKenney had suggested systematic reform in Indian affairs before Jackson came into office, and a bill based on his suggestions was introduced

[12] Reprinted in McKenney, *Memoirs*, 57.

but failed to pass the House in 1826. Secretary of War Eaton publicized the administrative obstacles and problems facing the Indian Office, and McKenney's suggestions were taken up by Lewis Cass and William Clark, two of the era's most experienced and thoughtful experts on Indian affairs. Their plan became the basis for a systematic reorganization and clarification of the Indian Office. The Cass-Clark report, like McKenney's, stemmed from a perceived need for modernization in the War Department and Indian Office, and provided the basis for congressional action. Cass and Clark prepared their report in 1829 and, like many governmental overhauls, time passed before Congress enacted its major provisions. The report influenced laws passed in 1832 and 1834. The 1832 law officially authorized the president to appoint a commissioner of Indian affairs at an annual salary of $3000, and it gave the commissioner responsibility for managing and directing Indian affairs and "all matters arising out of Indian relations" under the direction of the Secretary of War, and "agreeably to such regulations as the President may, from time to time, prescribe."[13] This Act, together with the 1834 Trade and Intercourse Act and the 1834 Indian Office Reorganization Act,[14] standardized provisions for Indian agents and accounting procedures, and reorganized the Indian department and its provisions for regulating trade; these general guidelines remained in force for many years. As noted in the previous chapter, the acts abolished older agencies and superintendencies, consolidated others, and opened new ones in areas coming into importance. The acts had specific provisions, such as those providing salaries for blacksmiths, teachers, and interpreters, those offering guidelines for purchasing and contracting, and a provision forbidding persons employed in the Indian department from having "any interest or concern in any trade with the Indians, except for, and on account of, the United States." Many of the provisions of the 1834 Trade and Intercourse Act granted to the president, the Secretary of War, and/or agents and subagents discretionary authority to make, implement, and interpret regulations for carrying out the act's goals and provisions.[15] By the end of the Jackson administration, the central office included six clerks and about twelve clerical assistants. While these numbers may seem small, they exceeded the number working directly for the Secretary of War prior to the Mexican War, and the Office took up seven rooms in the War Department building.[16]

Beneath the Secretary of War and the Commissioner's office, regional and local officials supervised, adapted, and implemented policies. Territorial

[13] *U.S. Statutes at Large*, 4:564, reprinted in Francis Paul Prucha, ed., *Documents of United States Indian Policy*, 2nd ed. (Lincoln: University of Nebraska Press, 1990), 62.

[14] *U.S. Statutes at Large*, 4:729–35 and *U.S. Statutes at Large*, 4:735–8, reprinted in Prucha, *Documents*, 64–71.

[15] Viola, *Thomas L. McKenney*, 236.

[16] Satz, *American Indian Policy*, 155; 161–6.

governors continued to act as ex officio superintendents, and possessed general authority to supervise and control loosely defined areas; the superintendent at St. Louis, for example, oversaw all Indians west of the Mississippi River.[17] These officials were still under federal control: for example, the territorial governor of Arkansas yielded to the Secretary in a dispute about calling up recruits to help manage Indian affairs in the territory.[18] The historian Ronald Satz describes mid-nineteenth century-superintendents' "tremendous responsibilities" this way:

> They were in charge of a large number of field officials and had to keep accurate accounts for all of the agencies and subagencies under their jurisdiction. They also maintained special records for migrating Indians, treaty negotiations, claims investigations, and other miscellaneous circumstances. The job was extremely exhausting, challenging, and frustrating. New appointees often found that they had to spend weeks clearing up old business left by their predecessors, and Congress was parsimonious when it came to requests for clerical assistance.[19]

In the field, Indian agents, military officers, and a long line of special commissioners and observers held sway over administration and policymaking.[20] The location, titles, and duties of superintendencies, agencies, and subagencies changed as circumstances on the ground changed. In the 1820s, local agencies opened at Mackinac, Sault Ste. Marie, Green Bay, Chicago, Fort Wayne, and Piqua, many on the foundations laid by earlier military posts and trading factories. Wisconsin's becoming a territory shrank the Michigan Superintendency's borders, and through the 1830s and 1840s business shifted from Mackinac and Detroit, to Detroit primarily, then to Saginaw, and back to Mackinac by the 1850s.[21] The changes reflected efforts to adapt administration to changing patterns and personalities in Michigan. As is the case with modern reorganizations, individuals remained in the bureaucracy as boundaries, offices, and titles shifted. Henry Schoolcraft, for example, supervised the Sault Ste. Marie agency in Michigan, and became superintendent of the Michigan Superintendency in 1837 as Wisconsin became a territory and reduced the Michigan Superintendency's boundaries.[22] Removal necessitated adaptation of physical resources, too: new posts were built, old ones expanded, and some shuttered facilities were

[17] Ibid., 179–80.

[18] Brad Agnew, *Fort Gibson: Terminal on the Trail of Tears* (Norman: University of Oklahoma Press, 1980), 157; see chs. 6 and 11 generally.

[19] Satz, *American Indian Policy*, 180.

[20] Field officers also had a significant impact on legislation to end abusive trading practices. Robert A. Trennert, "The Fur Trader as Indian Administrator: Conflict of Interest or Wise Policy?" *South Dakota History* 5 (Winter 1974), 17–19.

[21] Charles E. Cleland, *Rites of Conquest: The History and Culture of Michigan's Native Americans* (Ann Arbor: The University of Michigan Press, 1992), 204.

[22] Ibid., 204.

pressed back into service.[23] The former factory sites often served as locations for organizing removal.[24]

By the 1830s, the field service officially consisted of four superintendents, eighteen agents, twenty-seven subagents, thirty-four interpreters, and miscellaneous officers. Official figures often omit informal or temporary hirings for interpreters, suppliers, carters, contractors, and others associated with Indian affairs administration. Paul Light estimates the "true size" of today's federal government by adding contractors, state officials implementing federal mandates, and others to the numbers of formal federal employees;[25] a similar calculation needs to be kept in mind when measuring the "size" of the federal government and the Indian Office or military in the nineteenth century. For example, missionary societies often directed education efforts in these years, but they worked closely with the government to generate funds and support. One report to Congress shows government expenses through the missionary societies of $214,500 between 1819 and 1842, with the societies contributing $180,000 of their own funds. The estimate does not include education funds allocated in treaty annuities, which were $12,000 by 1842 in support of 37 schools, 85 teachers, and 1,283 students.[26] The 1837 treaty with the Saginaw for Chippewa lands in Michigan allocated funds for education and schools, and for smallpox vaccine and medical services,[27] much of which would have been administered by people holding special appointments or residing in the area. The formal tallies of employees at the Indian Office sharply underestimate the number of individuals involved in administering the wide variety of federal initiatives.

Public Administration and Patronage

The effective administration of expansion and removal policies took precedence over patronage, which is too often and erroneously regarded as the dominant political dynamic in nineteenth-century public administration. Removal policies continued for decades despite changes in party control, and appointments and administration in important cases trumped patronage concerns. Patronage did not hinder, and sometimes even furthered, administration of federal policy.

Jackson furthered party interests and careers when possible, but he was primarily concerned with effecting Indian removal successfully. When both ends could be met – usually by appointing loyalists who were dedicated to

[23] Agnew, *Fort Gibson*, ch. 8.

[24] Grant Foreman, *Indian Removal: The Emigration of the Five Civilized Tribes of Indians* (Norman: University of Oklahoma Press, 1972), 25.

[25] Paul C. Light, *The True Size of Government* (Washington, DC: Brookings Institution Press, 1999).

[26] Laurence F. Schemeckebier, *The Office of Indian Affairs: Its History, Activities and Organization* (Baltimore: The Johns Hopkins Press, 1927), 40.

[27] Cleland, *Rites*, 217.

removal and were also effective, experienced administrators – that's what the administration did. When patronage and effective administration conflicted, patronage gave way and administrative necessity was served. From March 1829, when Jackson took office, to September 1831, Jackson removed ten of twenty Indian agents and nineteen of thirty-six subagents in the Indian service – hardly a record of restraint, but also no indication of the Indian service's devastation due to patronage appointments in the field.[28] According to the era's leading historian, Jackson's actions supported efforts to remove incompetent agents and economize by consolidating agencies.[29] The historian Robert Remini argues that Jackson's replacements were "reliable loyalists whose commitment to removal was above question."[30]

Looking more closely, the pattern of marrying partisanship and administration when possible, or prioritizing administration over patronage when necessary, becomes clear. A close look reveals that administrators in Indian affairs were hardly the "prebureaucratic" hack clerks often presumed in earlier scholarship. For example, while patronage seems to have affected some minor positions in the Indian service, it does not seem to have dominated appointments to the most sensitive posts upon which the outcome of U.S. policy rested. At the top, experience, professionalism, and loyalty characterized the heads of the Indian Office who followed Thomas McKenney. Samuel Hamilton served directly after McKenney, from 1830 to 1831. Hamilton was a career bureaucrat with considerable experience in the Indian Office: he had been McKenney's chief clerk from 1824 to 1830, supervising incoming correspondence and compiling and editing a list of all Indian treaties concluded before 1825.[31] Elbert Herring, who served from 1831 to 1836, was characterized as a man of great integrity but had little experience in Indian affairs prior to receiving the post, apparently at the urging of Lewis Cass. In this case, the Commissioner did not need to be an expert in Indian affairs: Secretaries of War John Eaton and Lewis Cass, both close Jackson loyalists, were firmly in command of removal. Even so, Herring engaged directly in administration and leadership, initiating a formal system of annual inspections of local Indian schools meant to encourage enrollment, and overseeing the Office's implementation of the 1834 acts overhauling the Indian service bureaucracy and the trade and intercourse laws.[32] Carey Harris succeeded Herring; Harris was a member of the inner circle led by Jackson and Cass, a loyalist with a deep commitment to removal and to

[28] Viola, *Thomas L. McKenney*, 223–4.

[29] Satz, *American Indian Policy*, 186.

[30] Remini, *Indian Wars*, 229.

[31] R. David Edmunds, "Samuel S. Hamilton, 1830–31," in *The Commissioners of Indian Affairs, 1824–1977*, ed. Robert M. Kvasnicka and Herman J. Viola (Lincoln: University of Nebraska Press, 1979), 9.

[32] See Ronald N. Satz, "Elbert Herring, 1831–36," in Kvasnicka and Viola, *Commissioners*, 13–16; Satz, *American Indian Policy*, 156–7.

controlling Indians through military power and carefully crafted education policies.[33]

T. Hartley Crawford served as Commissioner from 1838 to 1845, under four different presidents – an indication of his ability and apolitical career. Crawford had experience in Indian affairs, having served as one of the commissioners investigating the Creek frauds; Crawford's criticism of the Creek frauds and his appointment to replace the discredited Harris helped the Van Buren administration counteract growing criticism of removal. Crawford possessed experience in another major issue area occupying the Indian affairs bureaucracy: education. While a member of the Pennsylvania legislature in 1833 and 1834, Crawford had helped establish the state's new system of general education. Crawford was a strong advocate of removal and a diligent administrator; he concentrated on reforming communications between the capital and field officers, and on raising Indian service salaries as a way of improving the applicant pool.[34] Amid political uncertainties and confusion due to Harrison's presidential victory and subsequent death, with a Tyler administration that kept Harrison appointees and which alienated Whigs in Congress, the administrative level in Indian affairs was "remarkably stable" under the hand of Crawford.[35]

Experience and loyalty also played key roles in the selection of personnel to positions in the field. Florida Indian affairs were entrusted to Jackson ally James Gadsden; Gadsden in turn selected experienced, trusted interpreters, significant figures in the region, to assist in important treaty negotiations at Payne's Landing in 1832 and at other events.[36] Jackson, Eaton, and John Coffee served as treaty commissioners in the South in these years, and relationships among treaty commissioners familiar with the issues and with each other contributed to the coordination and effectiveness of their efforts.[37] The same can be said of the northern treaties and removals, which commonly involved experienced hands like James Gardiner, John McElvain, and John Johnston – the latter described sympathetically by Charles Dickens, traveling through Ohio in 1842 a few days after Johnston concluded a treaty with Wyandot leaders. In the West, the Stokes Commission – including favorite Jackson agent John Schermerhorn – exemplified how federal agents

33 Ronald N. Satz, "Carey Allen Harris, 1836–38," in Kvasnicka and Viola, *Commissioners*, 17–22; Satz, *American Indian Policy*, 213–14, 257–8.

34 Ronald N. Satz, "Thomas Hartley Crawford, 1838–45," in Kvasnicka and Viola, *Commissioners*, 23–7; Satz, *American Indian Policy*, 159, 270.

35 Finger, "Abortive," 211.

36 See, e.g., John K. Mahon, *History of the Second Seminole War, 1835–1842* (Gainesville: University of Florida Press, 1992), 75–9; Prucha, *Great Father*, 247, 257; Roy W. Meyer, *History of the Santee Sioux: United States Indian Policy on Trial*, revised edition (Lincoln: University of Nebraska Press, 1993), 55.

37 See, e.g., Remini, *Indian Wars*, 102–21.

in important decision-making positions often possessed considerable experience and expertise.[38]

Key agents effective in other important field posts held their positions through numerous presidential administrations and across changes in party control.[39] Lawrence Taliaferro, agent in present-day Minnesota, served in every administration from Monroe to Van Buren; Henry Schoolcraft in the Michigan region served from 1822 to 1841 and again in the Polk administration; William Clark (of Lewis and Clark) served in St. Louis and the West from 1807 to 1838. Changes for political reasons tended to involve experienced replacements. Following the 1840 defeat of the Democrats, for example, the experienced Schoolcraft was replaced by Robert Stuart – a political maneuver, certainly, but Stuart had experience as the former Chief Superintendent of Astor's American Fur Company, and he was filling a position in Michigan in 1841 which remained at the forefront of expansion and development efforts.[40]

Military officers involved in Indian affairs were also a fairly stable, experienced group. Many retained their postings for years and sometimes for decades, like Matthew Arbuckle at Fort Gibson. Others, like Winfield Scott, Edmund P. Gaines, James Gadsden, and George Sibley moved around and engaged Indian affairs in different regions with growing expertise and experience.[41] Despite the ongoing rivalry between civilian and military

[38] Grant Foreman, *The Last Trek of the Indians* (New York: Russell & Russell, 1972 [1946]), 94–5; see also 122 n8 on Schermerhorn's talents. See also Francis Paul Prucha, *American Indian Treaties: The History of a Political Anomaly* (Berkeley: University of California Press, 1997), 209–10. State leaders often had considerable public service and Indian affairs experience, as well: Wilson Lumpkin, for example, a key figure in the removal debates, served as a representative to Congress from 1815 to 1831, as Governor of Georgia from 1831 to 1835, and as a U.S. Senator from 1837 to 1841 – close to thirty years of service from the factory system era through the peak of removal efforts in the South.

[39] See, e.g., Green, *Politics of Indian Removal*, 50.

[40] Cleland, *Rites*, 229. The disbursing agent for Creek removal also had a solid public service career, outlined in Gaston Litton, ed., "The Journal of a Party of Emigrating Creek Indians, 1835–1836," *The Journal of Southern History* 7 (May 1941), 227 n7. Trennert finds that Indian agents in the period from the 1830s to the 1850s were often experienced fur traders, and that "Most were more honest than they have received credit for." Trennert, "Fur Trader," 2, and see 2 n3; see also Alvin M. Josephy Jr., *The Nez Perce Indians and the Opening of the Northwest* (Boston: Houghton Mifflin, 1997 [1965], 415. Appointments often followed careful lobbying pressure and negotiation between trading companies and the government. Trennert, "Fur Trader," 3.

[41] Agnew, *Fort Gibson*, 6. On Gaines, see Silver, "Edmund Pendleton Gaines." On Gadsden, see Mahon, *Second Seminole War*, 40, 74. On Scott, Zachary Taylor, and William Tecumseh Sherman in the Seminole War, see Mahon, *Second Seminole War*, chs. 8, 11, and 13, and 298. On Sibley, see Andrew C. Isenberg, "The Market Revolution in the Borderlands: George Champlin Sibley in Missouri and New Mexico, 1808–1826," *Journal of the Early Republic* 21 (Fall 2001), 449. Numerous other departments featured long-tenured experts, including Civil War military supply departments, military surgeons, and personnel at the Treasury Department (Mark R. Wilson, *The Business of Civil War: Military Mobilization*

officers, in many cases the two wings of the War Department worked in concert in the field toward their mutual ends. Arbuckle, commander at Fort Gibson, assigned Indian affairs Subagent Nathaniel Philbrook to broker a peace with the Osages in the early 1820s, specifically because Philbrook had been responsible for the negotiation of an 1822 treaty with the Osage. "If anyone could persuade the Osages to surrender the accused warriors [at the heart of a dispute], it was he."[42]

Patronage and government administrative aims easily coincided. Appointments of treaty commissioners were driven by political considerations as well as the need to appoint men who could accomplish their jobs: Ronald Satz concludes that "[Jackson] appointed men who had the greatest influence over the tribe, since his object was to secure the signing of removal treaties as quickly as possible.... Jackson's successors continued the practice of choosing men with considerable influence over the tribes. The emphasis was clearly on the rapid negotiation of removal treaties."[43] John Schermerhorn was a favorite hired gun during the Jackson and Van Buren Administrations. Schermerhorn had long experience dealing with Indians in the east and on scouting parties in the West; he was a prominent proponent of divide-and-conquer strategies that fragmented Indian resistance to removal and allowed commissioners and others to claim to have Indian support for treaties and other agreements. Schermerhorn engaged in treaties with twenty Indian nations in the removal era, and whites and Indians alike saw him as "Jackson's man" in negotiations.[44] Schermerhorn was one of three members of the 1832 Stokes Commission at Fort Gibson, which aimed at pacifying the West and negotiating agreements covering removed Indians to the region; he guided negotiations for Cherokee removal at the Treaty of New Echota in 1835; and he was a driving force behind the Treaty of Buffalo Creek that removed the Seneca from New York. His attempts to negotiate removal agreements at Fort Gibson with the Seminole were a prime cause of the Second Seminole War of 1835–1842, when the Seminole rejected the shady deal. While Schermerhorn worked carefully with Democrats and enjoyed

and the State, 1861–1865 [Baltimore: The Johns Hopkins University Press, 2006], 35, 2, 40). Thomas Jesup led the Quartermaster's Department from 1818 to 1860; his chief clerk served for thirty-seven years starting in 1824; and George Gibson served as the nation's top food procurement officer from 1818 to 1860. Wilson, *Business of Civil War*, 40. William Thornton served at the head of the Patent Office from 1802 to 1828. Daniel Preston, "The Administration and Reform of the U. S. Patent Office, 1790–1836," *Journal of the Early Republic* 5 (Autumn 1985), 334. Joseph Totten, involved with the Bernard Board and seacoast fortifications for close to fifty years, was the Army's Chief Engineer from 1818 to 1864. Emanuel Raymond Lewis, *Seacoast Fortifications of the United States: An Introductory History* (Annapolis: Naval Institute Press, 1979), 37–53.

42 Agnew, *Fort Gibson*, 27.

43 Satz, *American Indian Policy*, 195.

44 Laurence M. Hauptman, *Conspiracy of Interests: Iroquois Dispossession and the Rise of New York State* (Syracuse: Syracuse University Press, 1999), 181.

appointments by Jackson and Van Buren, the importance of patronage was at least equaled by his skill, expertise, and effectiveness in the field.[45]

Two appointments in New York illustrate how patronage served administrative ends in the North. James W. Stryker and Ransom Gillett, Democratic operatives in upstate New York, helped Schermerhorn tailor the Treaty of Buffalo Creek, a corrupt deal by which the Seneca lost their lands and began to slide inexorably toward removal from New York. The point to remember here is that the government's policy focused on removal and the development of upstate New York, with the attendant consequence for Van Buren of solidifying Democratic control in the state. The goal was not the fair and just treatment of New York's Indians. To this end, the efforts by Stryker and Gillett to remove Indians, and build support for the Democrats by so doing, furthered both party and policy goals quite effectively. Without condoning the government's actions, we must acknowledge that patronage did not inhibit federal policy and administration in Indian affairs and expansion-related public policy. Rather, patronage often complemented and furthered administration.

Importantly, when the desire for patronage conflicted with the needs of administration, patronage gave way. Secretary of War Lewis Cass and others found ways to support the patronage system without crippling the administrative needs of national policy.[46] In the Choctaw case, for example, Secretary of War Eaton had appointed George Gaines as removal agent for the Choctaws because the Choctaws trusted him and because of Gaines' experience in the area. When Eaton resigned in 1831, his replacement, Lewis Cass, attempted to capitalize on removal's patronage opportunities to enhance his political position. Cass removed the trusted Gaines and assigned Francis Armstrong, a vocal supporter of Jackson, as superintendent of Choctaw removal. For a variety of reasons, the move helped Cass with Jackson, hurt anti-Jackson forces, and helped Jackson's support in the West.

The Choctaws balked at the displacement of their trusted liaison; they refused to remove until Gaines was put back in charge. Cass responded by delegating broad control over field operations, including the authority to nominate agents, to George Gibson, Commissary General of Subsistence. Satz continues the story: "... Cass had Gibson transfer Armstrong to the important position of Choctaw agent in the West and then placed Gaines in control of all removal operations to the west bank of the Mississippi River. Gibson agreed with the secretary of war that the appointment of Gaines was a necessary step to '*break the ice & pave the way for future removals.*'"[47] In another example, a trusted agent to the Quallatown Cherokee, William Thomas, was replaced by Thomas Hindman, a proponent of removing the

[45] Ibid., ch. 11.

[46] Satz, *American Indian Policy*, 74.

[47] Ibid., 74 emphasis in original.

Eastern Band of Cherokees. The Indians had developed a strong relationship with Thomas, and Hindman proved largely ineffective because the Indians did not trust him. Hindman was relieved of his position once it became clear that the Indians were unlikely to remove so long as he was in charge.[48] Elsewhere, Creek Indians were ready to comply with removal as long as John Hogan, a trusted agent, was appointed to oversee the process. But the momentum under Hogan was disrupted when other government agents let a contract for removal to a company that had been active in stealing Indians' lands, and which the Indians expected would try to steal as much as possible from the twenty dollars a head promised by the government. The enrollment and removal preparations collapsed.[49]

When patronage threatened implementation of removal, Cass and others found ways to support the patronage system while furthering the administrative needs of national policy. Patronage itself could further administration, by binding administrators to the goals of party and nation over the interests of Indians. When patronage was likely to hinder progress toward administrative goals, patronage appointments routinely gave way to more effective administrators.

Organizational Dynamics

Mission

It is important not to lose sight of policymakers' understanding that removal was an element of managed expansion and extended settlement. Greed was not the only motive involved in removal; many believed sincerely in the humanitarian rationale that removal was best for the Indians, whether in a national framework or merely as a rationale for what they saw in their own state or region. Motives and incentives in Indian affairs are always complex and multidimensional, as in any major policy area.[50] Like the British effort to establish a line across the Alleghenies, which satisfied both expansionist and nonexpansionist interests – and like the factory system, which appealed to development interests, large traders, land speculators, and even tribes and individual Indians – the removal policy appealed to a variety of contradictory, conflicting interests. People and groups that focused on expansion and national security, along with states' righters, miners, settler communities, speculators, and contractors saw removal as the best way to

48 John R. Finger, *The Eastern Band of Cherokees, 1819–1900* (Knoxville: The University of Tennessee Press, 1984), and Finger, "Abortive."

49 Foreman, *Removal*, 140.

50 See, e.g., McLoughlin, *Cherokees and Missionaries*, 244ff., Bernard W. Sheehan, *Seeds of Extinction: Jeffersonian Philanthropy and the American Indian* (Chapel Hill: University of North Carolina Press, 1973), ch. 9; on the pro-removal press' benevolence, see George B. Ellenberg, "An Uncivil War of Words: Indian Removal in the Press, 1830," *Atlanta History* 33 (Spring 1989), 56–9.

get rid of Indian problems. Some humanitarian interests saw removal as the best way to *protect* the Indians, by getting them out of harm's way and relocating them in a distant place where civilization initiatives and contact with other tribes – and reduced contact with whites – would in the long run help Indians assimilate successfully to white ways. Tribes, and factions within tribes, fought desperately to prevent removal and stay on their homelands, yet even in Indian communities many accepted removal as the most promising chance for survival, and many believed the promises made to them in treaty and other agreements that they would be protected and supported along the route and in the West. There was considerable opposition to removal, but – for a wide variety of conflicting rationales – there was also some support for it as national policy and as the answer to local difficulties.

The concept of removal as the primary mission aligned many of these diverse interests behind a simple and agreed upon goal. Whether for greed, expediency, speculation, humanitarianism – or simply because it was an administrator's job – the simple idea of removal unified policy and administration. Agents and subagents, treaty commissioners and investigators, military leaders and the rank-and-file received guidance from headquarters and discretionary authority in the field to achieve this goal. Removal was about removal.[51]

Removal as a concept began early in U.S. history. Thomas Jefferson usually gets credit for first suggesting that Eastern Indians and whites alike would be best served if the Indians moved west. Efforts to remove Indian communities up and down the East Coast had been ongoing for decades by the time Congress passed the Removal Bill in 1830, and presidents down to field agents had promoted, pressured, and manipulated processes in favor of removal for decades. As early as 1817, a Senate Committee on the Public Lands reported favorably on the concept of exchanging Indians' Eastern lands for lands in the West; the policy would aim at ordering "the irregular form of the frontier, deeply indented by tracts of Indian territory" by consolidating white settlements and by moving Indians away from contact with whites, "by which the civilized man cannot be improved, and by which there is ground to believe the savage is depraved."[52] The 1820 Treaty of Doak's Stand with the Choctaws noted the government's goal of exchanging lands in the East for territory in the West.

[51] On field discretion, see Mahon, *Second Seminole War*, 46 (treaty commissioners); Josephy, *Nez Perce Indians*, 229 (agents). On the difficulty of administering a removal, see, e.g., Mahon, *Second Seminole War*, 55.

[52] Quoted in Prucha, *Great Father*, 184. On Jefferson and removal, see Sheehan, *Seeds of Extinction*; S. Charles Bolton, "Jeffersonian Indian Removal and the Emergence of Arkansas Territory," *Arkansas Historical Quarterly* 62 (Autumn 2003); James R. Christianson, "Removal: A Foundation for the Formation of Federal Indian Policy," *Journal of Cherokee Studies* 10 (Fall 1985), 218–19.

By the 1830s, Jackson's dedication to removal was explicit, clear, and simple. Jackson wrote often of removal, including this typical statement to John Coffee in 1826: "You must get the whole territory [of the Chickasaws and Choctaws] or none.... the chickasaw and choctaw country are of great importance to us in the defence of the lower country, a white population instead of the Indian, would strengthen our own defence much."[53] The historian Robert Remini writes that the failure of the Adams and Monroe administrations to effect removal helped convince Jackson that stronger presidential leadership – his own – would be needed in order to remove the Indians and secure the territory. During negotiations with the Choctaw in 1830, President Jackson made his aim clear to the Senate: "The great desideratum is the removal of the Indians, and the settlement of the perplexing question involved in their present location."[54] The Indian Removal Act begins, "An Act to provide for an exchange of lands with the Indians residing in any of the states or territories, and for their removal west of the river Mississippi."[55] Jackson was clear about the mission in his public messages, which described the logic and goals of removal precisely and explicitly to the vast public audience.[56]

Removal was a bedrock policy goal, easily understandable and easily pursued. In Florida during the brutal Seminole War, General Thomas Jesup recommended that the government draw a line through the state and allow Indians to remain south of the line. Secretary of War Joel Poinsett bluntly rejected the suggestion: "The acts of the executive and the laws of congress evince a determination to carry out... [the removal policy], and it is to be regarded as the settled policy of the country."[57] The same year, 1838, General Winfield Scott addressed reluctant Cherokees and stated, with little room for misunderstanding, "The President of the United States has sent me, with a powerful army, to cause you, in obedience to the Treaty of 1835, to join that part of your people who are already established in prosperity on the other side of the Mississippi."[58] From 1836 to 1838, and including the Seminole, Creek, and Chickasaw contexts, Commissioner Carey Harris made it clear to subordinates that speed and economy of removal took priority over other, more humanitarian concerns. Harris aided whites in obtaining slaves from the Seminoles as the Indians were forced out, colluded directly with land speculators during Creek removal to facilitate the transfer of land allotments to whites, and threatened to withdraw assistance,

53 Quoted in Remini, *Indian Wars*, 224.

54 Quoted in Prucha, *American Indian Treaties*, 169.

55 *U.S. Statutes at Large*, 4:411–12, reprinted in Prucha, *Documents*, 52.

56 See "First Annual Message," reprinted in Prucha, *Documents*, 47ff.; "Seventh Annual Message," reprinted in Prucha, *Documents*, 71–2.

57 Quoted in Prucha, *American Indian Treaties*, 176.

58 Quoted in Prucha, *American Indian Treaties*, 181.

including rations, from Chickasaws if they delayed or deviated from the prescribed removal route – even though the Chickasaws were using their own funds to pay for their removal.[59] Harris's successor T. Hartley Crawford pursued the mission of removal in part by overlooking the miseries of removal itself; he reported to Congress, for example, that during Cherokee removal "Good feeling has been preserved, and we have quietly and gently transported 18,000 friends to the west bank of the Mississippi." Crawford conveniently omitted mention of the estimated four thousand Cherokees who died on the "Trail of Tears."[60] Populations applauded removals, as in Ohio: "There was great jubilation in Ohio over this final expulsion of the last remaining Indians from the state and the prospective placing on the market of a great area of desirable real estate."[61]

The mission of removal invited creative adaptations in pursuit of the overarching goal. Treaty provisions allotting Eastern lands in small parcels to individual Indians, for example, might at first glance suggest a willingness on the government's part to let Indians stay in Eastern regions as eventual citizens of the states. These provisions, however, pursued removal – just more gradually, as a nod to regional circumstances. Allotment was necessary in some cases because of Indian reluctance to remove; allotment also sounded good to humanitarians and other interests that opposed forced removals. But ultimately allotment made it easy to dispossess Indians of their lands: allotments were easy to alienate from Indians and quickly lost to speculators, traders, or alcohol vendors. Allotments to individual Indians could be used as bribes, and small reservations could be further dismantled at the next treaty. Allotments also allowed, and in some cases encouraged, whites to overrun Indian lands that had been broken up from the tribal base, as happened among the Creeks.[62]

Particularly in the North, U.S. policy followed a pattern of gradually shrinking reservations and encouraging piecemeal removals by so doing. Decisions were left to treaty commissioners, who had clear instructions on how the allotting process fit into the overall mission. Cass wrote to the commissioners at the Treaty of Chicago, in 1833: "Decline, in the first instances, to grant any reservations either to the Indians or others, and endeavor to prevail upon them all to remove." Cass went on to instruct the commissioners that if this proved impossible, they were to grant reservations "circumscribed within the narrowest possible limits."[63] The haphazard appearance

[59] Satz, "Carey Allen Harris," 18–20.

[60] Satz, "Thomas Hartley Crawford," 24.

[61] Foreman, *Last Trek*, 99 n25. See also Prucha, *Great Father*, 221, 234, 235, 240, 247, 268, 301; Prucha, *American Indian Treaties*, 179; Remini, *Indian Wars*, 115, 227; George Klos, "Blacks and the Seminole Removal Debate, 1821–1835," *The Florida Historical Quarterly* 68 (July 1989), 56, 67, 70, 74.

[62] Prucha, *American Indian Treaties*, 173.

[63] Cass, quoted in Prucha, *Great Father*, 247.

of removal efforts in the North can be explained by the fact that removal was the goal. If that was best served by piecemeal removals of small groups who were willing to go, then so be it. Treaties and allotment provisions helped the U.S. grind out a policy of removal of the Northern tribes.[64]

Actions in the West were also driven by the goal of facilitating Eastern removal. The military at Fort Gibson in Arkansas, for example, stood by as intertribal fighting took place in the 1820s. The historian Brad Agnew notes that the military's bystander attitude was no "sinister plan to encourage the Indians in a war of self-destruction but rather a reflection of the primary objective of the government to protect white settlers and encourage Indian removal with a minimum outlay for military expenses."[65] Later, tensions and conflicts in the West threatened removal by frightening Eastern Indians who were considering moving West. Some of the Eastern tribes were under the influence of common stereotypes, fearing the Western Indians as savages whose interests and ways were at odds with those of the more settled, agricultural Eastern Indians.[66] When disruptions in the West looked like they might deter Eastern Indians from removing, the military in the West was ordered to maintain peace and tranquility on the frontier, so as to reassure Eastern Indians contemplating removal. The military thereafter worked much harder to negotiate a series of shaky peaces among the tribes in order to pacify the region.[67]

Investigations and oversight also facilitated removal. Government policy generally aided and protected land speculators within the framework of U.S. policy, to the detriment of Indian interests. The Creek frauds, for example, by which white speculators obtained huge tracts of Indian lands illegally, inspired numerous special investigations and recommendations for reform. Some of the recommendations were heeded, and helped smooth the process in later removal efforts, which exhibited less overt fraud and during which Indians received better returns for their lands. At the same time, the results of the frauds and of the investigations never threatened to halt the actual removal of Indians, and the federal government was more than willing to assist in protecting gains made by fraud. It is easy to conclude that government oversight in such cases was inept or incompetent, but it is clear that the driving force was less government incompetence than government complicity that aided and effectively condoned the frauds. What the government would not do was dedicate itself to protecting Indian or tribal interests in the East.[68]

64 See Prucha, *American Indian Treaties*, ch. 7; Foreman, *Last Trek*.

65 Agnew, *Fort Gibson*, 76.

66 David LaVere, *Contrary Neighbors: Southern Plains and Removed Indians in Indian Territory* (Norman: University of Oklahoma Press, 2000), 6, 26–9.

67 Agnew, *Fort Gibson*, 53, 199, 205.

68 Mary E. Young, "The Creek Frauds: A Study in Conscience and Corruption," *The Mississippi Valley Historical Review* 42 (December 1955), 423.

Investigations that seemed to hinder removal could be defeated. White interests easily delayed the federal investigation surrounding the Creeks, and effectively stepped up pressure for removal by creating circumstances favorable to piecemeal immediate removals. Violence broke out, which some believed was instigated by whites to force the federal government's hand. Cass ordered the military to suppress the hostilities, instructing the commanding officer that "Your efforts will be directed to the unconditional submission of the Indians. As fast as this can be effected, and as any portion of them can be collected, they must be disarmed, and sent immediately to their country west of the Mississippi."[69] Cass suggested that even nonhostile Creeks would probably become hostile if they weren't removed, so they should be taken and moved as well. Further investigation of the Creek frauds could be continued after the Creeks had been removed. Almost twenty thousand Creeks were moved over the next two years, 1836 and 1837. Investigations of the 1838 Cherokee removal in the early 1840s were driven partly by sincere consternation over the expense, fraud, and inhumanity created by the removal, but partly too by the government's desire to get the remaining Cherokees to remove. The procedures for adjudicating claims were carefully designed to favor Indians who might be willing to settle their claims and remove to the West.[70]

Creek removal from Alabama demonstrates how the dynamics of politics, public administration, and investigations furthered the goals of Indian removal. Among the Creeks, as elsewhere, U.S. promises to investigate claims about fraudulent behaviors and promises to compensate Indians worked to extend the clock, weaken Indian resistance, provide hope for future justice, and assuage critics of removal's implementation. Yet the promise of investigations was often a future promise – such matters could be settled and adjusted later, during or even well after Indians had removed to the West.

Administrative Tasks

Aspects of administration in the removal era were extensions of earlier efforts. Treaties needed to be signed, censuses taken and populations classified, provisions procured and distributed. Add to this the nuts and bolts of physical removal – police presence, law enforcement orders, adjudication of disputes, provision for food and transport, and accompanying dynamics along the route. Add to this increased efforts to use treaties to allocate lands to individual Indians, and the administrative mechanisms supporting land exchanges, which sped the process of alienating those lands to white speculators and land companies. Add to this, too, constant and high-tension negotiation in the West to receive, process, and relocate embittered Eastern Indians – and at the same time mollify and manage Western Indian

[69] Quoted in Green, *Politics of Indian Removal*, 185.

[70] Finger, "Abortive," 216, 219–20.

populations, who often opposed the new immigrants and foresaw encroachments by white settlers. Removal quickly became a massive administrative undertaking, one that belies conceptions of government activity as defined by the addition of simple and routine tasks to existing units.

Administration differed, East to West. In the East, dispensing treaty annuities had become one of the main tasks of federal agents. Annuities, guaranteed under treaties, were annual payments for the lands ceded by tribes to the United States. Annuities, rations, and presents supported the tribes, yet annuities raised questions of means and regulation. Agents usually dispensed annuities at the agencies, giving funds or goods to local leaders who then distributed them to others. Annuities could be dispensed as goods, services, or as cash, each leading to its own problems. Cash easily found its way from Indians to whites, for example, and could be a source of antagonism and conflict. Dispensing cash, though, was easier than procuring and distributing goods or services. Cash also provided a way to influence relations between Indians and local whites, as debts could be paid quickly and directly. The dispensation of annuities provided leverage for local agents, and indirectly the federal government, to influence and manipulate local circumstances, and to reward or punish individual Indians by empowering or disempowering them.[71] In an administrative environment in which personal characteristics and relationships remained critical, the ability to decide who got what payments was important. The ever-changing regulations covering annuities distribution methods indicate the fluid nature of administration in Indian affairs.

Treaties remained the primary method for transferring lands from Indians to non-Indians in the removal era. As the Jackson and Van Buren administrations worked to get agreements that would encourage Indians to leave the Eastern states, the process of negotiating new removal treaties animated a host of administrative tasks. As in earlier years, treaty negotiations often required procurement and distribution of large amounts of goods and provisions. Five to six thousand Indians attended the Treaty of Dancing Rabbit Creek in 1830, for example.[72] Procurement for so many goods and services was no simple task, as Congress and executive branch officials worked to keep up with increasing payments. Treaty negotiators bestowed rations on Indian guests, under authority given the president in the 1834 reorganization act, at times using army provisions shifted into duty for treaties and negotiations.[73]

71 See Prucha, *Great Father*, 171.

72 Prucha, *Great Father*, 216.

73 Prucha, *Great Father*, 170. For excellent discussions of treaty negotiations, see Josephy, *Nez Perce Indians*; George S. Gaines, "Notes on the Early Days of South Alabama," reprinted in *The Alabama Historical Quarterly* 26 (Fall/Winter 1964), 199; Mary Elizabeth Young, *Redskins, Ruffleshirts, and Rednecks: Indian Allotments in Alabama and Mississippi, 1830–1860* (Norman: University of Oklahoma Press, 1961), ch. 2.

Treaty and related activities created complicated administrative tasks in Washington, DC, as Indian leaders were hosted, feted, entertained, and brought to negotiations and meetings with executive branch administrators and congressional representatives.[74] Designing, fashioning, paying for, transporting, and distributing peace medals generated a variety of regulations and procedures. The Cass-Clark report laid out clear and detailed rules regarding the distribution of peace medals, stipulating not only who could receive them, but also how a breakdown of size and materials would reflect the relationships between Indians and U.S. agents. The medals were integral parts of U.S.–Indian relations, in a political sense; they were also designed as works of art, destined for posterity. Designers and craftsmen were chosen carefully, and administrators at the U.S. Mint in Philadelphia did the striking.[75]

Census taking, a complicated and familiar aspect of public administration throughout the republic's history, supported the removal effort.[76] Census taking was not simple – people were hard to find, and often resisted being identified and counted. A census followed the Creek treaty of 1832, with the aim of ensuring that qualified Indians would be registered for lands; a locating commission followed.[77] The federal government took a census of the Cherokee in 1835, in anticipation of removal, counting people and outlining their locations, lands, improvements, and so on. Agents appraised improvements again in 1836, and decided which Indians who wanted to stay were qualified to remain. Some Indians received certificates denoting their permission to stay in North Carolina, although this process seems to have been implemented inconsistently.[78] Census taking supported efforts to sign treaties with Indians that allotted lands to individual landholders. These policies demanded complicated administrative efforts by special land agents. Surveys were run, parcels allotted, deeds registered. The policies also invited tremendous frauds. The frauds, in turn, invited more efforts to control administration, often through lawsuits, lobbying, and investigations. Taking a census itself could be a sensitive political issue: listing blacks among the Seminoles, for example, raised tensions by suggesting that they would be sold in advance of removal.[79]

[74] See, e.g., Herman J. Viola, *Diplomats in Buckskins: A History of Indian Delegations in Washington City* (Bluffton, SC: Rivilo Books, 1995).

[75] Prucha, *Great Father*, 174–6; Viola, *Diplomats in Buckskins*. On the continuing importance of medals in the reservation era, see Loretta Fowler, *Arapahoe Politics, 1851–1978: Symbols in Crises of Authority* (Lincoln: University of Nebraska Press, 1986), 33–4, 39, 79. Officials sometimes gave full U.S. military uniforms. See Fowler, *Arapahoe Politics*, 33.

[76] E.g., Klos, "Blacks," 56; Young, *Redskins*, 74.

[77] Young, "Creek Frauds," 413.

[78] Finger, *Eastern Band*, 16–18.

[79] Klos, "Blacks," 75.

As Indians prepared to remove, other administrative tasks came into play. Traders didn't want Indians leaving until debts were paid – whether those debts were real or fabricated by the traders. Suppliers and contractors competed for supply contracts and other lucrative benefits stemming from the Indians' move. Indian agents managed and negotiated accusations and complaints, adjudicated disputes, and worked to supply Indians who had sold their lands and their goods before, during, and after the trek west. Indians and soldiers needed provisions during removal, too, and sometimes weapons: the government ordered $1,200 worth of rifles for the Seneca, to help them hunt along the way.[80]

New lands had to be scouted and evaluated by tribal leaders considering removal. U.S. administrators supervised trips to western areas so that tribes facing removal could assess potential new lands. Congress appropriated $15,000 for exploration into western lands in 1828, part of a series of western inspections organized by the federal government and frequently including representatives of eastern tribes.[81] One trip involving Creeks, Choctaws, and Chickasaws in 1828 lasted more than six months, and included Indian representatives as well as federal subagents, translators, friends, and advisors totaling more than forty men and sixty horses.[82] In 1832, Congress authorized the appointment of three commissioners to seek out appropriate lands in the West to handle the incoming Choctaws, Creeks, and Chickasaws. Cass gave the Stokes Commission detailed instructions, and the commissioners represented significant actors in the politics of the day: in addition to Schermerhorn, the trio included a prominent businessman and a former governor of North Carolina.[83] In the years after the 1833 Treaty of Chicago with the Potawatomi, scouting parties left for Kansas to evaluate potential new homes.[84]

Federal agents often had to deal with segments of Indian populations that refused removal or that had arranged to stay. What would become the Eastern Band of Cherokee, for example, worked diligently in the field and through representatives in Washington, DC, to stay where they were, even as most Cherokees moved west. Following an 1819 treaty, federal agents registered forty-nine Cherokee family heads and surveyed their lands as part of a plan to allow those families to stay in North Carolina.[85] Similar dynamics complicated removal in Michigan, where the Pokagon band – which had been excluded from the removal treaty in effect – had to obtain a

80 Foreman, *Last Trek*, 67.

81 Prucha, *Great Father*, 228; LaVere, *Contrary Neighbors*, 23ff., 57; Alban W. Hoopes, *Indian Affairs and their Administration, 1849–1860* (New York: Kraus Reprint, 1972 [1932]), 8; Bolton, "Jeffersonian Indian Removal."

82 LaVere, *Contrary Neighbors*, 57.

83 Prucha, *Great Father*, 226.

84 Cleland, *Rites*, 223.

85 Finger, *Eastern Band*, 10.

court order to stop General Hugh Brady from forcing their removal.[86] Agents also tried to sort out controversies involving reserved lands, for example in North Carolina when the state inadvertently sold off lands reserved by treaty to Cherokees. A state court decision in 1824 upheld the treaty, the state worked to purchase the lands, and – in another indication of the federal role in Indian affairs – the federal government reimbursed the state.[87]

Piecemeal removal from the North created a steady stream of piecemeal tasks and ad hoc administrative requirements. Agent Pierre Menard at Kaskaskia, in a letter to William Clark typical of the era, noted in fall of 1830 that he expected close to five hundred Shawnee and Seneca from Ohio who would need provisions through the winter. Five hundred more Miami and Stone Eaters would also need provisions, and Menard requested $7,025. He also requested $1,500 to provide clothes for some of the women and children, who he expected would arrive almost naked in the cold autumn. Menard also told Clark that he would need an extra $500 to pay for ferrying the Indians across the Kaskaskia and Mississippi Rivers.[88] A different group, this time Seneca Indians moving in 1833, filled two rooms of a large riverfront warehouse in St. Louis with their belongings.[89]

In the West, other problems faced military and civilian agents. Forts and posts had to be built, and often they were moved or troops were shifted in response to changes in circumstances. It took time to build fortifications, often years; military personnel spent far more time cutting down trees and digging trenches than they did fighting. Military and civilian agents worked throughout the 1820s and 1830s to negotiate and communicate with Western tribes, many of whom were in conflict with each other and with military and settlement interests. When the United States decided in 1828 to move Cherokees from Arkansas to lands further West – Cherokees who had only moved to Arkansas a few years earlier – new treaties had to be signed and new arrangements made. The United States paid for improvements that the Cherokees had made to the Arkansas lands, and boundary disputes were worked out at organized gatherings of the Cherokees, Shawnees, Mohawks, Delawares, Creeks, and others who had taken up residence in the area.[90]

Complicating efforts to negotiate peace among so many tribes was the fact that the powers of chiefs of the various bands of Comanche, Kiowa, and Osage were extremely limited – meaning that agreements had to be

86 Cleland, *Rites*, 223.

87 Finger, *Eastern Band*, 11.

88 Foreman, *Last Trek*, 56–7. On Clark's complex tasks, large supervisory field, exercise of discretion, and his early focus on economic regulation and the factory system to stem competition and its ill effects, see James P. Ronda, "Red-Head's Domain: William Clark's Indian Brokerage," in *Between Indian and White Worlds*, ed. Margaret Connell Szasz (Norman: University of Oklahoma Press, 1994), 84 and generally.

89 Foreman, *Last Trek*, 68.

90 LaVere, *Contrary Neighbors*, 54–5.

worked out with many different bands and groupings. This complicated the process of making agreements, and also complicated the administrative tasks of supplying transportation, communications, presents, medals, and so on.[91] Translating negotiations, speeches, and agreements into multiple languages at such multinational negotiations was a daunting task in and of itself. As Eastern tribes made their way west, agents tried to calm their fears of western Plains tribes. Western officials also worked to dampen the Western tribes' opposition to having new Indians compete for goods and game. All of these affairs were affected by fluid political developments in Mexico and Texas, which posed constant problems as potential allies or as catalysts for conflict. Throughout the period, intermittent violence threatened to catapult the region and its dozens of tribes and tens of thousands of people into full scale war.

Effectiveness

Accounts of the removal of the Potawatomi from Indiana reveal the fruits of the government's blend of a clear mission, oversight, and order. The Indians' priest, Father Petit, wrote, in a passage that deserves to be quoted at length:

> On September 4, 1838, they were lined up, some afoot, some on ponies, followed by the wagons, and all heavily guarded with guards at the rear with bayonets, which were often used to keep the weak ones in the procession. Before starting the torch was applied to their village, so that they might see their homes destroyed and they would not want to return. When all was in readiness, this grewsome procession, nearly three miles long, like a funeral procession, which in reality it was, started on its final journey. It was a very sickly season....
>
> [The order of march was] The United States flag, carried by a dragoon; then one of the principal officers, next the staff baggage carts, then the carriage, which during the whole trip was kept for the use of the Indian chiefs; then one or two chiefs on horseback led a line of 250 or 300 horses ridden by men, women and children in single file, after the manner of savages. On the flanks of the line at equal distance from each other were the dragoons and volunteers, hastening the stragglers, often with severe gestures and bitter words. After this cavalry came a file of forty baggage wagons filled with luggage and Indians. The sick were lying in them, rudely jolted, under a canvas which, far from protecting them from the dust and heat, only deprived them of air, for they were as if buried under this burning canopy – several died thus[.][92]

Such is not the result of a weak, disorganized, and bungling government. Such is the result of a clear and accepted administrative mission, careful preparation, logistical planning, and execution.

[91] Ibid., 90.

[92] Quoted in Foreman, *Last Trek*, 111 and 124 n23.

The administration of Indian removal was problematic in many ways, from provisioning and preparation to cost effectiveness – not to mention the overwhelming injustice of the policy in the first place, which raises all sorts of ethical questions surrounding this particular instance of public administration. Yet as much as Indian removal was tragic and unjust, it was effective. The mission of the Indian service, the military, contractors, law enforcement officials, and others was to remove Indians from their homes and relocate them farther West. If this could be done humanely, fine – but we should remember that even a humane removal was not the goal for many people involved in promoting and implementing the process.[93]

Martin Van Buren wrote of removal that what Jackson had begun had been "crowned with complete success."[94] The Indian Office and the War Department removed Indians from Eastern regions and cleared land and title for white enterprise and settlement. The United States forcibly uprooted and relocated roughly one hundred thousand Indians from Southern states to areas West of the Mississippi River, a commonly used figure which does not include earlier ad hoc, voluntary, and coerced removals from areas in the South, or the thousands of people removed from the Old Northwest. It is the effectiveness of removal, and of other federal policies like the factory system, that created the "antebellum" South about which Richard Bensel writes, "An inhabitant of the South could travel through great swaths of the southern and central Appalachian upland, the Ozark region of Missouri and Arkansas, and the piney wood sections of Alabama, Georgia, Louisiana, and Texas without encountering another citizen who owed a significant portion of his livelihood to federal employment."[95] To the extent that this was true (and I'm not sure it was), it was because the federal officials had come and gone – they had built the roads that traveler was using, they had cleared the land of American Indians, and they had gone with those Indians to the West. The South exists as a states'-rights paradise before the Civil War only because it had successfully prevailed on the federal government to pacify and recreate that region. Removal worked.

93 Wilcomb Washburn is critical of an approach that sets the removal of Indian bodies as the criteria for evaluating the success of removal. Washburn's concern for the morality of the removal policy, the safe arrival of Indians being relocated, and the relationship of stated goals to what happened on the ground are tremendously important in understanding the full import of Indian policy. It is partly out of concern that such issues are not overlooked that I have generally chosen to use the word "effective" in describing removal, and to use "successful" in particular, specific contexts, such as in interpreting contemporary observers' reactions to removal and its implementation. Wilcomb E. Washburn, "Indian Removal Policy: Administrative, Historical and Moral Criteria for Judging Its Success or Failure," *Ethnohistory* 12 (Summer 1965).

94 Quoted in Laurence F. Schmeckebier, *The Office of Indian Affairs: Its History, Activities and Organization* (Baltimore: The Johns Hopkins University Press, 1927), 37.

95 Richard Franklin Bensel, *Yankee Leviathan: The Origins of Central State Authority in America, 1859–1877* (Cambridge: Cambridge University Press, 1990), 105.

Careful management over many years kept the lid on affairs in the West, despite the influx of new, bitter, dislocated tribes and the presence of culturally different Plains tribes who saw the removed Indians and the U.S. military and settlement presence as threats to *their* way of life. The argument has even been made that removal protected tribes that might have disappeared otherwise, in effect validating the arguments put forward in support of removal by Jackson and others. Francis Paul Prucha writes, "In spite of internal dissensions [within the tribes], the growth of these nations in the Indian Territory presaged an era of peace and prosperity that was taken as a sign of the wisdom of removal and the potentialities of the Indians to adapt to white ways."[96] Ronald Satz suggests that some of the social programs designed and implemented by the Indian Office and its personnel in this era were successful to varying degrees.[97]

Administration in itself was effective, showing a marked capacity for improvement and institutional learning as the removal years wore on. The Choctaw treaty and removal was an administrative nightmare. The treaty did not simply establish removal to the West; it included inducements, payments, and guidelines for allotting lands in the East to different categories of family and status, provisions to deal with improvements that had been made by the Indians, provisions for handling debts they had incurred, different types of reserved land, and many other complicated provisions. "All in all, the disposition of these lands and the settlement of claims arising from their sale led to nearly interminable conflicts between the Indians, bona fide settlers, and land speculators that delayed removal and unsettled land titles for years following the treaty."[98]

After the Choctaw test case, Cass turned removal over to the military and removed all civilian agents from removal-related posts. Cass hoped that this would make future removals more efficient and alleviate some of the continuing problems arising between civilian and military officials.[99] Gibson issued a set of governing regulations soon thereafter, and the 1832 and 1833 removals went more smoothly than the first one in 1831. The Creek Treaty improved upon the Choctaw treaty, being more administratively manageable and less of a forced removal treaty. Yet the federal government failed to evict intruders from lands allotted to remaining Creeks, and speculators took advantage of Indians' unfamiliarity with legal niceties to gain even more lands. Moreover, the contract to help the Creeks remove went to a company that the Creeks believed had been defrauding them for years.

96 Prucha, *Great Father*, 279. Pearson deems the vaccination program something of a success, as well: J. Diane Pearson, "Lewis Cass and the Politics of Disease: The Indian Vaccination Act of 1832," *Wicazo Sa Review* 18 (Autumn 2003), 28–9.

97 Satz, *American Indian Policy*.

98 Prucha, *Great Father*, 217.

99 Satz, *American Indian Policy*, 78–9.

In 1836, these dynamics led to open fighting between the Creeks and the Georgia militia. Once again, the federal government sought to take the lead in handling matters. Federal officers took over command of maneuvers, with Cass ordering removal of the Creeks as a military measure. The army removed remaining Creeks, often in chains or handcuffs, in July and August of 1836. Roughly 14,600 Creeks were removed to the West.[100]

The Chickasaws benefited from the experiences of the Choctaws and Creeks. By the time of Chickasaw removal, the federal government had adjusted its policies and procedures regarding allotment of lands based on what had been learned from earlier experiences. Speculators also had changed their methods, and the land in the cotton regions was worth more – all of these factors made affairs with the Chickasaws work somewhat more smoothly than they had with the Choctaws and Cherokees. The Chickasaws received greater return for their lands; the speculators developed a speculators' claim association to adjudicate disputes before they could make their way to the federal government's courts and investigators. The government abandoned the notion of having Indians settle on their allotments, and worked to oversee a process of sale to speculators that would be more fair and safe than earlier sales had been. These dynamics combined to achieve even more effectively the goals of the era, even though once again they looked past the idea of protecting Indians in their lands and traditions.[101] Historians have called Chickasaw removal "more tranquil" and "the least traumatic" in relation to earlier efforts.[102]

In the West the government's efforts could be effective, too, as defined at the time. Some tribes continued to show improvements in agriculture, education, civilization, adopting white dress, and other standards of the day for vindicating the removal policy. "[T]he southern nations showed tremendous resilience in reestablishing an orderly and productive existence beyond the Mississippi," Prucha writes. "Organized governments continued, agricultural development (including large plantations run in part by slave labor) quickened, school systems were established, and missionary endeavors were renewed and encouraged."[103] Matthew Arbuckle, twenty years the commander at Fort Gibson, summed up his successes in his final report in 1841, just after being relieved by General and future president

[100] Prucha, *Great Father*, 218–23.

[101] Mary E. Young, "Indian Removal and Land Allotment: The Civilized Tribes and Jacksonian Justice," *The American Historical Review* 64 (October 1958), 43. See also Young, "Creek Frauds."

[102] Prucha, *Great Father*, 224; Thomas D. Clark and John D. W. Guice, *The Old Southwest, 1795–1830: Frontiers in Conflict* (Norman: University of Oklahoma Press, 1996 [1989]), 249; Young, *Redskins*, ch. 6.

[103] Prucha, *Great Father*, 272; see also Remini, *Indian Wars*, 228 and 228 n4; Foreman, *Last Trek* discusses a variety of effects of removal on the tribes, some horrendous and some demonstrating promise in the West. See also Prucha, *Great Father*, 278.

Zachary Taylor. Arbuckle emphasized the fort's peacekeeping role in handling tens of thousands of Indians "removed under circumstances which rendered them anything but friendly disposed towards the United States or its inhabitants." Arbuckle wrote that "at no period have the Whites on our border or the Red people of this frontier been in a more perfect state of quiet and Security than they now enjoy."[104] Whether or not Arbuckle was right in his assessment, his primary goal and the focus of two decades of work is clear.

Removal stands as such a tragic monument to our past precisely *because of* its effectiveness. Treaty after treaty was signed; group after group was removed by themselves, by civilian agents, by private contractors, or by armed military; tribe after tribe was relocated in the West. U.S. officials achieved their ends both in the short term and the long. Historians have sometimes misconstrued the effectiveness of removal by viewing administration of Indian policy as part of a scattered and weak national administrative effort. The historian Ronald Satz, for example, terms the federal government "an incorrigible bungler."[105] Yet the government forcibly moved tens of thousands of people thousands of miles, all the while maintaining existing programs for education and training and beginning new ones. Removal was tragic; aspects were bungled; "civilization" was problematic in aim and result. Nevertheless, administrators at the War Department effectively accomplished their primary goal of removing Eastern Indians across the Mississippi and situating them on administratively manageable lands in the West. From the standpoint of understanding national public administration and bureaucratic capacity in the nineteenth century, this is the salient fact. Removal is not infamous because it was bungled; it is infamous because it was administered with imposing effectiveness.

[104] Quoted in Agnew, *Fort Gibson*, 204; Prucha, *Great Father*, 276.

[105] Satz, *American Indian Policy*, 178.

7

Public Administration, Politics, and Indian Removal

Perpetuating the Illusion of Failure

Evaluated by its objectives, Indian removal was tremendously and horribly effective. As administrative control was won – again – by federal authorities, however, it would not be Andrew Jackson and Thomas McKenney who did the difficult and disturbing work of forcibly relocating entire communities of Native Americans. Federal authorities, civilian and military, together with state officials, private contractors, and ordinary settlers and citizens did the heavy lifting. Indian officials, too, were involved, in resistance efforts and in efforts to manage or control or shape the process. The artful combination of standardized guidelines and common purposes with discretionary authority in the field, characteristic of the Indian Office's work in the factory system era, settled deep into the service by the removal years.

Over time, the Indian service's effective but localized administrative decision making during removals was forgotten, as contemporary and later observers focused on the U.S. failure to protect Indian interests and on the injustice of federal policy. Localized and personalized administration was an easy target for criticism, especially given the diverse interests actively engaged in Indian affairs at the time. As in the factory era, it served many interests to discredit the Indian service, even where charges of maladministration and corruption were not supportable. And as the course of Indian affairs evolved, many of the interests satisfied with removal's outcome became less active in Indian affairs or became opposed to expenditures being made for Indian affairs in the West. As in the factory era, one of the major reasons that we do not today consider the government's actions during removal as effective is because it was in the interests of the parties involved to obscure the effectiveness of Indian removal. By the end of the principal era of removal, the focus and the participants in Indian affairs had shifted again. New interests in the West became involved to ensure that Indians in the West were contained and isolated on reservations, the lands of which were to be gradually broken up and sold off.

Administration in Action: Local Discretion and Control

The Jackson administration proceeded with removal quickly and without a detailed plan of how it would implement the policy. During the Monroe administration, McKenney had prepared a list of all Indians residing in the states and territories. When McKenney asked Jackson and Eaton to wait while a systematic removal plan was drawn up for the Jackson team, Jackson refused. Recognizing the potential variations in specific local circumstances, and eager to cement executive control over the removal process, Jackson moved ahead. The administration's haste aimed directly at preventing Congress from defining explicitly the "mode and manner" of removal.[1] The ad hoc nature of many of the removals, particularly in the North, stemmed from having a clear and immediate mission combined with this lack of careful planning. Organization was not the goal of the Jackson and later administrations. Immediate removals, even if piecemeal or lacking thorough planning, were preferable to the delays that would be necessary if Indians were to move only in complete groups or if detailed, specific plans were to be worked out for each removal party. Field officers often did the best that they could in their local, specific contexts, but removal itself was the point of the endeavor.

Choctaw removal became a test case, and Jackson's eagerness to implement removal and have control over its administration made Choctaw removal a trial-and-error scenario. Authorizing broad discretion to field agents and contractors allowed the administration to forego much planning and coordination at the beginning of the process. Eaton told William Clark that "the nature of the service requires that you should be allowed a discretion as to all matters that may arise. You will, therefore, in your own way, pursue such a course as you may deem best."[2] Similar discretion was given to other regional supervisors for removals. Cass, after replacing Eaton at the head of the War Department, also authorized vast discretionary powers to field agents.[3] As Cass placed early Choctaw removal under civilian control, Commissary General of Subsistence George Gibson, overseeing efforts in the East, wrote to agent George Gaines that Gaines had complete discretion in making decisions for Choctaw removal. "It is not intended to confine the superintendent to any plan of operation.... The whole operation will be left open to the exercise of his judgment, formed – as it must be – upon a

[1] Herman J. Viola, *Thomas L. McKenney: Architect of America's Early Indian Policy: 1816–1830* (Chicago: Sage, 1974), 201; Ronald N. Satz, *American Indian Policy in the Jacksonian Era* (Lincoln: University of Nebraska Press, 1975), 65.

[2] Quoted in Arthur de Rosier Jr., *The Removal of the Choctaw Indians* (New York: Harper, 1970), 139–40. See also Satz, *American Indian Policy*, 64.

[3] Satz, *American Indian Policy*, 73.

nearer and more accurate view of the circumstances of the case."[4] Efforts to standardize removal and systematize the process did take place, but many of the adaptations were worked out during the Choctaw removal and the lessons applied to later removals of other tribes. As in other eras of Indian policy, federal authorities sought a mixture of standardization, oversight, and discretion that allowed far-flung field agents the freedom to find their own paths toward a common end. As in the factory system, field agents and street-level bureaucrats were key parts of the puzzle.

This approach created enormous pressure on agents in the field and led to difficulties as the agents struggled to handle new and unforeseen situations. Some of the obstacles facing removal agents throughout the era were out of their control. Language differences complicated the gathering of information about routes.[5] Disease, especially cholera and the fear of it, often made worse by damp or cold weather, also hindered efforts.[6] Almost eight hundred Cherokees delayed their removal in 1834 because they had been warned about disease along the route.[7] Weather and floods provided particularly unpleasant obstacles to removal efforts.[8] The historian Arthur de Rosier notes that severe weather during an early Choctaw removal required the supervising military officer, L. T. Cross, to make decisions and expenditures without formal authorization.

> Cross faced the challenge of transporting these 1,100 exhausted Choctaws to Indian Territory without any money, food, or even instructions. In this emergency, he took the initiative; without authorization he hired wagons and horses, and purchased food on the credit of the United States government. But, being in no position to bargain, he was forced to pay exorbitant prices to the local citizens for these goods; each Indian ration, for example, cost him... more than twice the normal price...[9]

The historian Grant Foreman echoes the sentiment:

> The government was launched without compass or rudder into the uncharted sea of Indian removal; for the first time it was about to engage on a large scale in the removal of its aborigines from their homes in which it was bound to collect and feed them, transport them across the great Mississippi river, carry them part way by steamboats and then overland through swamps and across streams, build roads and bridges, cut banks down to the streams, and finally locate these expatriates, men

[4] Quoted in de Rosier, *Removal*, 142. See also Gaines's account, in George S. Gaines, "Notes on the Early Days of South Alabama," reprinted in *The Alabama Historical Quarterly* 26 (Fall/Winter 1964), 213–14. Gaines describes problems with such discretionary arrangements on 225–8.

[5] Grant Foreman, *Indian Removal: The Emigration of the Five Civilized Tribes of Indians* (Norman: University of Oklahoma Press, 1953), 339; de Rosier, *Removal*, 145ff.

[6] Foreman, *Removal*, 76.

[7] Ibid., 252.

[8] Ibid., 151, 65, 97, 300, 336.

[9] de Rosier, *Removal*, 146–7.

and women, the aged and decrepit, little children, and babes in arms, in their new country.[10]

Such obstacles placed a premium on local decision making by officials in charge of removal, who were responsible for responding to unforeseen events. The agents relied on their discretion and judgments about particular circumstances to guide and organize removal behaviors.

As in the factory era, officials did not always enjoy being given broad grants of authority to use at their personal discretion. In charge of a removal party moving through Illinois, James Gardiner voiced his concerns in a letter to William Clark at St. Louis: "Deeply sensible of the responsibility which devolves upon me. . . . I am extremely solicitous to exercise all possible prudence and caution, in preserving the lives and health of the eight hundred defenceless human beings committed to my care. . . . I feel that I should be utterly without apology, if I rushed unnecessarily and unadvisedly, into the region of a terrible malady, and thus expose to probable destruction so many of the human race." Gardiner's concerns and questions indicate the seriousness with which he took his charge, and also afford some insight into the vast number of decisions that had to be made in the course of removal by agents in the field, sometimes with advice and sometimes without:

I therefore respectfully ask your advice as to the proper *time*, and *place* and *manner* of crossing the Mississippi; the route from thence, with *one* of the tribes, to the confluence of the Neosho and Arkansas rivers, and with the *other two*, to the southern side of the Kansas . . . and the best and cheapest mode of supplying subsistence and transportation on the way. Would you advise me to cross the river as soon as possible? And, if not, *how long*, and *where* do you think it best to tarry? Should I not be furnished immediately with one or *two* experienced physicians? If so, can you send me such, or recommend me whom to employ? We have two hundred dollars worth of medicines, *badly selected*, but do not know how to use them on important occasions. [paragraph] I trust we shall not long remain destitute of funds, unless the prevalence of the cholera at Cincinnati, of which we have just heard, shall delay or prevent the return of Lieutenant Lane, the disbursing agent.[11]

Clark wasn't completely comfortable with his authority, either. After being appointed the military agent for removal, Clark received authority to delegate points of issue for rations and to choose purchasing agents and other subordinates. Clark complained, uncomfortable with such responsibility.

[10] Foreman, *Removal*, 47.

[11] Portions of this letter are reprinted in Robert W. Richmond and Robert W. Mardock, eds., *A Nation Moving West: Readings in the History of the American Frontier* (Lincoln: University of Nebraska Press, 1966), 73–4; emphasis in reprint. Some contracts, such as that for Creek removal, included provisions for health care along the way, and gave the doctor considerable authority to mediate disputes between contracting companies and government agents. Gaston Litton, ed., "The Journal of a Party of Emigrating Creek Indians, 1835–1836," *The Journal of Southern History* 7 (May 1941), 227, 228 n10.

Regional supervisors like Clark also worried about being held responsible for the discretionary actions of subordinates like Gardiner, who might make disastrous choices in the field, and by those who might be tempted to turn removal into a profit-making venture.[12]

Yet, as in the factory era, federal agents took what was given them and made decisions when necessary. Despite the absence of an organized plan for Indian removal, field officials working on Choctaw removal made extensive preparations. Agent Gaines, charged with providing for removal, established precedents during Choctaw removal that influenced later field operations, such as the taking of censuses, encouraging farmers to plant corn instead of cotton to feed removing Indians, ordering corn and implements from ports on a standby basis, preparing wagons, weapons, tools and implements, establishing drinking water along the removal routes, advertising for cattle in the West, and erecting depots and stocking them with provisions. Commissary General Gibson, who had provided the Army with rations since 1818, took charge of the provisioning effort with an explicit awareness of the economic and moral precedents at stake in Choctaw removal. In careful instructions, Gibson communicated to his subordinates the goals of economizing and also of the moral rightness of removal.[13] Provisions were arranged, censuses taken, roads built, ferries constructed.

Examples of field agents relying on their own judgment in pursuit of the removal policy fill the histories of the era. During a Seneca removal through St. Louis, Clark had to approve more teams than had been authorized in order to account for the number of old, sick, and children too young to walk, plus the large amount of goods purchased by removing Seneca Indians (to sustain them in the absence of provisions along the route).[14] Added expenses for doctors and for coffins followed rough weather as the Indians struggled west from St. Louis.[15] Agents set their own trading and alcohol regulations, bending their instructions and guidelines when they believed it necessary.[16] One agent allowed Indians to carry dangerously burdensome amounts of baggage with them during removal; another accounts for the high expense of Chickasaw removal by pointing to the Indians' purchase of thousands of dollars of goods, and their insistence that they be allowed to take these goods with them. The agent, a military officer, concluded, "If I was wrong [in allowing them to bring their goods], it was in not obeying the Regulation. Feelings of kindness and justice compelled me to take the course

[12] Satz, *American Indian Policy*, 76.

[13] Satz, *American Indian Policy*, 70. Litton, "Journal," 227, includes attention to removal instructions.

[14] Grant Foreman, *The Last Trek of the Indians* (New York: Russell & Russell, 1972 [1946]), 68.

[15] Ibid., 69.

[16] E.g., Roy W. Meyer, *History of the Santee Sioux: United States Indian Policy on Trial*, revised edition (Lincoln: University of Nebraska Press, 1993), 41ff.

I did."[17] Those in charge of Indians being removed contracted on the fly for oxen, wagons, and other goods and transportation, and they constructed buildings to house headquarters operations and other administrative tasks. Field operatives appointed official aides and interpreters at their discretion.[18] At times, local or regional officials submitted plans to the War Department and lobbied for approval to go forward with removal efforts.[19] Finally, local agents made choices – sometimes unfortunate ones – about where exactly to locate removed Indians.[20]

Superiors learned to depend upon the discretionary choices made by the agents in the field. One reason for this was the constant barrage of ideas and opinions, which made it incumbent upon someone to make choices. Field agents approached questions using their specific knowledge of local conditions and people, but finding agreement on a plan could be difficult. A good example of the deference paid to the opinions of agents in the field comes from the effort to remove the Seminoles from Florida.[21] A key issue in removal of Seminoles from Florida centered on the place of the Seminoles' black slaves, coveted variously by white southerners, government agents, speculators, and Creek and Seminole Indians. These slaves and their context in the region contributed greatly to the significance of Indian affairs in Florida and in the South generally.

One plan for dealing with the Seminoles' slaves, supported by President Jackson and his allies in Florida, was to allow whites to purchase them in hopes that that would help clear the path for removal of the Seminoles. Jackson, Governor Richard Call, and Indian Office Commissioner Carey Harris all envisioned such a policy as furthering the main goal of removal. They also foresaw that such sales would alleviate a problem that threatened to complicate Indian affairs in the West, because if the slaves traveled West with the Seminoles the problems of ownership and competition, especially

17 Quoted in Foreman, *Removal*, 217–18.

18 Foreman, *Removal*, 42–3, 164, 257, 53.

19 See, e.g., Laurence M. Hauptman, *Conspiracy of Interests: Iroquois Dispossession and the Rise of New York State* (Syracuse: Syracuse University Press, 1999), 179; Francis Paul Prucha, *The Great Father: The United States Government and the American Indians* (Lincoln: University of Nebraska Press, 1984), 218ff., 240–1.

20 A removal agent dealing with the Creeks, for example, settled them on land in the North-eastern part of Indian territory, because they could more easily be supplied there and also be under the protection of Cantonment Gibson. Not only was this not where the Creeks had agreed to be settled, but the land itself had already been claimed by and reserved for Cherokees. David LaVere, *Contrary Neighbors: Southern Plains and Removed Indians in Indian Territory* (Norman: University of Oklahoma Press, 2000), 64–6. See also Foreman, *Last Trek*: as Kansas and the Indian Territory received more and more emigrations without an overarching plan, mistakes like this became common.

21 See George Klos, "Blacks and the Seminole Removal Debate, 1821–1835," *The Florida Historical Quarterly* 68 (July 1989), John K. Mahon, *History of the Second Seminole War, 1835–1842* (Gainesville: University of Florida Press, 1992), ch. 6.

with the Creeks who were also moving West, would continue to occupy the military and the Indian service for years to come. Selling these slaves in Florida benefited whites in the area, cleared the path for removal, and inoculated the government against future problems in the West.

Local Agent Wiley Thompson, though, worried that selling the Seminoles' slaves in Florida would "bring into the [Seminole] nation a crowd of 'speculators,' some of whom might resort to the use of improper means to effect their object, and thereby greatly embarrass our operations."[22] Thompson recognized that such sales were opposed by the Seminoles and by the blacks, who were close to the Seminoles and generally preferred life with the Indians to life with the whites. Thompson recognized that arranging sales of the blacks in Florida could galvanize resistance to removal and hinder the government's main object of removing the Indians and securing the country. Even rumors of such a policy could upset the delicate negotiations taking place in pursuit of Seminole removal.

Ultimately, Thompson's view prevailed, and he was given authority to deny the entry into Seminole country of traders to whom he had not issued a license, and he was authorized to issue such licenses at his discretion. The case illustrates several typical dynamics of removal, and of Indian affairs generally. The clear mission of removal drove planning. Immediate concerns – getting removal under way – took precedence over future concerns for the situation in the West. Illegal and immoral means were countenanced, and even promoted, if they promised effectiveness in furthering the policy. Federal goals played out at the local level in unique ways, with a close connection between state interests and federal leaders. Finally, the decision over how to handle the issue deferred to the agent in the field, a decision that here seemed to cut against the interests of whites who had looked to recover or purchase slaves at bargain prices from emigrating Seminole Indians. That deference to the field agent ultimately drove implementation in the field: the agent's opinion prevailed, and he was given considerable discretion thereafter to deny entry to traders and to issue licenses. This allowed the field operator to decide when selling slaves would promote removal, and when refusing to sell would promote removal. Removal remained the goal.

Personalized and Inconsistent Administration

The effectiveness of the removal policy rested on a delicate balance of shared mission, oversight, and local discretionary authority. Decision making and relationships with interested parties, Indian and non-Indian alike, relied heavily on the abilities of the individuals involved. This personal dynamic did not inhibit administration, but it inevitably created inconsistencies from place to place, and even in dealings with the same tribe over time as personalities changed.

[22] Quoted in Klos, "Blacks," 73.

Examples of the importance of individuals dot the landscape of the removal era. Individual appointments were critical to successful removal efforts, as we have seen. Tribal leaders insisted that removal be guided by trusted agents, and might refuse to work with strangers. Disruptions caused by the absence of trusted individuals or the removal of individuals with strong relationships to tribal leaders were common; some individuals who had been removed for patronage reasons were returned to their posts when it became clear that the individual was a necessary part of a successful removal.[23]

Field agents implemented all aspects of removal in different ways in different places. Among the Creeks, different agents responsible for managing and approving deeds to Indians established different administrative mechanisms, set different prices, and used different means to accomplish their ends, all with the approval of superiors because they pursued the same goals.[24] Unique motives, interested parties, and local circumstances characterized Seminole removal with dynamics and forces that were not present, or that were present in different ways, in the removal of other southern tribes. The specific provisions of treaties differed, and attitudes toward allotments and the actions of private interests helped make each context unique. Changing participants and attitudes, new events, feelings of being slighted, and rumor all buffeted agents' relationships with tribes and individuals, Indian and non-Indian alike. Reliance on individual discretion allowed for adaptation to circumstances without the delay that would have followed waiting for approval of decisions and actions from Washington,[25] but it led to a variety of different solutions and methods being used in different areas and to attendant confusion and contention among agents and subagents as to method and means of removal.[26]

Despite the heavy burden carried by administrators in the field, though, removal did not take place in a haphazard manner. The War Department and others sought to ensure that removal took place within an organized structure of rules and accountability. The Secretary of War and other officials issued detailed instructions to treaty commissioners, military officers, Indian agents, land regulators, fraud inspectors, and others, as requirements and politics on the ground evolved. Instructions were issued to guide commissioners in deciding claims and adjusting payments from traders at treaty negotiations.[27] The adjutant general distributed instructions to post commanders and quartermasters following the 1834 reorganization.[28] Later

[23] Foreman, *Removal*, 27, 46.

[24] Mary E. Young, "The Creek Frauds: A Study in Conscience and Corruption," *The Mississippi Valley Historical Review* 42 (December 1955), 421ff.

[25] Satz, *American Indian Policy*, 78.

[26] See de Rosier, *Removal*, 140ff.

[27] Prucha, *Great Father*, 267–8.

[28] Ibid., 299–300.

instructions exemplify efforts made by leaders at the Indian Office to keep policy on track and ensure against matters getting out of hand in the field. Instructions issued in the effort to get remaining Cherokees to remove to the West in the early 1840s, for example, provided for enrollment for emigration and specified the recommended size of removal groups. The instructions specified the exact amount of government support ($53.33 each), broken down by category: $20 for transportation, $33.33 to cover one year in the West. Commissioner Crawford also specified the manner of payment: no payments would be made in advance of removal; instead, removing Cherokees would receive the first third of their $20 transportation allowance once they were "fairly under way," the second third after crossing the Mississippi, and the rest upon arriving in the Cherokee nation in the West. No subsistence payments would be made until the individual had actually settled in the West. Not just an effort to control the removal, the instructions reflect an attempt to learn from earlier problems and to make sure that the Indians did, in fact, relocate – an important consideration given that the Eastern band were precisely those Cherokees who had for years effectively resisted government pressure to move.[29]

Examples exist, too, of field agents' judgments and recommendations being rejected. McKenney rejected suggestions from the field, for example, that the *government* purchase the Florida slaves as one way to settle claims of white southerners.[30] As James Gardiner supervised the removal of the Seneca and Shawnee of Lewiston, Ohio, he had to notify and assemble the Indians, choose a route to be followed, select points at which they would board boats, divide the Indians into companies, and look after myriad other details like vaccinations and disbursal of blankets and other provisions.[31] Gardiner complained about the difficulty of the process, particularly about the Indians' unwillingness to travel by steamboat – they apparently feared boiler explosions and preferred travel over land, a preference to which Gardiner felt compelled to surrender. In this case, Gardiner's requests to go by land were rejected by his superiors.

Localized administration can look haphazard, but a more accurate interpretation is that it was ad hoc. Administrators furthered the designs of clear policy in a manner adapted to the unique circumstances of the Northern tribes, for example, who had been moved about piecemeal constantly since the eighteenth century. Each treaty and its provisions were unique, and the politics and circumstances of the traders, speculators, and politics surrounding each treaty was unique. It may look like a hodgepodge, and be very difficult to recognize patterns. But this inconsistency, a kind of

[29] John R. Finger, "The Abortive Second Cherokee Removal, 1841–1844," *The Journal of Southern History* 47 (May 1981), 217.

[30] Klos, "Blacks," 61–2.

[31] Foreman, *Last Trek*, 73.

muddling through process for U.S. treaty commissioners, was exactly what was needed to prosecute the removal policy.[32] Grant Foreman identifies the system and the ordering principle on which administration of Northern removals was based – a system based on localized, immediate decision making in pursuit of a clear goal. "With candor or guile, by arguments, threats, or cajolery, by appealing to the cupidity of corruptible chiefs, by gorging the Indians at councils with food and drink – whatever the exigencies suggested to agents, inexperienced and often poorly qualified, as calculated to break down the resistance of the Indians was employed."[33] The treaties involved were unique; provisions were inconsistent, specific, and temporary, and treaties often had to be renegotiated hard on the heels of the treaty before, as circumstances changed. As Foreman puts it, "There was an infinite variety of methods, experiences, and details."[34]

Misleading Indicators

Inefficiencies

While the government's reliance on discretionary decision making in the field to pursue removal contributed mightily to the effectiveness of government administration, that same discretion created numerous problems and inefficiencies.

The government's haste in effecting removal backfired in several respects. Lack of advance planning led to some of the most tragic consequences of Indian removal. Travel preparations and provisioning were often inadequate. Blankets were often not issued to the Indians despite bitterly cold weather conditions, and foodstuffs and stock were often spoiled and in other ways inadequate. Even details like bringing cattle along to provide fresh meat proved problematic, as wild cattle were not used to being herded: "The difficulty of confining them to the line of march, preventing their plunging into the timber and brush, and recovering them from muddy, pathless and endless expanses of timber, brambles, vines and jungles, added much to the labor and delays of travel."[35]

Purchasing became a constant problem for field administrators. Since the early nineteenth century, discretionary authority had permitted field agents to take funds authorized by Congress for specific purposes and spend the money on other purposes deemed more pressing by field agents. Not only did this complicate bookkeeping, but field expense records were sent directly to

[32] See Prucha, *Great Father*, ch. 9.

[33] Foreman, *Last Trek*, 15.

[34] See Foreman, *Last Trek*, 14, 15. Foreman calls removal a "haphazard" process, but this fails to convey a sense of the clear and consistent administrative purpose involved, even as he himself describes.

[35] Foreman, *Removal*, 55, 337.

the Treasury Department, making it difficult for the Indian Office to oversee decision making.[36] In treaty negotiations throughout the early part of the nineteenth century, the pressure to get a treaty or the unexpected availability of certain lands often led individual agents and commissioners to offer more money than they were authorized to spend.

Broad grants of authority to field agents gave the Indian service and the War Department dominant positions in structuring and administering removal, and removal agents frequently relied on their own discretion to make purchases.[37] During removal, decision making for treaties, purchasing, and other aspects of removal focused on the short term and not on the overall costs, and thereby allowed local agents to take measures they believed necessary for care of their charges and in pursuit of the overall mission – even if costs rose as a result. Funds for removal were often not appropriated or had not arrived when needed, causing delays and recriminations and forcing agents to lay out funds from personal accounts.[38]

A crucial dynamic in Choctaw removal was the pressure put on the Indian service to implement removal quickly and at minimum possible cost. Jackson wanted removal under way, but he also wanted to demonstrate that the monetary cost of removal could be controlled. In hopes of minimizing costs, the War Department coordinated much of the work but contracted the actual undertakings to private concerns. Contracts were sometimes divided among several contractors, to defend against any one contractor's failure to provide promised goods and services.[39] The contracts entered into by the government were chillingly specific. The Creek removal contract with J. W. A. Sanford and Company, for example, included a per capita payment of $20 for each Indian removed, and provided a pro-rated amount for Indians who died on the way or who were left behind due to illness or were otherwise unable to proceed.[40] Contractors sometimes oversaw entire removal efforts, and were paid a flat rate per capita to collect and transport Indians west. These efforts, such as that for the Potawatomi removing from Michigan in the second half of the 1830s, were important revenue sources during the Panic of 1836 and 1837. Other removals took place with closer government supervision, often military, such as the 1840 push to finish the business of

[36] Satz, *American Indian Policy*, 153.

[37] Foreman, *Removal*, 169.

[38] Ibid., 64–5.

[39] Satz, *American Indian Policy*, 72–3; de Rosier, *Removal*, 138ff.

[40] Litton, "Journal," 226 n6. The contract provided detailed proscriptions for the mode of transportation, amount of baggage allowed, and average mileage per day. The contract stipulated that "The provisions and transportation should be of the best kind," and it detailed the types and amount of provisions to be offered, and how often, indicating just how unhaphazard this endeavor was. Litton, "Journal," 229 n14, 230 n15. For a later example, see Corinne L. Monjeau-Marz, *The Dakota Indian Internment at Fort Snelling, 1862–1864* (St. Paul: Prairie Smoke Press, 2006), 98 and ch. 7 generally.

removing the Potawatomi from Michigan.[41] Later removals were sometimes organized by Indians themselves.

The pressure to remove Indians and to do it quickly encouraged government agents to pay exorbitant fees for supplies, even when such payments exceeded formal rules and circumvented reporting procedures.[42] Field agents ignored their budgets and paid high prices for rations if necessary for the Indians' survival.[43] In supplying removal:

> When bids were called for, the dealers frequently combined to compel the government to pay excessive prices. One dealer on Red River owned nearly all the keel boats on the stream that could be used in carrying supplies for the Indians; another who owned the salt works near the Choctaw line, hired "the proprietor of another saltwork to let his work lie idle" in order to prevent competition in the sale of salt for the Indians. Captain Brown denounced "the whole sordid and avaricious combination against the Government... and those speculative combines which were... formed, and so strongly so, in some parts of the Territory, to overreach the agents, and prey upon the Government through their credulity."[44]

The same thing happened during other removals, as removal agents paid high prices to private interests who took advantage of the dearth of supplies and transport mechanisms available.[45]

Purchasing and contracting were not the only areas in which the exercise of discretionary authority had mixed results. Agents exercised their discretion in attending to the immediacy of removals, but they neglected timely paperwork and recordkeeping. In the midst of supervising removal of Indians from Lewiston, Ohio, James Gardiner wrote: "This rapid sketch is all I have been able to write you since I set out. I can truly say I have not slept three hours in any night for two weeks, and in the day time I am incessantly and most arduously engaged. I have not found it possible to take time to make out my estimate to the Commissary General for funds, but will do so as soon as practicable. I must keep all three detachments [of Indians] moving. We fail if we *stop three days between this [Richmond, Indiana] and the Mississippi*."[46] Similarly, in 1846, the agent for the Miami wrote from on board the *Colorado* on the Ohio River near Evansville, Indiana, "Too busy collecting Miamies to make an annual report until now."[47]

41 Charles E. Cleland, *Rites of Conquest: The History and Culture of Michigan's Native Americans* (Ann Arbor: University of Michigan Press, 1992), 223.

42 Foreman, *Removal*, 62–3.

43 Satz, *American Indian Policy*, 78.

44 Foreman, *Removal*, 69.

45 Ibid., 59.

46 Quoted in Foreman, *Last Trek*, 78; emphasis in Foreman.

47 Quoted in Foreman, *Last Trek*, 129; see also Litton, "Journal"; J. Diane Pearson, "Lewis Cass and the Politics of Disease: The Indian Vaccination Act of 1832," *Wicazo Sa Review* 18 (Autumn 2003), 16.

As in the factory era, agents continued to appeal to their orders as an excuse for *not* taking certain discretionary actions. A conductor in charge of the Seneca and Cayuga removal in 1832 blamed the tragedies of that removal on his orders – they kept him from delaying the move a few days, which he argued might have prevented some deaths and ameliorated some illnesses.[48] But many conductors made such adjustments habitually; the conductor here self-servingly blamed his orders for constraining his judgment.

Corruption

Corruption, profiteering, and fraud played important roles in Indian removal. The real presence of these dynamics affected efforts to get Indians to remove and buffeted removals themselves, yet these dynamics did not hinder administration – they often furthered U.S. policy. The illusion of Indian removal as a failure is built in large part on overlooking the ways in which corruption *advanced* administrative goals.

Given the goal of removing Indians in order to render them nonthreatening to U.S. interests and settlers, corruption that damaged Indian stocks, demoralized populations, and starved or degraded individuals and communities served the policy. Historians have often pointed to corruption in the Indian service as evidence of poor administrative controls and lack of oversight, and concluded that public administration was in an infant and largely ineffective state. On the contrary: corrupt actions were an important part of the Indian service's commitment to and culture of local discretionary authority. Corruption could further the ends of policy even if it undercut secondary goals that lacked strong political commitment, like education and agricultural development. In an administrative environment pursuing a goal of removal for gain by others, or even a goal of removal in the best interests of the Indians, corruption that advanced removal could even be rationalized at the time as appropriate. Oversight and administrative control mechanisms were in place to pursue the ultimate solution of removal, and only secondarily – and usually well after the fact – to consider questions of Indians' rights and protections.

Government officials were certainly complicit in fraud and corruption. Federal, state, and local officials conspired together and with private interests to commit frauds and depredations against Indians. William Ward, for example, defrauded many Choctaws who wished to stay in Mississippi. The Treaty of Dancing Rabbit Creek guaranteed these Choctaws that they could receive a reservation of land in Mississippi if they registered with the local agent – Ward – within six months. Ward, opposed to the prospect, delayed registering Indians as long as possible, at times claiming to be ill and at times even going into hiding. Ward was removed from his post in 1833,

48 Foreman, *Last Trek*, 71.

and a series of investigations in the late 1830s and 1840s confirmed the widespread abuses he made of his position.[49] A congressional investigation into Choctaw removal and a committee to adjust matters of maladministered Choctaw land claims in the East uncovered widespread frauds.[50] Investigations also targeted abuses in later removals, including political deals that defrauded Indians in land dealings, and traders' frauds and abuses. An agent to the Seminoles was removed for fraud,[51] and Solomon Betton, appointed to appraise Indian improvements to Creek lands as a precursor to Creek removal, worked with a firm in "nefarious speculation" in compensation claims – cheating hundreds of Creeks out of thousands of dollars.[52] Agents worked closely with contractors; one investigator noted that "the agents of the Government were also the agents of the contractors and hence when the Indians complained to the Government agent the contractor's agent would give them no dissatisfaction."[53] Nor was the leadership of the Indian Office immune from fraud and abuse. Commissioner Carey Harris resigned his post in 1838 following the disclosure of evidence showing that he was conspiring with interests in Mississippi to secure Indian reservation land for speculation.[54]

Factionalism among Indians multiplied opportunities for fraud; stores of goods invited plunder and theft.[55] Local officials used their authority to name minor officials to construct loyal political followings by manipulating the granting of trading licenses and by carefully doling out funds and jobs.[56] Agents overcharged for contractor's fees and pocketed the difference.[57] One removal conductor complained, "We have been shamefully imposed on in the cost of rations by a settled plan of extortion, connived at by the disbursing

49 de Rosier, *Removal*, 135–7; Thomas D. Clark and John D. W. Guice, *The Old Southwest, 1795–1830: Frontiers in Conflict* (Norman: University of Oklahoma Press, 1996 [1989]), 247–8; Mary Elizabeth Young, *Redskins, Ruffleshirts, and Rednecks: Indian Allotments in Alabama and Mississippi, 1830–1860* (Norman: University of Oklahoma Press, 1961), 51–2 and ch. 3 generally.

50 Satz, *American Indian Policy*, 86.

51 Foreman, *Removal*, 322–3.

52 Michael D. Green, *The Politics of Indian Removal: Creek Government and Society in Crisis* (Lincoln: University of Nebraska Press, 1985), 142.

53 Quoted in Satz, *American Indian Policy*, 193; see also Young, "Creek Frauds," 429; David Lavender, *The Great West* (Boston: Houghton Mifflin, 2000 [1965]), 188–9; Prucha, *Great Father*, 222; Foreman, *Last Trek*, 118–19, 123 n17, 130. The 1834 Act allowed for sealed bids in contracting Indian annuities, if time permitted, in an attempt to control gouging by contractors. Prucha, *Great Father*, 299.

54 Satz, *American Indian Policy*, 158–9; Satz, "Carey Allen Harris," in Robert M. Kvasnicka and Herman J. Viola, eds., *The Commissioners of Indian Affairs, 1824–1977* (Lincoln: University of Nebraska Press, 1979), 19–20.

55 Green, *Politics of Indian Removal*, e.g., 184; Foreman, *Removal*, 65.

56 Satz, *American Indian Policy*, 184–5.

57 Klos, "Blacks," 76 n83.

agent and his relatives."[58] Conflicts of interest abounded: removal of Seminoles from Florida was complicated by Indian agents who owned slaves and speculated in sales.[59]

Bribes were a common tool of federal administrators. Andrew Jackson recognized the role of bribery in Indian affairs when he served as a treaty commissioner after the War of 1812. According to Jackson biographer Robert Remini, Jackson opposed the practice – preferring that the U.S. impose its will on the Indians rather than buy them off – but he accepted his orders: "[S]ince the government had no intention of following his advice and since the acquisition of the lands in question was essential, he was forced to resort to bribery. He knew the chiefs would take the bribes and he knew they would work."[60] During federal consideration of the disputed treaty between the Senecas and the Ogden Land Company, bribery was condoned as a regular part of the treaty process by Senator John Norvell of Michigan. Norvell dismissed the chicanery in New York and referred to the treaty process with the Cherokees to soothe concerns that anything beyond the pale had occurred in New York.[61] Elbert Herring, Commissioner of Indian Affairs from 1831 to 1836, condoned the use of bribery, interference in tribal affairs, withholding of annuities, and the selection of chiefs by federal agents (rather than by tribal populations) as methods to further the goals of the removal policy.[62] James Gadsden's efforts at Payne's Landing in Florida relied on bribes to the interpreters, filtered through the Seminoles' treaty payments; a captain noted that Gadsden "could not have got the treaty through if he had not bribed the negro interpreter."[63]

Other corrupt practices benefited interests profiting from Indian removal. Traders, for example, were a key element in treaty negotiations during removals and at other times. Treaties often specified that goods be delivered to the Indians, and traders could supply these goods at highly inflated

58 Quoted in Foreman, *Last Trek*, 80. Contractors exploited Indians mercilessly. See, e.g., Foreman, *Last Trek*, 131 n7, which documents one case involving traders who filed undoubtedly fraudulent claims for goods provided to the Miami Indians, reaping rewards of approximately $300,000.

59 Klos, "Blacks."

60 Robert V. Remini, *Andrew Jackson and his Indian Wars* (New York: Viking, 2001), 112, 113–14; see also 127; Foreman, *Last Trek*, 125.

61 At the end of heated debates and considerable evidence of fraud, the Senate accepted the New York treaty on the basis of three tie votes, all broken in favor of the treaties by Vice President – and killer of Tecumseh – Richard M. Johnson. Francis Paul Prucha, *American Indian Treaties: The History of a Political Anomaly* (Berkeley: University of California Press, 1997), 205–7.

62 Satz, "Elbert Herring," in Kvasnicka and Viola, *Commissioners*, 14; see Prucha, *American Indian Treaties*, ch. 9 for a general discussion of treaty-making techniques on the part of the United States in this era.

63 Klos, "Blacks," 69–70; quoted in Klos, "Blacks," 70. On Gadsden and other bribery allegations, see also Mahon, *Second Seminole War*, 78, 285ff., 46.

prices and reap a government-sponsored windfall. Traders claimed – and often concocted – debts owed by the Indians for goods delivered on credit; treaties then paid these debts out of Indian funds, providing cash annuities that went directly to traders. As one historian notes, "So much influence did traders have over the Indians that in many cases the government would have been unable to procure the treaties of cession it wanted without providing adequately for the traders' interests."[64] When annual payments were made to Indians, the traders benefited again. Treaties provided for traders' debt claims to the tune of $10,000 at the Potawatomi treaty of 1828, $11,601 at the Winnebago treaty the next year, more than $200,000 at treaties with northern tribes in 1832, $175,00 at the Potawatomi treaty of 1833, $300,000 at the Ottawa treaty in 1836, more than $400,000 in treaties with the Chippewa, Sioux, Sac and Fox, and Winnebago in 1837, $400,000 in treaties with the Miami in 1838 and 1840, and close to $400,000 in treaties with the Wyandot, Chippewa, and Sac and Fox in 1842.[65]

Calculations of the benefits to be gained from Indian affairs were never simple. The land cessions and removals associated with treaties secured land and increased trade among Indians and settlers, but the process simultaneously *removed* Indian customers and the traders' best patron, the federal government. So while traders and others worked for removal, they also worked to *delay* removals as long as possible. Whites delayed removal in order to charge Indian groups, gathered but waiting to be moved, for food at extortionate rates. Whites charged the Indians for debts and legal fees, and took the Indians' money and goods, including livestock, before colluding local officials would allow the Indians to leave the jurisdiction. As state and local courts and officials conspired in these efforts, removals were delayed, costs increased, and opportunities for factionalized mischief multiplied.[66] Indian affairs officials in the field and at the capital commonly blamed traders for the delays and disturbances. Again, though, while such activity might appear to reflect inefficiency, uncoordination, and corruption, these local conspiracies served the twin purposes of weakening Indian interests socially and economically, while building up support and strength among the white populations.

Efforts to reduce the barricades to removal set up by traders included congressional restrictions on payments and on reservations of lands for specific individuals, but "claims dragged on and on, much to the irritation of the Indian Office."[67] Large sums were authorized to settle agreements

[64] Prucha, *Great Father*, 267.

[65] Prucha, *Great Father*, 267; Prucha, *American Indian Treaties*, 219–23; Meyer, *Santee Sioux*, 41–2, 56–7; Foreman, *Last Trek*, 57 n9, 75, 93, 109, 119–20, 127, 131 n7. On the vast variety of goods provided at treaty negotiations, see, e.g., the list in Foreman, *Last Trek*, 122 n4.

[66] Foreman, *Removal*, 62–3, 76, 97, 218.

[67] Prucha, *Great Father*, 269.

and debts between traders and Indians and allow removal to proceed, but these sums – and the complex obligations of these parties to each other, which varied in each case – complicated removal and provided innumerable new opportunities for fraud and abuse in the field. Land speculators also employed endlessly creative methods for taking advantage of Indians and gaining their land allotments. Pressure could be applied, goods could be traded for titles, and, when an Indian proved reluctant to sell his holding, another Indian could be sent to impersonate the allotment holder before the authorities.[68]

Local communities were thoroughly affected by Indian affairs and the dynamics of removal. Military posts then as now generated revenue and business opportunities in an area, and created longer-term indirect benefits through infrastructure improvements and mail delivery.[69] Settlers and local newspapers called upon the federal government for posts and expenditures, to grow communities as well as to protect them against real or imagined Indian threats.[70] Indians represented an important part of this kaleidoscope of interests, too. Indians made claims upon federal agents for protection, trusted commissioners, weapons, and new military posts – meaning that not only were federal agents responding to demands from white populations but also from a variety of diverse Indian populations, often with conflicting interests.[71] Battles or infighting among Indians could spark violence, sometimes for the same reasons of misunderstanding or misidentification as often sparked conflicts and mistakes between whites and Indians.[72] One removal party through Indiana, for example, was fraught with tension because the party included sparring tribes.[73]

The historian Charles Cleland puts it this way: "Indians were not just big players on the frontier, they were the only game in town. Most of the funds dispersed to Indians in the form of treaty annuities went more or less directly into the hands of the traders, who collected like vultures when the annual payments were made."[74] A British observer in 1833 described the scene surrounding six thousand Potawatomi gathered at Chicago for treaty negotiations:

> Horse dealers, and horse stealers, – rogues of every description, . . . half breeds, quarter breeds, and men of no breed at all; – dealers in pigs, poultry and potatoes; – men pursuing Indian claims, some for tracts of land, others . . . for pigs which the wolves

[68] Young, "Creek Frauds," 411; Prucha, *Great Father*, 222.
[69] Brad Agnew, *Fort Gibson: Terminal on the Trail of Tears* (Norman: University of Oklahoma Press, 1980), 167.
[70] Ibid., 26.
[71] LaVere, *Contrary Neighbors*, 66, 71, 82.
[72] Ibid., 71.
[73] Foreman, *Last Trek*.
[74] Cleland, *Rites*, 210; see also 226.

had eaten; – creditors of the tribe or of particular Indians, who know they have no chance of getting their money, if they do not get it from government agents; – sharpers of every degree; pedlars, grog-sellers; Indian agents and Indian traders of every description.... The little village (Chicago) was in an uproar from morning to night, and from night to morning...[75]

Corruption hurt Indians and tribes, but it benefited other interests. Together, corruption and corrupt practices *furthered* administration in pursuit of Indian removal.

Corruption as a Misleading Indicator

It is difficult to assess the level and prevalence of corruption in the Indian service precisely because there were so many interests involved in removal, jockeying for advantage in competitive relationships marked by conflicting and crosscutting objectives. It is not at all clear that corruption among government agents was widespread or characteristic of administration. Many charges of corruption, fraud, or simple maladministration were brought by interests dissatisfied with the process or progress of removal, dissatisfied with the efforts of officials to stem abusive practices, or dissatisfied that officials seemed to look the other way in a manner that advantaged the competition. Scholars have had a tendency to accept at face value the myriad charges of misbehavior leveled at Indian affairs officials, but administration in Indian affairs is as "political" as it is in any other environment – if not more so. A charge leveled against a field agent by a trader, or a settler, or even by an Indian or a tribal government, might be true or at least based on a reasonably objective interpretation of events and decision making – or it might be false, an effort to work the system to the accuser's advantage. When scholars fail to look critically at Indian affairs as an area of federal policymaking and public administration, the assumptions drive the analysis – we see a corrupt service because that is what we expect to see and because that supports the stereotypical and oversimplified view of expansion and Indian affairs: good guys and bad guys; pioneers and vagabonds; noble, suffering, doomed Indians and heartless, cruel, corrupt whites. Yet the reality is much more complicated: in the environment of Indian affairs, charges were often leveled not because they were true, but because they served the goals of the accuser.

The experience of William Thomas, a longtime agent for and ally of the Quallatown Cherokees, illustrates how charges of corruption and personal animosity existed in a foggy political universe.[76] The charges against Thomas clouded his reputation in the 1840s, and even now they make it difficult to

[75] Quoted in John Low and Paula Holley, "Treaty of Chicago – September, 1833," *Native Chicago*, 2nd ed., ed. Terry Straus (Chicago: Albatross Press, 2002), 103–4. See also Prucha, *American Indian Treaties*, 188ff., for discussion of the variety of interests involved in this treaty.

[76] Finger, "Abortive."

assess what exactly happened. An accuser charged Thomas with enriching himself at the Quallatown Indians' expense. The accuser also charged Thomas with having acted dishonestly as disbursing agent. In September 1841, Acting Secretary of War Albert Lea replaced Thomas with a new special agent tasked with getting the Indians to move West. The new agent was the same man who brought the charges, Thomas Hindman of Alabama.

Yet the story is not as simple as the replacement of a corrupt agent on a competitor's say-so; it appeared that Thomas, in fact, might have been too much of an *ally* to the Indians in his charge. Thomas's original appointment reflected the Indian Office's practice of appointing men based on calculations of expertise, experience, and trust. Thomas had been appointed to take a census of the tribe in 1840 and was also put in charge of disbursing moneys to them, and he seems to have been a faithful advocate for the remaining Indians' interests. He had been helping the Indians buy land in order to remain in North Carolina – which helped the Indians but cut directly against efforts to get the Indians to remove West. Thomas's close ties to the Quallatown Indians made him vulnerable, as every now and then a new push came from Washington to try to get the Indians to remove west and join the rest of the Cherokees in Indian Territory. Thomas himself blamed some of the charges against him on past conflicts with Hindman and on the complicated politics of Cherokee removal: Thomas and Hindman had ties to opposing factions in Cherokee politics.

The point here is the vulnerability of the field agent to political forces, divided interests, and policy goals. Operating in the field and dependent upon relationships with Indians as well with distant superiors, Thomas, like many field agents, was easily discredited by charges against him – especially when others had different immediate goals in mind. Lea, Hindman, and Indian Commissioner Crawford were all pushing for removal of the eastern Cherokee. Thomas opposed removal, but for an unclear mix of reasons – his incentive seems to have been some combination of sincere concern for the Eastern Cherokee together with a personal interest as the band's lawyer and perhaps a beneficiary of their lands in the east. Hindman and Thomas played against each other, often through complaints and charges made to Acting Secretary Lea. Personal dynamics extended to Thomas's relationship with Commissioner Crawford, who was exasperated by Thomas's failure to submit timely paperwork – and also by Hindman's relationship with Crawford due to Hindman's failures on the ground and by the disaffection of the Indians and others around him. Some of the charges against Hindman came from Colonel John Serburne, who had ties to the Indian Office and apparently wanted Hindman's job for his own.[77] A situation like this demonstrates how difficult it is to untangle the politics within removal, and thus to assess with any degree of certainty – even in specific cases, much

[77] Ibid., 213.

less on the whole – the extent of corruption and mismanagement in the administration of Indian affairs.

Personal dynamics and animosities were common during removals, too, in part because of the complicated nature of the endeavor. Civilian and military agents were involved beginning, middle, and end, and often in such ways as to comment on or be concerned about the actions of their colleagues. Each time a group of Indians being relocated were passed from one conductor or set of conductors to another was an occasion for commentary, complaint, or indemnification if an agent or officer feared recrimination from any direction. In just one example among many, personal animosity complicated removal of Indians from Lewiston, Ohio, as a feud between the conductor and the disbursing agent contributed to confusion that forced Colonel J. J. Abert to take charge of the removing Indians.[78] Grant Foreman notes that the parties to the feud "bombard[ed]" superiors in Washington with charges and countercharges related to drunkenness, inefficiency, and inattention to duty.[79] Indians continued to be deeply interested in their conductors and others engaged in their removals, and would levy their own charges and complaints. The Miami, for example, protested the appointment of Joseph Sinclear as their agent in the West, having dealt with him as their removal conductor.[80]

Even the military could find itself caught in the middle of powerful political forces looking to discredit opponents and secure self-interested gains. Charges plagued military officers involved in Indian affairs in the 1830s.[81] County officials brought charges against federal officers in Alabama who removed intruders and burned the town of Irwinton to reassure Creeks that the United States would act to enforce stipulations against squatters.[82] General John Wool, who often tried to protect Indian interests, was caught between Alabama state efforts and his federal duties; he was brought under investigation and charged by the state.[83] In an example from Georgia, Captain Archibald Turk, under federal orders, removed white squatters from Cherokee land. Some of the intruders were killed in the action, and Georgia tried the general for murder.[84]

Scheming underlings complicated affairs even more. Satz writes, "Superintendents always had to be on their guard against agents who coveted their position and were quick to report anything that might tarnish their record,

78 Foreman, *Last Trek*, 81.

79 Ibid., 87 n66. See also 107.

80 Ibid., 130. For a different example, see Mahon, *Second Seminole War*, 61.

81 Satz, *American Indian Policy*, 191.

82 Green, *Politics of Indian Removal*, 174ff.

83 Foreman, *Removal*, 279–80; Prucha, *Great Father*, 239–40.

84 Thomas L. McKenney, *Memoirs, Official and Personal* (Lincoln: University of Nebraska Press, 1973 [1846]), 258; William G. McLoughlin, *Cherokee Renascence in the New Republic* (Princeton: Princeton University Press, 1986), 311–14.

while subagents did much the same in their attempt to secure the higher-paying position of agent. Political factionalism in many states and territories turned the Indian service into a sordid battleground, with superintendencies, agencies, and subagencies being little more than pawns in the game of political patronage and power."[85] State leaders often condemned federal activities. Governor George Troup in Georgia issued scathing indictments of federal agents who he alleged were working to undermine Georgia's efforts to get the Creeks to remove; he also condemned the War Department for failing to punish the villains, thereby encouraging further machinations.[86]

Charges of corruption, mismanagement, poor judgment, maladministration, favoritism, inefficiency, incompetence, and even drunkenness could be true – but often making such charges was simply an effective technique used by some to gain advantage over others, to influence decision making, or to effect the replacement of one agent or officer with someone more sympathetic to the accuser's interests and objectives. Taking at face value the charges that were laid upon Indian service officials, without recognizing the complicated motives and interests involved, can make the Indian service look far more corrupt and ineffective than it probably was. And forgetting that corruption in many cases furthered the government's objectives obscures the relationship of corruption to organizational goals. In the pursuit of Indian removal, corruption, conflict of interest, and fraud could all help government administrators achieve their ends.

Politics, Pressure, and Removal

In this environment, government agents were under tremendous pressure to navigate powerful and complicated interests carefully, in order to further policy and at the same time protect individual careers and status in the Indian service. The clear goals of U.S. policy, the influence of local and regional interests, and the risk posed by potentially damaging charges combined to create a political environment that facilitated removal, regardless of the instances of actual corruption and fraud.

To be an effective advocate of Indian or tribal interests in this environment was not only extremely difficult, such advocacy violated the very purpose of policy if it hindered removal. Traders and other interested parties discredited agents who were not doing what the traders or the other interests wanted them to do. Lieutenant Colonel Ethan Allen Hitchcock reported that honest officials who challenged contractors were at risk of "galvanizing a whole community producing denunciations in quarters from which they might be least expected."[87] These dynamics ensured that federal

85 Satz, *American Indian Policy*, 187.
86 Green, *Politics of Indian Removal*, 102.
87 Quoted in Satz, *American Indian Policy*, 193.

agents would be heavily influenced by those interests, national and local, governmental and nongovernmental, that supported the removal policy and the development of non-Indian interests. Individual officials were constantly called upon to handle disputes among ever-changing combinations of local interests, putting a premium on individual abilities to mediate disputes and further the signing of removal treaties, conduct censuses and enrollments, contract for provisions, and oversee physical removals without allowing the process to be derailed.

Public officials worked hard to avoid problems and to defuse potential conflicts, sometimes before they could begin. Creek land contracts, for example, required presidential approval; presidential approval could be influenced by the local agents' reports. Agents discussed such matters among themselves, and agreed on the necessity of tailoring reports from the field so as to avoid head-on conflict with powerful figures. Many local agents were often trying to do their best to protect Indian interests, but compromise proved necessary. Failure to operate carefully in this politicized system easily resulted in charges that a particular agent was biased, corrupt, or otherwise failing to fulfill the mandates of government policy.[88] In pursuit of the mission, of personal safety, and of careers, Indian service officials did much better by compromising with pro-removal elements and furthering removal.

Investigations and oversight provide a good example of how government agents resolved thorny questions arising from their divided loyalties in favor of furthering removal. As discussed in the previous chapter, investigations and oversight efforts were common in Indian affairs. Special investigatory boards and oversight commissions repeatedly looked into charges of maladministration and abuse. Investigatory bodies and special commissions also multiplied the avenues by which interested parties could bring charges against field agents. The prospect of oversight efforts affected affairs in the field by encouraging field agents to work out compromises to avoid investigations or to settle problems before a formal investigation took place. Such compromises generally worked to the advantage of non-Indian interests. At best, investigations punished some people after the fact without derailing the purposes of policy. At worst, they exacerbated the disadvantaged position of American Indians and their communities.

The Creek cession, for example, and like many such cases, crawled with traders and whiskey peddlers selling on credit. A census taker acknowledged that the Creeks would be served bail writs before they could remove, putting them in jail and encouraging the federal government to pay off the Indians' debts before removing the Indians under guard. Intruders on Creek lands increased, prompting a flood of complaints, charges, and countercharges at the War Department offices. Creeks complained about whites, and whites

88 See Young, "Creek Frauds."

complained about mistreatment by federal officers. Secretary of War Lewis Cass tried to mollify all comers and delay action by promising to look into matters and investigate claims.[89]

Promises of oversight and investigations slowly produced compromises between federal and state officials, as Indian defenses weakened. To make sure matters went smoothly in Alabama, Cass removed the Creeks' agent, damaging the tribe's ability to work through regular channels in the controversy and simultaneously sending a clear message to other agents about the perils of operating too effectively on the Indians' behalf. Cass appointed a replacement with some experience in Indian affairs who shared the administration's pro-removal outlook. Meanwhile, a federal marshal in the area, trying to protect Creeks against encroachment by whites, became involved in violent altercations with white squatters resistant to being uprooted. The squatters banded together against federal agents and troops, lobbied state officers, and issued warrants for the arrest of federal officials and soldiers pursuant to the violence. Seeking to avoid a head-on conflict, state and federal interests slid toward a point of agreement: the Creeks would have to go. Cass worked toward the administrative prerequisites, including a new treaty and a scouting party to western lands. As the Creek government collapsed under the weight of decades of destabilization efforts, the Indians' leaders proved increasingly unable to mount effective challenges or even to take responsibility themselves for overseeing removal.[90]

Investigations undercut the authority of field agents, especially those who advocated Indian interests too vociferously. The mere threat of an investigation, which quickly became part of the landscape of Indian affairs administration, provided an easy alternative for interested parties as they went about their affairs relating to Indian policy. Traders, speculators, and others knew that if the local agents refused to play ball, those agents were vulnerable to well-placed charges made at higher levels. And as soon as agents' decision making was second-guessed by a commission or investigatory board, those charges produced results and could make agents all over the continent reluctant to defend Indian interests – or any other interests – against pro-removal forces. Together with the desire of headquarters, since the factory days, to allow local officials the discretion to make decisions in the field, these dynamics encouraged field decision making to accommodate powerful local interests and usually discouraged centralized oversight until there was a "fire" that needed to be put out. As long as things in the field ran smoothly and quietly, removal went forward.

To a casual observer in the 1830s, or now, the web of frauds, charges, and investigations enveloping Indian removal might look like bureaucratic

89 Green, *Politics of Indian Removal.*

90 Green, *Politics of Indian Removal*; see also Young, *Redskins*, ch. 3.

incompetence, administration hamstrung by patronage appointments, disgraceful negligence on the part of the civilian service, or militaristic aggression on the part of the military. The government appears unable to control the depredations and greed of white interests, and unable to defend Indian interests guaranteed by treaty. In reality, these are sophisticated, effective ways of managing expectations and gently pressuring field agents toward a consistent and unwavering purpose. Appointments and instructions to field officers pursued a largely unchanging goal; bureaucratic delays, frauds, and investigations of those frauds all furthered the ends envisioned by policy planners. Every delay, every explicit or implied message to the field service not to protect Indian interests too effectively, every promise of a future investigation, worked toward removal of the Indians while maintaining (at times) an appearance of sincere concern. A series of ad hoc, short term decisions and expedient compromises, backed up at the headquarters level, and supported by a strengthening military and by effective administration of removal's elements in the West, furthered the aim of the removal policy among the Creeks and among Indians in North and South alike.

It is thus not necessary to demonize whites in the removal era, or to identify a grand and explicit conspiracy of genocide or even of corrupt behavior, to explain the results of government action. As noted earlier, many claims of corruption and mismanagement in Indian removal are hard to support, and are probably exaggerated. Many officials and private citizens honestly sought the best for Indians, oftentimes rationalizing the horrors they saw during removal by appealing to the promising future they believed was being created for the Indians despite the hardships they endured. Far more significant than a grand conspiracy or a nation of greedy evildoers are dynamics of politics and public administration that to this day encourage well-meaning people to do things that later inspire regret. The compromises that took place in local, specific political environments, together with a clear objective supported by a plausible humanitarian rationale, allowed people of diverse characters and opinions on Indian affairs to conduct and pursue a policy that in retrospect is obviously abhorrent. Public administrators rarely pursue evil knowingly; far more often, disturbing results follow small, rational decisions by well-meaning people trying to get the job done as they understand it.[91]

Politics, Policy, and the Illusion of Failure

Affairs at the War Department and the Indian Office mirrored the difficult and vulnerable position of federal agents in the field. The simple idea of removal provided a clear goal, but the rationales supporting removal

[91] See, e.g., Guy B. Adams and Danny L. Balfour, *Unmasking Administrative Evil* (Thousand Oaks, CA: Sage, 1998).

provided a kaleidoscope of attractive arguments tailored to particular populations and interests. As a result, expectations were high, contradictions went unacknowledged, and all parties had a reason to see themselves as the intended beneficiaries of federal policy. When those interests were dissatisfied with outcomes, plenty of opportunities sprang up to discredit and condemn Indian affairs administration – both locally and systemically.

With removal billed as a magic bullet for all interests, expectations were high. Advocates of removal had promoted the plan not only as a favorable response to settlement and development interests in the North and South, but as a way to preserve the tribes and further the safety and effective development of Indian individuals. Removal's proponents courted humanitarians with explicit appeals to the benefits that removal would bestow on individual Indians. Thomas McKenney raised expectations in an 1829 public address:

> It is proposed, in the first place, to give them [removed tribes] a country, and to secure it to them by the most ample and solemn sanctions, suitable in all respects, in exchange for theirs; to pay them for all their improvements – and see them, free of cost, to their new homes – to aid them after their arrival there – and protect them; – to put over them, at once, the frame-work of a government, and to fill this up as their advancement in civilization may require it; to secure them the privilege of participating in it; to establish schools over their country, for the enlightening of the rising generation; and give them the Gospel. In fine, it is proposed to place them in a Territorial relation to us, and in all respects; and in the enjoyment of all the privileges consequent upon such a relation, civil, political and religious. Thus they will attain an elevation, to which, in their present relations, they can never aspire. And thus would new influences be created, ennobling in their tendencies, and animating in their effects. Under these, the Indian would rise into the distinction to which he has always been a stranger; and live and act with reference to the corresponding honors and benefits of such a state.[92]

McKenney used the example of the Eastern Indians – who he said had all but disappeared by the 1830s – to support the argument that Indians of the Southern states must be removed from the white advance if they were to survive. He acknowledged that his views had changed from his earlier affinity for civilization and assimilation in the East, and blamed the speed of white advance and the Indians' own desire for removal to support his case.[93] In this way, the removal policy could be made to satisfy not only development interests, but also interests concerned about the welfare of individual Indians and the desires of tribes.

But arguments in favor of removal were carefully tailored to specific audiences. To the Cherokees, for example, removal was held out to "progressives" as the best route to civilization – even as agents told traditionalists

[92] McKenney, *Memoirs*, 246–7.
[93] Ibid., 240ff.

and conservatives among the Indians that removal was the best path to maintaining traditional structures and lifeways.[94] The tribes had little alternative but to view the federal government as their best – perhaps only – potential ally.[95] Indians often delayed negotiating until a federal agent was in place to represent them, evidence that tribes could view the agent as their voice at treaties representing tribal interests.[96]

The different expectations that underlay the mission's goals and supporters created stress upon the Indian affairs bureaucracy that went far beyond the complicated environments surrounding the field agents. Indian interests targeted the executive and legislative branches in Washington with memorials, lobbying efforts, and other tactics designed to accelerate, alter, or delay removal.[97] Tribes pursued court strategies, too, often with the help of humanitarian interests. The results pulled the Indian Office in directions which conflicted with the demands coming from the executive and from Congress. Pending cases, and decisions such as the Supreme Court's ruling in *Worcester* v. *Georgia*, complicated removal and offered administrators conflicting cues as to what would be permitted or demanded in the removal process. The decision in *Worcester* defending tribal sovereignty excited the Indians and hindered removal efforts: enrollments ceased, and the pressure to halt preparations intensified. More delays were seen in 1832, as the Indians delayed preparations in hopes of a victory by Henry Clay in the presidential election.[98]

Non-Indian interests also lobbied and pressured the Indian service's leadership. Jackson supporter Sam Houston attempted to convince McKenney, by logic and then by bribe, to recommend the letting of contracts for removal provisions in such a way as to favor Houston's business and cut out other Western suppliers. Houston had the support of Secretary of War Eaton and, probably, of Jackson himself. McKenney refused, and Houston retaliated by publicizing alleged abuses in the Indian Department, including frauds perpetrated on Cherokee and Creek Indians, and he laid the blame with McKenney.[99]

Complaints came from Congress, stemming from serious inquiries into matters that were delayed or could not be answered by the Bureau of Indian Affairs, and from political charges that sought to vent frustration, support local interests and constituents, and open positions in the office to patronage.[100] Interests pursued reparations and reclamation of debts

94 John R. Finger, *The Eastern Band of Cherokees, 1819–1900* (Knoxville: University of Tennessee Press, 1984), 10.

95 See, e.g., Green, *Politics of Indian Removal*, 173; Prucha, *American Indian Treaties*, 158.

96 Agnew, *Fort Gibson*, 46. See also Viola, *Thomas L. McKenney*, 233–4.

97 Foreman, *Removal*, 107, 238; Green, *Politics of Indian Removal*, 179.

98 Foreman, *Removal*, 244, 246, 248ff.

99 See Viola, *Thomas L. McKenney*, 228ff.

100 Satz, *American Indian Policy*, 167.

through Congress. Cost mattered, and members of Congress worried as the total cost of Choctaw removal rose to $5.1 million, or $2 million more than Jackson had expected it to cost to remove *all* of the Eastern tribes. In the implementation of the removal policy, the Indian Office was forced to respond to demands from the president to enroll tribal members and expedite plans for removal, even as local interests working through Congress and directly with the War Department sought delays in removing Indians until debts had been paid and other claims had been answered.

Charges against field officers multiplied, as letters and accounts of specific activities in the field reached the public and created the impression of widespread abuses, administrative inconsistencies, and tragically ill-designed policy. For example, one Baptist missionary wrote of the camps gathering Indians waiting to be removed,

> The Cherokees are nearly all prisoners. They have been dragged from their houses, and encamped at the forts and military posts, all over the nation. In Georgia, especially, multitudes were allowed no time to take anything with them, except the clothes they had on. Well-furnished houses were left a prey to plunderers, who, like hungry wolves, follow in the train of the captors. These wretches rifle the houses, and strip the helpless, unoffending owners of all they have on earth. Females, who have been habituated to comforts and comparative affluence, are driven on foot before the bayonets of brutal men.... Many of the Cherokees, who, a few days ago, were in comfortable circumstances, are now victims of abject poverty. Some, who have been allowed to return home, under passport, to inquire after their property, have found their cattle, horses, swine, farming tools and house furniture all gone. And this is not a description of extreme cases. It is altogether a faint representation of the work which has been perpetrated on the unoffending, unarmed, and unresisting Cherokees.[101]

Publicity surrounding the details of the Trail of Tears and other removal efforts, and sympathetic first-hand accounts coming from towns and routes along Indians' long walks West, discredited the national government's relationships with Indians and tribes and contributed to a sense that Indian policy and administration were not functioning effectively.

Conclusion

Just as occurred during the factory system, the Indian Office's shrewd reliance on local, discretionary authority to adapt and implement policy effectively produced results, but also inconsistent administration, charges of corruption and maladministration, and dwindling enthusiasm among the policy's greatest beneficiaries. As removal wore on, support faded from

[101] Evan Jones, *Baptist Missionary Magazine*, September 1838, quoted in Laurence F. Schmeckebier, *The Office of Indian Affairs: Its History, Activities and Organization* (Baltimore: The Johns Hopkins Press, 1927), 36.

those interests that had pushed for, and were *satisfied* with, Indian removal's implementation. Just as supporters of the factory system eventually turned against that system or moved on to other pursuits, leaving Indian policy to a new group of settler and state interests in the removal era, here, too, the interests that had promoted removal and supported the efforts of the War Department quit the field. The humanitarians' interest in Indian affairs died down significantly after the debates over removal. This reflected the sense that a solution had been arrived at, an inability to foresee coming problems with reservation administration, and the growing pull of slavery as a national issue. Georgia, Alabama, and other eastern states no longer had the same interest in Indian affairs by the 1840s. Many powerful supporters of government-led removal became opponents of funding for Indian affairs and of the attention paid to them in the West. By the mid-1840s, the very interests that might have trumpeted the effectiveness of Indian removal would do no such thing – whether out of regret, recrimination, or just because politics and Indian affairs kept moving forward. And it served these interests, *after* removal, to underscore what a *bad* job expensive government programs did in addressing Indian issues.

The Indian service, still under the shadow of its presumed failure in the factory system era, now faced challenges stemming from a perceived failure in removal. The illusion of an ineffective, incompetent, and corrupt federal bureaucracy, first nurtured during debates over the factory system, stood out more clearly. The reality of forceful, dominating, and effective national administration faded, because it was in the interests of many to make it fade, and because the achievements of that bureaucracy are horrible to consider.

Attention soon turned toward reservations and the West. Reform, as rhetoric and as policy, would be adopted by new players in the West looking to promote their interests in a territory woven with land reserved for removed and western Indians. It is significant that Congress, when it passed the 1832 act authorizing a Commissioner of Indian Affairs, the 1834 Trade and Intercourse Act, and the 1834 reorganization of the Indian service, did not enact the accompanying recommendations of Cass, Clark, and others for organizing the West. The goal in 1834 was removal; the War Department's planning for the West was adequate for that purpose, but long range legislation covering the Indians once they got there was not yet Congress's concern. It would remain for another day to hash out the provisions of what the Indians would actually face once they reached the West.[102] The Indian Office would confront another new set of interested parties, including newly important tribes, even as it struggled to deal with the lasting effects of removal.

Reform is often the mantra of new players in Indian affairs, who see an opportunity to seize upon a discredited agency at the tail end of an

[102] See Prucha, *Great Father*, 302ff.

effective but no longer relevant policy. These new interests seek to redesign and redirect Indian policy to serve their own interests and address their own problems. As removal progressed, as Eastern interests gradually turned away from Indian affairs and Eastern Indians were forced west, new issues emerged that had been inadequately anticipated by the federal government. Big government would again be called upon to win the West by extending its jurisdiction over Indian territory and lands and events. Civilian control would continue to dominate U.S.–tribal relations. And once again, the goals of U.S. policy – no longer pacification and removal, but the subjugation and continued dispossession of American Indians – would be achieved by an effective national administrative effort.

Even though the civilian service temporarily lost control of one aspect of Indian affairs, when physical removal became an affair of force led by military might, the civilian service quickly recovered its unique role as affairs moved away from force and back to diplomacy, trade, and managed expansion before, during, and after the Civil War.

8

Clearing the Indian Barrier

Indian Affairs at the Center of National Expansion

Nathaniel Taylor, Commissioner of Indian Affairs, wrote in his 1868 Annual Report:

A little investigation, and even a superficial knowledge and a little reflection, will convince every candid mind that there is no branch of the public service more intricate and difficult, and involving more varied and larger public and private interests, than our "Indian affairs;" none requiring in their control and direction a larger brain, or a more sensitive and charitable heart.[1]

From the 1840s through the 1880s, Indian affairs continued to be centrally important to the life and development of the United States. Virtually every region and every social, political, and economic interest continued to be affected by Indian affairs in significant ways. The national government continued to be the leading force of authority and administration coordinating and managing expansion and settlement westward. The executive branch continued to lead in the design and implementation of policy, and in creative adaptation to ever-changing circumstances, as federal administrators in a host of contexts worked to conquer the continent before, during, and after the Civil War.

The Ongoing Significance of Indian Affairs

Today, one of our enduring images of the West – the image of "open, unspoiled wilderness" – involves Indians in a telling way. In truth, federal officials *created* the "uninhabited wilderness" we romanticize by removing Indians from the land. Even the "uninhabited landscapes" of national parks

1 "Annual Report of the Commissioner of Indian Affairs," 1868, reprinted in Francis Paul Prucha, ed., *Documents of United States Indian Policy*, 2nd ed. (Lincoln: University of Nebraska Press, 1990), 119.

such as Yosemite, Yellowstone, and Glacier are the result of careful, coordinated Indian removals.[2] Despite the romantic vision of an easily settled, unpopulated West, Indians before, during, and after the Civil War played a central role in popular political, social, and artistic endeavors, and they held a central place in the political and economic history of both East and West. Eastern and Western development interests, proponents of expansion, and observers of national affairs confronted the importance of Indian affairs throughout the years of the reservation era.[3]

Indians continued to hold an important and influential place in the country's art, popular culture, and social development during the middle and later years of the nineteenth century. Advances in publishing, along with an increasingly literate population, encouraged periodicals, adventure novels, and dime paperbacks, many of which featured stories of the West, pioneers, and cowboys and Indians. Captivity tales, long the staple of Indian-related storytelling by whites, continued.[4] Photographic imagery of the West, and especially of Indians, augmented the continuing work of painters. Indians traveling through towns and cities – whether during removals to the West or on trips to and from Washington, DC – received extensive press coverage and attention, becoming traveling celebrity events.[5]

Indian affairs continued to play a role in popular politics. Abraham Lincoln joked about his experiences on the margins of the 1832 Black Hawk War, relating tales of attacking onion fields, engaging in "a good many bloody struggles with the musquetoes [*sic*]," and noting his heroism when he "bent a musket pretty badly on one occasion." During campaigns in Illinois and for the presidency, though, Lincoln highlighted his election as a captain in the conflict with the Sauk Indians; when he eulogized President Zachary Taylor, Lincoln invoked Taylor's military record against Indians; and in 1852 Lincoln campaigned for Winfield Scott and spoke generously of "the applause of the great and good of the land" that Scott had earned for the manner in which he removed the Cherokee "from their homes to

2 Mark David Spence, *Dispossessing the Wilderness: Indian Removal and the Making of the National Parks* (New York: Oxford University Press, 1999), 4–5.

3 Richard White, *"It's Your Misfortune and None of My Own": A New History of the American West* (Norman: University of Oklahoma Press, 1991).

4 Robert F. Berkhofer Jr., *The White Man's Indian: Images of the American Indian from Columbus to the Present* (New York: Vintage, 1978), 96–100.

5 See, e.g., Norman J. Bender, *"New Hope for the Indians": The Grant Peace Policy and the Navajos in the 1870s* (Albuquerque: University of New Mexico Press, 1989), 122ff. and ch. 7; Loretta Fowler, *Arapahoe Politics, 1851–1978: Symbols in Crises of Authority* (Lincoln: University of Nebraska Press, 1986), 26, 64; William Haas Moore, *Chiefs, Agents & Soldiers: Conflict on the Navajo Frontier, 1868–1882* (Albuquerque: University of New Mexico Press, 1994), 142ff.; Joseph B. Herring, *The Enduring Indians of Kansas: A Century and a Half of Acculturation* (Lawrence: University Press of Kansas, 1990), 46ff., 91ff.

the west of the Mississippi."[6] Lincoln, historian David Nichols concludes, "learned how to use Indian affairs for political advantage."[7]

As in earlier eras, Indian affairs intertwined closely with careers in public service. Jefferson Davis, descended from Opechancanough of the Powhatan Confederacy, served seven years on the Michigan frontier removing squatters from Indian lands, fought in the Black Hawk War, and pressed for removal of Indians from Mississippi. Davis was appointed Secretary of War in 1853, during some of the harshest Indian affairs in California.[8] Also involved in Indian affairs in the far West before the Civil War were Ulysses S. Grant, Philip Sheridan, and George Pickett.[9] Isaac Stevens, governor of Washington Territory and signatory to key treaties in the 1850s, was in the engineer corps in the Mexican War, worked with the U.S. Coast Survey, and led the Pacific Railroad Survey group in the North. This brought him into the complex calculations of railroad routes and Indian lands. George McClellan commanded one of Stevens' survey groups, looking for passes through the mountains and dealing with Indian communities.[10] Ely Parker, a Seneca and later head of the Bureau of Indian Affairs, served as Grant's Military Secretary during the Civil War and drew up the articles of Lee's surrender at Appomattox.[11] After the war, future President James Garfield led a commission to the Flatheads in 1872 that responded to white settlers' fears regarding their Indian neighbors.[12]

John E. Wool provides a terrific example. Wool is probably most famous as commander of the Department of the East in New York City during the Civil War Draft Riots, at the end of his career. He was in that position because of his long service at the intersection of Indian affairs and the military before the Civil War. Wool served in the War of 1812, then served twenty-five years as inspector general of the U.S. Army. He was placed in command of Cherokee removal in 1836, until he ran afoul of state interests. He served in the Mexican War and then as head of the Department of the Pacific during the Gold Rush, a position which again brought him into

6 Quoted in David A. Nichols, *Lincoln and the Indians: Civil War Policy & Politics* (Urbana: University of Illinois Press, 2000), 3.

7 Nichols, *Lincoln and the Indians*, 3; see also David Herbert Donald, *Lincoln* (New York: Touchstone, 1996), 44–6.

8 Laurence M. Hauptman, *Between Two Fires: American Indians in the Civil War* (New York: Free Press Paperbacks, 1996), 12.

9 Alvin M. Josephy Jr., *The Nez Perce Indians and the Opening of the Northwest* (Boston: Houghton Mifflin, 1997 [1965], 285.

10 Josephy, *Nez Perce Indians*, 293. Stevens was killed at the Battle of Chantilly during the Civil War. Josephy, *Nez Perce Indians*, 378.

11 Hauptman, *Between Two Fires*, x, 181–3.

12 Josephy, *Nez Perce Indians*, 563.

contact with Indian affairs on a regular basis.[13] Like many Civil War era leaders, Wool had a long history interwoven with, and often focused on, Indian affairs.

Federal policy during the reservation era before, during, and after the Civil War remained crucial for a number of reasons. Before the Civil War, Indian affairs were part of mid-century's national expansion. The United States added Texas in 1845, Oregon in 1846, and California and large pieces of the Southwest in 1848. The belief that Indians who had earlier moved to the West could be protected and allowed time to acclimate and "civilize" – a cornerstone of the removal policy – suddenly came under fire, as whites looked to cross Indian territory for the far West and as hundreds of thousands of American Indians were suddenly in the middle of – rather than outside of – the United States' expansion. Demands for further Indian removals around the West abounded, and the federal government continued to shuffle Indian populations around the Indian territory and throughout the West. Heated debate characterized California's Indian affairs in the 1850s, for example, as white settlers demanded that the state's Indians be moved east across the mountains or north to Oregon. At the same time, though, the federal government confronted a crowding continent and a narrowing ability to execute further removals. The Bureau of Indian Affairs preferred in-state removals and concentration on reservations in California, an option that failed to satisfy white settlers' and speculators' dreams of occupying the entire state and which placed government agents at odds with citizens and, often, their elected representatives.[14] Indians complicated the politics of integrating areas like Texas, the Southwest, Oregon, and California into the constitutional system.

Expansion animated territorial politics in vast new regions, presented new trading opportunities, innumerable chances for costly conflict, and tremendous pressures on management and administration. By 1848 the Oregon Trail was the route to the West for more than fourteen thousand pioneers; 350,000 people would cross the Great Platte River Road by the end of the

[13] Laurence M. Hauptman, "John E. Wool and the New York City Draft Riots of 1863: A Reassessment," *Civil War History* 49 (December 2003), 370–7; see also Josephy, *Nez Perce Indians*, 347ff.; William M. Neil, "The Territorial Governor as Indian Superintendent in the Trans-Mississippi West," *The Mississippi Valley Historical Review* 43 (September 1956), 231–2; Terence O'Donnell, *An Arrow in the Earth: General Joel Palmer and the Indians of Oregon* (Portland: Oregon Historical Society, 1991), ch. 12.

[14] George Harwood Phillips, *Indians and Indian Agents: The Origins of the Reservation System in California, 1849–1852* (Norman: University of Oklahoma Press, 1997); George Harwood Phillips, *"Bringing Them under Subjection": California's Tejon Indian Reservation and Beyond, 1852–1864* (Lincoln: University of Nebraska Press, 2004); Ronald Spores, "Too Small a Place: The Removal of the Willamette Valley Indians, 1850–1856," *American Indian Quarterly* 17 (Spring 1993), 176 and generally; O'Donnell, *Arrow*, on Oregon, esp. 138.

1860s. By the 1850s, political and economic leaders wanted a transcontinental railroad. Recognizing the importance of Indians to Western and national affairs, Stephen Douglas wrote in 1853:

The Indian barrier must be removed. The tide of emigration and civilization must be permitted to roll onward until it rushes through the passes of the mountains, and spreads over the plains, and mingles with the waters of the Pacific. Continuous lines of settlement with civil, political and religious institutions all under the protection of law, are imperiously demanded by the highest national considerations. These are essential, but they are not sufficient. No man can keep up with the spirit of this age who travels on anything slower than the locomotive, and fails to receive intelligence by lightning. We must therefore have Rail Roads and Telegraphs from the Atlantic to the Pacific, through our own territory. Not one line only, but many lines, for the valley of the Mississippi will require as many Rail Roads to the Pacific as to the Atlantic, and will not venture to limit the number. The removal of the Indian barrier and the extension of the laws of the United States in the form of Territorial governments are the first steps toward the accomplishment of each and all of those objects.[15]

Territorial officials and national leaders fought for the fruits of that grand endeavor – an endeavor which ran right through the heart of Indian territory, no matter where it was built. Other interests demanded protection from potential conflicts between newly resettled Indians and the native inhabitants of the Plains. Whites wanted land for farming, for cattle raising, for oil and gas drilling. Mining, too, involved Indian affairs directly, and Morton Wilkinson in 1863 called for increased appropriations for the Indian service precisely because gold and other minerals lay under Indian territory.[16] Whites also wanted land for expansion of transportation and communications infrastructures, which connected intimately the lives of traders, suppliers, shippers, business owners, outfitters of pioneering expeditions, land speculators, and settlement companies – the backbone of the Western economy and a big part of the Eastern one, too. The connection of Indians to the land, and the fact that whites coveted even reservation land, kept Indians close to the center of local and national politics before the Civil War.[17]

15 Quoted in Francis Paul Prucha, *The Great Father: The United States Government and the American Indians* (Lincoln: University of Nebraska Press, 1984), 346.

16 Nichols, *Lincoln and the Indians*, 194; see also Joseph Ellison, "The Mineral Land Question in California, 1848–1866," *Southwestern Historical Quarterly* 30 (1926), reprinted in Vernon Carstensen, ed., *The Public Lands: Studies in the History of the Public Domain* (Madison: University of Wisconsin Press, 1968), 72–3; Fremont P. Wirth, "The Operation of the Land Laws in the Minnesota Iron District," *Mississippi Valley Historical Review* 13 (1927), reprinted in Carstensen, *Public Lands*; Lucile Kane, "Federal Protection of Public Timber in the Upper Great Lakes States," *Agricultural History* 23 (1949), reprinted in Carstensen, *Public Lands*.

17 On reservations and the Eastern economy, see, e.g., Neil, "Territorial Governor," 217. On military and government posts as part of local economies, see David M. Brugge, *The Navajo and Hopi Land Dispute: An American Tragedy* (Albuquerque: University of New Mexico Press, 1999), 20; Thomas R. Buecker, "The Post of North Platte Station, 1867–1878,"

Indian affairs were significant during the Civil War, as well. A series of uprisings and violent clashes flared across the West during the war years. Conflict with the Sioux in Minnesota culminated in violence in 1862; five hundred to a thousand settlers were killed, and more than three hundred Sioux were sentenced to death. Amid persistent rumors that Britain was about to enter the fight on the side of the Confederacy, and recalling long-standing concerns about Indian-European alliances, Minnesotans suspected British traders of working with the Sioux. Minnesotans demanded troops and materiel, straining the struggling Union but arguing that, as Minnesota Governor Alexander Ramsey wrote to Lincoln, "This is not our war, it is a National War."[18] Lincoln, in turn, worried that meeting demands in Minnesota would encourage other regions to make demands based on real or concocted Indian threats. The Minnesota fight had significant political implications for the Republicans, and – coming at almost exactly the same moment that Pope's Union forces were defeated at Second Bull Run, in August 1862 – the northern war seemed to contribute to Confederate momentum. Pope was moved to Minnesota.[19]

Thirty-eight Sioux were executed after the uprising, in the nation's largest public hanging. Lincoln's personal involvement in the military trials and sentences of Indians caught up in the Minnesota conflict – and his pardoning of close to three hundred people – further engaged the president. Afterward, Minnesota demanded that the federal government remove all remaining Sioux from the state, despite the ongoing crisis of the Civil War. Together with war refugees in Kansas and other demands – whites in the Minnesota and Dakota areas used the Minnesota uprising as a pretext for demanding that the national government remove even Indians who, like the Winnebagoes, had little to do with the conflict – the Lincoln administration faced a constant barrage of Indian-related events with significant relationships to national and regional politics, and to the war effort in the East. During the war, Lincoln dealt with ongoing questions of removals, reservations, insurgencies, and politics stemming from Indian affairs in the West. The fallout from the Minnesota uprising dragged on for years, and refugees, tribal politics, Indian soldiers, and international diplomacy typified the war years in Kansas and the Indian territory. By 1863, for example, two thousand Cherokee refugees remained around Fort Scott in Kansas, and nearly seven thousand were at Fort Gibson in Arkansas.[20] By 1865, the Union had twenty

in *The Nebraska Indian Wars Reader, 1865–1877*, ed. R. Eli Paul (Lincoln: University of Nebraska Press, 1998), 21–2.

18 Quoted in Nichols, *Lincoln and the Indians*, 85.

19 See Nichols, *Lincoln and the Indians*, especially at 78, 80, 81.

20 Hauptman reports that by 1863, one-third of married Cherokee women were widows and one-fourth of the children were orphans. The United States spent $250,000 on relief efforts at Fort Gibson just in the first six months after the war. Hauptman, *Between Two Fires*, 42.

thousand troops on the frontier, a considerable amount given the needs in the East.[21]

Violence also erupted in the Southwest during the Civil War, including the government's effort to keep the Navajo at the Bosque Redondo reservation and the 1864 Sand Creek massacre in Colorado. These events were interpreted in the context of the Civil War, with many Western citizens fearing alliances and combinations among Indians and between Indians and the Confederacy. Everything was connected, and Indian wars in the West added to the general upheaval of the era.[22] It is worth remembering that these disruptions followed the defeat of Tecumseh's confederacy by only about fifty years: the anxiety created by the prospect of Indian confederacies was still fresh in the imagination.

Nor were Indian affairs important *only* in western contexts during the Civil War: Indian affairs steadily intruded on the East's war efforts. The Five Civilized Tribes, southern in affinity and history, all sided with the confederacy.[23] Lincoln was slow to recognize the significance of Indians in the war, where tribes held key strategic positions and could supply personnel, and where refugees from areas that saw fighting were a constant headache.[24] The Confederacy immediately recognized the significance of Indians, though – the Confederate government sent a special agent to tribes west of Arkansas on the day of Lincoln's inauguration, and less than two weeks later the Confederacy created its own Bureau of Indian Affairs.[25] Lincoln belatedly engaged in attempts to resecure Indian territory and utilize thousands of Indian troops, with pay and benefits equal to that of white

[21] Nichols, *Lincoln and the Indians*, 164.

[22] Prucha, *Great Father*, 457–8.

[23] Prucha, *Great Father*, 416–17. Former federal personnel who had become officers in the Confederate military worked to convince the Southern Indians to ally with the South. Also pushing the Indians in this direction was the fact that much of their annuity moneys and trust funds were in Southern stocks and bonds; the Indians feared that they would lose these sums if they failed to ally with the South. Hauptman, *Between Two Fires*, 26–7; Nichols, *Lincoln and the Indians*, 30. Nichols, *Lincoln and the Indians*, ch. 3 outlines the significance of the Indians to the strategy and future of both the Union and the Confederacy.

[24] See Hauptman, *Between Two Fires*.

[25] The Confederacy recreated U.S. administrative structures. In Indian affairs, as in other fields, many officials left their Northern posts for parallel posts in the CSA, and federal laws became effective in the Confederacy unless actively amended or repealed by the CSA government. Paul P. Van Riper and Harry N. Scheiber, "The Confederate Civil Service," *The Journal of Southern History* 25 (November 1959). On CSA Indian affairs specifically, see Hauptman, *Between Two Fires*, 26–7. Reflecting the experience and professionalism characteristic of Indian Office leadership before the Civil War, the Commissioner of Indian Affairs for the new CSA was the experienced Albert Pike, a veteran of the Mexican War and a longtime inhabitant of Arkansas who spoke several Indian languages. Hauptman, *Between Two Fires*, 27.

troops.[26] Tens of thousands of American Indians served on both sides of the conflict, often capitalizing on local expertise to aid military efforts.[27]

After the Civil War, hundreds of thousands of Indians continued to occupy the land in the West. Disputes about title or legal right to occupancy could not hide the fact that there were Indians, and that they occupied vast stretches of territory. By the middle of the century, roughly 360,000 Indians faced the expanding United States, with at least 200,000 in the new U.S. territories. The historian Robert Utley divides Indian population totals into regions, with roughly 75,000 on the Great Plains from Texas to the British possessions; 84,000 removed Eastern Indians on lands west of the 95th meridian; 200,000 in the new U.S. territories, including 25,000 in Texas, 150,000 in California and New Mexico, and 25,000 in Oregon. By comparison, the U.S. population in the West by 1860 was only about 1.4 million.[28] The numbers remind us that, as in earlier eras, whites confronting Indians did not always benefit from overwhelming numerical advantages. Alban Hoopes points out that in most of the new territories, Indian populations generally exceeded white populations by considerable amounts.[29] And the Indian nations in the West were diverse, organized, and in many cases militarily, culturally, and politically powerful.[30]

After the War, as westerners confronted organized tribes and sizeable Indian populations, Indians remained relevant and important back East because of economic ties between Eastern companies and Western development, and because of debates about the amount of federal money being spent in the West and about the best ways in which to spend it. The frontier erupted in violence and disorder in 1865 and 1866, witnessing conflicts between whites moving along the Bozeman Trail and the Sioux Indians through whose land the trail passed. Sporadic conflicts, as Indians targeted

[26] Nichols, *Lincoln and the Indians*, 41.

[27] See Hauptman, *Between Two Fires*; Donald F. Danker, "The North Brothers and the Pawnee Scouts," in *Nebraska Indian Wars Reader*; W. Turrentine Jackson, "Indian Affairs and Politics in Idaho Territory, 1863–1870," *The Pacific Historical Review* 14 (September 1945). Hauptman points out that Indian roles in the war are often obscured by the terminology used to identify soldiers. Many Indians were identified in reports and paperwork as black, Negro, African American, or colored, and as a result "many Native Americans, especially in southern New England, have been written out of Civil War history." He estimates that roughly twenty thousand Indians served in the Civil War. Hauptman, *Between Two Fires*, 145, x.

[28] Robert M. Utley, *The Indian Frontier of the American West, 1846–1890* (Albuquerque: University of New Mexico Press, 1984), 4.

[29] Alban W. Hoopes, *Indian Affairs and their Administration, 1849–1860* (New York: Kraus Reprint, 1972 [1932]), 8; see also David J. Wishart, "The Dispossession of the Pawnee," *Annals of the Association of American Geographers* 69 (September 1979), 392 and generally; Spores, "Too Small a Place," 172.

[30] Utley, *Indian Frontier*, 4; Wilcomb E. Washburn, *The Indian in America* (New York: Harper & Row, 1975), 173.

the United States' line of forts along the trail, excited renewed worries about a frontier war. The Fetterman Massacre crystallized national fears of an all-out Indian war and disrupted Indian relations across the West, firing concern in the East and sparking a special investigatory commission to look into the event.

Violence in the West appalled observers in the East. President Grant's Peace Policy, under which religious societies selected government personnel for the reservations, aimed at reforming Indian affairs administration and ending the Indian wars. Yet the fighting went on: major battles of the era included the Modoc War on the Oregon–California border in 1872–1873; attacks by Kiowa, Comanche, and Cheyenne in Texas in 1874–1875; and raids and conflict with the Apache in the Southwest. The pursuit and eventual capture of the Nez Perce in the Northwest was "a national drama" coursing through the new national parks,[31] and Custer's defeat at Little Big Horn on June 25, 1876, shocked American citizens on the eve of the nation's centennial, as if designed to keep Indian affairs always in the forefront of the nation's consciousness. It would be ten more years before the United States captured Geronimo, and fourteen before the massacre of Indians at Wounded Knee.

The cost of Indian affairs mattered, too. Military expenditures rose during the period of the Mexican War and expansion to the West Coast, reaching to about 70 percent of federal expenditures in 1846.[32] The number of enlisted men in the Army, Navy, and Marines also spiked during the Mexican War and westward expansion in the 1840s and late 1850s, peaking close to sixty thousand.[33] A report from the Senate Committee on the Pacific Railroad estimated that wars with Indian tribes since the removal era had cost the United States twenty thousand lives and more than $750 million. At about the same time, the chairman of the House Committee on Indian Affairs estimated that conflict with Indians in the West cost the nation one million dollars each week, or $144,000 every day.[34] One estimate after the Civil War pegged the cost of killing an individual Indian at $1 million.[35] Indian

31 Josephy, *Nez Perce Indians*, 598; James McLaughlin provides a contemporary account of the Nez Perce story in *My Friend the Indian* (Lincoln: University of Nebraska Press, 1989 [1910]), ch. 19.

32 Ira Katznelson, "Flexible Capacity: The Military and Early American Statebuilding," in *Shaped by War and Trade: International Influences on American Political Development*, ed. Ira Katznelson and Martin Shefter (Princeton: Princeton University Press, 2002), 92–3.

33 Katznelson, "Flexible Capacity," 98; see also Max M. Edling, *A Revolution in Favor of Government: Origins of the U.S. Constitution and the Making of the American State* (Oxford: Oxford University Press, 2003), 138.

34 David E. Wilkins, *American Indian Sovereignty and the U.S. Supreme Court: The Masking of Justice* (Austin: University of Texas Press, 1997), 52.

35 See William E. Unrau, "Nathaniel Green Taylor," in Robert M. Kvasnicka and Herman J. Viola, eds., *The Commissioners of Indian Affairs, 1824–1977* (Lincoln: University of Nebraska Press, 1979), 117.

Commissioner Hiram Price estimated that the United States spent more than \$750,000 in the four years from 1879 to 1883 just to collect money owed *to* the Indians, particularly from excessive attorneys' fees.[36] The *New York Times* reported in 1882 that 80 percent of the War Department's budget and 73 percent of its personnel were being used to pacify Indians in the West.[37]

These costs were spread across the West. By 1867, the Commissioner of Indian Affairs estimated that the agency's experimental effort at administering the Navajo, at New Mexico's Bosque Redondo, had cost the government \$10 million.[38] In California, one of the federal government's first tasks with regard to the Indians was to protect whites' stock from raiding by Indians – an endeavor that involved tens of thousands of dollars. One contemporary estimate reported that Indian raiders stole at least \$80,000 worth of stock in California's Mariposa County alone, in about five months between 1850 and 1851; from another region, an estimate of the value of stolen stock was close to a half million dollars.[39] Governor John Bigler estimated that by the end of 1851, Indian wars had cost the state roughly a half million dollars in war bonds, interest, and war loan warrants; he also found that expeditions in Indian affairs to the north and south of the state had cost about one million dollars (he also pointed out to the state legislature that he expected the federal government to pay the bills).[40] Federal agent Redick McKee ridiculed Bigler's calculations as far too low, and argued that without the efforts of federal agents to maintain peace, resolve disputes, and settle the Indian question, California's debt would have been closer to \$8 or \$10 million. In the 1860s Congress spent nearly \$3 million on civil administration for Indians in California alone – a figure that does not include military expenses.[41] To the north, the Nez Perce War cost \$1.87 million, not including claims for private losses.[42]

Indians affected expansion and the economy in another very significant way – as underwriters of that expansion and as a key resource for U.S. economic development. Judith Nies argues that revenues from the sale of Indian lands constituted 80 percent of the federal government's revenues

[36] Floyd A. O'Neil, "Hiram Price," in Kvasnicka and Viola, *Commissioners*, 177.

[37] Hauptman, *Between Two Fires*, 189.

[38] Edward Everett Dale, *The Indians of the Southwest: A Century of Development Under the United States* (Norman: University of Oklahoma Press, 1949), 60; on Navajos generally, including expenditures, see Moore, *Chiefs, Agents & Soldiers*; John L. Kessell, "General Sherman and the Navajo Treaty of 1868: A Basic and Expedient Misunderstanding," *The Western Historical Quarterly* 12 (July 1981).

[39] Phillips, *Indians and Indian Agents*, 56.

[40] Ibid., 166.

[41] Dale, *Indians of the Southwest*, 44.

[42] Josephy, *Nez Perce Indians*, 633.

between 1789 and 1850.[43] In a careful study of railroads and development interests in Indian country in the half-century following the Civil War, H. Craig Miner finds that Indian annuity funds underwrote railroad and other development in violation of treaty provisions. Miner writes:

> [M]oney that Indian tribes gained by the sale of lands they were forced to leave went to gird the loins of the industrial system that was responsible. Indian funds were usually not distributed per capita to the tribes, on the grounds that savages could not use them responsibly. Instead they were held in trust in Washington. These trust funds were sometimes invested by the Indian Office directly in the securities of railroad companies and often were invested in state and U.S. bonds, which were in turn pledged to guarantee corporate issues in manufacturing as well as transportation. In 1864 the Cherokee national fund and the Cherokee orphan fund were invested in a U.S. bond issue pledged to support the Union Pacific, Eastern Division railway, which was at the time illegally cutting timber on the Delaware reserve in Kansas, while the Delawares moved in with the Cherokees to the south. The U.S. bonds representing the Creek orphan fund were pledged to the Chesapeake and Ohio Canal Company.... The significance of Indian trust funds as a source of capital for American industrialization cannot be overemphasized.[44]

The Complicated Politics of Indian Affairs

Debates raged around the costs and direction of Indian affairs. Many interests in the East and West benefited directly or indirectly from Indian affairs spending. Development interests looking to move through and conquer Indian territory in the West favored expenditures for Indian policy and administration: railroads and communications interests, mining and industrial interests, Western settlement interests, and interests profiting from supplying the reservations. Northeastern economic interests benefited from expansion and economic development, and so often supported new expenditures for treaties and supplies to support containment and military affairs. Humanitarians often supported spending for education and civilization initiatives, drawing the contempt of Westerners who – if money was to be spent – wanted it spent on a strong military and a muscular policy.

Other interests opposed expenditures for the West. Despite the violence, many Easterners didn't see any benefit to be gained by a large and active

43 Judith Nies, *Native American History: A Chronology of a Culture's Vast Achievements and their Links to World Events* (New York: Ballantine, 1996), 213.

44 H. Craig Miner, *The Corporation and the Indian: Tribal Sovereignty and Industrial Civilization in Indian Territory, 1865–1907* (Norman: University of Oklahoma Press, 1976), 9–10; see also Paul Stuart, *Nations Within a Nation: Historical Statistics of American Indians* (New York: Greenwood Press, 1987), 209. On relationships between Indian affairs, government administration, and railroad development, see also, e.g., Malone's discussion of the St. Paul, Minneapolis, and Manitoba railroad: Michael P. Malone, *James J. Hill: Empire Builder of the Northwest* (Norman: University of Oklahoma Press, 1996), 119ff. On railroad grants and government involvement, see Malone, *James J. Hill*, 33.

military, of railroad development in support of that military, or of supporting reservation Indians. Southern and Eastern interests had driven policy in the removal era, often over the objections of nervous Westerners who were happy to end the factory system but who were unhappy with the idea of tens of thousands of displaced Indians in their backyards. With the successful removal of most remaining Eastern Indians by the 1840s, Southern agrarian and slave interests, and Northern and Southern settlement interests, shifted their approaches and opposed much Indian Office activity, and its associated costs, in the West. Westerners debated the propriety of spending millions concentrating and supporting Indians who were viewed as threats. Farmers and miners in California opposed the federal government's treaty system, which set aside fertile lands and promising areas for Indians.[45] Of course, some interests, like traders in California and in other areas, wanted reservations nearby.[46]

Interests constantly shifted positions, too. Particular railroad magnates and companies supported certain initiatives and spending in particular areas, but not in others; towns supported military bases and expansion spending that benefited them locally, but opposed the same initiatives elsewhere. Along with private interests, Indian affairs engaged ever-shifting territorial political interests. As in earlier eras, territorial interests had close connections with territorial politics, creating a fluid political environment surrounding Indian affairs. Texas's Indian relations, for example, shifted considerably when Sam Houston was replaced as the Republic's president: the treaties and promises offered by Houston became dead letters when his successor assumed the reins of government.

By design, tribes persisted as important and influential interests in the reservation era. Reservations emerged from removal's philosophy that the means to save Indians from the pernicious effects of contact with whites was to establish Indian communities in safe areas in the West. An idea with antecedents among the colonial efforts of earlier European powers, a reservation system would protect Indians and tribes from white onslaughts. Segregated Indian communities, in turn, could be policed and managed by federal agents. The policy was meant to be a temporary one, designed to carry Indians along until such time as they had been sufficiently "civilized" to assimilate into white society, a peculiar application of isolation in service of assimilation. Until that occurred, tribes would be significant parts of both politics and policy in the middle of the nineteenth century. And until that occurred, conflicts would erupt between groups of Indians in the West, and between Indians and non-Indians. The same risks, worries, and threats that

[45] Phillips, *Indians and Indian Agents*, 159.

[46] E.g., Roy W. Meyer, *History of the Santee Sioux: United States Indian Policy on Trial*, revised edition (Lincoln: University of Nebraska Press, 1993), 156.

had dominated national thinking as early as the 1780s and 1790s continued in the 1840s through the 1880s, just in different locations.

Tribes in the West also differed in many ways from the Eastern tribes, and they posed new political and administrative issues. More prone to hunting and to a mobile culture than the settled, agrarian tribes of the East, the plains tribes had different technologies and ways of life, and they had different experiences with European and American colonists. They also, in many cases, had better weaponry than the Eastern tribes had possessed during their conflicts with the United States.

The interests of individual Indians were never far from the forefront of local issues and evaluations of Indian affairs administration. Crises in Indian affairs after the Civil War animated social activists and Eastern reformers; humanitarian interests in the reservation era focused on exposing abuses within the Indian service and on publicizing poor conditions on reservations. Investigations and exposure of reservation conditions provided the basis for the reforming humanitarians' influence in the second half of the nineteenth century. During the Civil War and Reconstruction, individuals such as John Beeson and Bishop Henry Whipple, who were interested in the welfare and development of Indians and upset at corruption and abuse in the Indian Service, maintained a steady and vocal critique of the agency and its officers. Whipple, in particular, lobbied the White House, members of Congress, the Board of Indian Commissioners, and the general public to expose and remedy abuses in the Indian Service.[47] Individual civilization and progress become the raison d'etre of reformers who condemned the failures of the reservation system, and the progress of individuals became a rallying cry supporting the destruction of tribes and their land bases as reservations were slowly allotted to individuals. These reformers gave the new trend in reservations a humanitarian logic, much as the factory system and removal took advantage of intellectual arguments that these policies were in the best interests of Indians.

Every Indian affairs context – which included contexts throughout and across the United States and its territories – involved an ever-changing network of interests with a particular angle on Indian affairs. Case studies are replete with unpredictable and shifting relations among local, territorial, state, and national politics and parties, traders, settlers, speculators, suppliers, farmers, shippers, railroad companies, communications concerns, road builders, government agents, local and national humanitarians, and religious groups from diverse and competing perspectives. And each of these smaller groupings had their own internecine competition: tavern and saloon keepers fighting to influence the location of military posts and roads, and lobbying to influence alcohol restrictions and the extent of local enforcement; competing groups of land speculators fighting over railroad routes or

[47] Prucha, *Great Father*, 465ff.; Nichols, *Lincoln and the Indians*.

over reservation lands or over particular mills, dams, and other improvements made by Indians or non-Indians on the land. Frontier politics were complicated, energetic, and cut-throat, sometimes literally. Race and slavery issues mediated through government agents and policies, even after the Civil War, continued to add greatly to the complexity.[48] Indian individuals and communities remained a big part of the action.

Indian Affairs and National Influence in the Reservation Era

The national government anchored, centered, and facilitated development in this complicated environment. As the United States obtained lands in the West, the issue of the federal role in Indian affairs continued to raise questions for local interests regarding the appropriate scope of the national government's powers. These questions were answered just as they had been in earlier years: with the extension of the federal government's authority and acquiescence in its leadership.

Nationalization and Treaties

The treaty system, with all of its administrative requirements, continued to be the cornerstone of national Indian affairs throughout the reservation era. The Indian Office promoted and defended the treaty policy as the appropriate means of negotiating with Indians and extending federal authority. While the treaty process adapted over time to changing relationships between the United States and various tribes, a consensus existed on the use of federal treaties that dated to the republic's earliest days. Treaties anchored Indian policy at the federal level despite shifts in party control and through rapidly evolving circumstances.

Treaties in the early parts of the nineteenth century aimed at securing federal authority over Indian affairs, land cessions, boundary demarcation, provision of services, and specification of the manner and means of removal. The reservation era's treaties did more, in some respects, than earlier treaties, and as such they continued to expand the federal executive's authority and

[48] Roughly 10 percent of the Creek population, 14 percent of Choctaws, 15 percent of Cherokees, and 18 percent of Chickasaws were enslaved at the start of the Civil War, for a total of about ten thousand people. About 12 percent of families in these nations owned slaves. Seminole numbers approached 30 percent, but the situation there was unique. Claudio Saunt, "The Paradox of Freedom: Tribal Sovereignty and Emancipation during the Reconstruction of Indian Territory," *The Journal of Southern History* 70 (February 2004), 65, 67. Saunt also discusses the complexities of applying the Emancipation Proclamation and the Civil Rights Act of 1866 to Indian nations, along with complexities involving post–Civil War treaties. Reflecting the ongoing significance of Indian affairs, commissioners for the treaties with the Five Civilized Tribes at the end of the war included Indian Affairs Commissioner Dennis Cooley; longtime number 2 at the BIA Charles Mix; Grant's Military Secretary and future Indian Commissioner, the Seneca Ely Parker; General William S. Harney; and Elijah Sells, Superintendent for the Southern Indians. Hauptman, *Between Two Fires*, 58–9.

powers. The treaties of the reservation era needed to be more cognizant of lands in the West and of the humanitarian goals of the reservation policy. The executive exercised authority not only to exchange Western lands between and among Indians and territories, but also to allot land parcels to individual Indians in the hopes that this would speed Indians on their way to becoming successful and independent citizen farmers. The executive also received expanded authority over the dispensation of treaty annuities; this not only increased the executive's collage of administrative tasks, it perpetuated the influence on local affairs wielded by Indian service field agents.

The commitment to treaties still demanded that important decisions be made at the local level and in response to local circumstances; it also accepted the fact that as circumstances changed in the field, so would agreements with the tribes. New negotiations and agreements were made as circumstances on the ground changed. Only field officers had the experience, knowledge, and presence to be able to make these decisions. And as decisions and agreements accumulated, expertise and awareness of relationships and histories increased the premium on local field administration, as it had in earlier eras. The pace of westward settlement pushed the federal government to respond to pressures quickly, and between 1853 and 1856 alone its agents negotiated and signed fifty-two treaties – more than in any other similar period.

Nationalization and the Territories

Treaties established a basis for federal involvement and control in the new territories. Congress authorized funds for presents and treaty making, and executive branch representatives went into the field to organize Indian populations and extend federal jurisdiction. This process was complicated in some areas by locals who were reluctant to cede important authority to the national government, but in each case officials in the territories eventually did just that. The process of implementing the reservation policy in these areas was simultaneously ongoing and fraught with administrative hurdles stemming from the absence of clear federal authority, local particularities, the weakness of the federal military, and the aggressiveness of white settler and pioneer populations. Events in the new territories, though, demonstrate the eventual accession by local populations to national control as a prerequisite for peace, order, and stability.[49]

Implementing the reservation system in Texas, for example, suffered from a number of serious constraints, none more important than the fact that annexation provisions had left public lands under the control of Texas itself, not the federal government. The first Texas legislature stated flatly that "we recognize no title in the Indian tribes resident within the limits of the state to any portion of the soil thereof; and that we recognize no right of the Government of the United States to make any treaty of limits with the said

49 See, e.g., Prucha, *Great Father*; White, *"It's Your Misfortune"*; Hoopes, *Indian Affairs*.

Indian tribes without the consent of the Government of this state."[50] This meant that the federal government had no lands onto which it could move Indian populations, and it was unable to extend federal trade and intercourse laws to the Indians without Texas' consent. Nevertheless, the federal government sent commissioners to work out treaties with Indians in Texas by which the Indians tied themselves to the United States and by which they gave exclusive trade and intercourse rights to the federal government. As with many earlier treaties, these treaties guaranteed to the Indians certain items like trading houses and agencies, enacted prohibitions against the traffic in alcohol, and formalized presidential discretion to provide blacksmiths, teachers, and missionaries. In 1847, Congress authorized funds to facilitate Texas treaties and future relations.[51]

Over the next ten years, the federal government pressured Texas to earmark territory for the Indians; federal officials were certain that peaceful relations between Indians and non-Indians in Texas depended upon it. Indian agents Robert S. Neighbors and his successor, John H. Rollins, worked to convince Texas legislators of the necessity of such concessions to the federal government. Texas began to concede in 1851, following a Texas legislature committee's report on the importance of these measures and following continued disruptions and violent conflicts between Indians and whites. Neighbors, by then a veteran of Texas Indian affairs, was the chairman of the committee which backed concessions to the national government. In 1854, the Texas legislature approved reservations for the Indians, spelling out the details of its new relationship with federal administrators. Texas also permitted extension of federal trade and intercourse laws, and allowed the federal government to establish agencies and military posts. While conceding important powers to the federal government may not have come easily in Texas, come it did.[52]

In New Mexico Territory, terms of the war settlement again constrained the federal government; for years the institution of civil authority was delayed. Efforts were made to institute a reservation policy and extend federal authority over the New Mexico Indians by treaty and legislation in the 1850s. Again, the best initiatives and leadership in the area came from the military and from the civilian Indian service. In Utah Territory, federal extension of control over the Indians brought conflict and jurisdictional issues with the Mormon government of Brigham Young. Governor Young

[50] Quoted in Washburn, *Indian in America*, 174. George Harmon notes that we should not be surprised at Texas' approach to Indians within its declared borders, since Texas President Mirabeau Lamar had been secretary under Georgia's governor during the removal battles. George D. Harmon, "The United States Indian Policy in Texas, 1845–1860," *The Mississippi Valley Historical Review* 17 (December 1930), 378 n4.

[51] See Prucha, *Great Father*, 354–66; Washburn, *Indian in America*, 174–80; Utley, *Indian Frontier*.

[52] See Harmon, "Indian Policy in Texas," 383ff.; Hoopes, *Indian Affairs*, 178ff.

bristled at bureaucratic problems with the federal government, and social issues stemming from Mormon doctrine invited the bloodless "Mormon War" of 1857. Young encouraged federal involvement in social policy with the Indians, and he worked closely with the local Indian agent to promote farming as well as a modified reservation policy in the early 1860s. Utah, like Texas and New Mexico, felt the presence of the national government and worked with federal administrators to mold national policy into appropriate local form and implement a policy of reservations and civilization.[53] In both the New Mexico and Utah cases, federal authority eventually became a prevailing force in Indian affairs.

California provides a good example of just how deep and how prominent were debates over the scope and difference of state and federal responsibilities. Conflicts emerged in the late 1840s and early 1850s, as Californians debated the division of responsibility for the state's Indian affairs. As the state legislature in 1851 debated the appropriate level of expenditures to deal with Indians in the region, the *Alta California* explained to its readers that it was the federal government's responsibility to handle Indian matters – using federal resources. Opposing state meddling in federal policy, the paper opined, "This whole matter belongs to the United States Government. She has troops enough and money enough on this coast to make the war, carry it on, and pay its expenses. She has as fine a set of officers here as can be produced any where, and a little skirmishing would be to them pastime. Let the State authorities, therefore, attend to their own legitimate business, plunge the State no further in debt, and leave to Uncle Sam and his servants to conduct this matter, which belong exclusively to them."[54] Governor John McDougal looked to the federal government to provide "the necessary means of protection and defence,"[55] and he argued to a state legislature reluctant to address an emergency in Indian affairs because of the cost to its taxpayers, that "[the federal government] under the political compact of the confederation of the States, is bound to protect them from invasion, insurrection, or rebellion, and Congress has always shown a liberal disposition in the payment of all expenses incurred by any of the States in putting down Indian disturbances, and I have no doubt but that Congress will promptly assume all the expenses attendant upon the expeditions that have heretofore or may hereafter be called into the service of the State."[56] Later, in assessing at almost $1.5 million the state's costs for fighting Indians through the end of 1851, Governor John Bigler noted his expectation

[53] On Utah, see, e.g., Dale L. Morgan, "The Administration of Indian Affairs in Utah, 1851–1858," *The Pacific Historical Review* 17 (November 1948); Hoopes, *Indian Affairs*, ch. 5. On New Mexico, see Hoopes, *Indian Affairs*, 161–78; Prucha, *Great Father*, 366–74.

[54] Quoted in Phillips, *Indians and Indian Agents*, 60; see also 158.

[55] Quoted in Phillips, *Indians and Indian Agents*, 61.

[56] Quoted in Phillips, *Indians and Indian Agents*, 65.

that the federal government would pay the bills – especially as the federal government had reimbursed Southern states for Indian-related expenses in the 1840s.[57]

Problems in California involved not only who was to pay, but also what policy would prevail. Federal agents favored a reservation system in California, while the state's leaders pushed hard for removal of the state's Indians to other states. At the urging of state officials, the U.S. Senate rejected important treaties signed by federal commissioners, keeping California Indian affairs unsettled for years. Bureau of Indian Affairs (BIA) Commissioner Charles Mix blamed the problems in California on the constraints that inhibited federal control:

> It would materially aid the [Indian] department in its efforts to carry out the [reservation] system successfully, in respect to the Indians in California, if that State would, like Texas, so far relinquish to the general government her jurisdiction over the reservations to be permanently retained there, as to admit of the trade and intercourse laws being put in force within their limits, so as to secure the Indians against improper interference and intercourse, and to prevent the traffic with them in ardent spirits.[58]

Throughout the debates and the deadly crises on the ground in California,[59] the Indian Office promoted reservations as best designed to promote a peaceful, managed Indian policy in California, and BIA officials refused to defer to the state government's wishes. To oversimplify a complicated history, federal field agents' implementation of the provisions of the unratified treaties influenced the state's Indian affairs deeply, and are often held up as the beginnings of the national reservation system.[60] Highlighting the importance of the federal government in expansion and Indian affairs, Mix also blamed problems in Indian affairs administration in Oregon and Washington Territories on the lagging federal influence there, and on the failure to ratify treaties signed by Governor Stevens in 1855.[61] To Mix, and to many others – sometimes immediately, sometimes only with time – the federal government was the critical force for pacifying and organizing expansion.

57 Phillips, *Indians and Indian Agents*, 166.

58 "Annual Report of the Commissioner of Indian Affairs," 1862, reprinted in Prucha, *Documents*, 95.

59 Frederick Law Olmstead documented white atrocities against Indians in California during the Civil War: in about twelve years from 1848 to 1860, the Indian population of California declined from about one hundred thousand to thirty-five thousand. Only twelve to twenty thousand would survive in 1900. Hauptman, *Between Two Fires*, 6.

60 For a thorough account of California's debate over state and federal responsibilities, see Phillips, *Indians and Indian Agents*, ch. 10; Hoopes, *Indian Affairs*, ch. 3.

61 "Annual Report of the Commissioner of Indian Affairs," 1858, reprinted in Prucha, *Documents*, 93–4. See also O'Donnell, *Arrow*, 126ff.; Hoopes, *Indian Affairs*, ch. 4.

National Public Administration in the Reservation Era

Numerous federal administrative efforts complemented the Indian service's work before, during, and after the Civil War. Before the war, federal administration involving both military and civilian objectives extended far into the territories and new states, bringing military organizations, social programs, and federal agents while coordinating development and the delivery of protection and services to new citizens and to Indian populations. The Civil War represents a significant escalation in military activity, systematized production of materiel, and integration of communications, technology, production, and administration, but it does not represent a watershed shift away from a dominant or near-exclusive localism. In an unbroken chain of federal presence and intrusions, citizens demanded federal action before and after the war, and they continued to confront the effects of federal policies.[62] People had regular contact with federal agents and federal policies and regulations, from visits by federal agents enforcing timber regulations in Wisconsin[63] to federal agents enforcing alcohol regulations in Alaska.[64] People complained when the federal government did too much, when it did too little, and when it seemed to be playing favorites.[65]

[62] See Moore, *Chiefs, Agents & Soldiers*, 215; Buecker, "North Platte Station," 22–4; Herring, *Enduring Indians of Kansas*, 6; Browne to Mix, September 29, 1858, reprinted in Robert F. Heizer, ed., *The Destruction of California Indians* (Lincoln: University of Nebraska Press, 1993 [1974]), 112–15, and the documents in ch. 4 generally; Donald R. McCoy, "The Special Indian Agency in Alaska, 1873–1874: Its Origins and Operation," *The Pacific Historical Review* 25 (November 1956), 356; Wishart, "The Dispossession of the Pawnee," 392; Spores, "Too Small a Place," 180; J. Orin Oliphant, "Encroachments of Cattlemen on Indian Reservations in the Pacific Northwest, 1870–1890," *Agricultural History* 24 (January 1950), 48ff., 53 n66; George D. Harmon, "Indian Policy in Texas," 381, 388; Jackson, "Indian Affairs and Politics in Idaho Territory," 315; O'Donnell, *Arrow*, 126, 132, 136, 159–60; Josiah Gregg, *The Commerce of the Prairies*, ed. by Milo Milton Quaife (Lincoln: University of Nebraska Press, 1967), 15–18, 98, 178, 180, 206; Josephy, *Nez Perce Indians*, 128; Tim Alan Garrison, "Beyond *Worcester*: The Alabama Supreme Court and the Sovereignty of the Creek Nation," *Journal of the Early Republic* 19 (Fall 1999), 431; Andrew C. Isenberg, "The Market Revolution in the Borderlands: George Champlin Sibley in Missouri and New Mexico, 1808–1826," *Journal of the Early Republic* 21 (Fall 2001); Larry C. Skogen, *Indian Depredation Claims, 1796–1920* (Norman: University of Oklahoma Press, 1996); Sidney L. Harring, *Crow Dog's Case: American Indian Sovereignty, Tribal Law, and United States Law in the Nineteenth Century* (Cambridge: Cambridge University Press, 1994), 252–8.

[63] Kane, "Federal Protection," 440–1.

[64] McCoy, "The Special Indian Agency in Alaska," 362ff.

[65] See, e.g., Browne to Mix, September 29, 1858, reprinted in Heizer, *Destruction*, 112–15; the complaints against reservation placement in the Petition of Tehama County citizens to Secretary of the Interior, reprinted in Heizer, *Destruction*, 137–9; Aloysius Frederick Plaisance, "The United States Government Factory System, 1796–1822," unpublished Ph.D. dissertation, St. Louis University (1954), 340ff.; Thomas D. Clark and John D. W. Guice, *The Old Southwest, 1795–1830: Frontiers in Conflict* (Norman: University of Oklahoma Press, 1996

Land sale regulation and redistribution continued to be a key area of national government administration. As in previous years, lands coming into the U.S. system were filtered through the federal regulatory scheme.[66] The Homestead Acts and Lincoln's vision for national expansion rested on the government's abilities to sign treaties with, dispossess, and remove Indians from the land, and Paul Wallace Gates estimates that since 1862, about half the total acreage entered under the Homestead Law were Indian lands.[67] Government involvement played a very significant role in redistribution of lands and in establishing the circumstances for development and entrepreneurialism. With respect to the railroad boom, for example, biographer Michael P. Malone challenges the "self-made man" legend of railroad entrepreneurs like James J. Hill. The only way to interpret the legend of Hill building railroads without benefit of a federal land grant is to ignore the process of federal land acquisitions, often from Indian nations, which were subsequently granted or sold to territorial legislatures, then granted or sold to railroads and developers. Malone writes, "Thus did the roots of the great Hill fortune sprout, like those of so many other 'self-made men' who 'built the West,' from the rich seedbed of federal subsidy."[68]

[1989]), 14, 51, 208ff.; Patricia Nelson Limerick, *The Legacy of Conquest: The Unbroken Past of the American West* (New York: Norton, 1987); Leslie A. Schwalm, "'Overrun with Free Negroes': Emancipation and Wartime Migration in the Upper Midwest," *Civil War History* 50 (June 2004), 163; Larry Gara, *The Presidency of Franklin Pierce* (Lawrence: University Press of Kansas, 1991), 1–17, 74, 86–100, 127–8, 159, 182–4.

66 During the Pierce administration, for example, Interior distributed almost ninety-four million acres of land, placed within the federal land system the Mexican Session, Oregon, Washington, Kansas, and Nebraska, and negotiated 52 treaties involving 174 million acres of land and costing $11 million. It also issued more than $1 million in pensions and granted an average of more than four thousand patents each year. Gara, *Presidency of Franklin Pierce*, 61–2. Land claim institutions were dominated by federal land commissions through the 1850s. States like California requested the commissions, and the commissioners were generally appointed by the president, commissioners enjoyed wide discretion, and the claims were confirmed by Congress, suggesting again the key role of the presidency in the mid-nineteenth century. Karen B. Clay, "Property Rights and Institutions: Congress and the California Land Act of 1851," *The Journal of Economic History* 59 (March 1999), 136ff. and Table 2, 137.

67 Nichols, *Lincoln and the Indians*, 198; Paul Wallace Gates, "The Homestead Law in an Incongruous Land System," *The American Historical Review* 41 (July 1936), 661–2. Gates recognizes the significant role of Indian affairs in western land policy, and sharply criticizes the interpretation of the Homestead Act as some kind of "free land" program benefiting small farmers. Gates, "Homestead Law," 662. See also, e.g., Mary Elizabeth Young, *Redskins, Ruffleshirts, and Rednecks: Indian Allotments in Alabama and Mississippi, 1830–1860* (Norman: University of Oklahoma Press, 1961); the essays in Carstensen, *Public Lands*.

68 See Malone, *James J. Hill*, 33, 119ff. See also Paul Starr, *The Creation of the Media: Political Origins of Modern Communications* (New York: Basic Books, 2004), 155–65, in which the discussion of the development of the telegraph is shot through with critical interventions by the federal government, including early monetary support for Samuel Morse's experimental

The Army's Corps of Topographical Engineers continued its work through the nineteenth century, as the Wilkes expedition explored the West Coast from San Francisco to Canada in 1838–42, and John Fremont explored the West to Oregon as well as Utah, California, and the Southwest for the Corps in the 1840s. Three trans-Mississippi expeditions headed West in 1845, with a variety of scientific, military, and diplomatic purposes. Key among these were the Mexican War Reconnaissance and the Boundary Survey, the latter in particular an exemplary story of the nineteenth-century bureaucracy and its import in national affairs.[69]

Before the Civil War, the Corps explored routes for wagon roads and railroads, with a full awareness of the significance of such an undertaking to the United States. Echoing Washington's concerns about the Old Northwest, and Jackson's concerns about the South – and anticipating Stephen Douglas's ideas about a transcontinental railroad – Colonel John Abert, the Topographical Corps' chief, wrote in 1849,

> The consequences of such a [wagon] road are immense.... [T]hey probably involve the integrity of the Union. Unless some easy, cheap, and rapid means of communicating with these distant provinces [on the Pacific] be accomplished, there is danger, great danger, that they will not constitute parts of our Union. Then what will become of our great moral power, our great commerce, our infinite resources ... ? We shall sink into two second rate governments if we are even able to maintain as good a position as that of second rate.[70]

A Pacific Wagon Road Office in the Interior Department was established in 1857 to deal with the pressure of demand on the government for action and development. Congress supported exploration, surveying, research, and planning for railroads in the 1850s, authorizing four major expeditions utilizing civilian scientists and experts and soldiers from the Corps of Topographical Engineers. The Corps was called upon in Texas, as leaders like Sam Houston demanded federal attention and assistance far above and beyond Indian affairs.[71] In California, the "postwar projects in the Tenth Military department included railroad, wagon road, and harbor surveys; reconnaissances for fort sites, military reservations, and emigrant trails; observation of Indian habits, mining practices, and the location of mineral deposits; as well as river expeditions and modest efforts at public works."[72] California placed some of the most vigorous demands on the federal government, including

developments, favorable federal court decisions, the usefulness of the patent system, and close connections between telegraph extension, railroad development, and federal land and subsidy policies.

69 William H. Goetzmann, *Army Exploration in the American West, 1803–1863* (Lincoln: University of Nebraska Press, 1959), ch. 5.

70 Quoted in Goetzmann, *Army Exploration*, 209–10.

71 Goetzmann, *Army Exploration*, 225.

72 Ibid., 249–50.

demands for railroad passages and wagon roads – the latter supported by, among other things, a petition to the federal government signed by seventy-five thousand Californians hoping to facilitate immigration, defend the land, and tie the West Coast to the rest of the country.[73] Fremont and Senator Thomas Hart Benton, among many others, worked to promote westward movement and provide practical assistance in a way that foreshadows the efforts of modern institutions like the Commerce Department.[74]

The federal presence along the Oregon and California Trails in the 1850s reveals the central role of public administration in the great population migrations of the nineteenth century.[75] Military posts along the trails, like Fort Kearny and Fort Laramie, were far more important for the services they provided and for their psychological impact upon migrating settlers than they were for the minimal role they played in actual armed conflict with Indians. The government worked to place and keep forts and posts at key points of heavily traveled trails, and worked hard under great duress to supply and man posts as the great waves of migration took off quickly and unexpectedly for the West. Military trains were familiar fellow travelers as they supplied posts, responded to events, escorted stagecoaches, and handled negotiations with Indians. Government forts provided landmarks and way stations along the route; their personnel provided supplies, stores, medical attention, blacksmithing and repair services, advice and recommendations for the migrants on their journeys, and the all-important mail services to bind the migrants to their families and communities back home.

The posts provided a physical reminder of home and of the extension of the national presence westward, and they provided psychological benefits that recur throughout the migrants' journals, letters, and diaries. Significantly, the federal personnel at the forts often had better reputations and received more positive reviews than the few scattered private trading posts along the trail. Despite occasional complaints, migrants appreciated the often free services and good-natured assistance they received from government agents, in contrast with the gouging and unpredictability they received

[73] Ibid., 343.

[74] See Goetzmann, *Army Exploration*. The military also did extensive work fostering railroad development by protecting workers and sites under construction: Buecker, "North Platte Station."

[75] Merrill J. Mattes, *The Great Platte River Road: The Covered Wagon Mainline Via Fort Kearny to Fort Laramie* (Lincoln: University of Nebraska Press, 1969), 223 especially; John J. Killoren, *"Come, Blackrobe": De Smet and the Indian Tragedy* (Norman: University of Oklahoma Press, 1994), 115–16; Judith A. Boughter, *Betraying the Omaha Nation, 1790–1916* (Norman: University of Oklahoma Press, 1998), 53. Buecker notes that the commanding officer of the North Platte Station post in Nebraska in 1867 was Arthur MacArthur, Douglas MacArthur's father. Buecker, "North Platte Station," 15.

at the hands of private traders.[76] They appreciated the rest and calm order that sometimes characterized the forts, in contrast with the trip between posts, which was often marked by tension, haste, and the anxiety of a crowded trail marked by traffic jams and short tempers.[77] Officers at the forts issued and enforced a variety of regulations governing the migrants: where they could camp, when they could head west, how much weight they could carry, how many people and wagons needed to be included in the westering parties. For several years migrants were strongly encouraged (with access to services serving as a carrot) to register their names and other information with the government – how many people in the party, how many oxen, how many horses, and so on.[78]

All of this may conflict with our myth of the pioneers, but the impact and management of the personnel on the great migration westward cannot be denied. It was there, it was critical to the events, and it made a considerable impact upon the migrants themselves – usually a positive impact, a sense that they were still connected to their country, and that the national state was acting for their benefit. Of Fort Kearny, Frank Young wrote in 1865,

> Fort Kearny is today without doubt the most important point in all this vast country north of the Arkansas, and between the Missouri River and the Rocky Mountains. It is the general military headquarters, and not only exercises autocratic sway over other and smaller posts which dot the Plains at intervals of a hundred miles or less along the Platte, but it practically has under its care the safety from Indian attack of at least a thousand miles of highway.[79]

Just as the military posts and mail routes in the early part of the nineteenth century were attractive boons to visionary speculators or entrepreneurial traders and tradesmen, the wagon roads, railroads, stage and freight operations, and communications and transportation companies before and after the Civil War fostered expansion and development and relied upon the federal government's choices and largesse.[80] The War Department and the regular military grew in sophistication, size, and scope before the Civil War years, of course, and after the war soldiers moved to the West to secure new

76 E.g., Mattes, *Great Platte River Road*, 438, 450ff. Private traders were usually subject to licensing systems, the records of which supply considerable information about the private posts' locations and proprietors.

77 Mattes portrays a trip infused with what would today be called "road rage." See also Gregg's journal for a good case study of a trader who always seems to be meeting somebody on the Santa Fe Trail. Mattes, *Great Platte River Road*; Gregg, *Commerce of the Prairies*. Mattes finds that tensions from crowding were far more of a disruptive factor than Indian attacks. Death from disease and accident far outnumbered those from conflicts with Indians.

78 At times, the military stopped "every wagon" and checked up on the numbers of people and animals making the journey. See Mattes, *Great Platte River Road*, e.g., at 503.

79 Quoted in Mattes, *Great Platte River Road*, 193.

80 White, *"It's Your Misfortune,"* ch. 5 and passim.

areas from Indians and to aid Indian service officials in signing treaties, containing Indians on reservations, allotting lands, and furthering communications and transportation expansions.[81] William Tecumseh Sherman, having moved from his central position during the Civil War to the nation-building tasks of the postwar West, wrote in 1881 of the military's roles in pioneering and protection:

> Heretofore the officers of cavalry and infantry have been doomed to everlasting service in the very remotest parts of what was known as the "West," always in advance of civilization. No sooner than the settlements reached their post, which they had built of sod, or stone, or wood, they had to pull up stakes, move two or three hundred miles ahead, till the same game was repeated, and so on, *ad infinitum*; but this is also changed. Railroads traverse the continent east and west in the interest of trade and commerce, and these troops are shoved to the right and left to guard the embryo settlements against the Indians, or the Indians against the intrusive settlers... [82]

Sherman took his work seriously. The historian Robert G. Athearn writes that Sherman was disappointed that his work nation-building in the West was continually overshadowed by his military achievements in the Civil War.[83] Part of this work continued to involve responding to demands for compensation from companies, families, and individuals in the West who saw the federal government as their protector and as the appropriate target for redress from depredations and other grievances.[84]

Like the Army on the Plains, the Navy's broader role in these years specialized in organization, management, exploration, and negotiation. As the United States worked its way into the Pacific, for example, whaling ships were critical in exploring and mapping the Pacific and in providing a foundation for later U.S. claims upon islands in the great ocean. Private knowledge regarding coastlines, depths, winds, and currents were compiled into public charts at the Naval Observatory by Matthew Maury starting in 1842, whose contributions to oceanography and thus to ocean-related trade and economics were indispensable to national development.[85] Pacific ports and way stations like Samoa were brought into the U.S. orbit through a combination of public and private collaborations, like the postal service's support of steamship liners running between San Francisco and Sydney

[81] Francis Paul Prucha, *The Sword of the Republic: The United States Army on the Frontier, 1783–1846* (Bloomington: Indiana University Press, 1977 [1969]), xv–xvi.

[82] Report of W. T. Sherman, November 3, 1881, in Annual Report of the Secretary of War, quoted in Robert G. Athearn, *William Tecumseh Sherman and the Settlement of the West* (Norman: University of Oklahoma Press, 1956), 339–40.

[83] Athearn, *Sherman*, 346.

[84] Mattes, *Great Platte River Road*, 310; Wishart, "Dispossession of the Pawnee," 392; Harmon, "Indian Policy in Texas," 387.

[85] Jean Heffer, *The United States and the Pacific: History of a Frontier* (Notre Dame: University of Notre Dame Press, 2002), 62.

or Auckland and U.S. involvement in Hawaii and Alaska after the Civil War.[86] The peace treaties and agreements negotiated by American diplomats from South America to Alaska to China and Japan not only established trade relationships and regulations, they protected American shipping and trading interests in the Pacific and they protected American citizens in foreign countries.[87]

Naval spending and federal subsidy of private construction of merchant ships bolstered the Navy and developed military-industrial collaborations. Iron interests, including mine and mill interests, lobbied federal representatives and agency leaders for subsidies and privileges in contracting for iron ships, inviting not only political infighting but also discussions of the extensive contracting system and the role of the Secretary in making key decisions independently of Congress. Michigan copper became a critical resource after the federally subsidized Sault Ste. Marie canal opened in 1855,[88] and after the Civil War the crew of the USS *Michigan* helped break labor actions of copper and iron miners near Copper Harbor in the Upper Peninsula. Federal efforts, including the revival of the federal garrison at Copper Harbor's Fort Wilkins, stabilized the area for investment and production, and protected the area from British influence.[89]

Federal agents had confronted the illegal timber trade since the 1830s, and by the 1850s agents from the Interior Department, the General Land Office, and the Revenue Cutter Service worked in violent and politically charged contexts to catch and prosecute timber barons, mill owners, and merchant vessel owners trying to get rich off of public resources.[90] Federal ships like the *Michigan* patrolled the Great Lakes, not only to impede illegal timber and other trade but also to assist vessels in distress. During the Civil

[86] Heffer, *United States and the Pacific*, 192–3, 195ff.; see also Mark R. Wilson, *The Business of Civil War: Military Mobilization and the State, 1861–1865* (Baltimore: The Johns Hopkins University Press, 2006), 49; and McCoy, "The Special Indian Agency in Alaska," 367, on the effectiveness of the federal presence in Alaska.

[87] Heffer, *United States and the Pacific*, 70, 94.

[88] Ibid., 37–8.

[89] Bradley A. Rodgers, *Guardian of the Great Lakes: The U.S. Paddle Frigate* Michigan (Ann Arbor: University of Michigan Press, 1996), 104.

[90] In 1831, Congress made it a crime to cut and remove timber from public lands. Kane, "Federal Protection," 439. Enforcement brought citizens into direct contact with federal agents, creating what can easily be understood as a "sense of the state." In 1854, for example, a person caught illegally cutting timber lamented: "... the timber agent Openly declares He will settle with no man on the Manistee River on ... [any] other Condition ... [but] to Strip them of their All ... and Says He will not leave a man there worth ten cents when he gets through with them ... "; "When ... [the agent] came to seize my lumber, I told him that I had lived under 3 Kings reign and a part of a Queens reign and I never [did] see property sized [*sic*] and taken away from poor people as they did from us." Kane notes that after asking if there were a higher authority than the agent to whom he could appeal, "the agent answered that there was no one higher than he except God Almighty." The quotations and comment are in Kane, "Federal Protection," 440–1.

War, the crew of the *Michigan* helped deter draft riots in Detroit, and helped suppress riots in Buffalo and Milwaukee. The *Michigan*'s efforts on behalf of the federal government proved so popular that the ship became both a tourist attraction and a recruiting tool.[91]

The universe of national administration in the reservation era included a host of organizations designing and managing other complicated tasks, including the work being done at the Customs Service and the Coast Guard.[92] The Freedmen's Bureau became involved in deep debates over federal power and responsibilities. Not surprisingly, the Commissioner of the Freedmen's Bureau, Major-General O. O. Howard, came from a military background deep in the Civil War and eventually moved on to play a central role in the Indian affairs of the West. Roughly nine hundred federal officials worked for the Bureau across the South, expending close to $12 million executing complicated administrative tasks: more than a half million patients received care at sixty hospitals and asylums, twenty-one million free rations were distributed at a cost of over $4 million, and over 4,300 Bureau schools served almost 250,000 students.[93] W. E. B. Du Bois listed the Bureau's complicated objectives as "the relief of physical suffering, the overseeing of the beginnings of free labor, the buying and selling of land, the establishment of schools, the paying of bounties, the administration of justice, and the financiering of all these activities."[94] The Bureau had some successes and some failures, notable among the latter the inconsistent approaches and results reached by its agents in a constellation of diverse administrative environments similar to that in Indian affairs.

The interventions of the Freedmen's Bureau met resistance in the post–Civil War South, but two things about its struggles are significant here. First is that the Bureau represents an effort to extend federal authority, administration, and rights – this was a battle waged across the counties of the South, and hardly reflects consensus about the virtues of localism. Moreover, despite the South's arguments against federal intervention, we should keep in mind that just thirty years prior to Reconstruction southern leaders had demanded – and received – federal intervention to remove Indians from

[91] Rodgers, *Guardian*, 6–7, 40–1.

[92] Irving H. King, *The Coast Guard Expands, 1865–1915: New Roles, New Frontiers* (Annapolis: Naval Institute Press, 1996); Stephen H. Evans, *The United States Coast Guard, 1790–1915: A Definitive History with a Postscript, 1915–1949* (Annapolis: United States Naval Institute, 1949); Dennis L. Noble, *That Others Might Live: The U.S. Life-Saving Service, 1878–1915* (Annapolis: Naval Institute Press, 1994).

[93] W. E. B. Du Bois, *The Souls of Black Folk* (New York: Vintage, 1990), 28–9 and ch. 2; Paul Cimbala and Randall Miller, *The Freedmen's Bureau and Reconstruction* (New York: Fordham University Press, 1999), xxviii and Introduction; James L. Huston, "An Alternative to the Tragic Era: Applying the Virtues of Bureaucracy to the Reconstruction Dilemma," *Civil War History* 51 (December 2005), 408.

[94] Du Bois, *Souls of Black Folk*, 28.

their homes and farms. Federal intrusion in everyday affairs in the South was hardly a new concept in the 1860s and 1870s.

The federal government's presence was felt even on the extreme fringes of the nation. Its agents surveyed lands, encouraged settlement, and enforced trade and liquor regulations among Indians and non-Indians in places as isolated as Michigan's Beaver Island, which rests in Lake Michigan off the northwest edge of the lower peninsula and on the route between the trading center at Mackinac and cities across the lake like Chicago and Green Bay.[95] At a particularly crucial moment in some very tense local battles, U.S. District Attorney George C. Bates wrote to President Millard Fillmore, "The truth is, sir, that nothing but the interference of the federal Government can put an end to the lawless violence which exists on that island. Our People are grateful to you for what has been done and look to the authority vested in the executive as the only means of arresting the course of these deluded people."[96]

Finally, morality, values, and national purpose animated concerns about public administration before and after the war. The 1850 Fugitive Slave Act created a "sense of the state" for hundreds of thousands of people, as federal agents and appointed commissioners supported the slave-catching work of bounty hunters throughout the North. The Act authorized federal agents to force citizens to aid slave-catching efforts, and nullified state laws like New York's personal liberty laws.[97] Episodes like the seizure of James Hamlet in New York City[98] and the removal of Anthony Burns from Boston – which required more than fifteen thousand soldiers to get Burns to a U.S. revenue cutter amid a throng of up to fifty thousand people[99] – galvanized opposition and terrified blacks throughout the country. Significantly, and like Indian removal, the Fugitive Slave Act illustrates the South's willingness to use federal power to support its ends.[100] Nor was the principle of using federal agents to catch and return slaves to the South anything new: President Washington had prevailed upon Treasury Secretary Oliver Wolcott and on a

95 Roger Van Noord, *Assassination of a Michigan King: The Life of James Jesse Strang* (Ann Arbor: University of Michigan Press, 1997), especially 68ff. and chs. 8 and 9; also Rodgers, *Guardian*, ch. 4.

96 Quoted in Van Noord, *Assassination*, 142–3.

97 Gara, *Presidency of Franklin Pierce*, 22; Manisha Sinha, "Black Abolitionism: The Assault on Southern Slavery and the Struggle for Racial Equality," in *Slavery in New York*, ed. Ira Berlin and Leslie M. Harris (New York: New Press, 2005), 257.

98 Craig Steven Wilder, "Black Life in Freedom: Creating a Civic Culture," in Berlin and Harris, eds., *Slavery in New York*, 236.

99 David Brion Davis, *Inhuman Bondage: The Rise and Fall of Slavery in the New World* (Oxford: Oxford University Press, 2006), 265; Gara, *Presidency of Franklin Pierce*, 105–11.

100 Davis, *Inhuman Bondage*, 265, 293; Henry Mayer, *All on Fire: William Lloyd Garrison and the Abolition of Slavery* (New York: St. Martin's Griffin, 1998), 440–5. See also the 1842 case of George Latimer, discussed in Mayer, *All on Fire*, 316–20.

customs collector in Portsmouth, New Hampshire, to catch and return Oney Judge to him, after she had escaped her enslavement at Mount Vernon.[101] The actions of Pierce administration officials and field agents were also direct influences on affairs in Kansas and Nebraska in the 1850s.[102]

Debates over the meaning of citizenship and over the definition and protection of the rights of minorities played out in Indian country and the federal courts even as they were hot-button issues in the South and elsewhere before the Civil War, during Reconstruction, and into the Progressive era.[103] Humanitarian reformers, government leaders, and other interests pushed for better administration and stronger moral purpose, and the Indian service and the Interior Department became central battlegrounds in the effort to link the development of individual character with the efficient and effective administration of national policy. The moral goals of the civil service reform movement complemented the tone and aim of Grant's Peace Policy and the rhetoric of Indian reformers.[104]

Conclusion

Indian affairs and the work of the Indian Office were not anomalies in a national administrative framework promoting a managed expansion westward; they were right in the middle of it. A return to a focus on Indian affairs reveals many of the threads of federal activity housed in a single agency: the Bureau of Indian Affairs and its agents helped blaze the path of expansion by signing treaties and conducting diplomacy, by maintaining and managing reservations, by building and overseeing Indian police forces, by creating and utilizing judicial systems on the reservations, by raising schools and education programs, by designing and delivering health care services, and by facilitating land transfers, economic development, and resource extraction.

101 Fritz Hirschfeld, *George Washington and Slavery: A Documentary Portrayal* (Columbia: University of Missouri Press, 1997), 112–17.

102 Gara, *Presidency of Franklin Pierce*, 111–26; Peter A. Wallner, *Franklin Pierce: Martyr for the Union* (Concord: Plaidswede Publishing, 2007), 193–209, 232–55.

103 See, e.g., Rogers M. Smith, *Civic Ideals: Conflicting Visions of Citizenship in U.S. History* (New Haven: Yale University Press, 1997); Peter H. Schuck and Rogers M. Smith, *Citizenship Without Consent: Illegal Aliens in the American Polity* (New Haven: Yale University Press, 1985), ch. 3; Frederick E. Hoxie, *A Final Promise: The Campaign to Assimilate the Indians, 1880–1920* (Cambridge: Cambridge University Press, 1995); and the selections in *Americanizing the American Indians: Writings by the Friends of the Indian 1880–1900*, ed. Francis Paul Prucha (Cambridge, MA: Harvard University Press, 1973).

104 See Paul P. Van Riper, *History of the United States Civil Service* (Evanston, IL: Row, Peterson and Company, 1958), 79–94; Robert Maranto and David Schultz, *A Short History of the United States Civil Service* (Lanham, MD: University Press of America, 1991), 44; Claude Moore Feuss, *Carl Schurz: Reformer (1829–1906)* (Port Washington, NY: Kennikat Press, 1932), 248; Hans L. Trefousse, *Carl Schurz: A Biography* (Knoxville: University of Tennessee Press, 1982), 241ff.

Many innovations began in the field as the product of creative discretionary actions by federal agents administering the reservations; only later would the innovations be officially sanctioned by Congress or condoned by the federal judiciary. As the guiding theory of the reservations evolved from scattered ad hoc areas, to the notion of two huge, consolidated reservations, and then to isolated, contained, ever-shrinking areas – and as policy moved through a variety of modifications including Grant's Peace Policy and stepped-up allotment – the Indian service met new challenges with new approaches. As in years past, the Indian service balanced a clear mission and diverse tasks with local authority to achieve its goals. And it did achieve its goals.

9

Containment and the Weakening of Indian Resistance

The Effectiveness of Reservation Administration

Indian reservations of one sort or another have been a part of Indian affairs since the colonial days. In the nineteenth century, as the United States expanded west, an evolving reservation system developed from an ad hoc assortment of temporary measures in the territories into a continental system for neutralizing "the Indian problem" by isolating and containing native populations. The reservation system evolved steadily from the 1840s, through the Civil War, and into the 1880s and 1890s. A vision of a permanent Indian country – the vision that had justified many of the arguments for removal – collapsed as the United States absorbed Western areas through the 1840s. Commissioner William Medill's vision of two giant reservations in the West, with settlements and railroads to the West Coast running between, drove much of the government's efforts in the late 1840s and 1850s. But even that plan rapidly had to be revised, as administrators in diverse contexts from the Indian Territory, to the Dakota Plains, to Texas, California, and Oregon confronted different environments and unique populations.

The Bureau of Indian Affairs steadily maintained its status as the preferred institutional vehicle for administering Indian policy, despite criticisms of the removal policy. The military played an important role, but the nation's officials never committed to a Western policy dominated and run by the military. As in years past, the cost, risk, and violent consequences of military action dissuaded leaders from making the military more than a temporary expedient or a consistent backup to the civilian service. In the end, reservations effectively achieved their primary goals: containing, weakening, and subjugating native populations. While other missions – education, civilization, job training, and economic development, for example – interested various administrators at various times, as in prior years these goals ran second to the purpose of reservations in supporting and promoting managed expansion and conquest of the continent by administrative means.

Administrative Structures

Organizational Structure and Development

Expansion necessitated adaptations in administration, the most formally significant of which was the creation of the Interior Department in 1849 and the transfer there of the Indian Office from its traditional home in the War Department. Nothing reflects the developing nature of Indian administration as much as this change. Believing that the time when Indians posed a threat to the viability of the republic had passed, the administration of Indian affairs looked optimistically toward control of the reservations and the gradual subsumation of Indians into the larger, advancing populace. In March 1849 President Polk signed the bill that created the Interior Department, bringing together under that heading the Indian Office, the General Land Office, the Patent Office, and the Pension Office. The law also reinforced alcohol trade restrictions and altered the issuing of annuities, as Congress continued to adjust existing policies for new circumstances. Changes in the 1850s relieved territorial governors of duty as Indian superintendents.[1] New local posts were created as the nation moved westward and as federal laws were extended to new areas. An 1851 law reorganized authority in the West, providing three superintendents to oversee Indian affairs north of Texas and New Mexico and east of the Rocky Mountains. New agents were assigned and the trade and intercourse laws were extended over tribes in New Mexico and Utah territories. The Commissioner's report for 1856 noted that thirteen new agencies and nine subagencies were created by Congress in this time.[2]

Presidents played a key role in the era. As reservation lands slid toward allotment to individuals, with the excess sold or given to non-Indian

[1] Territorial governors' dual duties in Indian Affairs and territorial government were split by Congress in 1857, a significant administrative change brought on by Indian Office pressure on Congress. The change was implemented gradually, with the last dual governorship/Indian affairs superintendent being abolished in 1871. William M. Neil, "The Territorial Governor as Indian Superintendent in the Trans-Mississippi West," *The Mississippi Valley Historical Review* 43 (September 1956), 213; Dale L. Morgan, "The Administration of Indian Affairs in Utah, 1851–1858," *The Pacific Historical Review* 17 (November 1948), 405–7.

[2] On reorganizations, see Francis Paul Prucha, *The Great Father: The United States Government and the American Indians* (Lincoln: University of Nebraska Press, 1984), 329ff., 591; Alban W. Hoopes, *Indian Affairs and their Administration, 1849–1860* (New York: Kraus Reprint, 1972 [1932]), ch. 2; Laurence F. Schmeckebier, *The Office of Indian Affairs: Its History, Activities and Organization* (Baltimore: The Johns Hopkins Press, 1927), 44; Willoughby M. Babcock Jr., "Major Lawrence Taliaferro, Indian Agent," *The Mississippi Valley Historical Review* 11 (December 1924), 369ff.; Ronald Spores, "Too Small a Place: The Removal of the Willamette Valley Indians, 1850–1856," *American Indian Quarterly* 17 (Spring 1993), 174ff.; Chester L. Guthrie and Leo L. Gerald, "Upper Missouri Agency: An Account of Indian Administration on the Frontier," *The Pacific Historical Review* 10 (March 1941), 52ff.

interests, Congress delegated authority to the president to identify, manage, and protect or exploit particular lands.[3] Presidents faced considerable pressure to put lands back on the market, especially after Indians made improvements and identified good farming land, and as white settlements expanded toward and around Indian areas. Executive orders withdrew lands from preemption by and sale to settlers, reserving land for acquisition or use by Indians; other executive orders could put lands back on the market, freeing them for use by non-Indians. Interior Secretaries played key roles, as when the Senate struck from treaties specific provisions setting monetary amounts for annuities and for paying traders' debts from treaties with Upper Sioux, and instead left the determination of exact expenditures up to the Secretary.[4] Similarly, many decisions continued to be left to the Indian Office itself: commissioners continued to negotiate treaties and establish policies,[5] for example, and Congress relied on field reports to determine individual grant amounts issued to the "Sioux of Different tribes" in the Flandreau community in Dakota Territory, which was comprised of Indians who had left the reservations in order to farm on their own. In making the appropriation, Congress gave the Indian Bureau discretion in deciding how to apportion funds in the region.[6]

Selecting personnel to make the decisions in these matters – at the top, middle, or bottom of the bureaucracy – continued to be a delicate exercise in combining patronage demands with the necessities of a very difficult and specialized administrative environment. At the top, the Commissioner of Indian Affairs in the reservation era was more than a figurehead, and

[3] See, e.g., Roy W. Meyer, *History of the Santee Sioux: United States Indian Policy on Trial*, revised edition (Lincoln: University of Nebraska Press, 1993), 89, 104, 140, ch. 8. Interior was not placed directly under the president's control in 1849. The Indian Office thus moved nominally from more direct presidential control to more congressional control, but little seems to have changed in the day-to-day functioning of officials and field agents. Hoopes, for example, notes that the move into the new Interior Department had no significant change on Indian policy. *Indian Affairs*, 16.

[4] Meyer, *Santee Sioux*, 199; see also 207, 278.

[5] George Manypenny, for example, personally negotiated many treaties in the early reservation era, and he pushed successfully to have annuities delivered in goods and stock rather than in cash. In another example of the Commissioner's authority, McCoy describes Indian Office efforts to locate administrative influence in the newly acquired Alaska territory. The BIA led in pressuring Congress to make appropriations, and went to considerable lengths to adapt existing policy, guidelines, and resources to account for Alaska before eventually having its efforts halted by Congress. Interior Secretary Delano, for example, appointed a Special Agent for Alaska on his own authority after Congress rejected his request for legislative approval and appropriation. Delano paid the agent out of the Department's general funds. Donald R. McCoy, "The Special Indian Agency in Alaska, 1873–1874: Its Origins and Operation," *The Pacific Historical Review* 25 (November 1956), 360. The Office's ability to act until being halted by opposition from the Treasury Department is a good example of the BIA's autonomy and capacity.

[6] Meyer, *Santee Sioux*, 247–8.

more than a crony. Commissioners were generally political appointees with close ties either to the administration or to important constituencies, but they were also usually qualified in some way for the post. Almost all of the commissioners had backgrounds in politics, a reasonable consideration in an environment as political as Indian affairs and into which came so many varied and diverse political, economic, and social interests. Indian commissioners before, during, and after the Civil War generally possessed considerable business experience, often combined with a military or administrative background. Some had been executive officials, others were career bureaucrats, and some were humanitarian reformers.[7]

Most of the choices reflected dominant trends in Indian affairs and administration. From 1848 to the Civil War, commissioners generally came from a political background and often had experience in expansion-related areas like the railroads and the military. Amid postwar political tensions, when officials often came under considerable challenge to their competence and integrity for partisan reasons, Indian commissioners such as Nathaniel Taylor, Francis Walker, Rowland Trowbridge, and Hiram Price were chosen at least in part because of their character and reputations for integrity, in order to deflect such charges and maintain trust and faith in government. Francis Walker, for example, appointed in 1871 to replace the embattled (and eventually cleared) Ely Parker, had overseen the Ninth Census and had a reputation as a brilliant administrator.[8] Amid concern for building ties between the missionary community, religious organizations, and government officials involved in Indian affairs, commissioners after the war such as Edward P. Smith, Ezra Hayt, Trowbridge, and Price all had strong connections to organized religion. Smith, for example, was a Congregational Church minister who had been agent at the Chippewa reservation in Minnesota – a choice that reflected a combination of experience with a close

7 See Robert M. Kvasnicka and Herman J. Viola, eds., *The Commissioners of Indian Affairs, 1824–1977* (Lincoln: University of Nebraska Press, 1979); Loretta Fowler, *Arapahoe Politics, 1851–1978: Symbols in Crises of Authority* (Lincoln: University of Nebraska Press, 1986), 39ff.; Michael L. Tate, "John P. Clum and the Origins of an Apache Constabulary, 1874–1877," *American Indian Quarterly* 3 (Summer 1977), 117 n27; Spores, "Too Small a Place," 174ff.; George D. Harmon, "The United States Indian Policy in Texas, 1845–1860," *The Mississippi Valley Historical Review* 17 (December 1930), 394. Contemporaries viewed personnel as experienced and qualified: see, e.g., James McLaughlin, *My Friend the Indian* (Lincoln: University of Nebraska Press, 1989 [1910]), 265, 272, 291. The Quartermaster's Office, the Bureau of Claims, and other institutions were also led and staffed by long-tenured experts. Many of the tenures included extended involvement with Indian conflicts. Mark R. Wilson, *The Business of Civil War: Military Mobilization and the State, 1861–1865* (Baltimore: The Johns Hopkins University Press, 2006); Neil, "Territorial Governor," 221. See also ch. 6, n40, *supra*.

8 Norman J. Bender, *"New Hope for the Indians": The Grant Peace Policy and the Navajos in the 1870s* (Albuquerque: University of New Mexico Press, 1989), 57.

connection to the values of Grant's Peace Policy.[9] Later in the reservation years, commissioners came to office with backgrounds in administration, education, and humanitarian concern for the Indians. Many of the commissioners in the reservation era had experience, either directly or indirectly, with Indian affairs. As a few examples, Charles Mix had worked at the office for decades; Alfred B. Greenwood had been a commissary agent to the Cherokees, providing supplies and accompanying the tribe during their removal through Tennessee;[10] Ezra Hayt, appointed Commissioner in 1877 by Hayes, had long, if controversial, experience with Indian affairs in the North and had served on the Board of Indian Commissioners;[11] Ely Parker was a full-blooded Seneca with long experience in the politics of Indian affairs; John Oberly had served as superintendent of Indian schools.

Commissioners were not characterized by corrupt behavior. Only one of the twenty commissioners in these years, Ezra Hayt, evinced serious corruption problems, and historian Roy Meyer concludes that those stemmed less from clear fraud and corruption than from charges of incompetence and a general pattern of troubling behavior that began even before Hayt became commissioner, when he was involved in Indian affairs in Minnesota.[12] Most commissioners are judged by their chroniclers as having been influential and effective administrators, even visionary in their understanding of Indian affairs and their expectations for the future demands of policy. Most outlined adaptations to major policy directions like the reservation system and allotments, and to more nuanced initiatives like Indian police forces, education, and judicial systems, long before Congress eventually acted upon their suggestions. Those who were not as influential, like Orlando Brown and Dennis Cooley, served in periods with strong Interior Secretaries who guided policies themselves. Of the twenty commissioners who served from 1848 to 1889, eight suffered under significant charges of corruption – but contemporaneous investigations or historians have acquitted seven of those eight of wrongdoing, regarded the merits of the charges against them to be ambiguous, or concluded that the charges were politically or personally motivated.[13] Many of the controversial commissioners served in the partisan and turbulent years from the end of the Civil War until about 1880, when the

9 Bender, "*New Hope,*" 96. On the Peace Policy generally, see, e.g., William Haas Moore, *Chiefs, Agents & Soldiers: Conflict on the Navajo Frontier, 1868–1882* (Albuquerque: University of New Mexico Press, 1994), ch. 4; R. Pierce Beaver, *Church, State, and the American Indians: Two and a Half Centuries of Partnership in Missions Between Protestant Churches and Government* (St. Louis: Concordia, 1966), ch. 4.

10 Gary L. Roberts, "Alfred Burton Greenwood," in Kvasnicka and Viola, *Commissioners*, 81–2.

11 Bender, "*New Hope,*" 177.

12 Roy W. Meyer, "Ezra A. Hayt," in Kvasnicka and Viola, *Commissioners*, 155–66.

13 The commissioners in this category are Brown, Denver, Dole, Cooley, Bogy, Parker, and E. P. Smith.

parties fought over Reconstruction and when Congress was locked in battle with Andrew Johnson. The reputation for corruption and mismanagement at the top of the Indian affairs bureaucracy is undeserved.

Despite a brief average tenure of about two years among Commissioners, expert and stable leadership characterized Indian affairs administration through the nineteenth century. From 1806 to the early 1830s Indian affairs in the War Department had been led by only two men, John Mason and Thomas McKenney. Consistency at the headquarters level in the middle of the nineteenth century centered on the chief clerk in the Indian Office, ostensibly the number two position in Indian affairs. This post was held by one man, Charles E. Mix, from 1850 to 1868; Mix had been involved in the Indian Office since 1837 as a clerk, building a tenure of more than thirty years by the time of his exit. Mix had a profound influence on policy and administration in the Indian Office, and his stabilizing influence provided the early reservation era with what Thomas McKenney had provided during the factory system and the removal debates: institutional memory, continuity, clarity, and professional leadership.[14] Mix was instrumental in attempts to clarify and organize legislation and rules regarding the Indian office and its administrative duties. He drew up an eighty-five-page pamphlet in 1850 which included texts of important legislation, specifications for superintendencies' boundaries and agencies, the duties of officials, and rules for handling claims, for managing emigrations, and for paying annuities. Mix included copies of the standard forms used for submitting the various reports required of the field service.[15] His manual remained a guideline for the agency, unchanged, until 1869 when minor revisions were made. Mix's presence, influence, and his actions all suggest a high level of order and standardization at the office.

Selection of other officials reflected the continuing importance of expertise in Indian affairs. Throughout the latter part of the nineteenth century, appointments of treaty commissioners and investigators continued to combine elements of patronage with a demand for expertise and experience. Often the sensitivity of a given situation determined the right balance. As in earlier eras, the more sensitive the issue, or the more important the investigations or negotiations, the greater the hand of experience and expertise. In general, though, appointees usually had long experience in Indian affairs or particular expertise qualifying them for their positions. When Secretary of War John Bell sought treaties with the Sioux in 1841, he turned to

[14] Prucha, *Great Father*, 325; see also Paul Stuart, *The Indian Office: Growth and Development of an American Institution, 1865–1900* (Ann Arbor: UMI Research Press, 1979), 27; Donald Chaput, "James W. Denver," in Kvasnicka and Viola, *Commissioners*, 70; Harry Kelsey, "Charles E. Mix," in Kvasnicka and Viola, *Commissioners*, 77–9.

[15] Ronald N. Satz, *American Indian Policy in the Jacksonian Era* (Lincoln: University of Nebraska Press, 1975), 190.

James Doty, Governor of Wisconsin Territory, who had experience dating back to travels with Henry Rowe Schoolcraft in the 1820s.[16] Indian Office Commissioners with little Indian affairs experience relied on experienced agents in the field: Luke Lea, for example, relied upon the veteran superintendent David Mitchell and the longtime trader, explorer, and agent Thomas Fitzpatrick to effect major treaty negotiations with Western tribes in 1851.[17] Lea gave the men clear instructions, considerable discretion, and was pleased with the results.[18] Field agents without experience, in turn, looked for knowledgeable local advisors. Federal agents sent to California received with their instructions four reports prepared by hands experienced in California's Indian affairs, and the agents worked closely with and often employed individuals like John Sutter and James Savage, who had considerable experience with Indian affairs in California.[19] The members of the Indian Peace Commission, too, had broad and long experience in Indian affairs and cannot be said to have been merely patronage appointments.

Many appointees to street-level posts in the field had deep experience with local politics and Indian affairs. William Forbes, appointed Indian agent at Devils Lake in 1870, had lived in Minnesota since 1837, run a trading post at the Indians' old reservation, and served as a provost marshal during the trials that followed the 1862 uprising.[20] His assistants and successors were also experienced in Indian affairs: John Cramsie, appointed in 1881, had come to the region in 1867 to work for the Quartermaster Department at nearby Fort Totten, had taken the first census of the Indians there, issued them their first rations, served as interpreter under Forbes, and run a store near the agency for four years. He would serve nine years, under presidents Garfield, Arthur, Cleveland, and Benjamin Harrison.[21] Robert Henton served in Minnesota under two Democratic and two Republican administrations, even though local Republicans sought the post when the party controlled the White House.[22] Amos Bruce, who the historian Roy Meyer writes was a political appointee, replaced longtime agent Lawrence Taliaferro and in some ways proved more effective than Taliaferro, who was himself a very effective agent.[23] Agents and other employees at Navajo and at other agencies in the

[16] Meyer, *Santee Sioux*, 73. See also 89, ch. 9 generally, and 216.

[17] Prucha, *Great Father*, 343–5. See also Neil, "Territorial Governor," 223; Terence O'Donnell, *An Arrow in the Earth: General Joel Palmer and the Indians of Oregon* (Portland: Oregon Historical Society, 1991), 132.

[18] See Robert A. Trennert, "William Medill," in Kvasnicka and Viola, *Commissioners*, 52. On instructions generally, see also Hoopes, *Indian Affairs*, 58 n94, 81–2.

[19] George Harwood Phillips, *Indians and Indian Agents: The Origins of the Reservation System in California, 1849–1852* (Norman: University of Oklahoma Press, 1997).

[20] Meyer, *Santee Sioux*, 222.

[21] Ibid., 234, and ch. 11 generally.

[22] Ibid., 292 n51.

[23] Ibid., 62ff.

Southwest possessed experience in Indian affairs.[24] Even an appointment like that of William F. M. Arny to the Navajo agency mixed patronage concerns with considerable support for Arny's qualifications and experience.[25]

In all of these cases, it is important to remember that Indian affairs did not operate in a vacuum. The goals of policy, and the significance of the issues, were not limited to protecting Indian interests in a narrow issue-area, as might be the case for a client agency operating on the fringe of major national issues. Commensurate with the broad significance and expansion-related goals of Indian policy, diverse criteria were important in selecting the personnel who would pursue the government's goals. Religious connections and character were important during the Peace Policy, for example, and many agents with no Indian affairs experience received appointments because character and devotion were thought to be central to the task of the reservation agent in civilizing and Christianizing Indians. Samuel Janney became superintendent in the Northern Superintendency, for example, and his brother Asa became agent to the Santee Sioux. They might appear to be unlikely or uninspired choices for the Indian service, having come to Nebraska from Virginia, but under the policies of the era they were logical appointments: they were longtime members of the Society of Friends, and their good standing reflected the driving force in appointments under the Peace Policy. Moreover, Samuel Janney had operated a girls' school in Virginia and been involved in education efforts among blacks before the Civil War – both of which complemented aspects of Indian affairs administration in the Grant years.[26] During the Peace Policy, Interior Secretary Columbus Delano listed the requirements for effective Indian agents, noting that a Christian lifestyle was not in itself sufficient – a successful agent would also need health, energy, and business experience. Delano did not include experience in Indian affairs as a prerequisite, reflecting the policy and goals of the era.[27] Interior Secretary Jacob Cox's Annual Report from 1869 outlines some of the personnel issues being considered during the Peace Policy, and he makes clear that experience or expertise in Indian affairs was not necessarily the most important selection criterion:

> The Friends were appointed [to select Indian service personnel] not because they were believed to have any monopoly of honesty or of good will toward the Indians, but because their selection would of itself be understood by the country to indicate the policy adopted, namely, the sincere cultivation of peaceful relations with the tribes, and the choice of agents who did not, for personal profit, seek the service, but were sought for it because they were at least deemed fit for its duties. The two

[24] See, e.g., Bender, "*New Hope*," 16–17, 20, 21–2, 145.

[25] See Bender, "*New Hope*," 99ff.; see also O'Donnell, *Arrow*, 186, 279.

[26] See Meyer, *Santee Sioux*, 163–4; see also the discussion of personnel selection during the Peace Policy in Bender, "*New Hope*," especially 37ff.

[27] See Bender, "*New Hope*," 45.

yearly meetings of "Friends" were asked to select men in whom they had confidence, and who might become at once the business agents of the government and zealous missionaries of civilization.[28]

The Board of Indian Commissioners echoed the idea when it defended "the wisdom of the President in selecting Indian superintendents and agents with a view to their moral as well as business qualifications."[29]

As the scope and tasks of Indian policy expanded through the middle of the 1800s, the number of Indian service personnel increased dramatically. Theodore Taylor reports that the BIA employed 108 regular employees in 1852; by 1872, the number of field agents had grown to 987, and by 1888 the total number of BIA employees stood at 1,725. The number of BIA employees almost doubled between 1881 and 1897, from roughly 2,100 to roughly 3,900.[30] The personnel rosters became increasingly specialized: Taylor notes that the 1852 figure included agents, subagents, interpreters, and clerks – while the 1872 figures included "twenty-one different types of specialists such as physicians, teachers, farmers, blacksmiths, carpenters, millers, shoemakers, teamsters, gunsmiths, wagonmakers, and plowmakers."[31]

As we've seen already, though, such numbers are misleading because many hires were made in Indian affairs for temporary translators and other positions, and the numbers never adequately account for the "true size" of the service, which would take into account contractors, missionaries and teachers operating with federal funds, and so on. Nor does Taylor's recognition of increasing specialization in the job categories indicate necessarily that specialization was increasing, only that the *reporting* of it had become more precise: the Indian service had been hiring people for specific purposes like translating or shipping or maintaining wagons for years, and government agents in a variety of special posts fill the Western landscape of the reservation era. Pierre De Smet's long activity in the West, as Jesuit missionary and frequent advisor to military and civilian officials, provides a good case in point. Never a regular employee of the government, De Smet utilized his considerable experience and the trust he had earned among a variety of Indian nations to aid U.S. diplomatic efforts, advise on policy, draw up maps,

[28] "Annual Report of the Commissioner of Indian Affairs," 1869, reprinted in Francis Paul Prucha, ed., *Documents of United States Indian Policy*, 2nd ed. (Lincoln: University of Nebraska Press, 1990), 130.

[29] "Annual Report of the Board of Indian Commissioners," November 23, 1869, reprinted in Prucha, *Documents*, 134.

[30] Theodore W. Taylor, *The Bureau of Indian Affairs* (Boulder: Westview Press, 1984), 35.

[31] Taylor, *Bureau of Indian Affairs*, 35. In 1879, the Indian field service included 1,457 officials (115 agents and clerks, 139 in education, 295 in law and order, 54 medical, and 854 other). By 1881, this number had jumped to 2,102, with increases from 139 to 238 in education and 295 to 824 in law and order. David Wallace Adams, *Education for Extinction: American Indians and the Boarding School Experience, 1875–1928* (Lawrence: University Press of Kansas, 1995), Table 3.1, 61.

and help negotiate treaties and other agreements. De Smet accompanied Harney's expedition and served as a special agent from 1864 through 1869, under four consecutive commissioners; he was frequently provided with provisions, transport, and lodgings. De Smet is a good example of the "shadow" government which existed even in the nineteenth century, whereby the formal administrative mechanism made use of available resources that may never emerge from official employment figures.[32] Moreover, De Smet took affirmative steps to try to maintain his independence and credibility even as he tried to help both the United States and the tribes achieve their ends.[33] And De Smet, like others, was still subject to the regulations and restrictions imposed by the government: one of William Clark's last official acts as Superintendent of Indian Affairs in the West was to sign De Smet's passport in 1838, allowing De Smet – already a noted, respected, and familiar figure traveling west of the Mississippi – to enter Indian country.[34]

Indian policy and administration were not disrupted by patronage. Scholars who have decried the rottenness of the patronage system have assumed that party loyalty and activity were the driving features of appointments and high turnover, suggesting an absence of qualifications for jobs. In the Indian case, it is abundantly clear that personnel at all levels were routinely chosen for their knowledge and experience in local circumstances and for their familiarity with specific Indian situations.[35] Field agents and the Indian Office's leadership worked to control and standardize bureaucratic activity,

[32] See John J. Killoren, *"Come, Blackrobe": De Smet and the Indian Tragedy* (Norman: University of Oklahoma Press, 1994), especially chs. 8 and 9; also Fowler, *Arapahoe Politics*, 46, 50, 59; Moore, *Chiefs, Agents & Soldiers*, 60; Morgan, "Indian Affairs in Utah," 398. Indian affairs was not the only area in which the true size of government is obscured. As many as 150 civilians worked for the Quartermaster's Department in San Antonio before the Civil War, and private contractor Russell, Majors, and Waddell employed six hundred teamsters to fulfill an army freighting contract in 1855. The firm built a new depot in Nebraska City in 1857, responding to government work based on President Buchanan's earlier efforts against the Mormons in Utah; RM&W added four thousand men to its operations. Expeditions like this also spurred hiring of contracted teamsters, suppliers, tentmakers, laundresses, millers, and thousands of others. Wilson, *Business of Civil War*, 46–53 and ch. 2 generally.

[33] Killoren, *"Come, Blackrobe,"* 233, 251, 288.

[34] Killoren, *"Come, Blackrobe,"* 56. Beeton writes that a third of reservation expenditures at the Utah Superintendency from 1855 to 1857 (excluding agents' and superintendents' salaries) was paid to settlers who worked as day laborers doing things like interpreting and building fences. Beverly Beeton, "Teach Them To Till The Soil: An Experiment With Indian Farms, 1850–1862," *American Indian Quarterly* 3 (Winter 1977–78), 306.

[35] See, e.g., William T. Hagan, *United States-Comanche Relations: The Reservation Years* (Norman: University of Oklahoma Press, 1990 [1976]), ch. 8; David J. Wishart, "The Dispossession of the Pawnee," *Annals of the Association of American Geographers* 69 (September 1979), 394; J. Orin Oliphant, "Encroachments of Cattlemen on Indian Reservations in the Pacific Northwest, 1870–1890," *Agricultural History* 24 (January 1950), 46; O'Donnell, *Arrow*, 286–7.

leave room for necessary adjustments, and foster patronage when it did not interfere with policy goals or administration.

As we have seen, too, in the Indian and expansion contexts patronage and effective administration were not antithetical. In the era of the factory system, pacifying relations and peacefully obtaining land cessions trumped concerns for civilization and education; in the removal era, removal itself far outweighed social goals. U.S. policy in the reservation era did not envision humanitarian goals as primary. The goal in the reservation era was neutralization of the Indian threat and a peaceful, managed expansion of U.S. citizens and interests across the continent, effected by isolating and containing Indian populations. To the extent that patronage appointments helped ensure that Indian interests would not be adequately defended against white interests, that Indian populations would be treated in ways that demoralized and weakened them, and that Western populations would be tied by politics and party to the rest of the United States, patronage *furthered* the Indian service's mission. A weak, starving, and poor Indian population on a reservation controlled by a party functionary working closely with the local railroad or cattle barons served the reservation policy better, in terms of the policy's ultimate purpose, than an active, organized, healthy Indian population catered to by an honest, experienced agent who defended Indian interests against whites and who strengthened Indians with adequate food, supplies, and money.

Organizational Dynamics

Mission

Personnel selection in Indian affairs suggests, though, that U.S. policy and administration should not be viewed quite so cynically, or quite so simplistically. Patronage did further the country's baser objectives, but the frequent combination of patronage concerns with concerns for administration, humanitarian goals, experience, and qualifications, reflects a far more diverse and complicated situation in Indian affairs administration.

Two goals anchored the reservation policy: containment and isolation of Indian populations, and civilization of the Indians. Political and administrative leaders outlined these clear goals and priorities for Indian policy and for the Indian service consistently throughout the reservation years. Commissioner William Medill outlined the goals in 1848:

> The policy already begun and relied on to accomplish objects so momentous and so desirable to every Christian and philanthropist is, as rapidly as it can safely and judiciously be done, to colonize our Indian tribes beyond the reach, for some years, of our white population; confining each within a small district of country, so that, as the game decreases and becomes scarce, the adults will gradually be compelled to resort to agriculture and other kinds of labor to obtain a subsistence, in which aid

may be afforded and facilities furnished them out of the means obtained by the sale of their former possessions.[36]

Medill went on to outline the role of education on the reservation, to be administered by religious denominations, in order that "a physical, intellectual, moral, and religious education will all be imparted together."[37] Charles Mix reiterated the mission ten years later:

Our present policy... is to permanently locate the different tribes on reservations embracing only sufficient land for their actual occupancy; to divide this among them in severalty, and require them to live upon and cultivate the tracts assigned to them; and in lieu of money annuities, to furnish them with stock animals, agricultural implements, mechanic-shops, tools and materials, and manual labor schools for the industrial and mental education of their youth.[38]

Commissioner William Dole wrote in 1863, "The plan of concentrating Indians and confining them to reservations may now be regarded as the fixed policy of the government." President Lincoln addressed Indian affairs in his 1863 Annual Message, calling upon Congress to reform the Indian system, widely viewed as corrupt – yet Lincoln first and more prominently spoke admiringly of the government's success in removing tribes, signing treaties, and "extinguishing the possessory rights of the Indians to large and valuable tracts of land."[39] After the Civil War, Dole pointed out that concentration, with the aim of exploiting Indian lands, drove Indian policy. Dole's polestars were the desire "to foster and protect our own settlements" with "the concentration of Indians upon ample reservations."[40] President Grant discussed the reservation system and related policy matters in some detail in his 1869 State of the Union address,[41] and Secretary of the Interior Jacob Cox described the reservation policy in the same year:

First, the location of Indians upon fixed reservations, so that the pioneers and the settlers may be freed from the terrors of wandering hostile tribes; and second, an earnest effort at their civilization, so that they may themselves be elevated in the scale of humanity, and our obligation to them as fellowmen be discharged.[42]

36 "Annual Report of the Commissioner of Indian Affairs," 1848, reprinted in Prucha, *Documents*, 77–8.

37 Ibid., 78.

38 "Annual Report of the Commissioner of Indian Affairs," 1858, reprinted in Prucha, *Documents*, 93.

39 Quoted in David A. Nichols, *Lincoln and the Indians: Civil War Policy & Politics* (Urbana: University of Illinois Press, 2000), 153–4.

40 Quoted in Nichols, *Lincoln and the Indians*, 131.

41 Bender, "*New Hope*," 7–8.

42 "Annual Report of the Secretary of the Interior," 1869, reprinted in Prucha, *Documents*, 129.

By 1876, Commissioner John Q. Smith had refined the mission down to three bullet points:

First. Concentration of all Indians on a few reservations.
Second. Allotment to them of lands in severalty.
Third. Extension over them of United States law and the jurisdiction of United States courts.[43]

Nuanced approaches and varied rationales supported the general goals of containment and civilization. Early in the reservation era, larger concentrations were expected to obviate the problems of numerous smaller settlements becoming encroached upon and otherwise disturbed by white settlement. Indian Office commissioners noted the advantages to control and administration that would result from confining Indians to constricted areas, and they supported variations on colonization and reservation policies in support of civilization goals. Reservations were also meant to end repeated upheavals of Indian communities, which had proven counterproductive to farming and the settled lifestyles desired by policymakers in the drive for civilization. And, of course, reservations aimed at civilizing Indians and removing the Indian problem with dispatch. Indian Commissioner William Medill, for example, wrote in 1848,

[I]t is to natural and unavoidable causes, easily understood and appreciated, rather than to willful neglect, or to deliberate oppression and wrong, that we must in a great measure attribute the rapid decline and disappearance of our Indian population. Cannot this sad and depressing tendency of things be checked, and the past be at least measurably repaired by better results in the future? It is believed they can; and, indeed, it has to some extent been done already, by the wise and beneficent system of policy put in operation some years since, and which, if steadily carried out, will soon give to our whole Indian system a very different and much more favorable aspect.[44]

A report by Indian Commissioner Luke Lea illustrates the reservation era belief that administration in specific contexts would quickly civilize Indians and solve complex problems:

With such arrangements for this tribe [the Chippewa], and the adoption of a like policy for the Winnebagoes, now located in their vicinity on the west side of the Mississippi, and the Menominees, soon to be removed there, the whole face of our Indian relations in that quarter would in a few years present an entire and

43 "Annual Report of the Commissioner of Indian Affairs," 1876, reprinted in Prucha, *Documents*, 148. On the mission of the Indian Office in the reservation era, see, e.g., Phillips, *Indians and Indian Agents*, ch. 1; Bender, *"New Hope,"* Preface, ch. 1; "Annual Report, 1858," in Prucha, *Documents*, 92–5; Grant's Second Annual Message, reprinted in Prucha, *Documents*, 135; Fowler, *Arapahoe Politics*, 46; Spores, "Too Small a Place," 175; O'Donnell, *Arrow*, 139. Neil, "Territorial Governor," 222, 235ff. offers a thoughtful discussion of the divided loyalty and goals facing territorial governors.

44 "Annual Report, 1848," reprinted in Prucha, *Documents*, 77.

gratifying change. We should soon witness in this, our northern colony of Indians, those evidences of general improvement now becoming clearly manifest among a number of our colonized tribes in the southwest, and which present to the mind of the philanthropist and the Christian encouraging assurance of the practicability of regenerating the red race of our country, and elevating them to a position, moral and social, similar if not equal to our own...[45]

Lea hoped that Indians would surrender their passions for war and hunting if confined in a controlled reservation environment.[46] The Peace Policy, too, envisioned a quick solution of the Indian problem through the appointment of local agents and administrators by missionary societies, the ideals and values of which would quickly serve to civilize and assimilate Indians to white ways.

Reservations were never meant to persist forever. As strange as it may seem that officials pursued assimilation through a policy of segregation, most officials at the time believed that reservations were a stage on the way to full assimilation of Indians into American society, and therefore another piece of the social policy experiments of the federal government. Isolating Indians would make life safer for them and for aggressive settlers, increasing security and reducing risk on the frontier. Isolation would also be well-suited to the kinds of social initiatives, education, and training that Indians would need to "advance" into white America. The social goals of the reservation policy – and the pursuit of them through social control – are evident in this passage from Lea, Commissioner of Indian Affairs under Zachary Taylor:

It is indispensably necessary that they [Indians] be placed in positions where they can be controlled and finally compelled by stern necessity to resort to agricultural labor or starve.... There should be assigned to each tribe, for a permanent home, a country adapted to agriculture, of limited extent and well-defined boundaries; within which all, with occasional exception, should be compelled constantly to remain until such time as their general improvement and good conduct may supersede the necessity of such restrictions. In the meantime, the government should cause them to be supplied with stock, agricultural implements, and useful materials for clothing; encourage and assist them in the erection of comfortable dwellings, and secure to them the means and facilities of education, intellectual, moral, and religious.[47]

Lea recognized that the critical task for administrators was control, and throughout the era the Indian agent's job in pursuit of these goals was clear. Roy Meyer describes longtime agent Lawrence Taliaferro's aims during Minnesota's early reservation period as "essentially those of his government: to gain and hold recognition by the Indians of United States sovereignty over the country they occupied, to protect the Indians of the baneful influence

[45] "Annual Report of the Commissioner of Indian Affairs," 1850, reprinted in Prucha, *Documents*, 83.

[46] Bender, "*New Hope,*" 1–2.

[47] "Annual Report, 1850," reprinted in Prucha, *Documents*, 82.

of the fur traders, to stop intertribal warfare, and to conduct his charges along the road toward civilization."[48] Little things suggest the government's goals, too. Agent Alexander Irvine at the Navajo reservation, for example, argued that the possession of horses by the reservation Indians should be discouraged or even prohibited, because horses did not further the goal of making the Indians farmers – and because, as historian Norman Bender puts it, "if the Indians had no horses, then they would be more inclined to remain in one place where they could be better controlled."[49]

Tasks

New administrative tasks and responsibilities did not replace old ones in the reservation era – they just added to the old ones. Diplomatic negotiations and treaty making continued to be important Indian Office responsibilities. Treaty negotiations still required extensive and complicated preparations, supply, distribution of goods, ratification of agreements, surveying of boundaries, and so on. A good example is the landmark 1851 Treaty of Fort Laramie, which eventually gathered together eight to twelve thousand Indians.[50] David Mitchell worked diligently to prepare for the treaty council, initially reporting that he expected ten companies representing the military. Mitchell invited bids for supplying goods to the council from firms in St. Louis, even before his official appointment came through from the commissioner's office. Mitchell had to notify participants through diplomatic messages and the printing and distributing of circulars, an unexpectedly complicated and expensive undertaking. Mitchell had to be very careful about how he promoted the goals and purpose of the council, in order to gain the support of both traders and tribes. He had presented utilitarian arguments in Washington to gain approval and funding for the council. To the traders, Mitchell promised that the conference's goals were their interests and safety, and he promised to compensate them for bringing Indians to the negotiations and serving as translators. To the tribes, Mitchell said that the council was "intended entirely for the benefit and future welfare of the Indians" and he emphasized that the conference would address the Indians' main

48 Meyer, *Santee Sioux*, 36.

49 Bender, "*New Hope*," 168.

50 Merrill J. Mattes, *The Great Platte River Road: The Covered Wagon Mainline Via Fort Kearny to Fort Laramie* (Lincoln: University of Nebraska Press, 1969), 517; Fowler, *Arapahoe Politics*, 28ff.; Killoren, "*Come, Blackrobe,*" 151. For typical examples of the treaty process and tactics, see Babcock, "Major Lawrence Taliaferro," 373; Moore, *Chiefs, Agents & Soldiers*, 17ff.; Spores, "Too Small a Place," 176ff.; John L. Kessell, "General Sherman and the Navajo Treaty of 1868: A Basic and Expedient Misunderstanding," *The Western Historical Quarterly* 12 (July 1981); Neil, "Territorial Governor," 223ff.; O'Donnell, *Arrow*, 152ff., 196ff. For examples of the large numbers of people who continued to gather at these negotiations and at distributions of annuities and presents, see Fowler, *Arapahoe Politics*, 49, 57; Moore, *Chiefs, Agents & Soldiers*, 42; McLaughlin, *My Friend the Indian*, chs. 16–17.

concern – compensation for depredations committed by whites. Presents were promised, too, of course.[51] Commissioner Lea reminded Mitchell that the purpose of the entire event, from the government's standpoint, was to fix boundaries of Indian lands, and ultimately to control the Plains by controlling the Indians: annual distributions to cooperating tribes would necessitate the tribes' "good conduct," giving the United States considerable leverage.[52] Mitchell worked to coordinate a military presence, maintain the peace among the tribes themselves, prevent against cholera and other medical problems at the site, and secure the arrival of huge supplies of goods and presents.[53]

The process of making and signing treaties continued to be fraught with intimidation, unfair dealings, outright corruption, and clever circumvention of general rules in order to satisfy particular local concerns and advance government policy. Governors and treaty commissioners tended to treat with weaker and less secure tribes first, so as to use their treaties as leverage with more powerful and secure tribes later. When believed to be in the interests of the United States, agents continued to chaperone Indians to Washington to impress them with the nation's power or to negotiate or complete treaties; the primary goal of these trips was to dominate and intimidate tribal leaders. Congress often corrupted treaties by making unilateral alterations prior to ratification, as when it reduced the agreed upon annuity written into the 1851 Fort Laramie treaty by 70 percent and changed the duration of payments from fifty years to fifteen.[54]

In the field, a military presence like that at Fort Laramie could be helpful in trying to intimidate assembled Indians. Other techniques were more subtle. After Congress had outlawed treaty provisions for direct payments to traders of debts incurred by Indians – because such payments were easy for traders to manipulate[55] – a treaty signed at Traverse des Sioux witnessed an innovative method of satisfying the traders. After stepping away from the treaty table, each Indian was made to sign a document drawn up by traders that acknowledged debts to the traders and committed the Indians to repayment. No sums were attached to the document; traders filled in the numbers later. Indians later claimed that they thought they were just signing another copy of the treaty.[56] And as was often the case, after the treaty signing whites began occupying ceded lands.[57] Later investigations of the

[51] Quoted in Killoren, *"Come, Blackrobe,"* 132; reprinted on 107; also Fowler, *Arapahoe Politics*, 25.

[52] Killoren, *"Come, Blackrobe,"* 134, 155.

[53] Meyer offers a good review of treaty making with the Sioux in the 1840s and 1850s: *Santee Sioux*, ch. 4.

[54] Killoren, *"Come, Blackrobe,"* 187.

[55] Lea reversed this reform. Killoren, *"Come, Blackrobe,"* 241.

[56] Meyer, *Santee Sioux*, 80–1.

[57] Ibid., 84.

"monstrous conspiracy" seem to have been politically motivated – and not a sincere effort to protect Indian interests.[58]

Field agents in the reservation era continued to engage in all of the tasks associated with removals, because removals remained a common part of Indian policy administration. Removal treaties were still negotiated and signed, and field agents still prepared tribes for removal, adjudicated claims and disputes, contracted for goods and services to be used during removal, conducted the removals, and worked to establish populations on new, and often disastrously inadequate, lands. Conditions on these removals were often no better than the more infamous removals of the Jackson era. Indians removed following the 1862 Sioux uprising, for example, experienced severe overcrowding, dangerous transportation, greedy and incompetent contractors, and widespread death and disease. Jammed into boats and railroad cars for the trip across Missouri, the experience was horrible, reminiscent of the Trail of Tears and other earlier population removals. Comparing the shipboard crowding of the Indians to the middle passage for slaves (in spite of the removal contract's stipulation of "ample space for comfort, health, and safety"), one observer wrote,

> when 1300 Indians were crowded like slaves on the boiler and hurricane decks of a single boat, and fed on musty hardtack and briny pork, which they had not half a chance to cook, diseases were bred which made fearful havoc during the hot months, and the 1300 souls that were landed at Crow Creek June 1, 1863, decreased to one thousand.... So were the hills soon covered with graves. The very memory of Crow Creek became horrible to the Santees, who still hush their voices at the mention of the name.[59]

Removals continued throughout the nineteenth century. As white settlements expanded, the value of lands was recognized, or railroads or other developments altered the values and decisions of people across the continent, tribes and native communities were forced to relocate again and again – despite occasional concerns of Indian Office officials who recognized the drawbacks of continual population upheavals and how such uncertainty undercut civilization efforts. Yet the primary mission of isolating, containing, and weakening Indian communities was well served by continued removals, exacerbating upheaval and dislocation, inciting disagreements within communities, encouraging fragmentation of those communities, and sapping the will of Indians.[60]

58 Ibid., 87.

59 Quoted in Meyer, *Santee Sioux*, 146. See also 90ff., 145ff., 156ff.

60 Joseph B. Herring, "Indian Intransigency in Kansas: Government Bureaucracy vs. Mokohoko's Sacs and Foxes," *The Western Historical Quarterly* 17 (April 1986), especially 197, includes details about the continuing difficulty of administering removals. See also Laurence M. Hauptman, *Between Two Fires: American Indians in the Civil War* (New York: Free

Agents in the reservation era also continued to confront the administrative complications created by Indians who stayed put. Just as federal officials earlier dealt with the complicated concerns of eastern Indians who had not removed, like the Eastern Band of Cherokee, Sioux who did not remove after the 1862 uprising – many of whom had been credited with helping whites during the conflict – became an administrative burden for federal agents years later as pressure for their lands and worries about their loyalty resurfaced.[61]

On the reservations themselves, administrative tasks multiplied. Tasks included the mundane, like arranging for payment to employees and supply of provisions, furniture, and so on.[62] Adam Johnston, for example, supplied provisions, tools, and services to four thousand Indians on five reservations in California in the early 1850s.[63] Sometimes passes had to be issued so Indians could sell their produce or the product of mills off the reservation.[64] Agents hired people for lower positions, often at their own discretion.[65] Federal agents often trained Indians, with varying degrees of success, to do work at the agencies.[66]

Press Paperbacks, 1996), 19; Joseph B. Herring, *The Enduring Indians of Kansas: A Century and a Half of Acculturation* (Lawrence: University Press of Kansas, 1990), 112ff.; Wishart, "Dispossession of the Pawnee," 398–401; Spores, "Too Small a Place"; Harmon, "Indian Policy in Texas," 402; Melissa L. Meyer, *The White Earth Tragedy: Ethnicity and Dispossession at a Minnesota Anishinaabe Reservation* (Lincoln: University of Nebraska Press, 1994), 56–65. Federal agents continued to try to manage affairs between tribes, as it had done in the years of the removal policy: Fowler, *Arapahoe Politics*, chs. 1 and 2; Herring, *Enduring Indians of Kansas*, ch. 4; Wishart, "Dispossession of the Pawnee," 388ff.

61 Meyer, *Santee Sioux*, ch. 13; Herring, *Enduring Indians of Kansas*, 11.

62 For typical examples during the Peace Policy, see Bender, *"New Hope,"* 19; Flora Warren Seymour, *Indian Agents of the Old Frontier* (New York: D. Appleton-Century Co., 1941), 147, 300–1, and ch. 8 generally. See, e.g., Phillips, *Indians and Indian Agents*, 73ff.; Meyer, *Santee Sioux*, 147ff. Bender, *"New Hope,"* chs. 4 and 9 offer excellent descriptions of the myriad tasks, responsibilities, and dynamics confronting Indian service personnel at the Navajo agency during the Peace Policy. Also see the documents in Robert F. Heizer, ed., *The Destruction of California Indians* (Lincoln: University of Nebraska Press, 1993 [1974]), ch. 4; Moore, *Chiefs, Agents & Soldiers*, 42ff.; James Riding In, "'*The United States* v. *Yellow Sun et al. (The Pawnee People)*': A Case Study of Institutional and Societal Racism and U.S. Justice in Nebraska from the 1850s to 1870s," *Wicazo Sa Review* 17 (Spring 2002), 22; Hoopes, *Indian Affairs*, 17ff., 81–2, 104ff.; Lucile Kane, "Federal Protection of Public Timber in the Upper Great Lakes States," *Agricultural History* 23 (1949), reprinted in Vernon Carstensen, ed., *The Public Lands: Studies in the History of the Public Domain* (Madison: University of Wisconsin Press, 1968).

63 Phillips, *Indians and Indian Agents*, 119; on reservation administration, see also Meyer, *Santee Sioux*, 170 n45 and 170ff.

64 E.g., Meyer, *Santee Sioux*, 211, 212.

65 E.g., Moore, *Chiefs, Agents & Soldiers*, 60; Bender, *"New Hope,"* 54ff., 143.

66 E.g., Meyer, *Santee Sioux*, 211; Fowler, *Arapahoe Politics*, 85. Lawrence Taliaferro left an interesting review of his complicated duties as Indian agent, which is reprinted in Babcock Jr., "Major Lawrence Taliaferro," 375.

Taking censuses and enrolling members on tribal rolls continued to be a familiar task for Indian service personnel and for special allotment agents. The process could involve rigorous examination in the presence of entire bands of Indians, because agents were concerned that enrollment processes for receiving benefits attracted Indians from other bands. Agents had to figure out who they believed did – and who did not – merit being enrolled.[67] Census taking could be a burden on local agents for other reasons: Frank Bennett complained of the added tasks when field agents were asked to be enumerators for the 1870 decennial census, and he evaluated the prospects for completing a census of the Navajo:

> I would report that it would be utterly impossible for me to take the census in accordance with instructions and blanks furnished, for the reason that at least nine out of every ten [Navajos] have no names. For instance, at the last issuance of annuity goods, I issued extra goods to over one hundred sub-captains, at least half of whom had no names, and I was obliged to improvise names for them.[68]

For the purpose of dispensing annuities and other benefits, reservation agents kept records of which Indians worked and which did not:

> the transactions [of every man's work] covered an average of over 250 pages of ordinary ten-quire journal pages. Goods were issued by the storekeeper on requisitions signed by the agent or the clerk. The storekeeper kept a ledger showing the amount of goods received and issued and posted it weekly. Supplies were issued monthly in this fashion to more than four hundred individuals. In addition, Indians whose credit was good or who brought in produce for sale were allowed to draw on the warehouse at any time, even though this procedure placed an additional burden on the storekeeper. Ironically, the further the Indians advanced – that is, the more labor they performed – the more work devolved upon the agency employees.[69]

Agents kept records and adjudicated claims, often for substantial amounts. The 1834 Trade and Intercourse Act had expanded provisions for whites to make claims against government for depredations committed by Indians upon the whites' property. Other congressional acts addressed specific cases and situations, as in congressional legislation that provided for compensation to whites who sustained damages after the 1862 conflict with the Sioux.[70] Agents wound up being responsible in many cases for approving such claims – a difficult, uncertain, and time consuming procedure given the promise of payoff and the all-too-common lack of evidence

[67] See Meyer, *Santee Sioux*, 277; Moore, *Chiefs, Agents & Soldiers*, 173; James C. Olson, *Red Cloud and the Sioux Problem* (Lincoln: University of Nebraska Press, 1965), 272; Robert M. Utley, *The Last Days of the Sioux Nation* (New Haven: Yale University Press, 1963), 54, 79, 95, 137.

[68] Quoted in Bender, *"New Hope,"* 36; see also 175; see also Meyer, *Santee Sioux*, 276.

[69] Meyer, *Santee Sioux*, 209–10.

[70] Meyer, *Santee Sioux*, 140. On claims arising out of the conflict, see Larry C. Skogen, *Indian Depredation Claims, 1796–1920* (Norman: University of Oklahoma Press, 1996), 89–90.

and presence of ulterior motives involved in making claims. The process also provided opportunities for whites and Indians alike to become disaffected with the agents' decision making or perceived incompetence or simple lack of concern, as we will see more fully in the next chapter.[71]

Distributing annuities and other provisions was a staple of Indian service activity. Goods had to be procured, shipped, and distributed. Distribution, of course, could affect local politics and power, depending on the method and timing. Are goods given, or cash? Are goods or cash distributed directly to individuals, to heads of families, or to tribal leaders? If the latter, whoever picks the leaders may be able to exert considerable influence over resources and local power politics. In these efforts, a diplomatic function combined intimately with straightforward acts of administration.[72] And any change, such as an order to make distributions to family heads, could cause a headache: agents might feel the change was another added-on administrative task or unnecessary oversight of their activities, and Indians might perceive changes as detrimental to their interests or as the front end of a policy shift.[73]

Indians had to be gathered and organized for the distributions. Historian Roy Meyer relates in detail the annuity payment to Sioux Indians in St. Paul in September 1849, a meeting of pageantry and ceremony as well as relaxed fraternizing.[74] Martha Royce Blaine offers a thorough description of an annuity payment to the Pawnee in 1871.[75] Norman Bender explains the process at Navajo, which included an organized line of Indians filing through the agency corral and red, blue, and pink tickets given to Indian men, women, and children. The agent kept the Indians in line all day, despite snow and sleet falling throughout, in order to ensure that no one went through the line more than once. The next day, Indians filed past the storehouse and surrendered their tickets to a soldier, who put the tickets in a tin box with a slotted lid. The individual then received one or more articles from the storehouse, and filed past a guard at the end who was posted to prevent people from returning into the line. This continued for two days and at other annuity issues, which sometimes serviced nine thousand Navajo seeking their annuity issues

[71] See Meyer, *Santee Sioux*, 54–5, 106, 140; also Nichols, *Lincoln and the Indians*, 11; Sidney L. Harring, *Crow Dog's Case: American Indian Sovereignty, Tribal Law, and United States Law in the Nineteenth Century* (Cambridge: Cambridge University Press, 1994), 255–8.

[72] Meyer, *Santee Sioux*, 170; Fowler, *Arapahoe Politics*, 33, 35, 85; Moore, *Chiefs, Agents & Soldiers*, 118–19, 210–11; Oliver Knight, "War or Peace: The Anxious Wait for Crazy Horse," in *The Nebraska Indian Wars Reader, 1865–1877*, ed. R. Eli Paul (Lincoln: University of Nebraska Press, 1998), 163; Utley, *Last Days of the Sioux Nation*, 23ff., 137; Tate, "John P. Clum," 104; Spores, "Too Small a Place."

[73] See, e.g., Bender, "*New Hope*," 167–8.

[74] Meyer, *Santee Sioux*, 71.

[75] Martha Royce Blaine, *Pawnee Passage: 1870–1875* (Norman: University of Oklahoma Press, 1990), 185–201.

together with distribution of rations. The process for dispensing annuities varied by time and place, but it was standardized enough that it was used as the basis for a ruse that allowed the United States to disarm and arrest Indians following the 1862 Sioux uprising.[76]

Other tasks involving field agents included holding Indians captured in battles or detained as a result of involvement in, or proximity to, uprisings and other events – administration that required complicated efforts to round up, detain, imprison, feed, and maintain physically and spiritually Indian populations in the hundreds and sometimes thousands. Administering incarceration raised questions surrounding the transportation of prisoners, definition of their privileges, medical treatment, exercise of religion, education, construction and maintenance of facilities, and contracting.[77] After the 1862 Sioux uprising, for example, the government held 322 Sioux prisoners at Mankato, plus roughly 20 cooks, laundresses, and other service personnel. Another group following the same incident numbered 1,600 – with 130 prisoner deaths taking place during the winter of 1862–63, and with those bodies replaced by roughly the same number of new captives.[78] Babies born as captives in prison-of-war (POW) camps complicated matters of both child-rearing and administrative jurisdiction.[79] Field agents developed, selected, and oversaw Indian police forces and created court systems to adjudicate disputes and extend the agent's control of the reservation.

Economic development was a big part of the reservation scene, including the leasing of lands, mineral and resource extraction, grazing, sale and recordkeeping of land deals, and so on. Land allotment increasingly became a major part of reservation administration throughout the nineteenth century, adding a raft of new tasks to the agent's duties: "He became the custodian of a tremendous body of records showing each individual Indian and his land and the use of it from year to year. In his office leases must be made, and collections; and checks must be prepared and delivered to the Indian lessors."[80]

Health, welfare, and morals on the reservations were important areas of policy and administration. John Menual, a missionary with medical training, was sent to Navajo in 1870 specifically to provide consistent medical care to the tribe after an army medical officer had helped combat a smallpox outbreak. The government engaged in housing policy, providing funds and encouragement for timber cutting and housing construction on reservations – both for the benefit of Indians directly, and to encourage them

[76] Meyer, *Santee Sioux*, 126.

[77] Meyer, *Santee Sioux*, 144ff.; Corinne L. Monjeau-Marz, *The Dakota Indian Internment at Fort Snelling, 1862–1864* (St. Paul: Prairie Smoke Press, 2006).

[78] Meyer, *Santee Sioux*, 137; see Meyer, *Santee Sioux*, ch. 7.

[79] H. Henrietta Stockel, *Survival of the Spirit: Chiricahua Apaches in Captivity* (Reno: University of Nevada Press, 1993); Monjeau-Marz, *Dakota Indian Internment*, 89–91.

[80] Seymour, *Indian Agents*, 369.

to settle in stable domiciles and live as white people. In the 1880s, for example, the government spent close to $10,000 to replace log cabins with frame houses among the Flandreau colony – just one of many examples in the region and across the West.[81] Attempts were made to regularize and regulate marriages.[82] Agents regulated dancing and religious worship.[83]

Education and job training efforts, including measures intended to make of the Indians successful farmers, lay near the heart of the complex array of an agent's tasks. As in earlier years, treaties, laws, and federal programs supported education for American Indians. Early in the reservation era, Commissioner T. Hartley Crawford made grants to boarding schools, conditioned upon the schools addressing "agriculture, homemaking and the mechanic arts."[84] Treaties with the Nez Perce in 1855 committed the United States to providing two schools and two teachers, and also to building a blacksmith shop and a hospital.[85] The same year, Lame Bull's Treaty committed $15,000 per year to educate children and adults among the Blackfeet Indians.[86] The treaties of Medicine Creek and Point Elliott also promised educational commitments.[87] In the 1868 Treaty of Fort Laramie, the government promised to provide a school and teacher for every thirty students. The treaty established age requirements, a student-teacher ratio, and the obligation of parents to police attendance.[88] California treaties typically included

81 Meyer, *Santee Sioux*, 252. On calls for social policy aid to Indians generally, see documents in Heizer, *Destruction*, ch. 5; O'Donnell, *Arrow*, 201. On the limited efforts made in housing, see, e.g., Hagan, *United States-Comanche Relations*, 181; O'Donnell, *Arrow*, 288. On administering alcohol regulations, see Moore, *Chiefs, Agents & Soldiers*, 152, 180; Robert S. McPherson, *The Northern Navajo Frontier, 1860–1900: Expansion Through Adversity* (Albuquerque: University of New Mexico Press, 1988), 67ff.; McCoy, "Special Indian Agency," 362ff.; Tate, "John P. Clum," 102ff.; Neil, "Territorial Governor," 229. On administering weapons and trade regulations, see McPherson, *Northern Navajo Frontier*, 71ff. On the military's enforcement of timber regulations, see, e.g., Herring, *Enduring Indians of Kansas*, 44; Kane, "Federal Protection."

82 Meyer, *Santee Sioux*, 231 n27.

83 Ibid., 214.

84 Joan Greene Orr, "Civilize the Indian: Government Policies, Quakers, and Cherokee Education," *The Southern Friend* 10 (1988), 29.

85 Alvin M. Josephy Jr., *The Nez Perce Indians and the Opening of the Northwest* (Boston: Houghton Mifflin, 1997 [1965]), 336. Also see Fowler, *Arapahoe Politics*, 46, 57, 74; Moore, *Chiefs, Agents & Soldiers*, 29, 143; Herring, *Enduring Indians of Kansas*, 50ff.; McLaughlin, *My Friend the Indian*, 267; Utley, *Last Days of the Sioux Nation*, 35ff.; Hagan, *United States-Comanche Relations*, 161–5; Spores, "Too Small a Place," 182; Morgan, "Administration of Indian Affairs in Utah, 1851–1858," 395; McCoy, "Special Indian Agency," 357.

86 It was not unusual for the federal commitment to languish. No school opened for seventeen years after Lame Bull's Treaty, and few children attended until the 1890s. Meyer Weinberg, *A Chance to Learn: The History of Race and Education in the United States* (Cambridge: Cambridge University Press, 1977), 193–4.

87 Weinberg, *A Chance to Learn*, 194–5.

88 Orr, "Civilize the Indian," 30.

education provisions, although these were not generally put into effect.[89] Two articles in an 1868 treaty with the Navajos dealt with education, the first committing the United States to building a schoolhouse and chapel, and the second giving attendance responsibilities to Navajo parents.[90] As Meyer Weinberg notes, Indians were also free to spend their treaty funds on education, and they did: during 1854–55, Weinberg finds more than $2 million being spent on Indian education, with 38.2 percent coming from treaty funds ($824,160), 18.6 percent from Indian national funds ($400,000); 38.5 percent from private societies ($830,000); and 4.7 percent from the Civilization Fund ($102,107).[91]

After the Civil War, the federal government began to take over Indian education directly and it "dominated the scene" after 1870, when Congress provided a fund of $100,000 for Indian education. This action began the replacement of mission schools with the establishment of government-run schools.[92] By 1872, hundreds of students at about a dozen schools were federally funded in California, Oregon, and Washington.[93] Between 78 percent and 83 percent of students attended government Indian schools in Washington state from 1875 to the 1890s.[94] Several agents provided consistent leadership in the development of an industrial school on the Niobrara Reservation, which eventually became a magnet for Indians across the region of Minnesota and the Dakotas.[95] Issues such as the content of the curriculum and the appropriate language of instruction engaged local agents and headquarters officials for years.[96] Boarding schools, notably the Carlisle Indian School but also variations nationwide, dominated Indian affairs education in the latter part of the nineteenth century.

Altering the methods and content of housing, health care, and education – encompassing knowledge and value systems and fundamental tenets of relationships between people and more ethereal elements, both religious and secular – represented powerful weapons in the government's effort to

[89] Weinberg, *A Chance to Learn*, 195–6.

[90] Ibid., 187.

[91] Ibid., 181–2.

[92] Irving G. Hendrick, "Federal Policy Affecting the Education of Indians in California, 1849–1934," *History of Education Quarterly* 16 (Summer 1976), 166; Orr, "Civilize the Indian," 31; Jon Reyhner and Jeanne Eder, "A History of Indian Education," in *Teaching American Indian Students*, ed. Jon Reyhner (Norman: University of Oklahoma Press, 1994), 44.

[93] Hendrick, "Federal Policy," 166.

[94] Weinberg, *A Chance to Learn*, 194–5. Education efforts continued into the allotment era. Congress extended jurisdiction over Alaska in 1884, and gave the Secretary of the Interior authority to create a federal school system. Gigi Berardi, "Schools, Settlements, and Sanitation in Alaska Native Villages," *Ethnohistory* 46 (Spring 1999), 334–5.

[95] Meyer, *Santee Sioux*, ch. 9.

[96] Ibid., see ch. 9, esp., 187ff.

weaken and control Indian nations and peoples. Programs that replaced traditional health care methods and providers with federal officers and officially sanctioned methods, forced alterations in living arrangements and family relationships, and mandated language use and educational content, were all means of weakening and controlling Indian populations.

In total effect, Indian agents and other federal personnel engaged across the continent in what would today be called nation-building. Many of the government's activities had antecedents in earlier eras of Indian policy, but the reservations located the efforts in clearly defined, administratively manageable areas away from migrations and settlements. Trade regulations, treaties, removals, and other initiatives from the United States' earliest Indian policy continued. And despite the service's efforts in social policies like housing, education, and health care, the main goal of the reservations must not be obscured. Indian agents existed to carry out first a policy of containment and control, in service of expansion and the exploitation of land, labor, and natural resources; after that came attention to "civilization" and social measures, and even then almost always in support of the mission of containment and control.

Effectiveness

Administration of Indian affairs in the reservation era was effective in three main ways. First, administrators achieved the primary goal of neutralizing the influence of Indian communities upon U.S. expansion and development through a combination of concentration, containment, isolation, and control. Second, administrators effectively managed Indian affairs – particularly the dispossession of Indians and redistribution of their lands – to the benefit of development interests like railroads, mining and grazing interests, and land speculators, even as they effectively pursued social control and "civilization" measures. Finally, regarding the agency itself, the BIA effectively deflected challenges to its autonomy by protecting its leading position in Indian affairs administration against efforts that would have transferred its responsibilities to the military.

Isolation, Containment, and Control

Indian policy develops slowly. The treaty system emerged from European precedents, and developed gradually through the eighteenth and nineteenth centuries as power relationships and other factors evolved. The factory system evolved from trade and other mechanisms to manage expansion and Indian relations. Removal's roots lay in the Jeffersonian era and in the tenure of John Calhoun as Secretary of War; it was not the immediate creation of the Jackson administration. Reservation theory, too, developed within the executive branch and the field service throughout the nineteenth century, and became the dominant policy as a result of the acquisition of new lands in the Southwest and Northwest. The Indian Office has held constantly to a variation of reservation policy from the early republic through the beginning of the twenty-first century. Adjustments to reservation policy have resulted from new exigencies facing administration and from adaptations within the Indian service, not from changes in party control.

There is no doubt that the reservation system achieved its goal of containing and isolating Indian communities, thereby promoting U.S. expansion and development and easing non-Indian settlement of the West. Reservations were placed in dismal areas away from the main streams of migration and the centers of non-Indian settlement. Indian populations were manipulated by the mechanisms outlined earlier, including federal agents' dispensation of annuities and provisions, federally influenced police forces, and agent-controlled judicial systems and social policies. Cronyism, kickbacks, and Indian rings disrupted provisioning of Indian populations, and political ties among whites and development interests consistently won battles with Indian and tribal interests or forced those interests into compromises.[97] In an 1872 report, Commissioner Francis Walker wrote that "by the reservation system and the feeding system combined, the occasions for collision [between whites and Indians] are so reduced by lessening the points of contact, and the number of Indians available for hostile expeditions involving exposure, hardship, and danger is so diminished through the appeal made to their indolence and self-indulgence, that the Army in its present force is able to deal effectively with the few marauding bands which refuse to accept the terms of the Government."[98]

Some reservations witnessed effective administration of even the secondary paths to containment and control of Indian populations. Reports from the schools and the reservations sounded optimistic noises about Indian progress toward civilization, and held out the hope that Indians would be successfully "civilized" in a generation. While criticizing much of the administration of the Indian school system and reviewing reasons for its problems in the removal era, the historian Ronald Satz writes, "At the end of the Polk administration, the Indian Office could boast that it was subsidizing sixteen manual labor schools, with over eight hundred students, as well as eighty-seven boarding and district schools, with nearly three thousand pupils. It could also claim that 'no other Government has contributed so largely to schools and farming instruction among the Indians, or contracted for and paid, in like manner, annuities to tribes who have been removed from the

97 Hoopes, *Indian Affairs*, 237–8; Wishart, "Dispossession of the Pawnee," 398ff.; Spores, "Too Small a Place"; O'Donnell on Palmer in Oregon, *Arrow*, 277, 287; Herring, *Enduring Indians of Kansas*, 67; Utley, *Last Days of the Sioux Nation*, 23–4.

98 "Annual Report of the Commissioner of Indian Affairs," 1872, reprinted in Prucha, *Documents*, 139.

land of which they originally held possession.'"[99] In Minnesota, Indians being supplied and aided by the government under the provisions of the treaty of 1837 seemed to do much better, in terms of "civilization" and also agricultural development and standard of living, than Indians who were not party to the treaty or those whose benefits had expired.[100]

The Indian Office developed extensive statistical measures of its effectiveness, which commissioners used to defend the agency's work. Commissioner Smith in 1875 pointed to data on the production of agricultural goods, acres of land under cultivation, numbers of families living in houses, and numbers of children attending schools, to demonstrate that the government's policies could work and were working. The Board of Indian Commissioners used similar techniques in 1876 to support the efficacy of the Peace Policy, citing such numbers as improvements from 1868 to 1876 in the number of houses occupied by Indians (7,476 to 55,717), the number of students attending reservation schools (4,718 to 11,328), and acres under cultivation (54,207 to 318,194). The Board also highlighted the number of church buildings on reservations (177), the number of Indians who were church members (27,215), and the number of Indians wearing "citizen's dress" (104,818 out of 266,000 Indians in the United States).[101] These data should be interpreted carefully, of course – their reliability is always in question, given the numerous incentives commissioners and others have for inflating numbers and trumpeting successes. More important, such data reflect a particular *kind* of effectiveness: effectiveness in the BIA's efforts to turn Indians into sedentary white Christian farmers. Roy Meyer writes that the assimilation efforts of missionaries and government officials in the reservation era are at the epicenter of damage to Indian populations: "it becomes possible to argue that the greatest crime committed by the white man against the Indian was not in stealing from him a continent, but in denying him the right to be an Indian – trying to deprive him of his racial and cultural identity."[102]

99 Satz, *American Indian Policy*, 271–2; see also Orr, "Civilize the Indian," 27, 31, 33; Terry A. Cross, Kathleen A. Earle & David Simmons, "Child Abuse and Neglect in Indian Country: Policy Issues," *Families in Society* 81 (January-February 2000), 50; David H. DeJong, "'Unless They Are Kept Alive': Federal Indian Schools and Student Health, 1878–1918," *American Indian Quarterly* 31 (Spring 2007), 257; Michael C. Coleman, "The Responses of American Indian Children and Irish Children to the School, 1850s–1920s: A Comparative Study in Cross-Cultural Education," *American Indian Quarterly* 23 (Summer 1999), 84; Berardi, "Schools, Settlements, and Sanitation," 332, 335ff.; Weinberg, *A Chance to Learn*, 199–202.

100 Meyer, *Santee Sioux*, 63ff. Administration created mixed results in some places (Bender, *"New Hope,"* 191ff.; Meyer, *Santee Sioux*, 102–7, chs. 8–11), failure in others, and some considerable successes, even if temporary ones (Meyer, *Santee Sioux*, 92, 165ff., 202; Bender, *"New Hope,"* 118, 164).

101 See Bender, *"New Hope,"* 147, 161–2.

102 Meyer, *Santee Sioux*, 363.

Meyer is right, of course – unfortunately, this was exactly what government agents were trying to accomplish.

Indian Affairs Administration and Expansion

It is sometimes easy to overlook the role that Indian affairs administration played in U.S. expansion. It is easy to overlook the role of Indians in the general land policies that spurred and sparked white settlement and development across the continent. Only through land transfers or otherwise sanctioned takings could the land be legally redistributed from Indians to others. The land that went to railroads, developers, settlers, and so on emerged from treaty processes, Indian removals, allotments of individual holdings – either through government directly, or through various mechanisms designed to allot lands to individual Indians which could then be taken, bought, leased, or stolen by non-Indian interests. The three California agents conducted eighteen treaties between March 1851 and January 1852, negotiating with 139 Indian communities, protecting white interests, preempting violent outbreaks and combinations, and setting aside for the Indians more than 7 percent of the state of California.[103] Commissioner Manypenny expressed pride in the achievements of the treaty makers when he noted, in 1855, that the United States had entered into more than fifty treaties in two years that brought to the United States more than 174 million acres of land – four to six thousand square miles of territory. "In no former equal period of our history," he wrote, "have so many treaties been made, or such vast accessions of land been obtained."[104]

Charles Mix implicitly defended the effectiveness of federal efforts to administer Indian affairs in a peaceful and orderly manner through the treaty system when, in his 1858 Annual Report, he stated baldly that had the treaties signed in the Northwest been ratified by the U.S. Senate, the Indians there would have been less disappointed and antagonistic toward whites and the United States, tensions and conflicts would not have taken place, and that "the cost of the military operations to subdue the Indians, and the losses sustained by our citizens from their depredations and hostilities, will amount to a far greater sum than would have been required to extinguish their title and establish and maintain them, for the necessary period, on properly selected reservations, had that policy in respect to them been sanctioned and timely measures taken to carry it out."[105] Later in the same report, Mix reflected on U.S. Indian policy over the years, concluding that while the removal and reservation policies had been costly, "we have been amply repaid its expense by the revenue obtained from the sale of the lands acquired from the Indians, and by the rapid extension of our

103 Phillips, *Indians and Indian Agents*, 108.

104 Quoted in Killoren, "*Come, Blackrobe,*" 198; "Annual Report of the Commissioner of Indian Affairs," 1856, reprinted in Prucha, *Documents*, 90.

105 "Annual Report, 1858," reprinted in Prucha, *Documents*, 94.

settlements and the corresponding increase in the resources and prosperity of our country."[106] Lincoln linked winning the Civil War with the expansion of the Union across the continent, and of course Indian affairs played an important role in such calculations.[107]

In 1872, Commissioner Francis Walker praised the effectiveness of Indian policy in isolating Indians and freeing paths to the West with a minimum loss of life and property, and noted with satisfaction that the remaining Indians would soon be reduced to surviving on charity.[108] Walker discoursed on how the pacification efforts of civilian administrators had not only saved the nation money, but provided the context in which settlers and developers thrived. He explicitly contrasted the effectiveness of the Indian Office's efforts with what the military was able to provide, explaining that while adventurous men might be comfortable living with a vast military force for their protection, "as a rule, men will not place women and children in situations of even possible peril, nor will they put money into permanent improvements under such circumstances." "The presence of no military force could give that confidence to pioneer enterprise which the general cessation of Indian hostilities has engendered."[109] Walker's understanding of the relationship between pacification, reservations, railroads, and development is coldly calculating, and he explained in clear terms how the reservations had helped the railroads, how the railroads helped settlement and military action, and how these forces in combination would soon bring about "the day of deliverance from the fear of Indian hostility." "[I]t is not too much to expect that three summers of peaceful progress," he wrote, "will forever put it out of the power of the tribes and bands which at present disturb Colorado, Utah, Arizona, and New Mexico to claim consideration of the country in any other attitude than as pensioners upon the national bounty."[110]

Of course, the government's mission always had benevolent motives, too: "This is, indeed, the only hope of salvation for the aborigines of the continent," Walker wrote.

> If they stand up against the progress of civilization and industry, they must be relentlessly crushed.... They must yield or perish.... And it is because the present system allows the freest extension of settlement and industry possible under the circumstances, while affording space and time for humane endeavors to rescue the Indian tribes from a position altogether barbarous and incompatible with civilization and social progress, that this system must be approved by all enlightened citizens...[111]

106 Ibid., 94.
107 Nichols, *Lincoln and the Indians*, 163–4; see also Monjeau-Marz, *Dakota Indian Internment*, 122.
108 "Annual Report, 1872," in Prucha, *Documents*, 140.
109 Ibid., 138.
110 Ibid., 140.
111 Ibid., 140.

The same year, President Grant in his State of the Union address echoed Walker's opinion, stating that the Peace Policy, while still young, had reduced administrative costs, decreased depredations committed by Indians against whites, allowed for the extension of the railroads, facilitated Western settlement, and even improved the lives of Indians.[112]

The beginnings of the allotment policy also proved effective. Allotting functioning reservations makes sense in the context of other U.S. Indian policies: factories sought peace, dispossession, and eventual civilization; removal sought removal, and eventual civilization; reservations aimed at isolation and containment, and eventual civilization; and allotment would aim for dispossession and eventual civilization. After it became the focus of federal policy from the 1880s to the 1930s, allotment cost native populations two-thirds of the lands they had managed to retain through the factories, removals, and reservations. Allotment began in the field, during the reservation era, and it proved effective even then as a means of dispossessing Indians from their land.[113]

The Indian Office in the reservation era, as it had in earlier years, pursued a complex set of tasks that supported the primary mission of reservation containment. Relying on a clear mission and organized, expert, and effective public administration, the Indian Office contained Indian populations on reservations, facilitated national expansion and the development of a host of non-Indian interests, and designed and promoted a variety of social programs that effectively weakened native communities and traditions, while forcing Indians toward Christianity and "civilization."

The Bureau, as always, relied heavily on the discretionary authority and creativity wielded by its operators in the field, and it effectively defended its administrative autonomy against constant threats from the military and supporters of a more aggressive expansion policy. Over time, though, the cruel effectiveness of the reservations became obscured by attention paid to inconsistencies in administrative approaches, corruption and charges of corruption and poor administration, and other familiar criticisms. These factors – and later observers' repugnance at the goals and results of the reservations – would shadow the Indian service into the next century, masking the tragedy of bureaucratic effectiveness in the nineteenth century and perpetuating the illusion of a poorly-run, ineffective, and corrupt agency.

[112] Bender, "*New Hope,*" 90; see also 149. Grant blamed criticism of the Peace Policy's effects on disgruntled traders and Westerners who saw diminished profits and business success under the new policy. Bender, "*New Hope,*" 111.

[113] E.g., see Herring, *Enduring Indians of Kansas*, 89ff., ch. 7.

10

What's an Administrator To Do?

Reservations and Politics

Charges of corruption, inefficiency, and failure dogged the Indian Service in the later years of the factory system and during Indian removal. As we have seen, many of these charges were off the mark – administration of the factories and of removal produced the results sought. It became advantageous to certain interests, after administrators had achieved their goals, to condemn the policies and the administrators. Simultaneously, the closest allies and supporters of those policies dropped out of the political debates swirling around Indian affairs, leaving the Indian Office vulnerable to its critics and open to newly active interests that sought to use Indian policy for their own ends.

This pattern recurs in the reservation era. Understanding the primary purpose of the reservations – containment of Indian populations as part of a managed expansion across the continent – reveals that the reservations did their job. So did reservation administrators. The gradual creation of reservations as parts of the removal experience and of constantly changing administrative environments forced field agents to adapt and develop administrative procedures and localized goals, even as they sought to synchronize those adaptations within the outlines and procedures of the agency's mission, previous decisions, and institutional structures. The adaptation and novel situations facing the Indian Office in the reservation era required the continued delegation of broad discretionary authority to field agents.

Yet the same dynamics of Indian affairs politics carried over from the earlier eras. Field agents acted in a hornets' nest of conflicting political interests and demands, and their actions – necessarily relying heavily on personal discretion and ad hoc decision making within the general parameters of the reservation system – always brought attacks from someone. These attacks would follow the service through the nineteenth century, as they had during the years of factories and removal, and they would leave a lasting impression of failure surrounding the BIA. The failure was illusory, partaking more of politics and retrospective remorse than of the true purposes of United

States policy. The BIA did what was asked of it. Once again, the tragedy of Indian affairs lay in the effectiveness of public administration at the national level.

Local Discretion and Innovation in the Field Service

A combination of detailed instructions and broad discretion to act on individual judgment in local contexts guided field agents' actions in the field. Charles Mix's 1850 handbook provided a common base of knowledge for Indian service officials. Treaty commissioners in California in the 1850s used it to help them get up to speed in negotiating treaties – a task with which they were unfamiliar when they first arrived on the West Coast. Commissioner William Medill gave the commissioners the handbook, together with copies of the 1834 Trade and Intercourse Act, the 1848 treaty with Mexico, and a collection of Indian treaties published in 1837.[1] Detailed instructions continued to be issued to field agents during the Peace Policy.[2] After posting bond and taking an oath, new agents by the 1870s were told in a letter from the Commissioner's office to report to their duty stations without unnecessary delay; they were instructed to examine the records of the previous agent, and issue receipts as agency property and funds were transferred. The agent was to devote time to the welfare and improvement of the Indians in his charge, and report important matters to the Commissioner's office. Recommendations for improving administration were encouraged; copies of official correspondence were required to be sent through the superintendent's office; and statements of accounts were to be submitted quarterly, in quadruplicate, on department forms.[3] 1884 regulations stated that "The chief duty of an agent is to induce his Indians to labor in civilized pursuits. To attain this end every possible influence should be brought to bear, and in proportion as it is attained, other things being equal, an agent's administration is successful or unsuccessful."[4]

Other bodies also received detailed instructions. The 1867 Indian Peace Commission was charged with securing peace among Western tribes, "and at the same time establish[ing] security for person and property along the lines of railroad now being constructed to the Pacific and other thoroughfares of travel to the western Territories, and such as will most likely insure civilization for the Indians and peace and safety for the whites." The Commission was then charged with selecting lands adequate for Indians to farm or graze,

1 George Harwood Phillips, *Indians and Indian Agents: The Origins of the Reservation System in California, 1849–1852* (Norman: University of Oklahoma Press, 1997), 7, 14, 74–7.

2 Norman J. Bender, *"New Hope for the Indians": The Grant Peace Policy and the Navajos in the 1870s* (Albuquerque: University of New Mexico Press, 1989), 46.

3 Bender, *"New Hope,"* 46.

4 Quoted in Francis Paul Prucha, *The Great Father: The United States Government and the American Indians* (Lincoln: University of Nebraska Press, 1984), 645.

suitable for excluding strangers not permitted to enter by the Indians, with the provision: "That the district or districts shall be so located as not to interfere with travel on highways located by authority of the United States, nor with the route of the Northern Pacific Railroad, the Union Pacific Railroad, the Union Pacific Railroad Eastern Division, or the proposed route of the Atlantic and Pacific Railroad by the way of Albuquerque." The instructions concluded with a provision authorizing the Secretary of War, under the president's direction, to accept state and territorial forces in order to suppress hostilities. Detailed instructions were issued to other bodies, like the Board of Indian Commissioners in 1869.[5]

Within these guidelines, exigencies in the field continued to direct the course and details of administration. Different circumstances in the new areas annexed by the United States created wide variation in local administrative circumstances, and the efforts of local officials in areas like Texas, New Mexico, and Utah were crucial to developing the federal reservation policy. Federal agents in California, for example, muddled through the early stages of Indian policy in that state. The California commissioners – despite possessing old treaties, copies of trade and intercourse laws, and Mix's handbook – wrote questions back to the capital regarding the extent of their authority and guidelines. Redick McKee wrote, early in the process,

> The commissioners regret that their instructions from the government at Washington, on these and other questions likely to arise and demand their immediate attention, are so meager and indefinite, and throw upon them necessarily so much responsibility. In the absence of direct and positive instruction, or even counsel and advice, we must do the best we can, relying upon your approval of what we may do, based upon an honest desire to promote at once the best good of the Indians, while we maintain the honor and evince the benevolent designs of our government towards the unfortunate aborigines.[6]

5 See Francis Paul Prucha, ed., *Documents of United States Indian Policy*, 2nd ed. (Lincoln: University of Nebraska Press, 1990), 105–6, 127–9. See also Ronald Spores, "Too Small a Place: The Removal of the Willamette Valley Indians, 1850–1856," *American Indian Quarterly* 17 (Spring 1993), 185ff.; Terence O'Donnell, *An Arrow in the Earth: General Joel Palmer and the Indians of Oregon* (Portland: Oregon Historical Society, 1991), 182. Census enumerators also received detailed instructions. Melissa Nobles, "History Counts: A Comparative Analysis of Racial/Color Categorization in US and Brazilian Censuses," *American Journal of Public Health* 90 (November 2000), 1740. Nobles offers interesting details about bureaucratic processes and control of field agents. Sometimes, instructions do not seem to have been given. See, e.g., W. Turrentine Jackson, "Indian Affairs and Politics in Idaho Territory, 1863–1870," *The Pacific Historical Review* 14 (September 1945), 314; William M. Neil, "The Territorial Governor as Indian Superintendent in the Trans-Mississippi West," *The Mississippi Valley Historical Review* 43 (September 1956), 214. Neil suggests that instructions became less necessary over time, as experience and habit eroded the need for close, detailed supervision. Neil, "Territorial Governor," 220.

6 Quoted in Phillips, *Indians and Indian Agents*, 15.

McKee hit the nail on the head, recognizing the fundamental dilemma of his responsibility to both Indians and the government and people for which he worked, recognizing the immediacy of his responsibility and the authority bestowed upon him to act on his best judgment, and offering the dark foreshadowing of already viewing the Indians as unfortunate. McKee and his fellow California commissioners asked their superiors a series of questions regarding their authority to conduct and sign treaties, but concluded that they would, "under the instructions heretofore given us, and in compliance with the demands of humanity, as we conceive, act affirmatively on all those questions until otherwise directed."[7] As Indian service personnel had been doing for generations, they often wound up answering their own questions, relying on their understanding of their mission and on their judgment to make decisions.

Commissioners possessing instructions for treaty negotiations frequently felt themselves free to make adjustments depending on particular circumstances. Often, when more land proved to be available than had been expected, commissioners acted to spend more and obtain more than their instructions required or allowed – the commissioners thereby fulfilled and furthered larger administrative goals. The California agents, for example, "were unsure of their authority and even the real purpose of their mission," writes the historian George Harwood Phillips, yet it is clear from his accounts of Indian affairs in California that the agents understood that the goals of policy were to reduce conflicts and depredations between whites and Indians, facilitate white development and control of the region, and try to uphold the rights and interests of Indian communities.[8] Reservations became their preferred means of controlling the behavior of Indian populations and weakening Indians' ability to threaten, obstruct, or hinder U.S. expansion. The reservations would also provide the isolation and circumstances through which government agents could effect change through

[7] Quoted in Phillips, *Indians and Indian Agents*, 70. Treaty commissioners in the Northwest similarly responded to immediate circumstances in 1851–53, in disregard of their instructions, allowing provisions for Indians to remain on diminished lands. The Senate refused to ratify the treaties, as the situation became similar to that in California: whites in the region demanding removals, and Indians and treaty commissioners working to secure reserved lands. Alvin M. Josephy Jr., *The Nez Perce Indians and the Opening of the Northwest* (Boston: Houghton Mifflin, 1997 [1965]), 287. Other examples of the interplay of instructions and discretionary judgment are in Joseph B. Herring, "Indian Intransigency in Kansas: Government Bureaucracy vs. Mokohoko's Sacs and Foxes," *The Western Historical Quarterly* 17 (April 1986), 192. The 1854 Gatewood Treaty with the Omahas, described in Judith A. Boughter, *Betraying the Omaha Nation, 1790–1916* (Norman: University of Oklahoma Press, 1998), 62ff., provides an interesting counterexample. The treaty was never ratified, and Gatewood's tenure was short and controversial. On exercise of discretion by governors, see Neil, "Territorial Governor," 218, 222; O'Donnell, *Arrow*, 130ff.

[8] Phillips, *Indians and Indian Agents*, xvii.

education, agricultural training, and missionary work. Phillips distinguishes what he calls "the new policy of confinement" from the former reliance upon removals by highlighting the government's "emphasis on controlling and changing Indians."[9]

When removals took place within California and elsewhere, discretionary actions by field agents predominated just as they had during the Jackson years – always with an eye on the goal of isolating Indians away from development and expansionist interests, resettling them on administratively manageable territory, and responding to demands from white communities. Adam Johnston, one of the California agents, took considerable actions without authorization, including issuing trading licenses and hiring a doctor to vaccinate Indians.[10] Johnston's actions echo earlier field activity: his superiors condoned hiring the doctor, and he was informed that a recommendation for appropriating payment would be made to Congress; his issue of licenses was approved after the fact – but he was informed that in accepting fees for the licenses he had "fallen into error."[11]

Agents outside California also continued to act, even when uncertain of their authority.[12] In a typical example, Sisseton Agent Benjamin Thompson worked with missionaries who had requested help in building a church in 1869. After asking superiors if he had authority to build, the agent

[9] Ibid., 5.

[10] Ibid., ch. 8.

[11] Ibid., 118.

[12] On the exercise of discretion, see also O'Donnell, *Arrow*, 127–8; William Haas Moore, *Chiefs, Agents & Soldiers: Conflict on the Navajo Frontier, 1868–1882* (Albuquerque: University of New Mexico Press, 1994), 73, 118, 147, 174; Julia B. McGillycuddy, *Blood on the Moon: Valentine McGillycuddy and the Sioux* (Lincoln: University of Nebraska Press, 1969 [1941]), 127–8; William T. Hagan, *United States-Comanche Relations: The Reservation Years* (Norman: University of Oklahoma Press, 1990 [1976]), 154; Donald R. McCoy, "The Special Indian Agency in Alaska, 1873–1874: Its Origins and Operation," *The Pacific Historical Review* 25 (November 1956), 361ff.; Michael L. Tate, "John P. Clum and the Origins of an Apache Constabulary, 1874–1877," *American Indian Quarterly* 3 (Summer 1977), 104, 116 n23; J. Orin Oliphant, "Encroachments of Cattlemen on Indian Reservations in the Pacific Northwest, 1870–1890," *Agricultural History* 24 (January 1950), 56–8; George D. Harmon, "The United States Indian Policy in Texas, 1845–1860," *The Mississippi Valley Historical Review* 17 (December 1930), 380–1; Alban W. Hoopes, *Indian Affairs and their Administration, 1849–1860* (New York: Kraus Reprint, 1972 [1932]), 195ff., 184, 206, 210; Dale L. Morgan, "The Administration of Indian Affairs in Utah, 1851–1858," *The Pacific Historical Review* 17 (November 1948), 387. For an example of Congress overruling discretionary actions, see Moore, *Chiefs, Agents & Soldiers*, 147, 174; Hoopes, *Indian Affairs*, 170–1. Other examples of innovative approaches taken in the field service are in Robert S. McPherson, *The Northern Navajo Frontier, 1860–1900: Expansion Through Adversity* (Albuquerque: University of New Mexico Press, 1988), 66; McGillycuddy, *Blood on the Moon*, 133; McCoy, "Special Indian Agency," 363–5; Morgan, "Indian Affairs in Utah," 398ff.

continued even though told to wait until it was determined which denomination would have control of the agency under the Peace Policy. As often was the case, the agent later received authorization to build anyway.[13] Education funds often arrived without specific instructions as to how they were to be spent, leaving it up to the local agent to spend (or not to spend) the resources as he saw fit, and the agitation of agents played an important role in the development of schools on reservations.[14] Education tasks varied at different reservations, depending on personal talents and educational philosophies, on the different missionary organizations and groups during and before and after the Peace Policy, and also depending on the particular administrative structures and rationales employed at different reservations.[15]

Discretion held sway in trade and local business affairs, too. The 1834 Indian Intercourse Act expanded agents' discretionary authority in dealing with alcohol trafficking and trade licenses;[16] Lawrence Taliaferro in Minnesota exceeded even this authority when he specified locations for trading posts and suspended traders' privileges of importing alcohol to Indian country to be used by the traders' boatmen, but he received little criticism from higher authority.[17] Local agents were a big part of the contracting process, especially when it came to supplying the Indians, estimating costs, soliciting bids, selecting contractors, and enforcing contract provisions.[18]

Agents' judgment about particular contexts shaped economic and business interactions among the interests arrayed in and around a reservation. Agents worked with cattlemen, for example, to negotiate deals that helped to feed local Indians who were inadequately supplied by government rations; often, such arrangements were crucial to avoiding conflicts and Indian raids.[19] The actions of P. B. Hunt, Indian agent for the Kiowa, Comanche, and Wichita tribes, provides a typical illustration. Informed that the government was planning to cut supplies and rations to the Indians, Hunt worried that the Indians might leave the reservation and threaten nearby white settlements. Hunt worked out his own approach, on his own authority. He arranged for several cattlemen who had been illegally grazing their herds on

[13] Roy W. Meyer, *History of the Santee Sioux: United States Indian Policy on Trial*, revised edition (Lincoln: University of Nebraska Press, 1993), 203.

[14] E.g., Meyer, *Santee Sioux*, 65ff., 177; Bender, "*New Hope.*"

[15] E.g., Meyer, *Santee Sioux*, 228; Bender, "*New Hope.*"

[16] Meyer, *Santee Sioux*, 54.

[17] Meyer, *Santee Sioux*, 42. For similar examples, see Moore, *Chiefs, Agents & Soldiers*, 118; Morgan, "Indian Affairs in Utah," 387; McPherson, *Northern Navajo Frontier*, 66.

[18] E.g., David A. Nichols, *Lincoln and the Indians: Civil War Policy & Politics* (Urbana: University of Illinois Press, 2000), 13; Meyer, *Santee Sioux*, 67.

[19] See, e.g., Richard N. Ellis, "General Pope and the Old 'Hand-to-Mouth Way,'" in *The Western American Indian: Case Studies in Tribal History*, ed. Richard N. Ellis (Lincoln: University of Nebraska Press, 1972), 69.

the reservation to stay, in contravention of policy, if they would give three hundred head of cattle to the Indians.[20]

Opening up reservation lands to non-Indian grazing by Hunt and by other agents in similar circumstances often began without formal approval. In Utah, Agent Garland Hurt adapted the reservation system in a method that emphasized farming over consolidation, in response to what he believed to be dangerous connections between Mormon missionaries and local Indians. Hurt's local adaptation of the prevailing system was "cautiously approved" by the Commissioner with some informal suggestions – a typical response to field adaptation that simultaneously accepted adaptations and innovation in the field without giving wholesale approval to them.[21]

Commissioners defended the discretionary actions of field agents. In one illustrative case, Francis Walker argued with an auditor from the Treasury Department who had disallowed an Indian agent's account because the agent had overpaid for lumber by a few cents. Walker wrote,

> Perhaps, with seven thousand wild Indians at his Agency... to be kept from quarreling with each other, to be subsisted (a duty, be it remembered, in addition to all the other duties of the agent's office, nor less exacting than the subsistence of a full division of troops in the field), the Agent may have felt unwilling to spare the seven days necessary to go to Cheyenne one hundred and twenty five miles and back to make the purchase of less than four thousand feet of lumber.[22]

The Indian service bureaucracy was quite innovative in developing new approaches to reservation issues. Faced with myriad issues of maintaining law and order on the reservations, field agents created and developed the concept of police forces staffed by Indians. Much more than simple law and order organizations, the police forces came to be an extension of the local agent's authority to maintain peace and promote social programs.[23] Indian

[20] Martha Buntin, "Beginning of the Leasing of the Surplus Grazing Lands on the Kiowa and Comanche Reservation," *Chronicles of Oklahoma* 10 (1932), 371. See Oliphant, "Encroachments," for another discussion of grazing and reservation administration.

[21] Prucha, *Great Father*, 377. Beeton provides a similar example, discussing how Indian farming in Utah Superintendency took place without formal sanction from headquarters and over the concerns of the Commissioner and the Governor of Utah. Beverly Beeton, "Teach Them To Till The Soil: An Experiment With Indian Farms, 1850–1862," *American Indian Quarterly* 3 (Winter 1977–1978), esp. at 312. See also Moore, *Chiefs, Agents & Soldiers*, 161; Hagan, *United States-Comanche Relations*, ch. 7; Morgan, "Indian Affairs in Utah," 399 n74; Neil, "Territorial Governor," 214; O'Donnell, *Arrow*, 139.

[22] Quoted in H. Craig Miner, "Francis A. Walker," in Robert M. Kvasnicka and Herman J. Viola, eds., *The Commissioners of Indian Affairs, 1824–1977* (Lincoln: University of Nebraska Press, 1979), 138–9. Expenditures could, however, be denied by the Treasury Department. See, e.g., Neil, "Territorial Governor," 219.

[23] Moore, *Chiefs, Agents & Soldiers*, 119ff.; James C. Olson, *Red Cloud and the Sioux Problem* (Lincoln: University of Nebraska Press, 1965), 266; Tate, "John P. Clum." The use of Indians as police dates back to at least 1798, when the federal government paid for a Lighthorse police force among the Cherokee, designed to deter horse thefts. William G. McLoughlin,

policemen acted, like the agents, in a vast and diverse number of areas. Agent Asa Janney asked for and received permission to start a police force at the Santee Sioux' Niobrara reservation in Nebraska in 1869. The project had considerable success and remained a part of reservation administration for the remainder of the century.[24] Agent John Clum initiated Indian police forces at the San Carlos Apache reservation in the 1870s; 1872 saw the beginnings of a police force at Navajo; John McLaughlin initiated a force at Devils Lake in 1879.[25] Field agents' judgment was critical to the effectiveness of administration on reservations, as in the selection of personnel to be police and judges. William T. Hagan writes that "The agent's ability to select the proper personnel as judges and police was the principal key to the success of the programs."[26]

These police forces are a good example of how field innovation gradually became standard operating procedure. By 1872, Secretary of the Interior Columbus Delano was considering the idea more generally.[27] After years of experiments in the field, and following a recommendation by Commissioner of Indian Affairs Ezra Hayt, Congress authorized pay for almost five hundred Indian police in 1877, expanding to nine hundred a year later.[28]

The field service also created Courts of Indian Offenses as mechanisms to maintain order and administer justice on reservations. The Courts of Indian Offenses evolved from long-standing practice in which the local agent acted as judge or delegated that power on the reservation.[29] The courts were headed by Indian judges appointed by BIA agents, and were charged with enforcing a Code of Federal Regulations designed to further the civilizing and assimilative goals of national policy in that era. The courts were

Cherokees and Missionaries, 1789–1839 (Norman: University of Oklahoma Press, 1995), 24; William T. Hagan, *Indian Police and Judges* (Lincoln: University of Nebraska Press, 1966), 20–4. On the Indian police force, see also Loretta Fowler, *Arapahoe Politics, 1851–1978: Symbols in Crises of Authority* (Lincoln: University of Nebraska Press, 1986), 85; Moore, *Chiefs, Agents & Soldiers*, 181; Theda Perdue, *Nations Remembered: An Oral History of the Cherokees, Chickasaws, Choctaws, Creeks, and Seminoles in Oklahoma, 1865–1907* (Norman: University of Oklahoma Press, 1980), 31; McGillycuddy, *Blood on the Moon*, ch. 10; Robert M. Utley, *The Last Days of the Sioux Nation* (New Haven: Yale University Press, 1963), 28; Hagan, *United States-Comanche Relations*, 149–50; Tate, "John P. Clum."

24 Meyer, *Santee Sioux*, 164–5.

25 Prucha, *Great Father*, 600–1; Tate, "John P. Clum"; Bender, *"New Hope,"* 81; Meyer, *Santee Sioux*, 233.

26 Hagan, *Indian Police and Judges*, 162.

27 Bender, *"New Hope,"* 81.

28 "Annual Report of the Commissioner of Indian Affairs," 1877, reprinted in Prucha, *Documents*, 151. See also Meyer, *Santee Sioux*, 164, 236; Bender, *"New Hope,"* 81ff., 117ff.

29 On the Courts of Indian Offenses, see Hagan, *Indian Police and Judges*, ch. 6; Utley, *Last Days of the Sioux Nation*, 31ff.; Tate, "John P. Clum," 100–1, 113; O'Donnell, *Arrow*, 292. Hagan argues in the book's conclusion that the courts were effective administrative mechanisms on the reservations. See 174–5.

empowered to punish individual Indians who engaged in tribal or traditional ceremonies, including any activities which the agent or the Commissioner of Indian Affairs deemed "heathenish."[30] Secretary of the Interior Henry M. Teller authorized the Commissioner of Indian Affairs to establish tribunals at all agencies excluding those of the Five Civilized Tribes; local agents were empowered to choose the members of the tribunals. Teller wrote in his Annual Report of 1883, "The Commissioner of Indian Affairs, with the approval of the Secretary of the Interior, promulgated certain rules for the government of this tribunal, defining offenses of which it was to take cognizance.... The Commissioner recommends an appropriation for the support of this tribunal, and in such recommendation I concur... "[31] Several years later, in 1892, Commissioner Thomas Morgan revised the rules and made several modifications, also at his discretion.[32] Executive branch agents at the capital and in the field created regulations outlining crimes, violations, and penalties that would be covered by the Indian police and adjudicated in the Courts of Indian Offenses.[33]

The extent of the authority over individual lives assumed by field agents utilizing their own police forces and their own courts was profound. The rapid development of the police forces sparked concern regarding the strength and discretionary power of the executive. In 1880, the chairman of the House Committee on Indian Affairs noted: "This provision turns him [the Indian] over, bound hand and foot, to the agents. These men had authority before almost without restriction, except as they are restricted by the want of physical force. Now we give them eight hundred men armed and equipped, and thus the fullest authority is allowed with fearful power to execute not only known laws, but the will of the agent."[34] The Courts of Indian Offenses lay at the heart of an important Supreme Court case, discussed in the conclusion, that formally sanctioned the creative actions of field agents and the courts they invented.

Land policy was also crafted by agents in the field. Federal agents designed and implemented the reservation system in California long before they had clear orders to do so, long before the treaties signed by these agents passed through California's government, and in spite of the rejection of the treaties by the U.S. Senate.[35] The federal agents sent to California in 1849 received broad authority to act on their own judgment, because neither Commissioner Medill nor the agents themselves had a clear understanding of Indians in

30 David E. Wilkins, *American Indian Sovereignty and the U.S. Supreme Court: The Masking of Justice* (Austin: University of Texas Press, 1997), 12.

31 "Annual Report of the Secretary of the Interior," 1883, reprinted in Prucha, *Documents*, 161–2.

32 Reprinted in Prucha, *Documents*, 186.

33 See, e.g., Meyer, *Santee Sioux*, 191ff., 205ff., 213–4, 231 n27, 236.

34 Quoted in Prucha, *Great Father*, 604.

35 Phillips, *Indians and Indian Agents*.

California. Medill wrote, "So little is known here [Washington, DC] of the condition and situation of Indians in that region that no specific instructions relative to them can be given at present; and the department relies on you to furnish it with such statistical and other information as will give a just understanding of every particular relative to them."[36] In less than three months, as Phillips writes, the federal commissioners had determined that removal of Indians from the state was not a viable policy; instead, the Indians would be moved and settled upon lands within the state, with treaty guarantees and federal supervision and management.[37] Even allotments were originally developed in the field by field agents, only later becoming the dominant thrust of national policy.

In all of these areas – reservation administration and provisioning, economics and development, law enforcement, criminal justice, and land policy – the field service of the Bureau of Indian Affairs recognized problems and confronted dilemmas long before policymakers in the capital could respond or design general policies. Field proposals were turned down on occasion,[38] but as it had done during the factory system and removal the field service capitalized upon its culture of local discretionary authority to resolve issues as they thought best. The responses were creative, adaptive, and unique to particular circumstances and particular times. Agents mediated and navigated among the influential interests arrayed around Indian affairs, locally as well as nationally. The field service generally did its best to pursue multiple and conflicting goals, but field agents also understood that the basic mission was the containment, neutralization, and eventual dispossession of American Indian communities. As in earlier eras, to the extent that education and other social policy initiatives could serve to further that primary mission, fine. To the extent that development and containment conflicted with those other goals, agents knew their jobs and pursued them effectively – and often ruthlessly.

Misleading Indicators, Reservation Style

Personalized and Inconsistent Administration

Differing situations in different areas – with development and local economies, with traders, and with a host of other variables comprising any reservation's existence – led to inconsistent administration across the continent during the reservation era. Tasks were always dictated in some part by the particular reservation context. Among the Upper Sioux at the Sisseton reservation, for example, the agent dealt with an unusual allotment context

36 Quoted in Phillips, *Indians and Indian Agents*, 7; see 70.

37 On discretion generally, see, e.g., Phillips, *Indians and Indian Agents*, 97, 110–11, 117; Meyer, *Santee Sioux*, 152, 226; Bender, *"New Hope,"* 34, 42, 52, 80–1, 96ff., 113, 115.

38 Bender, *"New Hope,"* ch. 2, 96–7.

that included valuable timberland on the reservation, which was located far from the best farmland; the agent recommended splitting allotments so that each Indian received two parcels of land. Even reservations close to each other presented differing circumstances and demanded unique administrative approaches.[39]

Annuities provide an excellent example of how the need for local decisionmaking led to inconsistencies in administration. Annuities were a difficult issue because the government-to-government relationship recommended the payment of annuities to tribal leaders, as a sign of respect for Indian sovereignty and to build good relations. The problem, as the BIA saw it, was that such large payments to a few leaders in any given situation invited corruption and abuses by leaders who might be manipulated by private interests looking to get a piece of the substantial annuity payments. The Bureau tried two methods of avoiding this problem. First, Commissioner Manypenny argued vociferously that annuity payments should not be made in money, but rather they should be made in stock and other goods that would directly serve the Bureau's civilization and education initiatives. At the same time, the Bureau maintained the authority of the field service to make decisions based on local circumstances. Most treaties of the era included a clause allowing the president discretion in establishing the nature of annuity payments to tribes. Despite rules governing the distribution of annuities, local agents exercised their discretion to determine the precise means of distribution. Agents had considerable leeway in deciding the extent to which work done by Indians was a factor in determining distribution of goods and annuities. Agents also controlled the timing of distributions, and the actual method of accomplishing the task. As a result, specific procedures for distributing annuities differed from reservation to reservation. When Indians learned of variations from reservation to reservation, friction and discontent could develop.[40]

Individuals thus continued to be crucial to administration in the reservation era. Proximity of an agent and particular attention to one or another of the reservations under his supervision led to selective attention and service delivery.[41] New agents sometimes altered their predecessor's plans for reservation locations or practices;[42] older agents ran into trouble if their administrative methods rubbed their superiors the wrong way;[43]

39 Meyer, *Santee Sioux*, 209, 210–11; Edward Everett Dale, *The Indians of the Southwest: A Century of Development Under the United States* (Norman: University of Oklahoma Press, 1949).

40 Meyer, *Santee Sioux*, 229–30; Moore, *Chiefs, Agents & Soldiers*, 164; McGillycuddy, *Blood on the Moon*, 133; Neil, "Territorial Governor," 225.

41 E.g., Phillips, *Indians and Indian Agents*, 123ff.

42 E.g., Meyer, *Santee Sioux*, 89–90, 109ff., 211–12, 232ff., 253; Bender, *"New Hope,"* 87, 102ff.; Moore, *Chiefs, Agents & Soldiers*, 59; Neil, "Territorial Governor," 235.

43 Meyer, *Santee Sioux*, 95.

secular administrators ran into tensions with Peace Policy appointees who looked to scripture to guide administration.[44] Personal priorities drove local initiatives.[45]

Personalized administration did not indicate uncontrolled, arbitrary decisionmaking. Nathan Meeker's authoritarian rule and independent decision making among the Utes typified the Indian agent and exemplified the personal role in directing activity in and around the reservation.[46] Yet Meeker justified many of his actions by appealing to the instructions he received from the Interior Department. His decisions grew out of an organizational culture that sought to channel agents' actions in the field but which afforded them great leeway in particular cases. Over time, the multiplication of instructions and the accumulated history of localized decision making allowed agents to justify their actions with a simple appeal to powers outside their own.

Meeker's personal priorities and relationships, like any agent's personal priorities and relationships, could be supported by appeal to discretion or by appeal to explicit rules and instructions. Agent Frank Bennett at the Navajo reservation provides another example of how agents could act, or not, depending on their judgment. Bennett seems to have had no qualms about commandeering a school building to house an agency employee,[47] and he arranged for subsistence supplies to be furnished to the hungry Navajo out of military stores. Yet in a complicated matter involving the Navajo, nearby Utes, and the status of several Navajo women living with Mexicans, Bennett opted *not* to act, choosing instead to tell the involved parties that he would have to wait to get an opinion on the matter from the Commissioner of Indian Affairs. This was the kind of issue that agents like Bennett could resolve if they saw an easy and safe way to do it.[48] But, as in earlier years, in difficult circumstances agents and superintendents could avoid acting by appealing to the delay necessitated by getting instructions from

[44] Bender, *"New Hope,"* xii; Moore, *Chiefs, Agents & Soldiers*, 79ff.; O'Donnell, *Arrow*, ch. 15.

[45] See, e.g., Bender, *"New Hope,"* 17ff., 23; Moore, *Chiefs, Agents & Soldiers*; David J. Wishart, "The Dispossession of the Pawnee," *Annals of the Association of American Geographers* 69 (September 1979), 398; Prucha, *Great Father*, 368–9.

[46] Wilcomb E. Washburn, *The Indian in America* (New York: Harper & Row, 1975), 217. See also Robert L. Whitner, "Grant's Indian Peace Policy on the Yakima Reservation, 1870–82," in Ellis, *The Western American Indian*, 53ff.; Ralph H. Ogle, "The End of Apache Resistance," in Ellis, *The Western American Indian*; David J. Wishart, *An Unspeakable Sadness: The Dispossession of the Nebraska Indians* (Lincoln: University of Nebraska Press, 1994), 105, 122, 205; William T. Hagan, "Squaw Men on the Kiowa, Comanche, and Apache Reservation: Advance Agents of Civilization or Disturbers of the Peace?" in *The Frontier Challenge: Responses to the Trans-Mississippi West*, ed. John G. Clark (Lawrence: The University Press of Kansas, 1971), 192.

[47] Bender, *"New Hope,"* 32.

[48] Ibid., 33–4.

superiors.[49] Prior to suggesting the grazing-in-exchange-for-beef arrangement discussed earlier, P. B. Hunt had refused a request from the cattlemen to lease the land for grazing, which would have been against standing rules; less than two weeks later Hunt suggested the trade of grazing in exchange for beef, even though such a trade also exceeded his explicit authority. Hunt rejected one option because it violated formal rules, and proposed another, also outside the formal rules, because in his judgment of the situation it was justified.

The impact of "squaw men" upon administration provides an example of just how important personalities were in the details of local administration. Squaw men were white men who married Indian women, and they could be troublesome because of vagaries in the distribution of government benefits, complicated administrative and judicial jurisdictions, and the influence these men could wield in tribal politics. Many observers worried that squaw men hindered the Indian Office's civilization goals, and others agreed with Indian agent Thomas Twiss that the propensity of squaw men was to conspire against agents. The historian William T. Hagan found that relations with squaw men depended on the agents, and that a series of changing agents at one reservation encouraged variety in responses and administrative results:

> Between the end of [J. Lee] Hall's administration in 1887 and the opening of the Kiowa, Comanche, and Apache Reservation in 1901, nine different men presided over the destinies of the Indians. All of them faced the problem of the squaw men, and their responses could be anticipated in terms of their general approach to their responsibilities. Those agents who eschewed innovation and were willing to live-and-let-live had the least trouble with intermarried whites. But an agent who conceived of himself as the real guardian of the Indians, or who resented the pressures both subtle and overt that squaw men could bring to bear on him, would soon be fighting to save his job or his authority.[50]

Numerous scholars have described frequent turnover in field personnel and the disruptions this caused in administration, leading to inconsistency, changing priorities, confusion, and the absence of long-term planning. Departing agents sometimes behaved badly and childishly, using up provisions or returning excess cash to the Treasury so as to embarrass the successor and make life more difficult. Agents took agency records and sometimes even the blank forms, leaving incoming agents in difficult circumstances.[51]

[49] See, e.g., Bender, *"New Hope,"* 17–18, 34, 166; Moore, *Chiefs, Agents & Soldiers*, 61–2; Martha Royce Blaine, *Pawnee Passage, 1870–1875* (Norman: University of Oklahoma Press, 1990), 185ff.

[50] Hagan, "Squaw Men," 184; see also Moore, *Chiefs, Agents & Soldiers*, 117ff., 151ff., 174; Olson, *Red Cloud*, 276; Oliphant, "Encroachments," 52.

[51] See Meyer, *Santee Sioux*, 231, 93, ch. 6, 112; Flora Warren Seymour, *Indian Agents of the Old Frontier* (New York: D. Appleton-Century Co., 1941), 26–34 and chs. 7–8; Bender, *"New Hope,"* 143, 153–6; Tate, "John P. Clum," 105; Neil, "Territorial Governor," 220.

More important, changes in agents and personnel often led to changes in the nature of relationships and priorities. An important dynamic in the Meeker case was the inconsistency in administration created by turnover in personnel. The agent who preceded Meeker had had some success with the local Indians. Meeker followed and moved the agency to a new location, where he hoped to put into practice his own principles about agriculture. Meeker's personal role disrupted reservation activities, and contributed directly to an outbreak of violence.[52]

In a study of Indian administration in the Southwest, Edward Everett Dale charts the courses of changing Indian agents, and changing priorities, at a number of reservations after the Civil War. At Navajo, for example, James Miller worked with tribal leaders and secured ad hoc solutions for feeding the Navajo when no appropriation was made to do so; Thomas Keam concentrated on establishing a 130-member police force; W. F. M. Arny concentrated on stock raising and ran into trouble with local squaw men and complained of interference from the military, which had worked closely with Miller and Keam; Alexander Irvine focused on farming and recommended moving the agency to an area with better farming land, and he suggested discontinuing the issuing of rations.[53] The effects of personnel turnovers were not necessarily counterproductive, however. Dale finds that "Despite the evils incident to frequent changes of agents, and regardless of frequent crop shortages due to drought, the economic condition of the Navajo steadily improved. Within fifteen years after leaving Bosque Redondo, they owned more than a million sheep and thirty thousand horses."[54]

Turnover often furthered policy goals. Agents could be replaced in order to effect or justify change. A good example is the removal of Agent Charles Potter among the Omaha, whose reports had been used to obstruct allotment efforts and support opposition to the Dawes Act. Potter's successor, Jesse Warner, was much more politic, working with local forces, building compromise solutions, and paving the ground for allotment. In this case, turnover helped political leaders and administrative superiors effectively pursue policy goals by removing agents who worked against those policies

[52] Prucha, *Great Father*, 542–4. See Fowler, *Arapahoe Politics*, 25, 39, 69ff.; Moore, *Chiefs, Agents & Soldiers*, 55ff., 73, 81, 97, 117, 165, 175, 233, ch. 7; Olson, *Red Cloud*, 266; Utley, *Last Days of the Sioux Nation*, 29ff.; Tate, "John P. Clum," 100; Morgan, "Indian Affairs in Utah," 389, 404; Neil, "Territorial Governor," 231–2.

[53] Dale, *Indians of the Southwest*, ch. 8.

[54] Dale, *Indians of the Southwest*, 124. See, e.g., Meyer, *Santee Sioux*, 177, 209, 231ff. On assumptions here, see Seymour, *Indian Agents*, e.g., ch. 10. Turnover did not necessarily lead to any changes at all (e.g., Moore, *Chiefs, Agents & Soldiers*, 112, 118; Tate, "John P. Clum," 113). An absence of change, as during the Tenure of Office Act, brought problems as well: see Jackson, "Indian Affairs"; Neil, "Territorial Governor," 234.

in an effort to defend Indian communities.[55] Alvin Josephy's account of the Nez Perce provides another good example. There, treaty negotiations were characterized by disagreements between relatively steady Indian leadership, on one hand, and rapidly changing U.S. representation, on the other. U.S. representatives failed to understand the history of Nez Perce–U.S. relations, enabling federal agents to discredit or ignore the nature and details of their predecessors' agreements and promises.[56]

Inconsistency in reservation administration arose from the fact that every reservation circumstance and every administrator contributed to create unique situations, but this inconsistency was a necessary part of the ultimate effectiveness of the reservations in isolating and weakening Indian populations. Turnover and inconsistency do not necessary lead to failure, especially when the policy's goal is to contain and control populations, or even when the tasks at hand require rapid adaptation to volatile circumstances. It is important to remember the underlying goals of reservation policy. Replacing an effective advocate for Indian interests with a new, weak, or green agent – thereby empowering traders and others – furthered policy goals. In such cases uncertainty, confusion, upheaval, the support of key interests – traders, for example – as well as nimbleness all work toward the fulfillment of the policy.

Corruption and Charges *of Maladministration*

Discretion and unique circumstances influenced by personal relationships and local politics shaped Indian affairs administration. These dynamics provided ample opportunity for corruption. They also provided unending opportunity for achieving particular ends by levying *charges* of corruption or mismanagement, regardless of the charges' truth.

Supplying goods to the reservations provided a multimillion dollar opportunity for fraud and corruption. "Indian rings," alliances of local government agents and private contractors, worked to defraud Indians and pocket profits. Dale describes the temptations facing individual agents at distant field posts during the reservation era. Dale is worth quoting at length, as the passage outlines not only the temptation for corruption around the reservations, but also the street-level nuts and bolts of everyday life that multiplied opportunities for corruption – precisely because the agent's job was to effect so many varied aspects of reservation administration.

[55] Boughter, *Betrayal of the Omaha Nation*, ch. 4, especially 116–8. See also, e.g., James C. Olson, "Red Cloud vs. McGillycuddy," in Ellis, *The Western American Indian*.

[56] Josephy, *Nez Perce Indians*, 420ff., 454, 487ff. See also John K. Mahon, *History of the Second Seminole War, 1835–1842* (Gainesville: University of Florida Press, 1992), 85–6, as Wiley Thompson replaces John Phagan and offers Seminoles a bizarre reading of their own history in 1834.

[An] appointment as an Indian agent afforded ample opportunities for graft. Ranchmen pasturing their herds on the public domain along the borders of a reservation were often willing to pay generously for the privilege of grazing their cattle on Indian lands when the pasturage elsewhere became poor. Beef contractors who supplied the Indians with a certain number of animals each week for slaughter sometimes took advantage of the opportunity to turn a dishonest penny by corrupting the agent. Scales were at first seldom available to weigh the cattle, and their weight had to be estimated by the agent or someone appointed by him. If the estimates were consistently too high, who could say that it was not an honest mistake? Any gains accruing to the contractor in such fashion were usually shared with the officials of the federal government who had made them possible. The government undoubtedly paid far more for beef than the Indians received, and this particular form of thievery was very difficult to detect.

The receipt and distribution of other rations or annuity goods gave the dishonest agent an opportunity to increase his income, which he might also augment because he often had on deposit large sums of money in tribal or individual funds. Indian traders were occasionally willing to pay for the privilege of defrauding the Indian, and bootleggers or whiskey peddlers once in a while sought to arrange for protection. Lumber companies or tiemakers might, for a consideration, be permitted to cut timber growing on the reservation, especially if its boundaries were not clearly marked. In short, there were many ways by which a crooked agent could add to his meager salary, and it is in no sense condoning such criminal practices to state that the temptation must at times have been great.[57]

Corruption and collusion between public and private interests could further policy. Nefarious activity could even bind Western communities together socially and politically. The historian Richard White writes that an Indian ring in Dakota Territory united settlers, traders and development interests, the local Republican party, and local BIA representatives in a collusion that funneled federal money to local interests.

Together they created an "Indian ring," in this case an organization designed to exploit the Sioux reservation by stealing supplies, embezzling funds meant for the Indians, and controlling contracts. When in 1878 the secretary of the interior, Carl Schurz, attempted to clean up the administration of Indian affairs, he was roundly attacked by friends of the ring in Dakota, and his efforts were stymied. In one of the oddest charges of persecution in American history, supporters of the ring accused the government of persecuting Episcopalians, since, in the afterglow of Grant's peace policy, Episcopalians still controlled the Sioux agencies. Not only was Henry Livingston, the Sioux agent at Crow Creek, acquitted (a result that reportedly astonished him as much as it did the prosecutors), but the citizens of Yankton also

[57] Dale, *Indians of the Southwest*, 159–60. For examples of corrupt activity, see Fowler, *Arapahoe Politics*, 81; Moore, *Chiefs, Agents & Soldiers*, 154; Joseph B. Herring, *The Enduring Indians of Kansas: A Century and a Half of Acculturation* (Lawrence: University Press of Kansas, 1990), 89–90; Utley, *Last Days of the Sioux Nation*, 95; Neil, "Territorial Governor," 221, esp. n30; O'Donnell, *Arrow*, 170ff.

gave him a sign of their devotion by electing him to the school board while he was on trial.[58]

Contemporary observers of Indian affairs saw Indian rings everywhere. Yet despite widespread charges of corruption and abuse in the Indian service during the reservation era, it was (and is) extremely difficult to identify precisely who was involved in Indian rings, where the rings were, and what they were doing. Earlier, we saw how Agent P. B. Hunt acted on his own discretion to allow cattlemen to use the reservation for grazing their herds, even though this violated policy. Hunt manipulated his authority to get the most out of the situation, arranging for the cattlemen to pay for the special privilege by donating cattle to feed the tribe during a ration crisis. It was a model of ad hoc, localized decision making, balancing powerful forces and humanitarian concern in the midst of a true crisis. The Indian Office's leadership authorized and condoned Hunt's actions after the fact, as it was prone to do when discretion and innovation in the field led to satisfactory outcomes. Yet because he allowed the cattlemen entry onto the reservation, Hunt was later implicated in an "Indian ring" with the cattlemen.[59]

Examples like this fill the pages of reservation era histories. The federal officials who negotiated treaties and maintained largely peaceful relations in California came under heavy criticism for their expenses, their decisions regarding contracts and lands chosen for reservations, and the damage they had done to whites hoping to expand and develop California. In a public debate that took place in the state legislature, California newspapers, and the nation's capital, the agents defended themselves by arguing that the charges laid against them were more artifacts of state politics and interest than they

58 Richard White, *"It's Your Misfortune and None of My Own": A New History of the American West* (Norman: University of Oklahoma Press, 1991), 176; see also Whitner, "Grant's Indian Peace Policy," 57ff.

59 See William T. Hagan, "Kiowas, Comanches, and Cattlemen, 1867–1906: A Case Study of the Failure of U.S. Reservation Policy," in *The American Indian: Essays from Pacific Historical Review*, ed. Norris Hundley (Santa Barbara: Clio Books, 1974). Examples like this are common in reservation histories: see, e.g., Nichols, *Lincoln and the Indians*, at 58–9; Meyer, *Santee Sioux*, at 42, 57ff., 70; Seymour, *Indian Agents*, chs. 1 and 18; Fowler, *Arapahoe Politics*, 35, 52ff.; Moore, *Chiefs, Agents & Soldiers*, 153ff. and ch. 7 generally, 203ff., 218; R. Pierce Beaver, *Church, State, and the American Indians: Two and a Half Centuries of Partnership in Missions Between Protestant Churches and Government* (St. Louis: Concordia, 1966), 146ff.; documents reprinted in Robert F. Heizer, ed., *The Destruction of California Indians* (Lincoln: University of Nebraska Press, 1993 [1974]), 166ff. Olson, *Red Cloud*, 284. For an interesting perspective from the wife of embattled Sioux agent Valentine McGillycuddy, see McGillycuddy, *Blood on the Moon*, esp. chs. 19–23; Tate, "John P. Clum," 105. Charges often followed territorial governors, as well, and often as a result of their role in Indian affairs. See, e.g., Jackson, "Indian Affairs," 319; Neil, "Territorial Governor," 221, 233, and 233 n66. Neil acknowledges that "Allegations of widespread corruption abound, but actual cases ferreted out which can stand up under scrutiny are remarkably few." Neil, "Territorial Governor," 221. See also O'Donnell, *Arrow*, 142.

were reflections of what had taken place in the early years of California's Indian policy.[60] The practice of complaining about agents continued into the Peace Policy era, with the addition of religious denominations competing alternately to praise or discredit various agents and secure control of reservation administration.[61] Amos Bruce, agent to the Santee Sioux, survived in his job despite charges brought by a Methodist missionary that he favored Catholics, and despite charges brought by independent traders that he favored licensed traders.[62] Robert Murphy suffered similar charges from traders, and Roy Meyer acknowledges that such charges "may have undermined his position and thus prepared the way for his eventual dismissal" in 1856, when Murphy was replaced during an administrative reorganization by Charles Flandrau, another experienced hand through years as a trader. Meyer implies that the charges against Murphy were probably of the same type that dogged agents across the continent, driven by unhappy interests more than by intentional or gross maladministration.[63] Agents at the Santee's Niobrara reservation were investigated due to complaints by Indians and others, but investigators found no evidence of dishonesty.[64] Political motives animated charges in the 1870s against the agent in charge of the Flandreau colony in South Dakota.[65] Charges against a teacher at Flandreau turned out to have been driven by the mother of the teacher's eventual replacement, and some of the signatures on the petition to have the teacher removed were forgeries.[66]

An example of the frequency of rumor and charges, and of the commensurate difficulty of assessing agents' actions, is offered by J. B. Harrison, who had traveled to the Pine Ridge agency in the Dakotas and had this to say about embattled and controversial agent Valentine McGillicuddy:

> The former agent, Dr. McGillicuddy, had just left the reservation when I was at Pine Ridge and I did not see him, but the people of the country were unanimous in praise

[60] See Phillips, *Indians and Indian Agents*, especially ch. 10.

[61] See Meyer, *Santee Sioux*, 204ff., 287–9; Bender, "*New Hope*," 15, 97ff., 132ff., 152; Seymour, *Indian Agents*, ch. 4.

[62] Meyer, *Santee Sioux*, 69–70, 70 n51.

[63] Ibid., 94–5.

[64] Ibid., 184.

[65] Ibid., 250ff.

[66] Meyer, *Santee Sioux*, 257. See Boughter, *Betrayal of the Omaha Nation*, ch. 3, especially 81ff. for more examples, as well as Josephy, *Nez Perce Indians*, 458ff.; Beeton, "Teach Them," 307–8, 313; Hoopes, *Indian Affairs*, 46, 55, 64ff., 70. See also Earl S. Pomeroy, *The Territories and the United States, 1861–1890: Studies in Colonial Administration* (Seattle: University of Washington Press, 1947), 19–20; Lucile Kane, "Federal Protection of Public Timber in the Upper Great Lakes States," *Agricultural History* 23 (1949), reprinted in Vernon Carstensen, ed., *The Public Lands: Studies in the History of the Public Domain* (Madison: University of Wisconsin Press, 1968), 440–6; Harold H. Dunham, "Some Crucial Years of the General Land Office, 1875–1890," *Agricultural History* 11 (1937), reprinted in Carstensen, *Public Lands*.

of his effective, intelligent, and just administration; but some months afterward, in Montana and Washington territory, I began to hear from the east all kinds of rumors about Dr. McGillicuddy's accounts being wrong and his having made vast sums of money out of rations which the Indians were not numerous enough to use. As there is no way in which an agent could possibly appropriate Indian rations to his own use beyond the number he could pick up and eat, the real impropriety of the agent at Pine Ridge must have been of a different character. One hears in the Indian country all kinds of vague, incoherent and absurd rumors about everybody.[67]

This is a telling passage. Not only is the author aware of the prevalence of rumor and the diversity of interests involved in Indian affairs, he refuses to suggest that the criticism of McGillicuddy is unfounded – he leaves open the possibility that McGillicuddy might have done something *different* that had caused controversy. Moreover, it is entirely possible that both sets of conclusions about McGillicuddy were right – the people in proximity to him, especially whites, may have been very happy with the agent *because* his accounts were wrong or because he was stealing provisions.

The difficulty of evaluating charges is a persistent obstacle in assessing the degree and pervasiveness of corruption and maladministration at the BIA in any given era. Agents were criticized by their successors, in efforts to condemn predecessors as well as to lay groundwork for the "success" of the new agent. Agents complained that charges against them were brought merely to harass or discredit them in the eyes of the BIA or among Indians.[68] The historian Ronald Satz notes that Indian Office regulations, even after the composite printing in 1850, left broad areas for confusion, double constructions, and inapplicability. Satz sees this as a factor creating confusion and inconsistency in the field service as well as evidence of the split between the headquarters level and the field service, but it can also be seen as evidence of the ramifications of administration based on local decision making and a culture of discretionary authority. Satz writes, "[E]ven honest agents might become subject to censure 'entirely through ignorance for the want of [specific] instructions.'"[69] Commissioner Francis Walker recognized that agents could be criticized merely because they were in the middle of intratribal politics.[70]

67 Quoted in Seymour, *Indian Agents*, 323; see also ch. 16.

68 Olson, "Red Cloud vs. McGillycuddy," 101ff., 112ff.; Hagan, "Kiowas, Comanches, and Cattlemen," 96ff. Donald J. Berthrong, "Federal Indian Policy and the Southern Cheyennes and Arapahoes, 1887–1907," in Ellis, *Western American Indian*, 135; David J. Wishart, *An Unspeakable Sadness*, ch. 5.

69 Ronald N. Satz, *American Indian Policy in the Jacksonian Era* (Lincoln: University of Nebraska Press, 1975), 190.

70 See Miner, "Walker," 138; see also Fowler, *Arapahoe Politics*, 67ff.; Moore, *Chiefs, Agents & Soldiers*, 95–6, 97, 159 and ch. 7 generally, 232; Olson, *Red Cloud*, 266–7 and ch. 14 generally; McGillycuddy, *Blood on the Moon*, 221; James McLaughlin, *My Friend the Indian* (Lincoln: University of Nebraska Press, 1989 [1910]), 275; Tate, "John P. Clum,"

The Bureau faced a series of investigations, special commissions, and ad hoc investigations, oftentimes with the leadership's support or acquiescence. These commissions were often counterproductive, just as they had been during removal, in that they had a tendency to be politically motivated and they provided another path for individuals and interests to challenge the decision making of field agents and thereby undercut their authority. Perhaps the most influential investigation into Indian affairs after the Civil War was the Doolittle Committee, consisting of three U.S. senators and four congressional representatives. Formed in 1865 and named for its chairman, the Doolittle Committee toured the West and distributed a detailed questionnaire to agents and others involved in Indian affairs. The Committee crafted a devastatingly critical report of Indian affairs in the field. An appendix to the report repeated numerous complaints of fraud, abuse, and mismanagement in the service. The Committee recommended the creation of a system of inspection districts and committees to police Indian affairs, and the report galvanized public opinion in the East. Reformers and others seized on its portrait of an out-of-control administration to demand change. When a series of violent Western conflicts erupted soon after the Committee issued its report, public attention focused on Indian affairs, leading to renewed calls for transfer of the Bureau's responsibilities to the military and, eventually, to the reform efforts of the Peace Policy.[71]

Yet the Doolittle Committee, like others before and after, was mired in politics and recriminations both in the field and in the capital. The motives of its commissioners and the motives of their sources in the field were deeply suspect, and the evidence uncovered about abuses and maladministration in the Indian service proved extremely unreliable. The historian Francis Paul Prucha writes that "Its bulky appendix was full of charges of fraud and corruption indicating the need for a new policy. The statements were inconsistent, the charges often unsubstantiated, and the facts many times in error."[72] Release of aspects of the report, often through leaks to the press, allowed the flawed report to be used for political gain in a variety of circumstances. Interests critical of local administration or of the BIA generally – for whatever reason, and there were many – used the Committee and the report, and manipulated the release of information, so as to condemn the Indian Office and perpetuate its reputation for failure and abuse.[73]

105, 108; Spores, "Too Small a Place," 189; Morgan, "Indian Affairs in Utah," 388, 391; O'Donnell, *Arrow*, 140–2, ch. 12, 290.

[71] See Bender, "*New Hope,*" 3.

[72] Prucha, *Great Father*, 486–7.

[73] Harry Kelsey, "The Doolittle Report of 1867: Its Preparation and Shortcomings," *Arizona and the West* 17 (Summer 1975). See also Meyer, *Santee Sioux*, 87; Bender, "*New Hope,*" ch. 1. Donald Chaput provides a review of the Doolittle Committee and its report, along with an analysis that accepts many of the report's findings and conclusions at face value. Donald Chaput, "Generals, Indian Agents, Politicians: The Doolittle Survey of 1865," *The*

In short, Indian field service agents existed in a monumentally difficult position: they faced complicated and conflicting administrative obligations, and had to try to pursue those responsibilities in a position made vulnerable by numerous highly motivated and competing interests. In 1903, Indian Commissioner Francis Leupp offered some sympathy for the Indian agent's precarious position in a statement defending an agent against charges leveled by Indians and a U.S. senator:

> When an agent has sat in one swivel chair for four consecutive years, practically every day from eight in the morning 'til five in the evening, hearing complaints, issuing orders, writing letters, opening bids, signing leases, supervising accounts, drawing checks, settling domestic disputes, exercising the functions of a guardian for orphan children, unravelling the intricacies of heirship... adjusting debts and credits between individual Indians, preparing cases for the prosecution of dram sellers or the ejection of intruders, devising forms for legal instruments which will save some remnant for the Indian after the white man gets through stripping him – performing these and a hundred other kindred duties day in and day out – who will cast the first stone at him if his spirit revolts now and then.... How many men in private life could endure such an unremitting grind as this, and meet with a smile a daily accusation of fraud, conspiracy, and misappropriation of funds, often from the very persons whose poor little possessions he is trying to save for them?[74]

Almost fifty years earlier, in 1856, the agent on the Upper Platte described the vulnerable position of the field agent in a manner which might have been written in 1806 or 1906, and which was true even in 2006. After condemning the character of most Western settlers as fugitive escapees from organized society, and reviewing the ways in which they manipulated Indians and "allure them to ruin step by step," the agent outlined the perils of the field officer:

> It may be asked by those unacquainted with the Indian country why this state of things is permitted to exist for a day; or why are not the humane and benevolent intentions of Congress, as enacted in the laws regulating trade and intercourse with the Indian tribes, enforced; and why are the orders and instructions of the Department of the Interior disregarded? I reply, for the simple and plain reason, that the Indian agent, your executive and administrative officer, is powerless to control these matters. If he attempts to execute and enforce the laws, he is Assailed by these men, claiming *citizenship*, with a force – an outside pressure, greater than the power of the throne itself. They form conspiracies against him, and hold talks with the Indians, the object of which is to make them discontented with the agent, and disaffected towards the government, should the department decline to comply with their demands to remove the unpopular agent. I have no intention to magnify these practices, fraught with such

Western Historical Quarterly 3 (July 1972). On administration at the Board of Indian Commissioners, see Bender, "*New Hope*," 6.

74 Quoted in William T. Hagan, "Adjusting to the Opening of the Kiowa, Comanche, and Kiowa-Apache Reservation," in *The Plains Indians of the Twentieth Century*, ed. Peter Iverson (Norman: University of Oklahoma Press, 1985), 25–6.

imminent peril, and tending to disturb the peace and tranquility of, and endanger the lives of the official agents of the department, and other whites, in the Indian country.[75]

The historian Roy Meyer makes the point more simply, writing of Agent Joseph Brown and the Minnesota Sioux in the years before the 1862 uprising: "The more successful Brown was in his efforts to make farmers out of the Indians, the more opposition was stirred up and the more violent it became."[76] Observers may have seen Indian rings everywhere, but it is far from clear that they actually *were* everywhere. And in those places where the rings existed and influenced administration, it is likely that they furthered, rather than retarded, the government's aims.

Interests, Politics, and Stress

Perhaps more than any other era, the reservation years illustrate the BIA's ability to adapt to new and changing interests in a volatile policy environment. Throughout the middle years of the nineteenth century, the Bureau repeatedly adapted its vision of the West and of Indian country to fit new circumstances and to satisfy new regional and local interests, all the while maintaining attention to tribal interests and also to the demands of humanitarian concerns. As in earlier eras, Indian policy promised all things to all interests. For developers and expansionists, cheap land and special deals for railroads, extraction industries, loggers, cattlemen, and so on; for tribes, continued existence in the West, protected by the federal government; for humanitarians, commitments to civilization and education; for white settlers, commitment to containment of Indian populations and a cost-effective defense. It all looked good on paper.

The Indian service tried to maintain good relations with all of these parties. At the local level, the Bureau's agents tried to forge alliances with local interests. Development interests demanded the breakup of tribal landholdings to facilitate expansion and settlement, for example, and years before the formal beginning of the allotment era the BIA allied with interests favoring the division of reservations and the allotment of land to individual Indians. The BIA's efforts to accommodate these interests is not surprising. The historian H. Craig Miner emphasizes the ability of developers and federal agents (including but not limited to the BIA) to negotiate satisfactory solutions

[75] Quoted in Laurence F. Schmeckebier, *The Office of Indian Affairs: Its History, Activities and Organization* (Baltimore: The Johns Hopkins Press, 1927), 45.

[76] Meyer, *Santee Sioux*, 108. See also Moore, *Chiefs, Agents & Soldiers*, ch. 3; Crook to Mackall, December 25, 1857, reprinted in Heizer, *Destruction*, 109; Harmon, "Indian Policy in Texas," 402–3; Morgan, "Indian Affairs in Utah," 389; O'Donnell, *Arrow*, 181, 278.

dependent upon local circumstances and local politics in the half-century after the Civil War.[77] Indian Office personnel shrank existing reservations, allotted lands in severalty, and leased tribal lands for grazing in the hope that clearing formal titles and dispensing lands would satisfy white settlers and other non-Indian interests while protecting Indians from potential threats.

Commissioners repeatedly professed an allegiance to civilization initiatives in the West, thereby building and maintaining relations that reflected the important role being played by humanitarian interests and "friends of the Indian." Many commissioners had backgrounds and political experience that tied them to development interests and the dominant political parties, but the policy direction of the nineteenth century's second half also reflected ties between the Indian Office and reformers, particularly religious organizations and "friends of the Indian" after the Civil War. The Peace Policy in particular aimed at keeping Indians on reservations while improving Indian lives through a commitment to civilization initiatives like education, and the active and subsidized participation of religious groups to help civilize the Indians and help agents deliver services.

Diverse interests with conflicting objectives coalesced behind reservation policy, just as diverse interests with a variety of motives – from tribes to greedy Southerners to humanitarian reformers from the Northeast – had forged consensus behind the factory system and removal policy. In the reservation era, containment and isolation provided the point of agreement for a variety of interests and motives. Humanitarians could argue that segregation from the negative influence of whites, protection from alcohol traders, and security in even substandard lands all worked toward their goals of educating and civilizing the Indians. Likewise, land developers and speculators could get on board with reservations as a way of carefully containing Indians, freeing up lands, and increasing pressure for allotments that would free even more land. Expansionists could point to the usefulness of reservations in clearing paths and making the western journey and development safe for whites. Containment and isolation could even be supported by Indians, persuaded that they could survive and even thrive through segregation from whites and the ever-present promise of perpetual rights to their land. Reformers, railroad barons, miners, tribes, individual Indians – there were separate rationales for each of these and for subsets within the general groupings, but they could all agree that a policy of containment on reservations served their ends. The point of the reservation era, and the goal pursued by

77 H. Craig Miner, *The Corporation and the Indian: Tribal Sovereignty and Industrial Civilization, 1865–1907* (Norman: University of Oklahoma Press, 1976), 215; see also, e.g., William W. Savage Jr., *The Cherokee Strip Live Stock Association: Federal Regulation and the Cattleman's Last Frontier* (Columbia: University of Missouri Press, 1973).

its administrators, was containment and isolation – in service of a variety of ends, on behalf of a variety of interests.[78]

As always, civil administration was understood to be more cost effective than extermination or violent military engagement, so interests concerned about economy could agree on reservations, too. From the days of the Washington administration, the cost of Indian affairs in blood and treasure had recommended civilian policies over military solutions: factories and treaties were less expensive than war. This remained the government's official thinking before the Civil War. California provides one good example: in 1851, three commissioners completed 18 treaties with 139 bands and tribes, involving 12,000 square miles of California land. The treaties promoted a reservation system, on which Indians would be taught how to farm and subsist on government rations. The California commissioners acknowledged that "It is, in the end, cheaper to feed the whole flock for a year than to fight them for a week."[79] Even in the wake of the Minnesota uprising of 1862, advocates of exterminating the Indians were a decided minority among policymakers.[80] As usual, the government opted for treaties, removals, and reservations, and not for extermination or for military conflict itself as a starting point. Special Indian agent E. B. Chandler put it into a familiar form: "The alternative of feeding or fighting the Indians must soon be chosen; and economy, as well as justice, would dictate the adoption of the former policy."[81] Similar activities and speed characterized affairs in New Mexico, Oregon, and Washington, as territorial governors and treaty commissioners worked to quiet title and consolidate and contain Indian populations.[82] After the Civil War, Commissioner Nathaniel Taylor restated the position, arguing that peace could have been achieved more quickly and with less expense in the West through civilian measures instead of military conflict – he contrasted his estimate of

78 For a thorough discussion of California's debate over removal and reservation policy, see Phillips, *Indians and Indian Agents*, ch. 10.

79 Quoted in Robert M. Utley, *The Indian Frontier of the American West, 1846–1890* (Albuquerque: University of New Mexico Press, 1984), 52. For more on California, see Phillips, *Indians and Indian Agents*, 65, 66, 95, 165, 173, 181–2; "Annual Report of the Commissioner of Indian Affairs," 1858, reprinted in Prucha, *Documents*, 92–5; Hoopes, *Indian Affairs*, ch. 3 and 44ff.

80 Meyer, *Santee Sioux*, 141. See Spores, "Too Small a Place," 173; 1856 newspaper article reprinted in Heizer, *Destruction*, 205; Neil, "Territorial Governor," 218–19, 236–7; O'Donnell, *Arrow*, 136–7.

81 Quoted in John J. Killoren, *"Come, Blackrobe": De Smet and the Indian Tragedy* (Norman: University of Oklahoma Press, 1994), 284.

82 Utley, *Indian Frontier*, 52–3 and ch. 2 generally. On Washington, see Stevens treaties discussed in Josephy, *Nez Perce Indians*, 310ff., and the essays in Clifford E. Trafzer, ed., *Indians, Superintendents, and Councils: Northwestern Indian Policy, 1850–1855* (Lanham, MD: University Press of America, 1986).

$250,000 to attain peace with the $5,000,000 he said had been spent by the military in pursuing Southern Cheyennes.[83]

Throughout the nineteenth century the debate raged on, with many arguing for more muscular frontier policies, more aggressive military action, and the cutting of costs for things like treaties, blankets, provisions, and farming equipment. General John Sanborn noted after the Fetterman massacre that while general public sentiment did not favor a war policy, it was the preference of plains ranchmen, army contractors, and some officers (who he believed were controlled by the ranchers and contractors).[84] General N. B. Buford noted, in 1867, "Nine-tenths of all the business that is being done on the route [to the West] is paid for by the government. At least two-thirds of the entire business of the Union Pacific railroad is for carrying troops and army supplies. Its employees are all for war."[85] Yet the government's policy stood firm: peace, order, and civilian administration would outgun Westerners' calls for extermination of the Indians.

Reservations were conceived as satisfying all of these diverse interests with comprehensive solutions that promised rapid advances, yet reservations also offered mixed messages and confused demands. The policy sought to advance assimilation by segregating Indians and subjecting them to the policies of the Indian Office and, for a time, missionaries in charge of local agencies. Field administrators worked on behalf of development interests to resolve conflicts and promote development goals, even as they simultaneously tried to protect Indian populations and encourage "progress" among them. The Peace Policy made religious organizations clients of the Indian service, as local agencies were apportioned among the groups and the groups themselves were empowered to nominate and in effect appoint local administrators and employees.

Yet the denominations themselves quarreled, as did developers, Indians, humanitarians, and everybody else. The kaleidoscope of interests involved in Indian affairs through the reservation era often had motive to criticize or condemn individual agents regardless of whether their decisions were just or reasonable. The careful and opportunistic use of formal instructions and discretionary authority, and real instances of maladministration and abuse, made the administrative environment facing any field agent precarious. There was no way the Indian Office could ever have satisfied all of these

83 William E. Unrau, "Nathaniel Green Taylor," in Kvasnicka and Viola, *Commissioners*, 117–18. See the calculations by Taylor and Walker, in Prucha, *Documents*, 138; Phillips, *Indians and Indian Agents*, 98ff., 156. Typical instances of the civil-military relationship in the field are included in Moore, *Chiefs, Agents & Soldiers*, 42, 233; McCoy, "Special Indian Agency," 361; Tate, "John P. Clum," 103–4; Neil, "Territorial Governor," 231–2.

84 Quoted in Killoren, *"Come, Blackrobe,"* 280.

85 Quoted in Killoren, *"Come, Blackrobe,"* 281. See also McPherson, *Northern Navajo Frontier*, 65; Neil, "Territorial Governor," 228–9.

interests simultaneously and, as in earlier eras, these interests expressed their unhappiness and displeasure by criticizing the agency and its people at any opportunity.

The BIA was stressed, receiving conflicting cues from Congress, the president, and the courts. The controversy surrounding removal of the relatively small and peaceful Ponca tribe from their treaty-guaranteed reservation in northeastern Nebraska offers a good illustration of the conflicting cues operating in Indian affairs. The federal government deeded the Ponca's reservation to the Sioux and encouraged Brule Sioux to locate there; the Poncas were to be removed to Indian Territory in 1877. Ignorant of their impending removal until the arrival of a removal agent, opposition by the Ponca led to soldiers being called in to force the tribe to move. With no preparations made for removal or for their arrival in Indian territory, many people died on the journey. Settling on the Omaha reservation without permission, the survivors were arrested by the military and ordered to move back to Indian Territory. A court strategy mounted in the Poncas' defense earned the Poncas' release, and a subsequent investigation ordered by President Hayes led to a congressional appropriation to compensate the Poncas for their losses.[86]

The Ponca case attracted an unusual amount of public notice, but the position of the BIA and the involvement of a host of interests is fairly typical of the era. Ponca removal was driven by the general effort to concentrate Indians in the Indian territory. Commissioner of Indian Affairs Ezra Hayt argued, nevertheless, that the Poncas had been wronged and that they should be compensated. Congress at first paid no heed to his opinions. Humanitarian opponents of the government's treatment of the Ponca, including author and activist Helen Hunt Jackson, then targeted new Interior Secretary Carl Schurz. Schurz first blocked an effort to get the Ponca case to the Supreme Court, an effort led by reformers and supported openly by the governor of Massachusetts. Senator Henry Dawes of Massachusetts attacked Schurz and implied that Schurz favored the removal of the Ponca and may have been involved in plotting the shooting death of a prominent Ponca in 1879. A special Senate committee investigating the entire affair advocated returning the Indians to their old home, but a minority of the committee submitted a report aligning with Schurz's view that the Ponca should be kept in Indian Territory. President Hayes convened a special commission to meet with the Poncas; the president's commission recommended leaving the Poncas in Indian Territory but providing for those who had fled back to their old reservation. Hayes pushed this recommendation through Congress.

Administration of Indian affairs in the Ponca case was buffeted first by the general policy demand to consolidate Indians in Indian Territory; this led to the abrogation of the earlier treaty agreement by which the government was

[86] See Angie Debo, *A History of the Indians of the United States* (Norman: University of Oklahoma Press, 1970), 210–2; Prucha, *Great Father*, 566ff.

bound, and then to removal. Administration was then buffeted by concern generated by publicity and by orders of a federal court to release Indians who had violated government orders implementing the removal and resettlement policy; then by the involvement of humanitarians in the East who demanded further court action; then by competing interests in Congress and the executive, each investigating affairs and advocating different solutions to the problem; and finally by the creation of a solution that did not fully support either the removal and concentration policy or the argument for full restitution. The Indian Office received a variety of cues from government institutions as well as demands from interests outside of government, only to settle on a compromise worked out under specific circumstances that offered little help in dealing with other cases.[87]

Conclusion

Throughout the reservation era, charges followed Indian service personnel and the BIA itself – charges that were sometimes justified and sometimes not. Repeatedly the agency came under fire, under the eye of investigatory bodies, under threat of its duties being reassigned to the military. The BIA defended itself against such charges and maintained its autonomy, as we will see, yet the charges and the image of an incompetent agency stuck. Just as in the factory system and the days of removal, federal agents and the bureaucracy looked ineffective and incompetent even as they achieved their mission – here, containing and subjugating Indian populations – and even as the BIA continued to function as an active, energetic, and innovative federal agency engaged in a diverse array of contexts.

As in earlier eras, policy began to attract new forces and strike out in new directions as the era moved gradually on. The factory system's effects evolved slowly into removal; removals evolved slowly and naturally into reservations, and big reservations evolved into a network of smaller reservations. With time, new interests highlighted apparent failings in the reservation system and its administration, like the Ponca case, and argued successfully that reservations only served to prop up outdated and harmful tribal governments. These new interests would condemn the policies and efforts of the BIA, arguing that breaking up the tribal land mass into individual allotments, and destroying tribes as political entities, was the only way to make the land productive and turn Indians toward "civilization." As reservations

[87] *Standing Bear* v. *Crook* was ignored by field operatives and the BIA hierarchy less than ten years later, when a similar circumstance involved the Sacs and Foxes. Herring, "Indian Intransigency," also 187, 198. See also Claudio Saunt, "The Paradox of Freedom: Tribal Sovereignty and Emancipation during the Reconstruction of Indian Territory," *The Journal of Southern History* 70 (February 2004); Sidney L. Harring, *Crow Dog's Case: American Indian Sovereignty, Tribal Law, and United States Law in the Nineteenth Century* (Cambridge: Cambridge University Press, 1994), ch. 6.

shrank, as whites appropriated the land, as roads and rails crisscrossed the West, and as Indians and their communities weakened, those who had supported the reservations faded away in satisfaction or defeat, leaving the next era to the leadership of forces pursuing general land allotment as the way to solve the Indian problem.

Congress committed the nation to full-scale allotment with passage of the Dawes Act in 1887. As in the past, the forces administering allotment – the Indian service, the land offices, local, state, and federal administrative agencies, legislatures, and courts – would prove effective. Allotment would cost Native Americans two-thirds of the lands they'd managed to keep until allotment began in earnest, before this latest tragically effective administrative endeavor was brought to a close during the New Deal. Effective dispossession through allotment is a signal example of just how effective the reservations were at containing, isolating, and weakening American Indian communities, setting them up for the next step in the careful, planned administration of federal policy toward American Indians.

Conclusion

The Myth of Limited Government

Toni Morrison has said that studying American history without recognition of the experience of Africans and African Americans renders American history "incoherent." The same can be said about Native Americans and Indian affairs. Studying the federal government in the nineteenth century – its activities, its development, its relative strengths and weaknesses, and its institutions – without carefully and thoroughly considering the exhausting requirements of westward expansion, the single most important function of that government, is absurd. Studying expansion without carefully and thoroughly considering the role of American Indians and tribes renders American political development incoherent. To recognize the administrative requirements of expansion is to replace the movie myth of the West with a real sense of the scope and activity of the national government from the founding through the nineteenth century. To do so is to erase the myth of limited government.

In Chapter 1, I defined big government loosely as the combination of (1) national, programmatic social, economic, trade, and regulatory policies touching the lives of millions; (2) the bureaucratic capacity, discretionary authority, and administrative autonomy to plan, to innovate, and to effectively implement policies and programs; and (3) an awareness, a sense of the state, seamlessly and inextricably woven into the fabric of everyday life and never far from the consciousness and activity of American society. Big government won the West.

Bureaucratic Capacity and Autonomy

The effective implementation of managed expansion reveals the federal bureaucracy's reliance upon discretionary authority exercised by field agents in the executive branch, the ability to plan and to innovate, and the autonomy characteristic of modern bureaucratic agencies.

The Indian Office and the Illusion of Incompetence

Beginning in the early republic, civil administration – not military force and not simple, unsupervised demographics – conquered the North American continent and its millions of inhabitants. In each major era of Indian policy, the Indian Office effectively pursued and achieved its missions. In the early republic, the factory system in the War Department effectively controlled relations with Indians on the frontier, driving the lucrative fur trade into the control of large and accountable major firms while limiting the potential for costly conflicts that would threaten the new nation's survival. In the 1830s, the federal government oversaw the forced removal of tens of thousands of American Indians, relocating them on administratively manageable reservations West of the Mississippi River. Throughout the heart of the nineteenth century, the federal government isolated and contained Indians in these reservations and on areas in the newly acquired West, extending federal jurisdiction and administrative structures into new areas and finally across the continent. Through all of these years, the federal government implemented a tremendous land transfer program, through treaties and through the allotment of millions of acres of tribal lands to individual Indian and non-Indian landowners. In each era, social policies extended goods and services to Indian populations, opened and administered reservation and off-reservation schools, initiated training and vocational programs, undertook programs in health care, and developed infrastructure and natural resources.

Field service agents performed endlessly diverse and constantly multiplying tasks to keep the peace, keep the factories running, and obtain lands through federal treaties; to keep the peace, sign removal treaties, and remove Indians to the West; to isolate Indians on administratively manageable reservations; and to dispossess those Indians of their remaining lands. Factors and agents at the Indian Office and in other agencies maintained furs and records, enforced trade and social regulations, negotiated treaties, implemented contracts, promoted social policies in education, housing, and health care, secured provisions, supplied security, enforced policing functions, maintained boundaries, initiated police forces and court systems, ran prisons and detention camps, oversaw purchasing and provisioning systems, implemented licensing, and managed land transfers. Tasks also involved an almost endless series of ad hoc measures undertaken to pursue the agency's mission, and the complexity of the field service's charge channeled some tasks to specialized personnel like factors, translators, teachers, school superintendents, forestry experts, and irrigation specialists.

Discretionary authority and a commitment to localized decision making allowed the field service to achieve the primary goals of Indian policy in the nineteenth century, even while dealing with diverse tribes and unfamiliar, constantly shifting political relationships. The treaty system – driven by political necessity and by respect for the power and sovereignty of Indian communities, especially in its early years – instantly made Indian affairs administration reliant upon the actions of dedicated individuals in unique, localized circumstances. The federal government was unable to dictate treaties and their terms to Indian nations following the Revolution, and it was fruitless and even counterproductive to try to standardize treaties and the treaty making process. Nationalization of Indian affairs and administration quickly committed the United States to piecemeal expansion treaties based on particular and changing circumstances and particular relationships with Indian tribes. The Indian Office's leaders were far too distant from the explosive action on the moving frontier – whether that frontier was Georgia in 1805, Arkansas in 1835, California in 1845, or the Dakotas in 1875 – to micromanage responses to rapidly changing events.

Indian Office leaders tried to standardize routine operations and control individual behavior as best they could, but from the opening days of United States Indian policy leaders in the capital understood and accepted the need for important decisions to be made at the discretion of field agents. The slow rate of communication, the mixed signals field personnel received as to who should receive their reports, the absence of stiff penalties for failing to follow formal directions, and the encouragement of innovation and creative problem solving – and field agents' embrace of their discretionary authority – all helped create an organizational culture based on local decision making. Local decision making and the exercise of discretionary authority were explicitly encouraged in formal instructions and guidelines. Accumulation of ad hoc decisions made at the local level further precluded uniformity and standardization in administration. The clarity of the Indian service's primary missions is such an important part of its effectiveness precisely because it gave to field agents a clear understanding of overall objectives when the leadership could not possibly foresee all, or even most, questions that would arise in the field.[1]

High expectations for solving "the Indian problem" encouraged interests involved in Indian policy to see themselves as the rightful beneficiaries of Indian policy and the primary client of the Indian Office. The Bureau of Indian Affairs and other federal entities responded to rapidly shifting political and administrative environments as the nation moved West and as the interests involved in frontier affairs evolved and developed. Fur traders and land companies gave way to railroad and mining companies, settlement interests, farmers, and Western developers. Affairs with eastern tribes grew to encompass tribes of the Southwest, the Northwest, California, and the Great Plains. Missionary societies looking to save and improve individual Indians in the Southeast and Old Northwest were followed by philanthropic

[1] James Q. Wilson, *Bureaucracy: What Government Agencies Do and Why They Do It* (New York: Basic Books, 1989); Anne M. Khademian, *Working with Culture: The Way the Job Gets Done in Public Programs* (Washington, DC: CQ Press, 2002); Herbert Kaufman, *The Forest Ranger: A Study in Administrative Behavior* (Washington, DC: RFF Press, 2006).

humanitarians and nonsectarian Friends of the Indian. The BIA developed in response to these evolving interests and to the new challenges brought on by acquisition of new territories in the Great Plains, Texas, Arizona, New Mexico, California, Washington, Oregon, and eventually Alaska and Hawaii. The ever-changing environment, though, repeatedly separated the Indian Office from consistent political allies. Former allies could not be counted upon to support the agency when it was criticized, and those groups with a vested interest in older policies were often unwilling to defend those policies against new, energized, and more dynamic forces entering the field of Indian affairs. Interests satisfied with the outcome of Indian policy and administration tended to quit the field, leaving dissatisfied older interests and interested newcomers to pressure the Indian Office for change. This changing roster of players prevented the Indian Office from relying on powerful allies for more than a decade or two at a time.

Each set of interests, whether oriented toward development and expansion, tribal interests, or the interests of individual Indians – and any particular element within those groupings – was free at any point to work through the presidency, Congress, or the courts – and also free to work through state and local venues – to influence the development of policy and the course of administration. Interests attempted to influence Indian affairs policy and administration through a variety of avenues, often as they responded to what they believed to be the failure of the Indian Office to meet its objectives. It is thus not always a corrupt Indian field service that led to charges of abuse and maladministration in Indian affairs policy and administration. The nature of Indian affairs and American politics provided incentives to criticize and condemn even the best agents and most successful administrators. Those administrators who defended Indian interests best, in fact, often attracted the most vehement complaints.

Because it was asked to administer national policies in so many sensitive and diverse contexts, and to be responsive to so many interests both inside and outside of government, exaggerated expectations and the political incentives for castigating the BIA and its agents have obscured the effectiveness with which agency administrators carried out their primary responsibilities in the nineteenth century. These dynamics also obscure the fact that the Indian Office's actions exhibit what is commonly thought of as autonomy, in a very modern sense. Indian Office policies and the actions of its agents sat in opposition to congressional interests and local populations in numerous situations: when it administered treaties without a direct role for the House of Representatives, sparking the end of treaty making in 1871; when it supported reservations over removals; when it promoted reservation police forces; when it refused to pay depredation claims, at times in order to protect funds to be used for Indian annuities; when it worked to extend federal criminal justice administration into Indian country; when it led administration in the new Alaska territory; when it held Indians in prison camps; when it promoted and administered tribal landholding, education, and health care. All of these offended key interests, who often proved unable to control or command the Indian service's personnel.[2]

Defending Organizational Autonomy

Throughout the nineteenth century, the Indian Office defended its autonomy against efforts to transfer its duties to the military, against investigatory bodies and other special commissions, against policy changes, and against personnel reforms.

The Indian Office defended its autonomy against efforts to transfer its duties to the military by appealing to its expertise as a specialized agency involved in an arcane and complicated policy field. The BIA's repeated successes in this battle speak to the nation's enduring commitment to a managed conquest of the continent – an expansion that, for all its peril, would be overseen primarily by civilian administrators operating within a systematic administrative environment. From the factory system forward, the civilian service presented an image of itself as more adaptable, more knowledgeable, and more professional than the military. Messages and reports to other branches of government and to nongovernmental interests highlighted these traits, and were designed to emphasize the technical nature of Indian affairs and the unique attributes offered by the civilian service in comparison with their military counterparts. John Mason and Thomas McKenney relied on such arguments to defend the benefits, especially noneconomic benefits, of the factory system, and these arguments helped reestablish the civilian service's role in the West during and after removal.

The conflict between civilian administrators and the military continued through the nineteenth century, peaking in the reservation period after the Civil War, when a confident military sought a new purpose and as Western

[2] Sidney L. Harring, *Crow Dog's Case: American Indian Sovereignty, Tribal Law, and United States Law in the Nineteenth Century* (Cambridge: Cambridge University Press, 1994), 101–3, 115–18, 223–5; Larry C. Skogen, *Indian Depredation Claims, 1796–1920* (Norman: University of Oklahoma Press, 1996), 73, 85, 90–1, 115–16, 185; Corinne L. Monjeau-Marz, *The Dakota Indian Internment at Fort Snelling, 1862–1864* (St. Paul: Prairie Smoke Press, 2006), 24–36; Donald R. McCoy, "The Special Indian Agency in Alaska, 1873–1874: Its Origins and Operation," *The Pacific Historical Review* 25 (November 1956). Numerous other agencies also exhibited autonomy and the ability to circumvent, ignore, or oppose the demands and desires of elected officials and segments of the public: e.g., U.S. House of Representatives, Committee on House Administration, "The Power of the Purse," *Journal of Public Budgeting, Accounting & Financial Management* 9 (Fall 1997), 371ff.; Daniel Preston, "The Administration and Reform of the U.S. Patent Office, 1790–1836," *Journal of the Early Republic* 5 (Autumn 1985), 339–45; Brad Agnew, *Fort Gibson: Terminal on the Trail of Tears* (Norman: University of Oklahoma Press, 1980), 4; Paul Wallace Gates, "The Homestead Law in an Incongruous Land System," *The American Historical Review* 41 (July 1936), 656ff., 680; Larry Gara, *The Presidency of Franklin Pierce* (Lawrence: University Press of Kansas, 1991), 64.

interests grew weary of reservations blocking expansion and development. The Indian Office's defense of the various aspects of the reservation system – treaties, federal jurisdiction, government administration, federal control of lands, federal spending, local agents' authority over policing, politics, and criminal justice – often flew in the face of the demands and desires expressed by citizens and their elected representatives. Many Western interests and settlers preferred a more forceful approach to Indian affairs, repeatedly scorned the pacifist and "civilization" approaches of romantic Easterners and distant government leaders, and demanded the removal of Indians and the sale of their lands. A movement to transfer the Indian department back to the War Department gained momentum as a response to the continuing charges of abuse and maladministration in the BIA's fieldwork. Transfer was a direct attack at civilian control of Indian affairs, as it would have placed administration of the reservations and of Indian affairs generally under the immediate supervision of professional military personnel.

The BIA's defense traded on its expertise, which became a significant part of its successful efforts to defend its mission, turf, and resources. BIA Commissioner Dole, for example, faced with proposals designed by General Pope to turn control of Indian affairs over more fully to the military in the 1860s, responded to Pope's charges of BIA corruption by writing, "I have yet to learn that the greed of military contractors is any less than is that of contractors drawn from the ranks of civilians; or that camp-followers and the 'hangers-on' around the military posts are more virtuous than are the classes of whites who assemble around our Indian reserves under the present policy."[3] Dole contended that the problems of Indian affairs were not due to the problems of a civilian agency's incompetence, but were endemic to the nature of Indian affairs; they could therefore be handled just as well by a civilian agency as by the military. Before changing its position in response to a spike in western violence in 1868, the Peace Commission opposed transfer and described the unique attributes of the BIA's civilization efforts: "We have the highest possible appreciation of the officers of the army, and fully recognize their proverbial integrity and honor; but we are satisfied that not one in a thousand would like to teach Indian children to read and write, or Indian men to sow and reap. These are emphatically civil, and not military, occupations."[4]

[3] Quoted in Francis Paul Prucha, *The Great Father: The United States Government and the American Indians* (Lincoln: University of Nebraska Press, 1984), 476. See also Donald J. D'Elia, "The Argument Over Civilian or Military Indian Control, 1865–1880," *The Historian* 42 (February 1962).

[4] "Report of the Indian Peace Commission," January 7, 1868, reprinted in Francis Paul Prucha, ed., *Documents of United States Indian Policy*, 2nd ed. (Lincoln: University of Nebraska Press, 1990), 108; cf. "Annual Report of the Commissioner of Indian Affairs," 1868, reprinted in Prucha, *Documents*, 119.

Commissioner Taylor submitted an extensive report outlining the problems and dangers of military control of Indian affairs. To motivate allies he invoked the image of a large peacetime standing army, and he criticized past performances by the military in Indian affairs. Taylor also argued that costs were lower under civilian control. He relied emphatically on the peaceful and civilization-oriented goals of Indian policy, stating bluntly in 1868, "Our true policy toward the Indian tribes is peace, and the proposed transfer is tantamount, in my judgment, to perpetual war."[5] Taylor explained why the mere presence of soldiers inflamed the nation's Indian relations, and he warned, "If a chronic war, with additional annual expenses of $50,000,000 to $150,000,000 annually on account of Indian affairs, is desired, the transfer, it seems to me, is a logical way to the result."[6] Later in the report, Taylor estimated that, over the preceding forty years, war policy in Indian affairs had cost the nation $500,000,000, while "civil management or peace policy" had cost less than $60,000,000, "including annuities, presents, payments for immense bodies of land, and everything else."[7]

The BIA shrewdly coordinated its appeals to expertise by combining savvy leadership with careful alliances. The historian Francis Paul Prucha gives much credit for the defeat of the transfer idea to Carl Schurz, whose efforts to reform the Indian Office stood as proactive defenses against military criticism.[8] The BIA's appeals to its civilian expertise rested heavily on its commitments and promises to interests concerned for the welfare and development of Indians as individuals. Concerns for civilization policies, education, health care, and assimilation all tied important humanitarian interests to the BIA at the national level. Humanitarian interests used each failure or abuse by the military to illustrate the problems of military control and the desirability of civilian, particularly missionary, administration of Indian affairs. Even amid charges of maladministration and abuse, the BIA's carefully nurtured reputation for special expertise helped it maintain its role in policy development and administration, and its receptiveness to humanitarian concerns protected its support in the East.

The refusal to turn Indian policy over to the military underscores the fact that the military played a subordinate role in managing expansion. The BIA's success in warding off transfer of its duties also underscores the fact that while the public reputation of the agency concentrated on corruption and mismanagement, government leaders recognized the Indian service's merits and accomplishments and held its reputation in some respect. The Indian Office's success in these transfer battles reflects its autonomy and

5 "Annual Report, 1868," in Prucha, *Documents*, 119.
6 Ibid., 119.
7 Ibid., 122.
8 Prucha, *Great Father*, 558.

independence, which by the 1880s rested on nearly a century of effective activity, political networking, and shrewd leadership.

Organizational Autonomy, Oversight, and Reform

Along with efforts to transfer the BIA's duties to the military, a never-ending series of special investigations and ad hoc commissions buzzed around the periphery of Indian affairs administration. These efforts are hard to characterize in any general sense, as each was a unique response to particular circumstances. The thing to remember here is the complicated relationship of these oversight efforts, on the one hand, and the relatively straightforward goals of Indian policy, on the other. Special commissions and investigatory bodies were, on occasion, sincere efforts to protect Indian rights and interests. Yet such outside investigations could also be impotent sops to outraged activists and friends of the Indian, or they could be aimed at circumventing field personnel who were too effectively protecting Indian interests, or they could be means of furthering expansionist goals by smoothing and regularizing land transfer mechanisms or other procedures. In other words, they were not necessarily efforts to reign in a corrupt bureaucracy. They were often nudges *toward* corruption, with the effect of complicating politics and multiplying avenues of redress and avenues of wrongdoing.

As such, these commissions and investigations offer a hazy window into the autonomy of the Indian Office. First, these outside efforts can, in certain cases, be seen as attempts to oversee an agency and personnel that were acting too independently, often in opposition to the desires of members of Congress or of state and local interests. The dynamic cut both ways: field agents advocating Indian interests were investigated by anti-Indian officials, and anti-Indian field agents were investigated by pro-Indian officials. Second, the boards and commissions inflated the big government of the era by empowering *another* set of officers with discretionary authority aimed at influencing and furthering policy goals, often at very local levels. The commissions and investigations were usually efforts to use *different* bureaucratic agents with different bases of authority to further the goals of policy. Each commission or board became yet another layer of administration, with another set of guidelines and instructions, another set of records and record-keeping duties, another combination of standardized and uniform procedures animated by personal discretion and individual approaches, another relationship between private interests and government. Each represented a formalized, semiautonomous response to some stimulus, whether from reformers, developers, citizens, or from the course of events across a wide continent.

Investigations and commissions often recommended structural reforms at the Bureau. Yet the organizational culture of the Indian field service has long proven impervious to efforts to clarify lines of authority and reorganize institutional structures. Factors continued to send intelligence reports to the Superintendent of Trade even after they were instructed to send them directly to the Secretary of War, and they continued to function as both traders and diplomats. Efforts to get agents to submit quarterly reports and other paperwork to proper supervisors in a timely fashion often fell victim to more pressing concerns in the field, regardless of sharpened requirements. Alteration in the Office's institutional placement – for example, its move to the new Interior Department in 1849 – brought little change to the actual functionings of the Indian Office before or after the Civil War. The Bureau's general duties and responsibilities remained the same.[9]

Even policy changes have had trouble affecting administration at the Indian Office. The end of treaty making in 1871 exemplified the House of Representatives' increasing desire to be involved in the details of Indian policy and administration, but it also highlights Congress's limited ability to affect administrative activity on the ground.[10] Treaty making had given the executive initial dominance in most relations with Indians since the birth of the republic; monies and authority were delegated to the executive, and the outcome of land cessions and the exact nature of those cessions were left to the executive's agents. Representatives in the House hoped to increase their role in Indian affairs and land policy by putting an end to the treaty system, but the formal policy change failed to alter many of the administrative prerogatives already anchored in the executive branch. The act ending treaty making explicitly protected and continued existing treaties. Many of the administrative requirements embodied in the treaty system thus continued, such as the dispensation of annuities, respect for boundaries, and commitments for services, criminal justice protocols, and so on. Other interactions formerly handled through treaty arrangements were replaced by executive agreements with tribes and by executive orders, which created reservations and dispensed lands at the behest of the president without the advice and consent of the Senate. What looks at first glance like fundamental reform in Indian policy and administration – the removal of the main pillar of federal policy for close to a century – did little more than change the formal vehicle by which the executive branch and its officials directed and managed expansion policy and Indian affairs.

Personnel reform has also failed to have a deep impact on the functioning of the Indian service. Selecting better people, reformers have repeatedly argued, would reform a corrupt and dangerous system. Bishop Whipple's mid-century criticisms of the Indian service, for example, outlined abuses and

[9] Prucha, *Great Father*, 322; Laurence F. Schmeckebier, *The Office of Indian Affairs: Its History, Activities and Organization* (Baltimore: The Johns Hopkins University Press, 1927), 43. On this change's failure to affect education programs, see Jon Reyhner and Jeanne Eder, "A History of Indian Education," in *Teaching American Indian Students*, ed. Jon Reyhner (Norman: University of Oklahoma Press, 1994), 39.

[10] See, e.g., "Report of the Commissioner of Indian Affairs," 1869, reprinted in Prucha, *Documents*, 134–5; *U.S. Statutes at Large*, 16:566, in Prucha, *Documents*, 136.

agitated for personnel reform to replace the corrupt and incompetent men that he believed dominated the field service. The Peace Commission recommended in the 1860s that, in Prucha's terms, "all agents and superintendents be relieved of office and only the competent and faithful reappointed."[11] The agitation of reformers during and after the Civil War resulted in Grant's Peace Policy, which had roots before the war and which extended well into the late nineteenth century. The Peace Policy had a number of general goals, including a commitment to selecting "Competent, upright, faithful, moral, and religious" agents.[12] The Peace Policy assigned particular reservations and the selection of agents to religious societies, in hopes that the religious societies would choose better individuals for the tasks and thereby alleviate problems of corruption and mismanagement and improve administration. Missionary boards nominated agents and others to work in the field.

These examples may look like they led to significant change in Indian affairs administration; they didn't. The Peace Policy, for example, merely substituted new administrators for old ones without radically altering the administrative environment of the field service. Reformers in some areas continued to be hindered by "Indian rings" and localized corruption, which were able to block or ignore recommendations of the Board of Indian Commissioners. Competition developed between longtime government administrators and new Peace Policy appointees. Joint authority between the Board and the BIA did not magically create teamwork, and cooperation between the two never blossomed. The diversity and scope of Indian affairs work in the field continued to complicate matters. Appointees were unprepared for the "tremendous responsibility" of the work, and individual personalities often displayed less than pure character. Education and missionary work often remained secondary goals, and interdenominational rivalries dominated the stances taken by different groups. "Maintaining a position against a conflicting group was, unfortunately, often a more powerful motivation than concern for the welfare of the Indians," Prucha writes.[13] Charges continued to be brought against the new agents – only now, religious denominations added to the numerous interests with particular motives for discrediting reservation administrators. Interdenominational rivalries, problems in selecting and maintaining field officers, patronage concerns, local circumstances, and mutually disadvantageous political charges worked to discredit the BIA, the Board, and field administrators. In a study of the Navajo reservation during the Peace Policy, historian Norman Bender describes a central problem when he writes, "Regrettably, the zealous churchmen blithely approached their tasks with the assumption that vigorous application of Christian axioms would overcome all obstacles. They soon discovered that their pious principles had little effect when directed, for example, to

[11] Prucha, *Great Father*, 492.
[12] Ibid., 482.
[13] Ibid., 522, 523.

hard-headed negotiations for annual appropriations and to efforts to overcome opposition from Indians and whites who, quite simply, did not agree with their methods."[14]

Later, reformers and officials at the top of the Indian Service tried again, agreeing that civil service reform in the Indian service was the means to ensure qualified field agents and improve administration.[15] The Peace Policy was already in decline when Rutherford B. Hayes succeeded Grant. Carl Schurz, the new Secretary of the Interior, criticized the appointment policies of the Board of Indian Commissioners and the missions, and began to turn toward a more "scientific" selection process that would involve the Indian service with the growing move toward civil service reform. By 1882, the churches were out of the appointing business, but reformers who recognized the continuing and even increased significance of the agent in local administration of civilization and education programs again turned to personnel selection reform as a means of stabilizing and improving local administration in the field service. John D. C. Atkins tried to reform personnel selection in the 1880s by centralizing hiring of agents, farmers, clerks, and doctors in Washington, DC. Atkins ran into a predictable complaint: such centralized hiring precluded hiring with an informed eye toward local needs and situations, which had long been a hallmark of Indian service personnel selection for lower posts. In fact, despite Atkins's tenure during civil service reform, critics charged with some merit that all this practice did was make it easier for Atkins to make selections based on patronage.[16]

Reformers took advantage of the movement for civil service reform, and humanitarians and reformers worked to have the entire Indian Service classified under civil service reform legislation and to circumvent the perceived ills of patronage appointments. Like the Peace Policy, these efforts and the occasional changes they brought failed to have a significant impact on the administration of Indian policy in the field. Civil service reform's single advantage may have been in reducing administrative disruptions and inconsistencies that arose from rapid turnover in certain posts, but even this is not assured.[17]

14 Norman J. Bender, *"New Hope for the Indians": The Grant Peace Policy and the Navajos in the 1870s* (Albuquerque: University of New Mexico Press, 1989), xii; see also Joseph B. Herring, *The Enduring Indians of Kansas: A Century and a Half of Acculturation* (Lawrence: University Press of Kansas, 1990), 109. For a discussion of the mechanisms involved in selecting personnel during the Peace Policy, see Bender, *"New Hope,"* especially 37ff.

15 Prucha, *Great Father*, 726ff.

16 Gregory C. Thompson, "John D. C. Atkins," in Robert M. Kvasnicka and Herman J. Viola, eds., *The Commissioners of Indian Affairs, 1824–1977* (Lincoln: University of Nebraska Press, 1979), 184–5; see also Flora Warren Seymour, *Indian Agents of the Old Frontier* (New York: D. Appleton-Century Co., 1941), 273.

17 Civil service reform produced little change or improvement in hiring of teachers for Indian schools, for example: Reyhner and Eder, "History," 43–4; Meyer Weinberg, *A Chance to Learn: The History of Race and Education in the United States* (Cambridge: Cambridge University Press, 1977), 207–8.

BIA reforms – whether structural reforms, policy changes, or personnel reforms – generally failed to affect significantly the behavior of field officers. Reorganizing lines of authority within the BIA or rearranging personnel procedures cannot change the fact that the most important decisions must be made by individuals at the field level. The details of field decisions are shaped as much by local circumstances, individual relationships, and shifting exigencies, as they are by laws or by the character of the field agent. All of these forces are important; none are determinative.

Reforms also failed to silence criticism of the agency's administrative structures, personnel, and achievements. Such criticism could never be silenced: local political charges and shifting political interests inevitably brought charges of maladministration and corruption whether they existed or not. Even the best people, in the most clearly defined bureaucratic structure, would not have been able to avoid the rumors and the charges brought by any one of the myriad interests involved in Indian affairs. Standardizing or even significantly altering administration in the field, or quelling criticism, were unlikely outcomes in Indian affairs.

From its inception, the Indian Office had a measure of autonomy that helped it pursue its mission in a volatile environment, despite the rampant charges against it and despite the illusion of incompetence that even today obscures the agency's early and persistent effectiveness.

National Policies, Programs, and Bureaucratic Capacity

Our understanding of government and administration in the nineteenth century has heretofore rested on a number of unshakable pillars. First, scholars have argued that programmatic social policies on a national scale were relatively small and rare prior to the post–Civil War era. Second, scholars have generally believed that administrative activity was minimal, often corrupt, and dominated by patronage appointments that precluded effective and professionalized administration. Third, scholars have argued that the nineteenth century is best characterized as "a state of courts and parties," lacking strong executive leadership on domestic policies and significant regulation at the national level. All of these points need to be reexamined.

National Social Policy Targets Millions

Indian affairs differ from other activities of the early American state like the post office, the military, and the land offices in part because a major part of Indian policy and of the mission and tasks assigned to the Indian bureaucracy were social in nature: the care and protection of a defined class of people, based on certain assumptions about their status, about how that status related to the general polity, and about what changes in that status the nation envisioned or wished to promote. The "benefits" of social policy were not granted as gifts; they represented benefits targeted to a defined class of people resulting from exchanges of land and also from complex moral rationales and belief systems regarding the federal government's responsibilities to address issues of personal behavior, morals, and human progress. Programmatic initiatives in core areas of domestic public administration characterized Indian relations from the republic's early years. The United States committed itself to spending millions of dollars to supply Indians with education, income stabilization, health care, economic development funds, and many other forms of social provision. Long before the Civil War, the federal government was distributing millions of dollars in cash and goods to Indian communities and individuals for a variety of reasons, including concern for individuals' economic and social well-being. The federal government's involvement in housing and family policies, too, are grounded in Indian affairs.

These early efforts at social provision are the scene of early government efforts to reconcile the duties of the national government and the duties of private and other nongovernmental organizations. The national government was deeply involved with tribal, state, territorial, and local governments, activists, interest groups, and religious organizations. Early social provision played a significant role in defining the boundaries of national obligation and responsibility, aided in the development of views of federalism and local control, and tested the boundaries of public-private partnerships and of the constitutional separation of church and state. American attitudes toward Indian affairs clearly supported and recognized the role of the national government as an ally and a leader in providing social benefits, programs, goods, and services to Indian populations.

The benefits granted to Indians were, in an important sense, programmatic: they were similar across tribes, can be understood as related parts of an organized and planned whole, and they generally involved the same sets of political actors, bureaucratic structures, field operators, and business and voluntary organizations. We should recognize, too, that benefits to Indians were expanded constantly: each new treaty or agreement guaranteeing new benefits throughout the nineteenth century incorporated a new population or a new understanding of benefits and obligations. It is not the case that expansion happened all at once, at defined points in political time, or that early treaties alone created a set of benefits into which later native populations were included. The situation is very complex, as each new benefit created what in some important ways was a new program, targeted at a particular tribe for a particular reason, and with unique understanding of benefits, obligations, and deserving or nondeserving people or communities. Even delivery varied, as Congress and the executive branch zigged and zagged among different methods for delivering services and goods and for determining eligibility. Finally, the various efforts in particular and generally invigorated debates very similar to debates we see now: over the proper level of benefits, the worthiness of recipients, the nature of appropriate delivery mechanisms, an optimistic approach to generosity, and a pessimistic approach that anticipated fraud, dependence, and a sapping of the will to be thrifty and hardworking.

A thorough study of social provision as it relates to the Indian affairs context and big government in the nineteenth century is beyond the scope of this book, which focuses on the bureaucratic capacity and skill of the Indian Office and other national government agencies. However, it is clear that bureaucratic capacity at the national level to plan and implement, and to reorganize and adapt, in complex policy areas, existed long before the Civil War. It is also clear that programs existed to target benefits of various types – cash, goods, and services – to specific populations. Structure, capacity, and will existed to channel a wide variety of social benefits to U.S. soldiers after the Revolution, to blacks, women, and children after the Civil War, and to noncitizen American Indians from the dawn of the republic to the present. Easy to overlook is the intellectual precedent for locating these programs, and the bureaucratic organs necessary to design and implement them, at the federal level. It remains for another project to explore whether social programs in Indian affairs served as policy or bureaucratic precedents to later programs with broader, citizen-oriented programs, and to examine the extent to which administrators with Indian affairs experience may have cross-pollinated programs and policies targeted at non-Indians.

As important as these programs are in terms of understanding the development of social provision in the United States, their importance to the United States and its officials and public should not be overstated. Many people were deeply committed to establishing and expanding these programs and meeting treaty obligations, for any number of reasons. Yet these programs never rose to the same level of priority as did issues surrounding expansion, land, and security. Social policies often complemented efforts to pacify, remove, isolate, control, and dispossess Indians, but they rarely took first priority.

Administrative Necessity Trumps Patronage

A fundamental assumption guiding scholars' understanding of public administration in the nineteenth century has been that there was little administration to speak of, and that what did exist was dominated and rendered ineffective by the burden of patronage politics. The effectiveness of expansion policy administration, including but not limited to the effectiveness of Indian affairs administration, suggests that we need to revisit the relationship between patronage and administration in the nineteenth century.

Indian affairs administration *was* effective, as I have tried to demonstrate throughout this book. Assessments and assumptions of patronage's deleterious effects in the Indian service assume that administration *failed*. Such analyses often shift subtly from a focus on the Indian Office as an arm of the nation's expansionist policies to one which evaluates the agency in terms of its responsibilities to Indians – such as relate to presumed failures in the government's civilization and education initiatives. Such evaluations obscure the fact that social policies were secondary to expansion goals and non-Indian interests throughout the eighteenth and nineteenth centuries, and play upon readers' assumption that Indian affairs administration was an abject failure.

As we have seen, patronage was not a dominating factor in appointments in the Indian service, nor was it a bar to effective administration of the BIA's major tasks and missions. Appointments at the top of the Indian service combined political and patronage incentives with responsiveness to the needs of interest groups and the demands of reformers, and usually led to the appointment of qualified individuals at the top of the Bureau. Just below the top, career officers like Charles Mix maintained institutional memory and professionalism, promulgating careful and organized lists of rules and regulations and creating stability at the Bureau. Field agents in sensitive posts were, from the BIA's earliest days, chosen with an understanding of how particular appointments might hinder or advance the Office's mission, and patronage appointments that conflicted with the demands of policy were either not made or were reversed when problems arose.

To the extent that patronage moved the agency away from concern for Indians, patronage actually *furthered* the primary administrative goals of the Indian Office. One historian, for example, traces several examples of local Indian service officials who used the availability of appointments and contracts to build political bases and loyal followers. Ronald Satz criticizes the process because it corrupted the Indian service: "The result was that the officials' obligations to the Indians became subjugated to political considerations."[18] Satz overlooks the crucial fact that the Indian Office's primary mission at this time was the removal of Indians. If the agents' concern for Indians became subjugated to political considerations as a result of policies like removal and the dominance of party and patronage, that actually *helped* the agency meet its administrative goals. The same might be said of political ties leading reservation administrators away from concern for Indians' well-being.

The BIA is not the only agency at which patronage did not preclude efficient administration. The Topographical Engineers witnessed numerous cases in which personnel selection and administration took precedence over patronage, or in which the patronage system directly served the organization's demands. Goetzmann writes of the selection system for the Engineers,

> The total effect of this system of advice and recommendation [for appointments] was the creation of a powerful scientific lobby that not only controlled individual appointments but was actually instrumental in persuading Secretary [Jefferson] Davis to embark on his ambitious scientific project to the extent that he did.... Thus within

[18] Ronald N. Satz, *American Indian Policy in the Jacksonian Era* (Lincoln: University of Nebraska Press, 1975), 185.

the framework of a simple Jacksonian democracy there existed an unofficial federal patronage of science that was indissolubly linked to the practical development of the country.[19]

Students of the Post Office also have difficulty explaining exactly how patronage and spoils hindered the administration of mail delivery. Wesley Everett Rich writes that there is no evidence of patronage adversely affecting efficiency.[20] Richard John acknowledges the absence of good evidence for evaluating postal efficiency, and his conclusion that Jacksonian patronage policies "had a major effect on postal administration" relies heavily on editorial comments from partisan newspapers and unsupported assumptions.[21] It is never clear, in fact, why individuals appointed for political reasons through patronage would be any less adept at their jobs and responsibilities than nonpatronage appointments (especially when many scholars assume that these jobs required only the ability to carry out routine clerk functions).

If the assumptions are that patronage dominated nineteenth-century administration, and also that there was no social provision, it is easy to assume a correlation between the two. The coincidence of industrialization, civil service reform, and social provision after the Civil War then seems to connect new and related developments – until we examine social provision in the years of patronage politics more closely. The Indian Office's administrative effectiveness and the limited role played by patronage shatters the image of a patronage-dominated national government paralyzed by party politics and devoid of programmatic initiatives. The Indian Office was much closer to what we today consider a professional agency, in that its officials relied on written guidelines and established procedures in order to ensure effective accomplishment in a critical area of national policy. This is not to say that local issues did not affect administration; it is to say that problems were more a result of the *nature* of state structures at the time than they were due to the *absence* of those structures. In Indian affairs, the situation is not a combination of patronage and the absence of social provision. In fact, it's just the reverse: patronage is a relatively minor obstacle to administration, and there is broad commitment to, and capacity for, social provision.

In short, Indian affairs suggest two important ideas for how we view patronage in the nineteenth century. First, we cannot assume that patronage dominated appointments. Second, at those points in time and space where

19 William H. Goetzmann, *Army Exploration in the American West, 1803–1863* (Lincoln: University of Nebraska Press, 1959), 308.

20 Wesley Everett Rich, *The History of the United States Post Office to the Year 1829* (Cambridge, MA: Harvard University Press, 1924), 169.

21 Richard R. John, *Spreading the News: The American Postal System from Franklin to Morse* (Cambridge, MA: Harvard University Press, 1995), 222ff., 241.

patronage did play a role, we cannot assume that the effects were detrimental to the pursuit of policy and administration.

The important role of operators forces us to reexamine the uses and effects of turnover in the field service at a nineteenth-century agency like the BIA. The standard assumption even in Indian affairs histories is that turnover hurts performance; that information and programmatic capacity depend on the ability of the bureaucracy to attract, keep, and secure the commitment of skilled technical and administrative personnel. Turnover is assumed to be the enemy of performance, learning, adaptation, and programmatic ability.

The reality is not so simple. Some objectives may be *better* served with a new workforce that lacks institutional memory or experience. A new workforce, for example, may rely on its presuppositions and prejudices. In a matter of treaty negotiations, an inexperienced and ignorant workforce could benefit the United States by being sincerely unaware of previous agreements and promises, as in the case of negotiations with the Nez Perce in the latter half of the nineteenth century. Nor is it always true that experience and networks of known dynamics help performance: impersonal relations[22] can help autonomy and programmatic capacity, and impersonal relations can be fostered through turnover. In particular, if operators are being asked to do harmful or immoral things, as is often the case in Indian affairs, turnover can and did help the BIA to fulfill its objectives.

The relationship of turnover and learning is also more complicated than Daniel Carpenter and others recognize. Experience and long tenure can help learning, and in many cases tenures in the field service are long and benefit from institutional memory, personal relationships, knowledge of the soil, and so on. Constancy can help performance. In many cases, though, the BIA did not *want* its agents to learn, as in the treaty negotiation case cited earlier: learning could hinder agency goals if operators knew too much or their memories were too long. Moreover, the Indian service, by the nature of its business, was constantly innovating. New regions, new Indians, new circumstances constantly confronted the agency, and overarching policy directions shifted every generation. In this circumstance, the BIA was better off with relatively new operators, not set in their ways, who understood and were committed to new policies or new leadership. In other words, patronage and turnover could further, not retard, innovation and implementation.[23]

[22] See H. George Frederickson, *The Spirit of Public Administration* (San Francisco: Jossey-Bass, 1996), 50–1.

[23] Cf. Daniel P. Carpenter, *The Forging of Bureaucratic Autonomy: Reputations, Networks, and Policy Innovation in Executive Agencies, 1862–1928* (Princeton: Princeton University Press, 2001), 29, 49; John, *Spreading the News*, 335n117; Theda Skocpol, *Protecting Soldiers and Mothers: The Political Origins of Social Policy in the United States* (Cambridge, MA: Harvard University Press, 1995), 75.

The Stronger Presidency

Understanding expansion as an area of public policy, attended early by mature and autonomous bureaucratic organizations, profoundly reorients our understanding of the development of the presidency and the executive branch. Scholars of social provision tend to assume a weak executive, and to use the weak executive to help explain lag in the development of American social provision. This approach rests in part on scholars of the presidency, most of whom have generally failed to recognize in the office a leading role in domestic policymaking and bureaucratic activity prior to the turn of the twentieth century. Stephen Skowronek, for example, argues that "The Presidency had never risen far above the status of a clerk during the heyday of party competition."[24]

This traditional view cannot be sustained when expansion and Indian affairs are included in the analysis. Indian affairs shows clearly that nineteenth century presidents were much more than clerks or party hacks in the important realm of Indian affairs. Presidential leadership designed and directed Indian policy throughout the nineteenth century, and engineered major policy shifts in the removal and reservation eras. Presidents from George Washington forward had significant and often dominant control over the important Indian service bureaucracy, control that was formally delegated by Congress to the president and then passed by the president to the Secretary of War and later to the Secretary of Interior. In turn, authority was delegated to a civilian army of field agents whose task it was to reconcile the mandates of national policy with the interests and conditions of local areas.

The role of the presidency in the all-important area of national expansion suggests that we need to reexamine the usual understanding of relative power relationships between the president and Congress. Rather than an initially forceful presidency under Washington which quickly gives way to a nineteenth century dominated by Congress, expansion as public policy suggests forceful executive leadership in policymaking and administration that was outside the scope of congressional activity. Presidents helped to design and promote policies, and helped to administer and support them in the face of party and localistic opposition. Presidents looked for much wider constituencies in the realm of territorial politics, helping the parties build more than local organizations. Presidents had independent institutional resources, as Congress delegated authority and resources to the executive branch. Control of expenditures and recordkeeping responsibilities fell to the executive, with congressional efforts at oversight through hearings or commissions often ineffective. Finally, presidents had opportunity and incentive to lead

[24] Stephen Skowronek, *Building a New American State: The Expansion of National Administrative Capacities, 1877–1920* (Cambridge: Cambridge University Press, 1982), 169.

on Indian affairs and impact the life of the nation. In the century's primary issue-areas, Indian affairs and expansion policy, the president led.

The U.S. Supreme Court and National Administrative Activity

We may also need to reevaluate the role of the federal judiciary in the nineteenth century. For Skowronek, for example, courts and parties

> tied together this state's peculiar organizational determinants and established its effective mode of operations. They coordinated action from bottom to top of this radically decentralized governmental scheme. Under a Constitution designed to produce institutional conflicts and riddled with jurisdictional confusion, they came to lend order, predictability, and continuity to governmental activity....
>
> As the final arbiter in institutional and jurisdictional disputes the [U.S. Supreme] Court... defined the legitimate forms of interaction between states, between states and national governments, and within the national government itself. In the evolution of the constitutional law, the fragmented system of governmental authority became malleable and responsive.[25]

Sometimes.

Court activity and influence in Indian affairs varied widely, unified not by an institutional role in organizing the system but in the Court's tendency to sanction the extension of federal jurisdiction and administrative authority across the continent being driven by the president, the bureaucracy, and Congress. Importantly, though, the Court often acted less with determinative authority over policy and administration, and more as a body merely sanctioning the actions of others well after the fact. And on occasions when the Court stood in the way of extensions of jurisdictional and administrative authority, it was overruled by actions in the field, by executive policy, or by legislation.

At times, the Court shaped policy and organized relationships in the manner suggested by Skowronek. It removed jurisdictional logjams and made influential policy decisions in Indian affairs cases like *Fletcher* v. *Peck* (1810), *Worcester* v. *Georgia* (1832), and *U.S.* v. *Rogers* (1846). *Rogers* involved an 1817 Act that had extended federal criminal jurisdiction to interracial crimes in Indian country, but which had reserved to tribal authorities jurisdiction over Indian-against-Indian crimes. U.S. officials, seeking to extend federal jurisdiction over tribal matters, began in earnest to bring Indian-against-Indian crimes under federal authority in the 1840s. *Rogers* centered

[25] Skowronek, *Building*, 24, 27. See also, e.g., Skocpol, who writes that "[T]here was no national civil bureaucracy that could compete with the courts by promoting 'the national interest' in a more substantial fashion." Skocpol, *Protecting*, 69. She also writes, "[I]n the United States judicial officials achieved continuous purview over a broad scope of policy issues well before groups of civil administrators did, for the latter gained independent footholds in local, state, and national governments only from the Progressive Era onward." Skocpol, *Protecting*, 71. Both statements are incorrect.

on a murder case in which both the victim and the accused were white men who had moved into Cherokee territory, married and raised families, and been formally accepted into the Cherokee Nation. The questions for the Court involved the jurisdiction of U.S. courts over cases involving Indians on Indian land, and also the definition of Indians and their membership in a tribe. The Taney Court argued that Rogers could not become an Indian for purposes of the law because he had a different biological and racial makeup. The effect of the decision was to open the way for expanding congressional and executive administrative authority in Indian country. Shortly after the *Rogers* decision, Congress, soliciting opinions from the current and former Commissioners of Indian Affairs, began extending federal criminal law into Indian territory.[26]

The Court issued similar jurisdiction-settling decisions in other cases. In *The Kansas Indians* (1866), the Court reinforced tribal sovereignty and federal control of Indian affairs by blocking Kansas' extension of taxing powers over the Shawnees, Weas, and Miami.[27] In *The Cherokee Tobacco* case (1871), the Court extended *federal* taxing authority over alcohol and tobacco sales on reservations. Here, the Court ruled that Congress had extended its taxing powers over Indian country with the 1868 General Revenue Act. Importantly, Congress had not done this explicitly, and precedent should have excluded its application in Indian country. In upholding the Revenue Act's applicability in Indian country, the Supreme Court created a congressional intent in order to extend the law. The case exemplifies the Court's tendency to support the national government in jurisdictional disputes and even to actively extend federal authority and administrative power.[28] In *U.S.* v. *Kagama* (1886), another example, the Court "cleared the way for Congress to pass some 5,000 laws pertaining to the regulation of American Indians without the consent of, and often without so much as consulting with, the Indians themselves."[29]

These cases, ranging from the republic's early years to the close of the nineteenth century, supported national authority over the states and over tribal governments. Legal scholar David Wilkins notes that this pattern contrasts with relations between blacks and the states in the nineteenth century,

[26] See David E. Wilkins, *American Indian Sovereignty and the U.S. Supreme Court: The Masking of Justice* (Austin: University of Texas Press, 1997), 38ff., for a thorough discussion of this intriguing case. Wilkins includes an eye-opening discussion of how Taney's understanding of Indian history and sovereignty in *Rogers* differs markedly from his presentation of the same topics in his *Dred Scott* decision.

[27] Vine Deloria Jr. and Clifford M. Lytle, *American Indians, American Justice* (Austin: University of Texas Press, 1992), 53.

[28] Wilkins, *American Indian Sovereignty*, 51–63.

[29] Ward Churchill and Glenn T. Morris, "Key Indian Laws and Cases," in *The State of Native America: Genocide, Colonization, and Resistance*, ed. M. Annette Jaimes (Boston: South End Press, 1992), 18.

in which states generally possessed "virtually free reign to assert their dominance over blacks. Tribal nations, on the other hand, were generally shielded from the states, though the shielding device used by the federal government was effective congressional omnipotence over Indian sovereignty and Indian civil, political, and property rights."[30] With the executive and the Indian Office playing crucial leadership roles related to policy and administrative initiatives, the judiciary was a staunch ally and sometimes a catalyst in the expansion of federal administrative authority before and after the Civil War.

At other times, though, instead of breaking logjams and opening paths to national expansion, the Court merely condoned the lead taken by other actors, often well after important decisions had been made elsewhere in the system. Rather than making policy for a weak state, the nineteenth-century Court often acted merely to support a strong one. In *Johnson* v. *McIntosh* (1823), for example, Marshall sanctioned U.S. expansion in a remarkable statement that explicitly surrendered right, justice, and law to real-world exigencies. In *Cherokee Nation* v. *Southern Kansas Railway Company* (1887), the Court upheld Congress' abrogation of treaty requirements, thus choosing not to stand in the way of railroad development through reservation land. Congress had authorized the Secretary of the Interior to monitor and assist railway extensions through reservation land, even if no Indians had been consulted and no official consent had been given. Clearly another violation of tribal sovereignty and treaty provisions, the Court merely upheld federal actions.[31] Cases like these deferred to extensions of congressional power, and thus sanctioned bureaucratic and administrative extensions indirectly. In cases like *U.S.* v. *Clapox* (1888), the Court directly sanctioned the discretionary actions taken by field officers of the Indian service. *Clapox* examined the legitimacy and legality of the BIA's Courts of Indian Offenses, which (as noted earlier) had been created in the field by Indian agents to help them manage reservations. These "courts" adjudicated disputes and were staffed by Indians, but they were controlled by the reservation agents. The Supreme Court, asked whether or not such administrative weapons were constitutional, quietly upheld their legality.

More important to an understanding of the state of courts and parties, though, is recognition of just how little determinative power the courts had when opposing expansion led by other institutional or administrative actors. The above decisions paralleled and reinforced congressional, presidential, and bureaucratic decisions about the direction of policy and administration. Yet the Court's unwillingness to confront Jackson in *Worcester* v. *Georgia* has long been an example of the judiciary's weakness in the nineteenth century. In some ways, the Court in *Worcester* did what would be expected in a state of courts and parties – it offered final arbitration regarding the

[30] Wilkins, *American Indian Sovereignty*, 15–16.
[31] Ibid., 81–91.

appropriate locus of authority in Indian affairs in a critical test of tribal, state, and national power. But in a different way, by acceding to the directions and policies of the national executive and legislative branches, and the actions of federal administrators, the Court revealed its weakness in the face of determinations made by the bureaucracy and by other policymakers. *Worcester* is far from unique: the Supreme Court ruled in *Ex parte Crow Dog* (1883), for example, that the federal government had no jurisdiction to prosecute an Indian for killing another Indian on an Indian reservation. The Court's decision in *Crow Dog* aimed at limiting federal jurisdiction, but it resulted in little more than a bump in the administrative road. Congress responded by passing the Major Crimes Act two years later, which codified the authority prohibited in *Crow Dog* and which delegated broad police power to the executive branch. The Court meekly upheld the Major Crimes Act in *Kagama*, despite the fact that the Act violated treaty provisions. In his analysis of *Kagama*, Wilkins argues that "this sudden transformation in Supreme Court thought and policy occurred to legitimize the congressional policy of forced assimilation and acculturation of tribal citizens into American society."[32] The Court proved unable to block Congress' subsequent extension of federal administrative authority being exercised by executive branch agents. Similarly, when removal of Sacs and Foxes later in the nineteenth century created a situation very similar to the one controlled by the Court's Ponca decision in *Standing Bear* v. *Crook* (1879), only a few years after that decision had been issued, administrators merely ignored the Court's guidelines.

Cases expanding federal powers at the expense of the states and of Indian sovereignty were essential to the expansion of administrative control at the national level. Congress, the president, and the bureaucracy asked for and received greater administrative control, and when the Court leaned toward restraining the extension of federal power, in cases like *Worcester* and *Crow Dog*, Congress and the executive branch extended their authority anyway. Far more than acting as a final arbiter or coordinating activity for a weak, decentralized state, the courts followed field agents west and contentedly sanctioned the decisions and administrative efforts and preferences of pro-expansion congressional and executive branch officials.[33]

National Regulation Manages the Economy

The Indian Office was deeply involved in debates about the scope of federal responsibilities in ordering and regulating trade as early as the 1790s. The

[32] Ibid., 80.

[33] Skowronek, *Building*, 27, 29. On the complex interactions of congressional and other activity involving and often controlling courts in the United States and in Indian country, see Jeffrey Burton, *Indian Territory and the United States, 1866–1906: Courts, Government, and the Movement for Oklahoma Statehood* (Norman: University of Oklahoma Press, 1995); Harring, *Crow Dog's Case*.

federal government's laws and regulations enforced restrictions on land purchases and distribution, and on key sectors of the economy like land, the fur trade, alcohol, weapons, timber, and shipping. Licensing and regulatory systems sought to circumscribe access to land and the Indian trade for a variety of reasons. The Indian Office was involved in promulgating and enforcing legally binding rules for behavior, and these rules were backed by the threat of coercion. The Indian Office was responsible in part for issuing trading licenses and regulations, and also for apprehending, judging, and penalizing violators – in effect, an executive agency fulfilling legislative, executive, and judicial functions, much as today's agencies do. Lest we overlook the Indian Office's regulatory role as unimportant, it is worth noting the importance of the fur trade – and the way in which it was regulated and directed by the federal government – to the development of the early United States. The historian Jack Weatherford writes,

> Profits from the fur trade financed much of the development of the early settlements into national and international cities. Indian furs paid for the building of wharves and docks, and for the expansion of warehouses. The most important source of revenues for the colonial government came from tariffs and taxes on trade, most of which was supported by the Indian fur trade. The Indian trade helped to underwrite the cost of building roads into the wilderness, and later financed construction of canals and dredging of rivers.[34]

Weatherford points out that the single most influential developer in early New York, John Jacob Astor, built much of his empire on the foundation of his American Fur Company in the early nineteenth century. As we have seen, Astor was intimately tied to federal government regulatory activities in the early nineteenth century which sought to limit access to the fur trade and regularize markets. Astor's opposition to federal involvement – after he had secured dominance in the industry – was a catalyst for the demise of those regulatory structures.

The Indian Office's involvement in regulatory policy and enforcement suggests that we need to reexamine the general belief that the United States begins its regulatory efforts in the late nineteenth century. This era should be viewed not as the initial response to regulatory needs, but as an *intermediate* response which follows earlier measures that located regulatory authority at the national level. Nor can it be argued that these efforts were too minimal to be worthy of our attention. While not all of the trading regulations were totally effective, it is still the case that much of this effort was effective, that the intellectual precedent and administrative foundation for national regulation existed early on, and that later regulation arose as state capacities and public needs evolved.

34 Jack Weatherford, *Native Roots: How the Indians Enriched America* (New York: Crown, 1991), 85–6. See also Robert W. Richmond and Robert W. Mardock, eds., *A Nation Moving West: Readings in the History of the American Frontier* (Lincoln: University of Nebraska Press, 1966), ch. 9.

A Sense of the State

U.S. leaders entrusted the survival and expansion of the United States not to the development of military capacity, but to the development of civilian administrative capacity. To judge the development of the early American state by looking only at the military side of Indian affairs, and within that to look only for violent conflict, is to miss the larger picture. The success and development of civil administration is the real story of American political and state development. The administrative tasks and successes of the Indian service and of the military acting in an administrative capacity worked to build the state even as they limited the apparent direct relevance of frontier crises and conflicts. In other words, the military fails to look very significant in the late eighteenth and nineteenth centuries because conquest by administration was so effective. This was no accident. From the republic's earliest days, national leaders relied on what they hoped would be relatively peaceful, cost-effective, and orderly administrative mechanisms to manage expansion by controlling and regulating the use of land and the course of trade – their success in these endeavors meant that development of the military never dominated the federal government's use of its coercive and administrative authority.

The Bureau of Indian Affairs and its predecessors were involved in important and volatile tasks at the end of the eighteenth century, throughout the nineteenth, and into the twentieth. Indian affairs personnel were not simply sitting around handing out benefits to party members; they were, rather, influencing the course of policy and administration on the frontier and within the United States. They functioned as an effective public bureaucracy within the executive branch, and they functioned as experts in policy and administration regardless of party concerns and control. Indian affairs demonstrate that the federal government was an active participant and a considerable presence in American public affairs from the days when national policy efforts supported expansionist policies, helped build roads and canals to promote settlement and economic development, and provided social benefits and pursued social objectives in Indian affairs. The essential nature of American governance and administration from the dawn of the republic included a variety of private and public interests that accepted the national government as a critical participant in matters of expansion, development, social policy, and Indian affairs. The Progressive era and the New Deal are important pieces of the general course of American political and administrative development, but they do not represent radical upheavals in politics or attitudes about government.

Among the elements of big government, the idea of reorienting our view of a sense of the state requires perhaps the least new research. In examining the cultural identification of the state, as part of "the more general recognition of the state as a significant factor in political and social life," J. P. Nettl asks,

"To what extent have individuals generalized the concept and cognition of state in their perceptions and actions, and to what extent are such cognitions salient? This last is perhaps the most important of the approaches..."[35] Aside from the rhetoric of government officials and foreign observers, the American people themselves made it quite clear throughout the nineteenth century that the central government was an important and steady presence in their lives. Traders demanded protection. Trading companies worked for advantageous regulation and enforcement. Land companies demanded order and legitimacy. Land companies and settlers demanded roads, canals, infrastructure, and communications networks. Settlements demanded protection, and recognition, and legitimacy, and stability. Migrants demanded paths and protection and services. Residents demanded that the federal government indemnify them against losses from Indians, and compensate them when losses occurred. Whether it was in the demand for services, treaty negotiations, removal of Indians, trade licensing and regulation, supervision of migration, redistribution of lands to manage expansion and satisfy veterans, land and deed registrations, provision of legality and legitimacy for territorial areas and development and growth, the extensions of government control during the Sabbatarian controversy, the return of fugitive slaves, wagon road and railroad development, or questions of nationally oriented morality and justice in the slave and Indian contexts, a sense of the state pervades the era and is unavoidable in its persistent connection to aspects of everyday life. All of these interests took advantage of government efforts to meet their demands, and felt aggrieved when government failed to do so. Perhaps even more significantly for our purposes here, these interests felt aggrieved when big government met the demands of *other*, *competing* interests, adverse to their own. And interests often resented the money, goods, services, and federal personnel attending to the needs and demands of American Indians and Indian nations, even as those non-Indian interests demanded that the federal government pacify, remove, contain, isolate, and dispossess those communities. And, lest we forget, millions of Indians and Mexicans and French and Spaniards and Africans living in North America in the nineteenth century certainly had a "sense of the state."

Expansion did not just happen. States delegated to the federal government primary responsibility for designing and coordinating expansion policies, a key portion of which included Indian affairs. Because national leaders

[35] J. P. Nettl, "The State as a Conceptual Variable," *World Politics* 20 (July 1968), 566. Andrew Cayton examines the question of "dominion," and suggests that a key factor is "the degree to which they [citizens] identified with the nation-state, accepted its authority, and saw its interests and their interests as complementary." Andrew R. L. Cayton, "'Separate Interests' and the Nation-State: The Washington Administration and the Origins of Regionalism in the Trans-Appalachian West," *The Journal of American History* 79 (June 1992), 42.

chose to make administration and not military conquest the driving force of expansion, the development of the American military provides only a part of the picture of the national state's activities in the eighteenth and nineteenth centuries. The success of administration in Indian affairs and other policy areas meant that the military did not need to develop as quickly or to such an extent as we might expect in a developing state. Indian affairs administration was overwhelmingly effective in controlling the dynamics of U.S.–Indian relations, helping the United States move westward in a relatively organized and coherent manner.

Expansion required a host of administrative activities and spurs to state development that have heretofore been largely overlooked, a result of assumptions about expansion that have discouraged political scientists and historians from examining thoroughly the contours of administrative conquest. Looking more closely at Indian affairs, we see not a minor niche area involving a few isolated cavalry officers and a few doomed Indians, but rather national policies and administrative developments involving important sectors of the economy, significant social movements and initiatives, and salient political issues across the continent and throughout the nineteenth century. Early decisions continue to create conflicts and constrain responses even today; the intellectual and institutional dynamics which govern Indian policy and administration in the twenty-first century were established in the nation's first years. The Indian Office's mission, culture, tasks, and constraints still feel the legacy of those early years, and these aspects of the Office's existence continue to encourage volatility and unpredictability in Indian affairs.

Including expansion and Indian policy in American political history significantly alters our understanding of the roots of centralized administration in the American state. Our traditional understanding of limited and often ineffective administration characterized by local, fragmented powers is replaced by one of *national* administration directed by federal officials coordinating federal agents in the field, who operated with vast grants of discretionary authority. The Office of Indian Affairs provides just one example of the federal government managing the grand public policy initiative of the nineteenth century: the conquest and unification of North America.

References

Adams, David Wallace. *Education for Extinction: American Indians and the Boarding School Experience, 1875–1928*. Lawrence: University Press of Kansas, 1995.

Adams, Guy B., and Danny L. Balfour. *Unmasking Administrative Evil*. Thousand Oaks, CA: Sage, 1998.

Adams, Mary P. "Jefferson's Reaction to the Treaty of San Ildefonso." *The Journal of Southern History* 21 (1955).

Agnew, Brad. *Fort Gibson: Terminal on the Trail of Tears*. Norman: University of Oklahoma Press, 1980.

Allen, Michael. "Justice for the Indians: The Federalist Quest, 1783–1796." *Essex Institute Historical Collections* 122 (1986).

Almeida, Deirdre A. "The Hidden Half: A History of Native American Women's Education." *Harvard Educational Review* 67 (1997).

Amenta, Edwin. *Bold Relief: Institutional Politics and the Origins of Modern American Social Policy*. Princeton: Princeton University Press, 1998.

Anderson, Fred, and Andrew Cayton. *The Dominion of War: Empire and Liberty in North America, 1500–2000*. New York: Viking, 2005.

Anderson, Terry L. *Sovereign Nations or Reservations? An Economic History of American Indians*. San Francisco: Pacific Research Institute for Public Policy, 1995.

Andrew, John A. III. *From Revivals to Removal: Jeremiah Evarts, the Cherokee Nation, and the Search for the Soul of America*. Athens: University of Georgia Press, 1992.

Aron, Stephen. "Lessons in Conquest: Towards a Greater Western History." *The Pacific Historical Review* 63 (1994).

Athearn, Robert G. *Forts of the Upper Missouri*. Englewood Cliffs, NJ: Prentice Hall, 1967.

______. *William Tecumseh Sherman and the Settlement of the West*. Norman: University of Oklahoma Press, 1995 [1956].

Babcock, Willoughby M. Jr. "Major Lawrence Taliaferro, Indian Agent." *The Mississippi Valley Historical Review* 11 (1924).

Balogh, Brian. *A Government Out of Sight: The Mystery of National Authority in Nineteenth-Century America*. Cambridge: Cambridge University Press, 2009.

Beach, John C., et. al., "State Administration and the Founding Fathers During the Critical Period." *Administration & Society* 28 (1997).

Beatty, Willard W. "The Federal Government and the Education of Indians and Eskimos." *The Journal of Negro Education* 7 (1938).

Beaver, R. Pierce. *Church, State, and the American Indians: Two and a Half Centuries of Partnership in Missions Between Protestant Churches and Government.* St. Louis: Concordia, 1966.

Beeton, Beverly. "Teach Them To Till The Soil: An Experiment With Indian Farms, 1850–1862." *American Indian Quarterly* 3 (1977–1978).

Bender, Norman J. *"New Hope for the Indians": The Grant Peace Policy and the Navajos in the 1870s.* Albuquerque: University of New Mexico Press, 1989.

Bennett, Linda L. M., and Stephen Earl Bennett. *Living With Leviathan: Americans Coming to Terms with Big Government.* Lawrence: University Press of Kansas, 1990.

Bensel, Richard Franklin. *Yankee Leviathan: The Origins of Central State Authority in America, 1859–1877.* Cambridge: Cambridge University Press, 1990.

Berardi, Gigi. "Schools, Settlements, and Sanitation in Alaska Native Villages." *Ethnohistory* 46 (1999).

Berkhofer, Robert F. Jr. "Jefferson, the Ordinance of 1784, and the Origins of the American Territorial System." *The William and Mary Quarterly* 29 (1972).

______. *The White Man's Indian: Images of the American Indian from Columbus to the Present.* New York: Vintage, 1978.

Berlin, Ira, and Leslie M. Harris, eds. *Slavery in New York.* New York: New Press, 2005.

Bernstein, Iver. "Securing Freedom: The Challenges of Black Life in Civil War New York." *Slavery in New York.* Ed. Ira Berlin and Leslie M. Harris. New York: New Press, 2005.

Bertelli, Anthony. "Building the Administrative State." *Public Administration Review* 64 (2004).

Berthrong, Donald J. "Federal Indian Policy and the Southern Cheyennes and Arapahoes, 1887–1907." *The Western American Indian: Case Studies in Tribal History.* Ed. Richard N. Ellis. Lincoln: University of Nebraska Press, 1972.

Blaine, Martha Royce. *Pawnee Passage: 1870–1875.* Norman: University of Oklahoma Press, 1990.

Bland, Larry I. "The Rise of the United States to World Scientific Power, 1840–1940." *The History Teacher* 11 (1977).

Bogue, Allan G. "The Iowa Claim Clubs: Symbol and Substance." *The Public Lands: Studies in the History of the Public Domain.* Ed. Vernon Carstensen. Madison: University of Wisconsin Press, 1968.

Bolton, S. Charles. "Jeffersonian Indian Removal and the Emergence of Arkansas Territory." *Arkansas Historical Quarterly* 62 (2003).

Bond, Beverly W. Jr. "American Civilization Comes to the Old Northwest." *The Mississippi Valley Historical Review* 19 (1932).

______. "William Henry Harrison in the War of 1812." *The Mississippi Valley Historical Review* 13 (1927).

Boughter, Judith A. *Betraying the Omaha Nation, 1790–1916.* Norman: University of Oklahoma Press, 1998.

Bradley, Jared W. "William C. C. Claiborne, the Old Southwest and the Development of American Indian Policy." *Tennessee Historical Quarterly* 33 (1974).

Brave Heart, Maria Yellow Horse, and Lemyra M. DeBruyn. "The American Indian Holocaust: Healing Historical Unresolved Grief." *American Indian and Alaska Native Mental Health Research* 8 (1998).

Britten, Thomas A. "Hoover and the Indians: The Case for Continuity in Federal Indian Policy, 1900–1933." *Historian* 61 (1999).

Brugge, David M. *The Navajo and Hopi Land Dispute: An American Tragedy.* Albuquerque: University of New Mexico Press, 1999.

Bruyneel, Kevin. *The Third Space of Sovereignty: The Postcolonial Politics of U.S.–Indigenous Relations.* Minneapolis: University of Minnesota Press, 2007.

Buecker, Thomas R. "The Post of North Platte Station, 1867–1878." *The Nebraska Indian Wars Reader, 1865–1877.* Ed. R. Eli Paul. Lincoln: University of Nebraska Press, 1998.

Buntin, Martha. "Beginning of the Leasing of the Surplus Grazing Lands on the Kiowa and Comanche Reservation." *Chronicles of Oklahoma* 10 (1932).

Burton, Jeffrey. *Indian Territory and the United States, 1866–1906: Courts, Government, and the Movement for Oklahoma Statehood.* Norman: University of Oklahoma Press, 1995.

Calhoun, Frederick S. *The Lawmen: United States Marshals and Their Deputies, 1789–1989.* New York: Penguin, 1991.

Calloway, Colin G. *The American Revolution in Indian Country: Crisis and Diversity in Native American Communities.* Cambridge: Cambridge University Press, 1995.

Campbell, John. "The Seminoles, the 'Bloodhound War,' and Abolitionism, 1796–1865." *The Journal of Southern History* 72 (2006).

Carpenter, Daniel P. *The Forging of Bureaucratic Autonomy: Reputations, Networks, and Policy Innovation in Executive Agencies, 1862–1928.* Princeton: Princeton University Press, 2001.

Carstensen, Vernon, ed. *The Public Lands: Studies in the History of the Public Domain.* Madison: University of Wisconsin Press, 1968.

Carstensen, Vernon. "Introduction." *The Public Lands: Studies in the History of the Public Domain.* Ed. Vernon Carstensen. Madison: University of Wisconsin Press, 1968.

Carter, Kent. *The Dawes Commission and the Allotment of the Five Civilized Tribes, 1893–1914.* Orem, UT: Ancestry.com, 1999.

Carter, Patricia A. "'Completely Discouraged': Women Teachers' Resistance in the Bureau of Indian Affairs Schools, 1900–1910." *Frontiers* 15 (1995).

Cayford, John E. *Fort Knox: Fortress in Maine.* Bangor, ME: Cay-Bel Publishing, 1983.

Cayton, Andrew R. L. "'Separate Interests' and the Nation-State: The Washington Administration and the Origins of Regionalism in the Trans-Appalachian West." *The Journal of American History* 79 (1992).

Chambers, Nella J. "The Creek Indian Factory at Fort Mitchell." *Alabama Historical Quarterly* 21 (1959).

Champagne, Duane. *Chronology of Native North American History: From Pre-Columbian Times to the Present.* New York: Thomson Gale, 1994.

Chaput, Donald. "Generals, Indian Agents, Politicians: The Doolittle Survey of 1865." *The Western Historical Quarterly* 3 (1972).

Chittenden, Hiram Martin. *The American Fur Trade of the Far West.* Volume 1. Lincoln: University of Nebraska Press, 1986 [1935].

Christianson, James R. "Removal: A Foundation for the Formation of Federal Indian Policy." *Journal of Cherokee Studies* 10 (1985).

Churchill, Ward. *Fantasies of the Master Race: Literature, Cinema and the Colonization of American Indians.* Monroe, ME: Common Courage Press, 1992.

Cimbala, Paul, and Randall Miller. *The Freedmen's Bureau and Reconstruction.* New York: Fordham University Press, 1999.

Clark, Thomas D., and John D. W. Guice, *The Old Southwest, 1795–1830: Frontiers in Conflict.* Norman: University of Oklahoma Press, 1996 [1989].

Clay, Karen B. "Property Rights and Institutions: Congress and the California Land Act of 1851." *The Journal of Economic History* 59 (1999).

Cleland, Charles E. *Rites of Conquest: The History and Culture of Michigan's Native Americans.* Ann Arbor: University of Michigan Press, 1992.

Clemmons, Linda. "'We find it a difficult work': Educating Dakota Children in Missionary Homes, 1835–1862." *American Indian Quarterly* 24 (2000).

Cole, Arthur H. "Cyclical and Sectional Variations in the Sale of Public Lands, 1816–1860." *The Public Lands: Studies in the History of the Public Domain.* Ed. Vernon Carstensen. Madison: University of Wisconsin Press, 1968.

Coleman, Michael C. "The Responses of American Indian Children and Irish Children to the School, 1850s–1920s: A Comparative Study in Cross-Cultural Education." *American Indian Quarterly* 23 (1999).

Coles, Harry L. Jr. "Applicability of the Public Land System to Louisiana." *The Public Lands: Studies in the History of the Public Domain.* Ed. Vernon Carstensen. Madison: University of Wisconsin Press, 1968.

Coman, Katherine. "Government Factories: An Attempt to Control Competition in the Fur Trade." *The American Economic Review* 2 (1912).

Cooley, Rita W. "The Office of the United States Marshal." *The Western Political Quarterly* 12 (1959).

Corwin, Edward S. "The President as Administrative Chief." *The Journal of Politics* 1 (1939).

Cotterill, R. S. "Federal Indian Management in the South, 1789–1825." *The Mississippi Valley Historical Review* 20 (1933).

Crenson, Matthew A. *Building the Invisible Orphanage: A Prehistory of the American Welfare System.* Cambridge, MA: Harvard University Press, 1998.

———. *The Federal Machine: Beginnings of Bureaucracy in Jacksonian America.* Baltimore: The Johns Hopkins University Press, 1975.

Cross, Terry A., Kathleen A. Earle, and David Simmons. "Child Abuse and Neglect in Indian Country: Policy Issues." *Families in Society* 81 (2000).

Cumfer, Cynthia. "Local Origins of National Indian Policy: Cherokee and Tennessean Ideas About Sovereignty and Nationhood, 1790–1811." *Journal of the Early Republic* 23 (2003).

Dale, Edward Everett. *The Indians of the Southwest: A Century of Development Under the United States.* Norman: University of Oklahoma Press, 1949.

Danhof, Clarence H. "Farm-Making Costs and the 'Safety Valve': 1850–1860." *The Public Lands: Studies in the History of the Public Domain*. Ed. Vernon Carstensen. Madison: University of Wisconsin Press, 1968.

Danker, Donald F. "The North Brothers and the Pawnee Scouts." *The Nebraska Indian Wars Reader, 1865–1877*. Ed. R. Eli Paul. Lincoln: University of Nebraska Press, 1998.

Davis, David Brion. *Inhuman Bondage: The Rise and Fall of Slavery in the New World*. Oxford: Oxford University Press, 2006.

Debo, Angie. *A History of the Indians of the United States*. Norman: University of Oklahoma Press, 1970.

DeJong, David H. "'Unless They Are Kept Alive': Federal Indian Schools and Student Health, 1878–1918." *American Indian Quarterly* 31 (2007).

D'Elia, Donald J. "The Argument Over Civilian or Military Indian Control, 1865–1880." *The Historian* 42 (1962).

Deloria, Vine Jr., and Clifford M. Lytle. *American Indians, American Justice*. Austin: University of Texas Press, 1983.

Deloria, Vine Jr., and David E. Wilkins. *Tribes, Treaties, & Constitutional Tribulations*. Austin: University of Texas Press, 1999.

DeRosier, Arthur H. Jr. *The Removal of the Choctaw Indians*. New York: Harper, 1972.

Dinnerstein, Leonard, and Kenneth T. Jackson, eds. *American Vistas, 1607–1877*. 2nd ed. New York: Oxford University Press, 1975.

Dobyns, Henry F. "Estimating Aboriginal American Population: An Appraisal of Techniques with a New Hemispheric Estimate." *Current Anthropology* 7 (1966).

______. *Their Number Become Thinned: Native American Population Dynamics in Eastern North America*. Knoxville: University of Tennessee Press, 1983.

Donald, David Herbert. *Lincoln*. New York: Touchstone, 1996.

Dow, George Francis. *Slave Ships and Slaving*. Mineola, NY: Dover, 2002 [1927].

Downes, Randolph C. *Council Fires on the Upper Ohio*. Pittsburgh: University of Pittsburgh Press, 1989 [1940].

Draper, Lyman Copeland, ed. *Collections of the State Historical Society of Wisconsin*. Vol. VII. Madison: Wisconsin Historical Society, 1908 [1876].

Drinnon, Richard. *Facing West: The Metaphysics of Indian Hating & Empire Building*. New York: Schocken, 1990.

Dubnick, Melvin. "Customs Service." *A Historical Guide to the U.S. Government*. Ed. George T. Kurian. New York: Oxford University Press, 1998.

Du Bois, W. E. B. *The Souls of Black Folk*. New York: Vintage, 1990.

Dunham, Harold H. "Some Crucial Years of the General Land Office, 1875–1890." *The Public Lands: Studies in the History of the Public Domain*. Ed. Vernon Carstensen. Madison: University of Wisconsin Press, 1968.

Duthu, N. Bruce. *American Indians and the Law*. New York: Viking, 2008.

Edling, Max M. *A Revolution on Favor of Government: Origins of the U.S. Constitution and the Making of the American State*. Oxford: Oxford University Press, 2003.

Eid, Leroy V. "American Indian Military Leadership: St. Clair's 1791 Defeat." *The Journal of Military History* 57 (1993).

Ellenberg, George B. "An Uncivil War of Words: Indian Removal in the Press, 1830." *Atlanta History* 33 (1989).

Ellis, Clyde. "Boarding School Life at the Kiowa-Comanche Agency, 1893–1920." *Historian* 58 (1996).

Ellis, Richard N. "General Pope and the Old 'Hand-to-Mouth Way.'" *The Western American Indian: Case Studies in Tribal History*. Ed. Richard N. Ellis. Lincoln: University of Nebraska Press, 1972.

Ellis, Richard N., ed. *The Western American Indian: Case Studies in Tribal History*. Lincoln: University of Nebraska Press, 1972.

Ellison, Joseph. "The Mineral Land Question in California, 1848–1866." *The Public Lands: Studies in the History of the Public Domain*. Ed. Vernon Carstensen. Madison: University of Wisconsin Press, 1968.

Evans, Stephen H. *The United States Coast Guard, 1790–1915: A Definitive History with a Postscript, 1915–1949*. Annapolis: United States Naval Institute, 1949.

Feller, Daniel. *The Jacksonian Promise: America, 1815–1840*. Baltimore: The Johns Hopkins University Press, 1995.

———. *The Public Lands in Jacksonian Politics*. Madison: University of Wisconsin Press, 1984.

Feuss, Claude Moore. *Carl Schurz: Reformer, 1829–1906*. Port Washington, NY: Kennikat Press, 1932.

Finger, John R. "The Abortive Second Cherokee Removal, 1841–1844." *The Journal of Southern History* 47 (1981).

———. *The Eastern Band of Cherokees, 1819–1900*. Knoxville: University of Tennessee Press, 1984.

Forbes, Jack D. *Africans and Native Americans: The Language of Race and the Evolution of Red-Black Peoples*. 2nd ed. Urbana: University of Illinois Press, 1993.

Foreman, Grant. *The Five Civilized Tribes: Cherokee, Chickasaw, Choctaw, Creek, Seminole*. Norman: University of Oklahoma Press, 1934.

———. *The Last Trek of the Indians*. New York: Russell & Russell, 1972 [1946].

———. *Indians and Pioneers: The Story of the American Southwest Before 1830*. Revised edition. Norman: University of Oklahoma Press, 1936.

———. *Indian Removal: The Emigration of the Five Civilized Tribes of Indians*. Norman: University of Oklahoma Press, 1953.

Fowler, Loretta. *Arapahoe Politics, 1851–1978: Symbols in Crises of Authority*. Lincoln: University of Nebraska Press, 1986.

Frederickson, H. George. *The Spirit of Public Administration*. San Francisco: Jossey-Bass, 1996.

Friedberg, Aaron L. "American Antistatism and the Founding of the Cold War State." *Shaped by War and Trade: International Influences on American Political Development*. Ed. Ira Katznelson and Martin Shefter. Princeton: Princeton University Press, 2002.

Gaines, George S. "Notes on the Early Days of South Alabama." Reprinted in *The Alabama Historical Quarterly* 26 (1964).

Gara, Larry. *The Presidency of Franklin Pierce*. Lawrence: University Press of Kansas, 1991.

Garrison, Tim Alan. "Beyond *Worcester*: The Alabama Supreme Court and the Sovereignty of the Creek Nation." *Journal of the Early Republic* 19 (1999).

______. *The Legal Ideology of Removal: The Southern Judiciary and the Sovereignty of Native American Nations*. Athens: The University of Georgia Press, 2002.

Garroutte, Eva Marie. "The Racial Formation of American Indians: Negotiating Legitimate Identities within Tribal and Federal Law." *American Indian Quarterly* 25 (2001).

Gates, Charles M. "The West in American Diplomacy, 1812–1815." *The Mississippi Valley Historical Review* 26 (1940).

Gates, Paul Wallace. "The Homestead Law in an Incongruous Land System." *The American Historical Review* 41 (1936).

______. "The Role of the Land Speculator in Western Development." *The Public Lands: Studies in the History of the Public Domain*. Ed. Vernon Carstensen. Madison: University of Wisconsin Press, 1968.

Gere, Anne Ruggles. "Indian Heart/White Man's Head: Native-American Teachers in Indian Schools, 1880–1930." *History of Education Quarterly* 45 (2005).

Gillman, Howard. "How Political Parties Can Use the Courts to Advance Their Agendas: Federal Courts in the United States, 1875–1891." *The American Political Science Review* 96 (2002).

Glatthaar, Joseph T., and James Kirby Martin. *Forgotten Allies: The Oneida Indians and the American Revolution*. New York: Hill and Wang, 1996.

Goetzmann, William H. *Army Exploration in the American West, 1803–1863*. Lincoln: University of Nebraska Press, 1959.

______. "The West and the American Age of Exploration." *American Vistas, 1607–1877*. 2nd ed. Eds. Leonard Dinnerstein and Kenneth T. Jackson. New York: Oxford University Press, 1975.

Goodwin, Frank P. "The Rise of Manufactures in the Miami Country." *The American Historical Review* 12 (1907).

Green, Michael D. *The Politics of Indian Removal: Creek Government and Society in Crisis*. Lincoln: University of Nebraska Press, 1985.

Green, William D. *A Peculiar Imbalance: The Fall and Rise of Racial Equality in Early Minnesota*. St. Paul: Minnesota Historical Society Press, 2007.

Gregg, Josiah. *The Commerce of the Prairies*. Ed. Milo Milton Quaife. Lincoln: University of Nebraska Press, 1967.

Grinde, Donald A. Jr. "Iroquoian Political Concept and the Genesis of American Government." *Indian Roots of American Democracy*. Ed. José Barreiro. Ithaca, NY: Akwe:kon Press, 1992.

Gunderson, Robert Gray. *The Log-Cabin Campaign*. New York: Greenwood Press Reprint, 1977 [1957].

Guthrie, Chester L., and Leo L. Gerald. "Upper Missouri Agency: An Account of Indian Administration on the Frontier." *The Pacific Historical Review* 10 (1941).

Hagan, William T. "Adjusting to the Opening of the Kiowa, Comanche, and Kiowa-Apache Reservation." *The Plains Indians of the Twentieth Century*. Ed. Peter Iverson. Norman: University of Oklahoma Press, 1985.

______. *Indian Police and Judges*. Lincoln: University of Nebraska Press, 1966.

______. "Squaw Men on the Kiowa, Comanche, and Apache Reservation: Advance Agents of Civilization or Disturbers of the Peace?" *The Frontier Challenge:*

Responses to the Trans-Mississippi West. Ed. John G. Clark. Lawrence: The University Press of Kansas, 1971.

______. *United States-Comanche Relations: The Reservation Years*. Norman: University of Oklahoma Press, 1990 [1976].

Hamilton, Alexander. *Writings*. New York: Library of America, 2001.

Hargreaves, Mary W. M. *The Presidency of John Quincy Adams*. Lawrence: University Press of Kansas, 1985.

Harmon, Alexandra. "American Indians and Land Monopolies in the Gilded Age." *The Journal of American History* 90 (2003).

Harmon, George D. "Benjamin Hawkins and the Federal Factory System." *The North Carolina Historical Review* 9 (1932).

______. "The United States Indian Policy in Texas, 1845–1860." *The Mississippi Valley Historical Review* 17 (1930).

Harring, Sidney L. *Crow Dog's Case: American Indian Sovereignty, Tribal Law, and United States Law in the Nineteenth Century*. Cambridge: Cambridge University Press, 1994.

Harrington, Earl G. "Cadastral Surveys for the Public Lands of the United States." *The Public Lands: Studies in the History of the Public Domain*. Ed. Vernon Carstensen. Madison: University of Wisconsin Press, 1968.

Harrison, Robert W. "Public Land Records of the Federal Government." *The Public Lands: Studies in the History of the Public Domain*. Ed. Vernon Carstensen. Madison: University of Wisconsin Press, 1968.

Hauptman, Laurence M. *Between Two Fires: American Indians in the Civil War*. New York: Free Press Paperbacks, 1996.

______. *Conspiracy of Interests: Iroquois Dispossession and the Rise of New York State*. Syracuse: Syracuse University Press, 1999.

______. "John E. Wool and the New York City Draft Riots of 1863: A Reassessment." *Civil War History* 49 (2003).

Hawkins, Benjamin. *A Sketch of the Creek Country, in the Years 1798 and 1799 [1848] and Letters of Benjamin Hawkins, 1796–1806 [1916]*. Spartansburg, SC: Reprint Co., 1974.

Heffer, Jean. *The United States and the Pacific: History of a Frontier*. Notre Dame: University of Notre Dame Press, 2002.

Heizer, Robert F., ed. *The Destruction of California Indians*. Lincoln: University of Nebraska Press, 1993 [1974].

Hendrick, Irving G. "Federal Policy Affecting the Education of Indians in California, 1849–1934." *History of Education Quarterly* 16 (1976).

Henri, Florette. *The Southern Indians and Benjamin Hawkins, 1796–1816*. Norman: University of Oklahoma Press, 1986.

Henry, Robert S. "The Railroad Grant Legend in American History Texts." *The Public Lands: Studies in the History of the Public Domain*. Ed. Vernon Carstensen. Madison: University of Wisconsin Press, 1968.

Herndon, Ruth Wallis, and Ella Wilcox Sekatau. "The Right to a Name: The Narragansett People and Rhode Island Officials in the Revolutionary Era." *Major Problems in American Indian History*. 2nd ed. Ed. Albert L. Hurtado and Peter Iverson. Boston: Houghton Mifflin, 2001.

Herring, Joseph B. *The Enduring Indians of Kansas: A Century and a Half of Acculturation*. Lawrence: University Press of Kansas, 1990.

______. "Indian Intransigency in Kansas: Government Bureaucracy vs. Mokohoko's Sacs and Foxes." *The Western Historical Quarterly* 17 (1986).

Hirschfeld, Fritz. *George Washington and Slavery: A Documentary Portrayal.* Columbia: University of Missouri Press, 1997.

Hoopes, Alban W. *Indian Affairs and their Administration, 1849–1860.* New York: Kraus Reprint, 1972 [1932].

Hopkins, Raymond F. "The international role of 'domestic' bureaucracy." *International Organization* 30 (1976).

Horsman, Reginald. *Expansion and American Indian Policy, 1783–1812.* Norman: University of Oklahoma Press, 1992 [1967].

______. *The Frontier in the Formative Years, 1783–1815.* Albuquerque: University of New Mexico Press, 1975.

Howe, Daniel Walker. "Church, State, and Education in the Young American Republic." *Journal of the Early Republic* 22 (2002).

Hoxie, Frederick E. *A Final Promise: The Campaign to Assimilate the Indians, 1880–1920.* Cambridge: Cambridge University Press, 1995 [1984].

Hurt, R. Douglas. *The Ohio Frontier: Crucible of the Old Northwest, 1720–1830.* Bloomington: University of Indiana Press, 1996.

Huston, James L. "An Alternative to the Tragic Era: Applying the Virtues of Bureaucracy to the Reconstruction Dilemma." *Civil War History* 51 (2005).

Irving, Washington. *The Adventures of Captain Bonneville.* Washington, DC: National Geographic, 2003 [1837].

Irwin, Lee. "Freedom, Law, and Prophecy: A Brief History of Native American Religious Resistance." *American Indian Quarterly* 21 (1997).

Isenberg, Andrew C. "The Market Revolution in the Borderlands: George Champlin Sibley in Missouri and New Mexico, 1808–1826." *Journal of the Early Republic* 21 (2001).

Jackson, Curtis E., and Marcia J. Galli. *A History of the Bureau of Indian Affairs and Its Activities Among Indians.* San Francisco: R&E Research Associates, 1977.

Jackson, W. Turrentine. "The Governorship of Wyoming, 1885–1889: A Study in Territorial Politics." *The Pacific Historical Review* 13 (1944).

______. "Indian Affairs and Politics in Idaho Territory, 1863–1870." *The Pacific Historical Review* 14 (1945).

Jennings, Francis. *The Creation of America: Through Revolution to Empire.* Cambridge: Cambridge University Press, 2000.

______. *The Invasion of America: Indians, Colonialism, and the Cant of Conquest.* New York: Norton, 1976.

Jensen, Laura. *Patriots, Settlers, and the Origins of American Social Policy.* Cambridge: Cambridge University Press, 2003.

Johansen, Bruce E. *Debating Democracy: Native American Legacy of Freedom.* Santa Fe, NM: Clear Light, 1998.

John, Richard R. "Elaborations, Revisions, Dissents: Alfred D. Chandler, Jr.'s The Visible Hand after Twenty Years." *Business History Review* 71 (1997).

______. *Spreading the News: The American Postal System from Franklin to Morse.* Cambridge, MA: Harvard University Press, 1995.

Johnson, Willard R. "Tracing Trails of Blood on Ice: Commemorating 'The Great Escape' in 1861–62 of Indians and Blacks into Kansas." *Negro History Bulletin* 64 (2001).

Josephy, Alvin M. Jr. *The Nez Perce Indians and the Opening of the Northwest.* Boston: Houghton Mifflin, 1997 [1965].

Kane, Lucile. "Federal Protection of Public Timber in the Upper Great Lakes States." *The Public Lands: Studies in the History of the Public Domain.* Ed. Vernon Carstensen. Madison: University of Wisconsin Press, 1968.

Katz, Michael B. *In the Shadow of the Poorhouse: A Social History of Welfare in America.* 10th ed. New York: Basic Books, 1996 [1986].

Katznelson, Ira. "Flexible Capacity: The Military and Early American Statebuilding." *Shaped by War and Trade: International Influences on American Political Development.* Ed. Ira Katznelson and Martin Shefter. Princeton: Princeton University Press, 2002.

———. "Rewriting the Epic of America." *Shaped by War and Trade: International Influences on American Political Development.* Ed. Ira Katznelson and Martin Shefter. Princeton: Princeton University Press, 2002.

Katznelson, Ira, and Martin Shefter. *Shaped by War and Trade: International Influences on American Political Development.* Princeton: Princeton University Press, 2002.

Kaufman, Herbert. *The Forest Ranger: A Study in Administrative Behavior.* Washington, DC: RFF Press, 2006.

Kaufmann, J. E. & H. W. Kaufmann. *Fortress America: The Forts that Defended America, 1600 to the Present.* Cambridge, MA: Da Capo Press, 2004.

Kelman, Ari. "Deadly Currents: John Ross's Decision of 1861." *Major Problems in American Indian History.* 2nd ed. Ed. Albert L. Hurtado and Peter Iverson. Boston: Houghton Mifflin, 2001.

Kelsey, Harry. "The Doolittle Report of 1867: Its Preparation and Shortcomings." *Arizona and the West* 17 (1975).

Keohane, Robert O. "International Commitments and American Political Institutions in the Nineteenth Century." *Shaped by War and Trade: International Influences on American Political Development.* Ed. Ira Katznelson and Martin Shefter. Princeton: Princeton University Press, 2002.

Kerber, Linda K. "The Abolitionist Perception of the Indian." *The Journal of American History* 62 (1975).

Kerwin, Cornelius M. "Introduction." *Federal Regulatory Directory.* 6th ed. Washington, DC: Congressional Quarterly, 1990.

Kessell, John L. "General Sherman and the Navajo Treaty of 1868: A Basic and Expedient Misunderstanding." *The Western Historical Quarterly* 12 (1981).

Key, Joseph Patrick. "Indians and Ecological Conflict in Territorial Arkansas." *The Arkansas Historical Quarterly* 59 (2000).

Khademian, Anne M. *Working with Culture: The Way the Job Gets Done in Public Programs.* Washington, DC: CQ Press, 2002.

Killoren, John J. *"Come, Blackrobe": De Smet and the Indian Tragedy.* Norman: University of Oklahoma Press, 1994.

Kilpinen, Jon T. "The Supreme Court's Role in Choctaw and Chickasaw Dispossession." *Geographical Review* 94 (2004).

King, Desmond S., and Rogers M. Smith. "Racial Orders in American Political Development." *American Political Science Review* 99 (2005).

King, Irving H. *The Coast Guard Expands, 1865–1915: New Roles, New Frontiers.* Annapolis: Naval Institute Press, 1996.

King, James T. "The Republican River Expedition, June–July, 1869." *The Nebraska Indian Wars Reader, 1865–1877.* Ed. R. Eli Paul. Lincoln: University of Nebraska Press, 1998.

Klos, George. "Blacks and the Seminole Removal Debate, 1821–1835." *The Florida Historical Quarterly* **68** (1989).

Knight, Oliver. "War or Peace: The Anxious Wait for Crazy Horse." *The Nebraska Indian Wars Reader, 1865–1877.* Ed. R. Eli Paul. Lincoln: University of Nebraska Press, 1998.

Kunitz, Stephen J. "The History and Politics of US Health Care Policy for American Indians and Alaskan Natives." *American Journal of Public Health* **86** (1996).

Kvasnicka, Robert M., and Herman J. Viola, eds. *The Commissioners of Indian Affairs, 1824–1977.* Lincoln: University of Nebraska Press, 1979.

Landis, Michele L. "'Let Me Next Time Be "Tried by Fire"': Disaster Relief and the Origins of the American Welfare State 1789–1874." *Northwestern University Law Review* **92** (1998).

Lavender, David. *The Fist in the Wilderness: A Narrative History of the American Fur Trade.* New York: Doubleday, 1964.

______. *The Great West.* Boston: Houghton Mifflin, 2000 [1965].

LaVere, David. *Contrary Neighbors: Southern Plains and Removed Indians in Indian Territory.* Norman: University of Oklahoma Press, 2000.

Lawrence, Bonita. "Gender, Race, and the Regulation of Native Identity in Canada and the United States: An Overview." *Hypatia* **18** (2003).

Lee, Mordecai. *The First Presidential Communications Agency: FDR's Office of Government Reports.* Albany: State University of New York Press, 2005.

Lewis, Emanuel Raymond. *Seacoast Fortifications of the United States: An Introductory History.* Annapolis: Naval Institute Press, 1979.

Light, Paul C. *The True Size of Government.* Washington, DC: Brookings Institution Press, 1999.

Limerick, Patricia Nelson. *The Legacy of Conquest: The Unbroken Past of the American West.* New York: Norton, 1987.

Linklater, Andro. *Measuring America: How an Untamed Wilderness Shaped the United States and Fulfilled the Promise of Democracy.* New York: Plume, 2003.

Lipsky, Michael. *Street-Level Bureaucracy: Dilemmas of the Individual in Public Services.* New York: Russell Sage Foundation, 1983.

Litton, Gaston, ed. "The Journal of a Party of Emigrating Creek Indians, 1835–1836." *The Journal of Southern History* **7** (1941).

Livermore, Shaw. *Early American Land Companies: Their Influence on Corporate Development.* New York: Octagon, 1968.

Low, John, and Paula Holley. "Treaty of Chicago – September, 1833." *Native Chicago.* 2nd ed. Ed. Terry Straus. Chicago: Albatross Press, 2002.

Lowi, Theodore J. *The End of Liberalism: Ideology, Policy, and the Crisis of Public Authority.* New York: Norton, 1969.

______. *The End of the Republican Era.* Norman: University of Oklahoma Press, 1995.

Lowrie, Walter, and Matthew St. Clair Clarke, eds. *American State Papers: Indian Affairs*. Washington, DC: Gales and Seaton, 1832.

Lynn, Laurence E. Jr. "The Myth of the Bureaucratic Paradigm: What Traditional Public Administration Really Stood For." *Public Administration Review* 61 (2001).

Madrick, Jeff. *The Case for Big Government*. Princeton: Princeton University Press, 2009.

Magrath, C. Peter. *Yazoo: The Case of Fletcher v. Peck*. New York: Norton, 1966.

Mahon, John K. *History of the Second Seminole War, 1835–1842*. Gainesville: University of Florida Press, 1992.

Malone, Dumas. *Jefferson the Virginian*. Boston: Little, Brown, and Company, 1948.

Malone, Michael P. *James J. Hill: Empire Builder of the Northwest*. Norman: University of Oklahoma Press, 1996.

Mancall, Peter C. "Men, Women, and Alcohol in Indian Villages in the Great Lakes Region in the Early Republic." *Journal of the Early Republic* 15 (1995).

Maranto, Robert, and David Schultz. *A Short History of the United States Civil Service*. Lanham, MD: University Press of America, 1991.

Marshall, S. L. A. *Crimsoned Prairie: The Indian Wars*. New York: Da Capo Press, 1972.

Mashaw, Jerry L. "Recovering American Administrative Law: Federalist Foundations, 1787–1801." *The Yale Law Journal* 115 (2006).

Mattes, Merrill J. *The Great Platte River Road: The Covered Wagon Mainline Via Fort Kearny to Fort Laramie*. Lincoln: University of Nebraska Press, 1969.

Mayer, Henry. *All on Fire: William Lloyd Garrison and the Abolition of Slavery*. New York: St. Martin's Griffin, 1998.

McCoy, Donald R. "The Special Indian Agency in Alaska, 1873–1874: Its Origins and Operation." *The Pacific Historical Review* 25 (1956).

McCraw, Thomas K. "Business & Government: The Origins of the Adversary Relationship." *California Management Review* 26 (1984).

McDonnell, Janet A. *The Dispossession of the American Indian, 1887–1934*. Bloomington: Indiana University Press, 1991.

McGillycuddy, Julia B. *Blood on the Moon: Valentine McGillycuddy and the Sioux*. Lincoln: University of Nebraska Press, 1969 [1941].

McLaughlin, James. *My Friend the Indian*. Lincoln: University of Nebraska Press, 1989 [1910].

McLoughlin, William G. *After the Trail of Tears: The Cherokees' Struggle for Sovereignty, 1839–1880*. Chapel Hill: The University of North Carolina Press, 1993.

———. *Cherokees and Missionaries, 1789–1839*. Norman: University of Oklahoma Press, 1995.

———. *Cherokee Renascence in the New Republic*. Princeton: Princeton University Press, 1986.

McPherson, Robert S. *The Northern Navajo Frontier, 1860–1900: Expansion Through Adversity*. Albuquerque: University of New Mexico Press, 1988.

Melnick, R. Shep. "An American Dilemma." *Wilson Quarterly* 23 (1999).

Merrill, Karen R. "In Search of the 'Federal Presence' in the American West." *The Western Historical Quarterly* 30 (1999).

Meyer, Carter Jones, and Diana Royer, eds. *Selling the Indian: Commercializing & Appropriating American Indian Cultures*. Tucson: University of Arizona Press, 2001.

Meyer, Melissa L. *The White Earth Tragedy: Ethnicity and Dispossession at a Minnesota Anishinaabe Reservation*. Lincoln: University of Nebraska Press, 1994.

Meyer, Roy W. *History of the Santee Sioux: United States Indian Policy on Trial*. Revised edition. Lincoln: University of Nebraska Press, 1993.

Milakovich, Michael E., and George J. Gordon. *Public Administration in America*. 7th ed. Boston: Bedford/St. Martin's, 2001.

Miller, John C. *The Federalist Era, 1789–1801*. New York: Harper & Row, 1960.

Million, Dian. "Policing the Rez: Keeping No Peace in Indian Country." *Social Justice* 27 (2000).

Miner, H. Craig. *The Corporation and the Indian: Tribal Sovereignty and Industrial Civilization in Indian Territory, 1865–1907*. Norman: University of Oklahoma Press, 1989 [1976].

Mitchell, Fredric, and James W. Skelton. "The Church-State Conflict in Early Indian Education." *History of Education Quarterly* 6 (1966).

Mohr, Walter H. *Federal Indian Relations, 1774–1788*. New York: AMS Press, 1971.

Monjeau-Marz, Corinne L. *The Dakota Indian Internment at Fort Snelling, 1862–1864*. St. Paul: Prairie Smoke Press, 2006.

Moore, William Haas. *Chiefs, Agents & Soldiers: Conflict on the Navajo Frontier, 1868–1882*. Albuquerque: University of New Mexico Press, 1994.

Morgan, Dale L. "The Administration of Indian Affairs in Utah, 1851–1858." *The Pacific Historical Review* 17 (1948).

Morris, Richard B., ed. *Encyclopedia of American History*. 6th ed. New York: Harper & Row, 1982.

Morris, Wayne. "Traders and Factories on the Arkansas Frontier, 1805–1822." *The Arkansas Historical Quarterly* 28 (1969).

Nash, Gerald D. "Bureaucracy and Reform in the West: Notes on the Influence of a Neglected Interest Group." *The Western Historical Quarterly* 2 (1971).

Neil, William M. "The Territorial Governor as Indian Superintendent in the Trans-Mississippi West." *The Mississippi Valley Historical Review* 43 (1956).

Neiman, Max. *Defending Government: Why Big Government Works*. Upper Saddle River, NJ: Prentice Hall, 2000.

Nelson, Michael. "A Short, Ironic History of American National Bureaucracy." *The Journal of Politics* 44 (1982).

Nettl, J. P. "The State as a Conceptual Variable." *World Politics* 20 (1968).

Nichols, David A. *Lincoln and the Indians: Civil War Policy & Politics*. Urbana: University of Illinois Press, 2000.

Nies, Judith. *Native American History: A Chronology of a Culture's Vast Achievements and their Links to World Events*. New York: Ballantine, 1996.

Noble, Dennis L. *That Others Might Live: The U.S. Life-Saving Service, 1878–1915*. Annapolis: Naval Institute Press, 1994.

Nobles, Melissa. "History Counts: A Comparative Analysis of Racial/Color Categorization in US and Brazilian Censuses." *American Journal of Public Health* 90 (2000).

Novak, William J. *The People's Welfare: Law & Regulation in Nineteenth-Century America*. Chapel Hill: The University of North Carolina Press, 1996.

———. "Private Wealth and Public Health: a critique of Richard Epstein's defense of the 'old' public health." *Perspectives in Biology and Medicine* 46 (2003).

Nye, Russel Blaine. *The Cultural Life of the New Nation*. New York: Harper, 1960.

O'Donnell, Terence. *An Arrow in the Earth: General Joel Palmer and the Indians of Oregon*. Portland: Oregon Historical Society, 1991.

Ogle, Ralph H. "The End of Apache Resistance." *The Western American Indian: Case Studies in Tribal History*. Ed. Richard N. Ellis. Lincoln: University of Nebraska Press, 1972.

Oliphant, J. Orin. "Encroachments of Cattlemen on Indian Reservations in the Pacific Northwest, 1870–1890." *Agricultural History* 24 (1950).

Olson, James C. *Red Cloud and the Sioux Problem*. Lincoln: University of Nebraska Press, 1965.

———. "Red Cloud vs. McGillycuddy." *The Western American Indian: Case Studies in Tribal History*. Ed. Richard N. Ellis. Lincoln: University of Nebraska Press, 1972.

O'Neil, Floyd A. "Hiram Price." The Commissioners of Indian Affairs, 1824–1977. Ed. Robert M. Kvasnicka and Herman J. Viola. Lincoln: University of Nebraska Press, 1979.

Onuf, Peter S. *The Origins of the Federal Republic: Jurisdictional Controversies in the United States, 1775–1787*. Philadelphia: University of Pennsylvania Press, 1983.

———. *Statehood and Union: A History of the Northwest Ordinance*. Bloomington: Indiana University Press, 1987.

Orloff, Anna Shola. "The Political Origins of America's Belated Welfare State." *The Politics of Social Policy in the United States*. Ed. Margaret Weir, Ann Shola Orloff, and Theda Skocpol. Princeton: Princeton University Press, 1988.

Orr, Joan Greene. "Civilize the Indian: Government Policies, Quakers, and Cherokee Education." *The Southern Friend* 10 (1988).

Osburn, Katherine M. B. "'To Build Up the Morals of the Tribe': Southern Ute Women's Sexual Behavior and the Office of Indian Affairs, 1895–1932." *Journal of Women's History* 9 (1997).

Otis, D. S. *The Dawes Act and the Allotment of Indian Lands*. Norman: University of Oklahoma Press, 1973.

Owens, Robert M. "Jeffersonian Benevolence on the Ground: The Indian Land Cession Treaties of William Henry Harrison." *Journal of the Early Republic* 22 (2002).

Owsley, Frank L. Jr. "Benjamin Hawkins, the First Modern Indian Agent." *Alabama Historical Quarterly* 30 (1968).

Parsons, Lynn Hudson. "'A Perpetual Harrow upon My Feelings': John Quincy Adams and the American Indian." *The New England Quarterly* 46 (1973).

Paul, R. Eli, ed. *The Nebraska Indian Wars Reader, 1865–1877*. Lincoln: University of Nebraska Press, 1998.

Peake, Ora Brooks. *A History of the United States Indian Factory System, 1795–1822*. Denver: Sage, 1954.

Pearson, J. Diane. "Lewis Cass and the Politics of Disease: The Indian Vaccination Act of 1832." *Wicazo Sa Review* 18 (2003).
Perdue, Theda. *Nations Remembered: An Oral History of the Cherokees, Chickasaws, Choctaws, Creeks, and Seminoles in Oklahoma, 1865–1907*. Norman: University of Oklahoma Press, 1980.
Philbrick, Francis S. *The Rise of the West, 1754–1830*. New York: Harper & Row, 1965.
Phillips, George Harwood. *"Bringing Them under Subjection": California's Tejon Indian Reservation and Beyond, 1852–1864*. Lincoln: University of Nebraska Press, 2004.
______. *Indians and Indian Agents: The Origins of the Reservation System in California, 1849–1852*. Norman: University of Oklahoma Press, 1997.
Pitney, John J. Jr. "The Coming Ascent of Congress." *Policy Review* 100 (2000).
Plaisance, Aloysius. "The Arkansas Factory, 1805–1810." *Arkansas Historical Quarterly* 11 (1952).
______. "The Chickasaw Bluffs Factory and Its Removal to the Arkansas River, 1818–1822." *Tennessee Historical Quarterly* XI (1952).
______. "The United States Government Factory System, 1796–1822." Unpublished Ph.D. dissertation, St. Louis University. 1954.
Platt, Anthony M., and Jenifer L. Cooreman. "A Multicultural Chronology of Welfare Policy and Social Work in the United States." *Social Justice* 28 (2001).
Pomeroy, Earl S. *The Territories and the United States, 1861–1890: Studies in Colonial Administration*. Seattle: University of Washington Press, 1947.
______. "Toward a Reorientation of Western History: Continuity and Environment." *The Mississippi Valley Historical Review* 41 (1955).
Preston, Daniel. "The Administration and Reform of the U.S. Patent Office, 1790–1836." *Journal of the Early Republic* 5 (1985).
Prucha, Francis Paul. *American Indian Policy in the Formative Years: The Indian Trade and Intercourse Acts, 1790–1834*. Lincoln: University of Nebraska Press, 1962.
______. *American Indian Treaties: The History of a Political Anomaly*. Berkeley: University of California Press, 1997.
______. *The Great Father: The United States Government and the American Indians*. Lincoln: University of Nebraska Press, 1984.
______. *The Sword of the Republic: The United States Army on the Frontier, 1783–1846*. Bloomington: University of Indiana Press, 1977.
______. "Thomas L. McKenney and the New York Indian Board." *The Mississippi Valley Historical Review* 48 (1962).
Prucha, Francis Paul, ed. *Americanizing the American Indians: Writings by the "Friends of the Indian" 1880–1900*. Cambridge, MA: Harvard University Press, 1973.
______. *Documents of United States Indian Policy*. 2nd ed. Lincoln: University of Nebraska Press, 1990.
Purser, Joyce. "The Administration of Indian Affairs in Louisiana, 1803–1820." *Louisiana History* 5 (1964).
Quaife, M. M. "An Experiment of the Fathers in State Socialism." *Wisconsin Magazine of History* 3 (1920).

Rayman, Ronald. "Joseph Lancaster's Monitorial System of Instruction and American Indian Education, 1815–1838." *History of Education Quarterly* 21 (1981).

Remini, Robert V. *Andrew Jackson and his Indian Wars*. New York: Viking, 2001.

———. *The Battle of New Orleans: Andrew Jackson and America's First Military Victory*. New York: Viking, 1999.

Reyhner, Jon, and Jeanne Eder. "A History of Indian Education." *Teaching American Indian Students*. Ed. Jon Reyhner. Norman: University of Oklahoma Press, 1994.

Rich, Wesley Everett. *The History of the United States Post Office to the Year 1829*. Cambridge, MA: Harvard University Press, 1924.

Richmond, Robert W., and Robert W. Mardock, eds. *A Nation Moving West: Readings in the History of the American Frontier*. Lincoln: University of Nebraska Press, 1966.

Riding In, James. "'*The United States* v. *Yellow Sun et. al. (The Pawnee People)*': A Case Study of Institutional and Societal Racism and U.S. Justice in Nebraska from the 1850s to 1870s." *Wicazo Sa Review* 17 (2002).

Roberts, Gary L. "Alfred Burton Greenwood." *The Commissioners of Indian Affairs, 1824–1977*. Ed. Robert M. Kvasnicka and Herman J. Viola. Lincoln: University of Nebraska Press, 1979.

Rodgers, Bradley A. *Guardian of the Great Lakes: The U.S. Paddle Frigate* Michigan. Ann Arbor: University of Michigan Press, 1996.

Rohr, John A. *To Run a Constitution: The Legitimacy of the Administrative State*. Lawrence: The University Press of Kansas, 1986.

Rohrbough, Malcolm J. *The Land Office Business: The Settlement and Administration of American Public Lands, 1789–1837*. New York: Oxford University Press, 1968.

Rollins, Peter C., and John E. O'Connor, eds. *Hollywood's Indian: The Portrayal of the Native American in Film*. Lexington: The University Press of Kentucky, 1998.

Ronda, James P. "Red-Head's Domain: William Clark's Indian Brokerage." *Between Indian and White Worlds*. Ed. Margaret Connell Szasz. Norman: University of Oklahoma Press, 1994.

Rosenbloom, David H. "History Lessons for Reinventors." *Public Administration Review* 61 (2001).

———. "Retrofitting the Administrative State to the Constitution: Congress and the Judiciary's Twentieth-Century Progress." *Public Administration Review* 60 (2000).

Royster, Charles. *The Fabulous History of the Great Dismal Swamp Company: A Story of George Washington's Times*. New York: Vintage, 1999.

Satz, Ronald N. *American Indian Policy in the Jacksonian Era*. Lincoln: University of Nebraska Press, 1975.

———. *Tennessee's Indian Peoples: From White Contact to Removal, 1540–1840*. Knoxville: University of Tennessee Press, 1979.

Saunt, Claudio. "The Paradox of Freedom: Tribal Sovereignty and Emancipation during the Reconstruction of Indian Territory." *The Journal of Southern History* 70 (2004).

———. "Taking Account of Property: Stratification among the Creek Indians in the Early Nineteenth Century." *The William and Mary Quarterly* 57 (2000).

Savage, William W. Jr. *The Cherokee Strip Live Stock Association: Federal Regulation and the Cattleman's Last Frontier*. Columbia: University of Missouri Press, 1973.

Scheiber, Harry N., ed. *The Old Northwest: Studies in Regional History, 1787–1910*. Lincoln: University of Nebraska Press, 1969.

Schmeckebier, Laurence F. *The Office of Indian Affairs: Its History, Activities and Organization*. Baltimore: The Johns Hopkins University Press, 1927.

Schuck, Peter H., and Rogers M. Smith. *Citizenship Without Consent: Illegal Aliens in the American Polity*. New Haven: Yale University Press, 1985.

Schwalm, Leslie A. "'Overrun with Free Negroes': Emancipation and Wartime Migration in the Upper Midwest." *Civil War History* 50 (2004).

Seymour, Flora Warren. *Indian Agents of the Old Frontier*. New York: D. Appleton-Century Co., 1941.

Shaw, Ronald E. *Canals for a Nation: The Canal Era in the United States, 1790–1860*. Lexington: The University Press of Kentucky, 1993.

Sheehan, Bernard W. *Seeds of Extinction: Jeffersonian Philanthropy and the American Indian*. New York: Norton, 1973.

Shefter, Martin. "International Influences on American Political Development." *Shaped by War and Trade: International Influences on American Political Development*. Ed. Ira Katznelson and Martin Shefter. Princeton: Princeton University Press, 2002.

———. *Political Parties and the State: The American Historical Experience*. Princeton: Princeton University Press, 1994.

Sheriff, Carol. *The Artificial River: The Erie Canal and the Paradox of Progress, 1817–1862*. New York: Hill and Wang, 1996.

Sibley, George. Extracts from the Diary of Major Sibley. Reprinted in *Chronicles of Oklahoma* 5 (1927).

Silver, James W. "Edmund Pendleton Gaines and Frontier Problems, 1801–1849." *The Journal of Southern History* 1 (1935).

Singer, P. W. *Corporate Warriors: The Rise of the Privatized Military Industry*. Ithaca, NY: Cornell University Press, 2003.

Sinha, Manisha. "Black Abolitionism: The Assault on Southern Slavery and the Struggle for Racial Equality." *Slavery in New York*. Ed. Ira Berlin and Leslie M. Harris. New York: New Press, 2005.

Skocpol, Theda. *Protecting Soldiers and Mothers: The Political Origins of Social Policy in the United States*. Cambridge, MA: Harvard University Press, 1995.

———. *Social Policy in the United States: Future Possibilities in Historical Perspective*. Princeton: Princeton University Press, 1995.

Skocpol, Theda, Marshall Ganz, and Ziad Munson. "A Nation of Organizers: The Institutional Origins of Civic Voluntarism in the United States." *The American Political Science Review* 94 (2000).

Skocpol, Theda, Ziad Munson, Andrew Karch, and Bayliss Camp. "Patriotic Partnerships: Why Great Wars Nourished American Civic Voluntarism." *Shaped by War and Trade: International Influences on American Political Development*. Ed. Ira Katznelson and Martin Shefter. Princeton: Princeton University Press, 2002.

Skogen, Larry C. *Indian Depredation Claims, 1796–1920*. Norman: University of Oklahoma Press, 1996.

Skowronek, Stephen. *Building a New American State: The Expansion of National Administrative Capacities, 1877–1920*. Cambridge: Cambridge University Press, 1982.

Slotkin, Richard. *Regeneration Through Violence: The Mythology of the American Frontier, 1600–1860*. New York: HarperPerennial, 1996 [1973].

Smith, Rogers M. *Civic Ideals: Conflicting Visions of Citizenship in U.S. History*. New Haven: Yale University Press, 1997.

Southerland, Henry de Leon Jr., and Jerry Elijah Brown. *The Federal Road through Georgia, the Creek Nation, and Alabama, 1806–1836*. Tuscaloosa: The University of Alabama Press, 1989.

Spence, Mark David. *Dispossessing the Wilderness: Indian Removal and the Making of the National Parks*. New York: Oxford University Press, 1999.

Spindel, Carol. *Dancing at Halftime: Sports and the Controversy over American Indian Mascots*. New York: New York University Press, 2000.

Spores, Ronald. "Too Small a Place: The Removal of the Willamette Valley Indians, 1850–1856." *American Indian Quarterly* 17 (1993).

Stannard, David E. *American Holocaust: The Conquest of the New World*. New York: Oxford University Press, 1992.

Starr, Paul. *The Creation of the Media: Political Origins of Modern Communications*. New York: Basic Books, 2004.

Stiffarm, Lenore A., with Phil Lane, Jr. "The Demography of Native North America: A Question of American Indian Survival." *The State of Native America: Genocide, Colonization, and Resistance*. Ed. M. Annette Jaimes. Boston: South End Press, 1992.

Stockel, H. Henrietta. *Survival of the Spirit: Chiricahua Apaches in Captivity*. Reno: University of Nevada Press, 1993.

Straus, Terry, ed. *Native Chicago*. 2nd ed. Chicago: Albatross Press, 2002.

Strong, John A. *The Montaukett Indians of Eastern Long Island*. Syracuse: Syracuse University Press, 2001.

Stuart, Paul. *The Indian Office: Growth and Development of an American Institution, 1865–1900*. Ann Arbor: UMI Research Press, 1979.

———. *Nations Within a Nation: Historical Statistics of American Indians*. New York: Greenwood Press, 1987.

Sturm, Circe. "Blood Politics, Racial Classification, and Cherokee National Identity: The Trials and Tribulations of the Cherokee Freedmen." *American Indian Quarterly* 22 (1998).

Sword, Wiley. *President Washington's Indian War: The Struggle for the Old Northwest, 1790–1795*. Norman: University of Oklahoma Press, 1993.

Tate, Michael L. "John P. Clum and the Origins of an Apache Constabulary, 1874–1877." *American Indian Quarterly* 3 (1977).

Taylor, Theodore W. *The Bureau of Indian Affairs*. Boulder: Westview Press, 1984.

Thornton, Russell. *American Indian Holocaust and Survival: A Population History Since 1492*. Norman: University of Oklahoma Press, 1990.

Tichenor, Daniel J., and Richard A. Harris. "Organized Interests and American Political Development." *Political Science Quarterly* 117 (2002/2003).

de Tocqueville, Alexis. *Democracy in America*. 2 vols. New York: Vintage, 1945.

Trafzer, Clifford E., ed. *Indians, Superintendents, and Councils: Northwestern Indian Policy, 1850–1855*. Lanham, MD: University Press of America, 1986.

Trattner, Walter I. *From Poor Law to Welfare State: A History of Social Welfare in America*. 5th ed. New York: Free Press, 1994.

Treat, Payson Jackson. "Origin of the National Land System under the Confederation." *The Public Lands: Studies in the History of the Public Domain*. Ed. Vernon Carstensen. Madison: University of Wisconsin Press, 1968.

Trefousse, Hans L. *Carl Schurz: A Biography*. Knoxville: University of Tennessee Press, 1982.

Trelease, Allen W. *Indian Affairs in Colonial New York: The Seventeenth Century*. Lincoln: University of Nebraska Press, 1997 [1960].

Trennert, Robert A. "The Fur Trader as Indian Administrator: Conflict of Interest or Wise Policy?" *South Dakota History* 5 (1974).

______. *The Phoenix Indian School: Forced Assimilation in Arizona, 1891–1935*. Norman: University of Oklahoma Press, 1988.

______. "William Medill." *The Commissioners of Indian Affairs, 1824–1977*. Ed. Robert M. Kvasnicka and Herman J. Viola. Lincoln: University of Nebraska Press, 1979.

Tulis, Jeffrey K. *The Rhetorical Presidency*. Princeton: Princeton University Press, 1987.

United States Bureau of the Census. *Historical Statistics of the United States: Colonial Times to 1970*. 2 parts. Washington, DC: U.S. Bureau of the Census, 1975.

Unrau, William E. "Nathaniel Green Taylor." *The Commissioners of Indian Affairs, 1824–1977*. Ed. Robert M. Kvasnicka and Herman J. Viola. Lincoln: University of Nebraska Press, 1979.

Unruh, William E. *White Man's Wicked Water: The Alcohol Trade and Prohibition in Indian Country, 1802–1892*. Lawrence: University Press of Kansas, 1996.

U.S. House of Representatives. Committee on House Administration. "The Power of the Purse." *Journal of Public Budgeting, Accounting & Financial Management* 9 (1997).

Usner, Daniel H. Jr. "American Indians on the Cotton Frontier: Changing Economic Relations with Citizens and Slaves in the Mississippi Territory." *The Journal of American History* 72 (1985).

Utley, Robert M. *The Indian Frontier of the American West, 1846–1890*. Albuquerque: University of New Mexico Press, 1984.

______. *The Lance and the Shield: The Life and Times of Sitting Bull*. New York: Henry Holt, 1993.

______. *The Last Days of the Sioux Nation*. New Haven: Yale University Press, 1963.

Van Every, Dale. *Disinherited: The Lost Birthright of the American Indian*. New York: Avon, 1966.

Van Noord, Roger. *Assassination of a Michigan King: The Life of James Jesse Strang*. Ann Arbor: University of Michigan Press, 1997.

Van Riper, Paul P. *History of the United States Civil Service*. Evanston, IL: Row, Peterson and Company, 1958.

Van Riper, Paul P., and Harry N. Scheiber. "The Confederate Civil Service." *The Journal of Southern History* 25 (1959).

Viola, Herman J. *Diplomats in Buckskins: A History of Indian Delegations in Washington City*. Bluffton, SC: Rivilo Books, 1995.

______. *Thomas L. McKenney: Architect of America's Early Indian Policy: 1816–1830*. Chicago: Sage, 1974.

Wallace, Anthony F. C. *Jefferson and the Indians: The Tragic Fate of the First Americans*. Cambridge, MA: Harvard University Press, 1999.

Wallner, Peter A. *Franklin Pierce: Martyr for the Union*. Concord: Plaidswede Publishing, 2007.

Ward, Harry M. *The Department of War, 1781–1795*. Pittsburgh: University of Pittsburgh Press, 1962.

Washburn, Wilcomb E. *The Indian in America*. New York: Harper & Row, 1975.

———. "Indian Removal Policy: Administrative, Historical and Moral Criteria for Judging Its Success or Failure." *Ethnohistory* 12 (1965).

Way, Royal B. "The United States Factory System for Trading with the Indians, 1796–1822." *Mississippi Valley Historical Review* 6 (1919).

Weatherford, Jack. *Indian Givers: How the Indians of the Americas Transformed the World*. New York: Fawcett Columbine, 1988.

Webb, Stephen Saunders. *1676: The End of American Independence*. Syracuse, NY: Syracuse University Press, 1995.

Weinberg, Meyer. *A Chance to Learn: The History of Race and Education in the United States*. Cambridge: Cambridge University Press, 1977.

Weir, Margaret, Ann Shola Orloff, and Theda Skocpol, eds. *The Politics of Social Policy in the United States*. Princeton: Princeton University Press, 1988.

Wesley, Edgar B. "The Government Factory System Among the Indians, 1795–1822." *Journal of Economic and Business History* 4 (1932).

Westmoreland, Timothy M., and Kathryn R. Watson. "Redeeming Hollow Promises: The Case for Mandatory Spending on Health Care for American Indians and Alaska Natives." *American Journal of Public Health* 96 (2006).

White, Leonard D. *The Federalists: A Study in Administrative History*. New York: Macmillan, 1948.

———. *The Jacksonians: A Study in Administrative History, 1829–1861*. New York: Macmillan, 1954.

———. *The Jeffersonians: A Study in Administrative History, 1801–1829*. New York: Free Press, 1951.

White, Richard. *"It's Your Misfortune and None of My Own": A New History of the American West*. Norman: University of Oklahoma Press, 1991.

White, Richard D. Jr. "Exploring the Origins of the American Administrative State: Recent Writings on the Ambiguous Legacy of Alexander Hamilton." *Public Administration Review* 60 (2000).

Whitner, Robert L. "Grant's Indian Peace Policy on the Yakima Reservation, 1870–82." *The Western American Indian: Case Studies in Tribal History*. Ed. Richard N. Ellis. Lincoln: University of Nebraska Press, 1972.

Wilder, Craig Steven. "Black Life in Freedom: Creating a Civic Culture." *Slavery in New York*. Ed. Ira Berlin and Leslie M. Harris. New York: New Press, 2005.

Wilkins, David E. *American Indian Sovereignty and the U.S. Supreme Court: The Masking of Justice*. Austin: University of Texas Press, 1997.

Wilkins, David E. and K. Tsianina Lomawaima. *Uneven Ground: American Indian Sovereignty and Federal Law*. Norman: University of Oklahoma Press, 2001.

Wilkinson, Charles F. *American Indians, Time, and the Law: Native Societies in a Modern Constitutional Democracy*. New Haven: Yale University Press, 1987.

Williams, Daniel W. "Measuring Government in the Early Twentieth Century." *Public Administration Review* 63 (2003).

Williams, Robert A. Jr. *Like a Loaded Weapon: The Rehnquist Court, Indian Rights, and the Legal History of Racism in America*. Minneapolis: University of Minnesota Press, 2005.

Wilson, James Q. *Bureaucracy: What Government Agencies Do and Why They Do It*. New York: Basic Books, 1989.

______. "The Rise of the Bureaucratic State." *Current Issues in Public Administration*. 6th ed. Ed. Frederick S. Lane. Boston: Bedford/St. Martin's, 1999.

Wilson, Mark R. *The Business of Civil War: Military Mobilization and the State, 1861–1865*. Baltimore: The Johns Hopkins University Press, 2006.

______. "The Extensive Side of Nineteenth-Century Military Economy: The Tent Industry in the Northern United States during the Civil War." *Enterprise & Society* 2 (2001).

Wirth, Fremont P. "The Operation of the Land Laws in the Minnesota Iron District." *The Public Lands: Studies in the History of the Public Domain*. Ed. Vernon Carstensen. Madison: University of Wisconsin Press, 1968.

Wishart, David J. "The Dispossession of the Pawnee." *Annals of the Association of American Geographers* 69 (1979).

______. *An Unspeakable Sadness: The Dispossession of the Nebraska Indians*. Lincoln: University of Nebraska Press, 1994.

Wood, Gordon S. *The Americanization of Benjamin Franklin*. New York: Penguin, 2004.

Wright, J. Leitch. *Creeks and Seminoles: The Destruction and Regeneration of the Muscogulge People*. Lincoln: University of Nebraska Press, 1990.

Young, Mary E. "The Creek Frauds: A Study in Conscience and Corruption." *The Mississippi Valley Historical Review* 42 (1955).

______. "Indian Removal and Land Allotment: The Civilized Tribes and Jacksonian Justice." *The American Historical Review* 64 (1958).

______. *Redskins, Ruffleshirts, and Rednecks: Indian Allotments in Alabama and Mississippi, 1830–1860*. Norman: University of Oklahoma Press, 1961.

Young, James Sterling. *The Washington Community, 1800–1828*. New York: Harcourt Brace Jovanovich, 1966.

Zolberg, Aristide R. "International Engagement and American Democracy: A Comparative Perspective." *Shaped by War and Trade: International Influences on American Political Development*. Ed. Ira Katznelson and Martin Shefter. Princeton: Princeton University Press, 2002.

Index